FILM FESTIVAL YEARBOOK 6:

FILM FESTIVALS AND THE MIDDLE EAST

Edited by

Dina Iordanova and Stefanie Van de Peer

St Andrews Film Studies
St Andrews
2014

This book is dedicated to

the memory of

Alberto Elena

(1958-2014)

First published in Great Britain in 2014 by
St Andrews Film Studies
101A North Street, St Andrews, KY16 9AD
Scotland, United Kingdom

Secure on-line ordering:
http://www.st-andrews.ac.uk/filmbooks

British Library Cataloguing-in-Publication Data
A catalogue record for this book is available from the British Library.

ISBN (paperback) 978-1-908437-11-2

The book is published with the assistance of the Centre for Film Studies at the University of St Andrews. Research was facilitated through grants from the Carnegie Trust for the Universities of Scotland and The Royal Society of Edinburgh.

St Andrews Film Studies promotes greater understanding of, and access to, international cinema and film culture worldwide.

University of
St Andrews

The University of St Andrews is a charity registered in Scotland, No. SC013532

Cover design: Duncan Stewart
Cover and pre-press: University of St Andrews Print & Design.

Cover illustration: Dubai International Film Festival, open-air film screening © Satish Kumar, *The National* (http://www.thenational.ae). Reproduced with permission by *The National*.

Inside illustratons:
Contexts – Journées Cinématographiques de Carthage: Festival 2012 Poster © JCC
Case Studies – Beirut International Film Festival 2013: Audiences © BIFF
Iran – Fajr International Film Festival Logo © Fajr Film Festival
Turkey – Instanbul International Film Festival 2013: Audiences Queuing © Basin Toplantisi
Middle East – Cairo International Film Festival: Opening Ceremony © The North Africa Post
Gulf – Dubai International Film Festival: Ticket Sales © DIFF
Maghreb – Journées Cinématographiques de Carthage: Audiences Queueing © JCC

Printed in Great Britain by Lightning Source.

Contents

Acknowledgements

The Film Festival Yearbook Series is now in its sixth year, with this volume exploring an area that features prominently in the media today: the Middle East. It goes without saying that the Middle East is a vast geographical area, and with the broad scope of this volume, we wish to reflect on its diversity, internal complexity as well as on the transnational circuits, the relevance and aspirations of the region's film culture.

The editors would like to express their gratitude to all the generous film festival organisers and filmmakers who contributed in various ways to this project. Without the festivals, there would be no festival yearbooks.

We also wish to thank the contributors to this volume, all of whom showed great commitment and flexibility. Authors of the chapters as well as the interviewees revealed incredible insights and knowledge of the Middle Eastern and North African film festival circuits. We are grateful to them for assisting us in expanding the geographical focus of the field of film festival studies. A special mention goes to those who assembled the tables that form a defining part of the series: Koen Van Eynde, Maryam Ghorbankarimi, Vivian Saglier, Murat Akser, Nick Denes, Marion Fohrer, and our assiduous bibliographer, Amber Shields.

We thank the publishers of *The Moving Image*, who granted us permission to reprint part of Laura U. Marks' 2004 piece 'The Ethical Presenter: Or How to Have Good Arguments over Dinner', published in *The Moving Image* 4, 1, 34-47. We are also greatly indebted to Satish Kumar, photographer for the Emirati newspaper *The National*, who so generously provided us with a stunning image for the front cover of the book.

The circumstances under which some chapters for this book were commissioned also require us to thank, emphatically, Kholoud Hussain and Koen Van Eynde, who translated from Arabic the chapter on Egyptian film festivals by Mahmoud Kassem and in the process solved some mysteries regarding film titles and directors' names, and Steve Blackey for his invaluable assistance with the text and attention to matters of expression. We thank Duncan Stewart for designing the cover of this book, Margaret Smith for designing the manuscript, the anonymous peer reviewer and Jeffrey Ruoff, Josef Gugler and Robert Stam for providing us with a wonderful endorsement for the back cover of the volume.

Lastly, family, friends and colleagues have been encouraging in offering moral support and constructive suggestions, and have helped us considerably with the expansion of our network of film festival professionals and visitors. In particular we want to thank Marjan

Weyn, Richie McCaffery, Hassouna Mansouri, Mohamed Ghazala, Perla Kherlakian, Elias Doumar, Eli Yazbek, Yasmin Fedda, Colette Naufal, Rasha Salti, Alberto Elena, Jean-Michel Frodon, Joe Khalil, Asaf Shalev, Cho Young-jung, Dimitris Kerkinos, Kamel Ben Kaaba, Eva Jorholt, Tabish Khair, Ludmila Cvikova, Hamid Naficy, Pedram Khosronejad, Ibrahim El Marashi, Stefan Moal, Haim Bresheeth, Yosefa Loshitzky, Lena Jayyusi, Annabelle Sreberni, Sally Shafto, Nezih Erdogan, Ahmet Boyacioglu, Engin Ertan, Yusuf Pinhas, Zeki Demirkubuz, Canan Balan, Cemal Kafadar, and Lalehan Ocal for their encouragement and generosity throughout our work and for their support over the years. Dina Iordanova would like to thank Onur Zerenli and Yuksel Kukul, for the happy moments in Balat, and the light on the table.

A Note on Language, Referencing and Interviews

Language

A number of the chapters in this collection were originally written in Arabic (Mahmoud Kassem), Spanish (Javier H. Estrada) or French (Jean-Michel Frodon). These pieces have been translated by professionals and / or experts, or by the contributors themselves, as indicated.

Disclaimer

Comments in the interviews and essays are the express opinions or the property of their individual authors and the interviewees. Therefore, some of the views in this collection do not necessarily reflect those of the editors or interviewers.

Film Titles

On first mention, all films are referenced in the following fashion: *Original title (English language title* [where applicable], Director, Country of Origin, Date); subsequent references are by the most common English language title only.

Many of the films mentioned in this collection have original titles in Arabic, Farsi or Turkish. In the Film Festival Yearbook series, we give the original titles of the films first, when referenced, using IMDB as a source and thus achieving consistency. However, IMDB does not list all the films referenced in this volume. Where this is the case, we have used the most widely used transliterations and translations of the titles in question. After the title in the original language, we include the English title. If the films do not have an English title, we use the most common transliteration, or the French given title, and translated the French into English.

Arabic Names

Given names, transliterated from Arabic into English (or the Roman alphabet), often use el / El or al / Al, sometimes with a hyphen. As there are no firm rules on how the transliteration is to be rendered, for the sake of consistency, in this volume we have opted for capitalisation and have foregone the hyphen.

Referencing of Other Volumes

Some of the essays in this volume reference texts published in the earlier volumes of the *Film Festival Yearbook* series. In the interest of brevity and to avoid pointless repetition of publication details, these have simply been referenced throughout as *FFY1: The Festival Circuit*, *FFY2: Film Festivals and Imagined Communities*, and so on.

Websites

The URLs for film festival websites are cited in parentheses the first time the festival is mentioned. In the case of interviews these are presented in square brackets, since they constitute editorial interventions and do not form part of the interview itself.

List of Abbreviations

ACCM	Association des critiques de cinéma au Maroc / Association of Moroccan Cinema Critics
ACWC	Association of Cinema Writers and Critics (Egypt)
AFLAM	Distributors of Arab Cinema, based in Marseilles (France)
AIF	Arab Institute of Film
CCM	Centre Cinématographique Marocain / Moroccan Cinema Centre
EAFCWC	Egyptian Association of Film and Cinema Writers and Critics
FCF	Farabi Cinema Foundation (Iran)
FEPACI	Fédération Pan-Africaine de Cinéastes / Pan-African Federation of Filmmakers
FESPACO	Festival panafricain du cinéma et de la télévision de Ouagadougou / The Pan-African Film and Television Festival of Ouagadougou (Burkina Faso)
FIAPF	Fédération Internationale des Associations de Producteurs de Films / International Federation of Film Producers Associations
FNCCM	Fédération Nationale des Ciné-Clubs du Maroc / National Federation of Moroccan Cine-clubs
FTCA	Fédération Tunisienne des Cinéastes Amateurs / Tunisian Federation of Amateur Filmmakers
FTCC	Fédération Tunisienne des Ciné-clubs / Tunisian Federation of Ciné-Clubs
GFD	Gulf Film Development
IFM	Iranian Film Market
IKSV	İstanbul Kültür Sanat Vakfı
MCIG	Ministry of Culture and Islamic Guidance (Iran)
MENA	Middle East and North Africa
NETPAC	Network for the Promotion of Asian Cinema
OIF	Organisation Internationale de la Francophonie / International Organisation of the Francophonie
RFC	Royal Film Commission (Jordan)
VMI	Vidual Media Institute (Iran)

Contributors

Asma Ajroudi holds a BS in Journalism from Northwestern University in Qatar, with a concentration in Broadcast and a Certificate in MENA Studies. Asma has also produced documentaries in Qatar and Greece.

Murat Akser is Lecturer in Cinematic Arts in the School of Creative Arts, University of Ulster. Previously, he was Associate Professor of Cinema and Media Studies, Chair of the New Media Department and the founding director of the Cinema and Television MA programme at Kadir Has University, Istanbul. He holds a PhD in Communication and Culture from York University, Canada. He works on the political economy of film festivals and has published a book-length study of Turkish cinema entitled *Green Pine Resurrected: Film Genre, Parody, and Intertextuality in Turkish Cinema* (2010).

Zena Al Tahhan is a freelance writer and journalist. She obtained a BS in Journalism from Northwestern University in Qatar, with a concentration in Broadcast Journalism and a Certificate in Middle Eastern Affairs. Zena has produced documentaries in Qatar, Brazil and Greece; her films have been screened at the Al Jazeera International Documentary Film Festival and at Zayed University Middle East Film Festival in Abu Dhabi.

Savaş Arslan is Professor of Film and Television at Bahçeşehir University in Istanbul, Turkey. In addition to contributing various articles on cinema, arts, and culture to different journals, magazines, and edited volumes, he has written three books: *Cinema in Turkey: A New Critical History* (Oxford University Press, 2011), *Media, Culture and Identity in Europe* (co-editor, Bahçeşehir University Press, 2009), and *Melodram* (in Turkish, L&M, 2005).

Jamal Bahmad is a Postdoctoral Research Associate at the Center for Near and Middle Eastern Studies of Philipps-Universität Marburg in Germany. He holds a PhD in Film and Postcolonial Cultural Studies from the University of Stirling (UK). His doctoral dissertation examined the politics of neoliberalism, everyday life and postcolonial subjectivity in Moroccan urban cinema since the 1990s. Dr Bahmad specialises in North African cultural studies with a focus on cinema, literature, youth and urban cultures. His research has appeared in various peer-reviewed journals and book collections.

Melis Behlil is Associate Professor of Cinema Studies and Chair of Radio, Television and Cinema Department at Kadir Has University in Istanbul, Turkey. She is also Affiliated Researcher at Stockholm University

Institute for Turkish Studies (SUITS). Her areas of research interest are media industries, production studies and contemporary Turkish cinema. She writes film reviews for various publications, co-hosts a weekly radio show, and is a member of the board for the Turkish Film Critics Association. She also serves as a jury member at various national and international film festivals.

Chris Berry is Professor of Film Studies at King's College London. His academic research is grounded in work on Chinese cinema and other screen-based media, and he co-ordinates, with Dr Luke Robinson, the AHRC-funded Chinese Film Festival Studies Research Network. His publications include: (with Mary Farquhar) *Cinema and the National: China on Screen* (Columbia University Press and Hong Kong University Press, 2006); (with Janet Harbord and Rachel Moore), *Public Space, Media Space* (Palgrave Macmillan, 2013); and (with Lu Xinyu and Lisa Rofel), *The New Chinese Documentary Film Movement: For the Public Record* (Hong Kong University Press, 2010).

Anne Demy-Geroe is co-Director of the Iranian Film Festival Australia and was the inaugural Artistic Director, and then Executive Director of the Brisbane International Film Festival from 1991 until 2009. She is a doctoral candidate on Iranian Cinema at the University of Queensland. Anne has curated regional festivals and retrospectives and served on international juries. She is a NETPAC Board Member, a Nominations Council Member of the Asia Pacific Screen Awards, and in 2003 was awarded an Australian Centenary Medal for services to the film industry.

Nick Denes founded the London-based Palestine Film Foundation along with Khaled Ziada in 2004. He has co-directed the organisation and its annual London Palestine Film Festival since that date. He is a senior teaching fellow at the Centre for Media and Film Studies in the School of Oriental and African Studies, University of London.

Gönül Dönmez-Colin is the author of *Women, Islam and Cinema* (2004); *Cinemas of the Other: A Personal Journey with Filmmakers from the Middle East and Central Asia* (2006/2012); *The Cinema of North Africa and the Middle East* (ed.) (2007); *Turkish Cinema: Identity, Distance and Belonging* (2008) and *The Routledge Dictionary of Turkish Cinema* (2014), among others. She has been the programme consultant of Calcutta Film Festival and Kerala International Film Festival in India, Mannheim-Heidelberg International Film Festival in Germany and the international curator of Samsung Women's International Film Festival in Chennai (SWIFT).

Alberto Elena is Professor of Media Studies at the Carlos III University of Madrid. A member of the Editorial Boards of *New Cinemas*, *Secuencias* and *Catalan Journal of Communication and Cultural Studies*, he has organised different film retrospectives and has been on the jury of a variety of international festivals. His publications include *Satyajit Ray* (1998), *Los cines periféricos (Africa, Oriente Medio, India)* (1999), *The Cinema of Latin America* (2003; with Marina Díaz López), *The Cinema of Abbas Kiarostami* (2005) and *La llamada de África. Estudios sobre el cine colonial español* (2010), as well as various contributions to specialised journals.

Javier H. Estrada holds an MA in History of Film and Visual Media from Birkbeck College, University of London. He is a contributing editor to the film magazine *Caimán* and for the film journal *Secuencias*. He curated the film programmes 'Tales from the Bosphorus: Istanbul in Contemporary Turkish Cinema' for Casa Árabe Madrid (2011) and 'Amir Muhammad' for the International Film Seminar Punto de Vista in Navarra (2012). He works as a programmer for the Lima Independiente Film Festival (Peru).

Azadeh Farahmand has a doctorate in Cinema and Media Studies from University of California, Los Angeles (UCLA). She has taught Film History at UCLA and California State University. Her research and publications deal with topics such as international film festivals, Iranian cinema, and national vs. exile cinemas. In addition to her scholarly pursuits, she has entertainment industry experience, having worked in motion picture distribution and exhibition. Since 2009, she has conducted marketing research for motion picture, television, and on-line media clients at IPSOS, a global marketing research and consulting firm.

Marion Fohrer studied Cultural Anthropology, Islamic Studies and Education in Tübingen, Germany. She is now doing her PhD at the HU Berlin in European Anthropology. Her focus is on film festivals in the Gulf region.

Jean-Michel Frodon is a world-renowned journalist and film critic at weekly *Le Point* (1983-1990) and *Le Monde* (1990-2003). He was Editorial Director of *Cahiers du cinéma* between 2003 and 2009. Since then he has written for the website slate.fr. He is also Professorial Fellow at the Department of Film Studies in St Andrews and Professor at Sciences Po in Paris. He has covered and programmed many film festivals worldwide, including Carthage, Marrakech, Doha and the Rencontres Internationales des Cinémas Arabes in Marseille.

Maryam Ghorbankarimi is Teaching Fellow at the School of Modern Languages, University of St. Andrews. She completed her PhD in Film Studies at the University of Edinburgh in 2012, an analysis of the evolution in representation of women in Iranian cinema since the 1990s. Maryam is also a filmmaker and editor.

Kholoud Baher Hussein is a PhD student at Cornell University, pursuing a project on the literature of John Steinbeck and Yusuf Idris. Previously, she taught Arabic at the University of St Andrews.

Dina Iordanova is Professor of Global Cinemas and Creative Cultures at the University of St. Andrews in Scotland, where she founded the Film Studies programme and the Centre for Film Studies. She fostered research into film festivals by initiating the *Film Festival Yearbook* series in 2009, and the series *Films Need Festivals, Festivals Need Films* in 2013. Her most recent books include (with Stuart Cunningham), *Digital Disruption: Cinema Moves On-line* (2012) and *The Film Festivals Reader* (2013). She works with a range of international film festivals and on editorial boards for publishers and journals. Her work is translated in many languages.

Mahmoud Kassem is Professor in Criticism and Analysis at Minia University in Egypt. He is a writer, novelist and film critic. He was educated at the University of Alexandria. His novels include *My Odyssea* (1984) and *The Days of Charleston* (1998). He has also won seven awards in the field of children's literature and radio series. He has been a freelance journalist for many newspapers and magazines, among which *Al Arabi*, *Al Founoun* and *Al Khyal*. He works as a journalist at the publishing house *Dar Al Hilal* (The Crescent) in Cairo.

Alisa Lebow is Reader in Film Studies at University of Sussex. Her research is concerned with issues related to documentary film, and 'the political'. Her books *The Cinema of Me* (Wallflower, 2012) and *First Person Jewish* (University of Minnesota Press, 2008) explore the representation of self and subjectivity in documentary. She co-edited *The Blackwell Companion to Contemporary Documentary* with Alexandra Juhasz (2014). She is a filmmaker, whose work includes *For the Record: The World Tribunal on Iraq* (2007), *Treyf* (1998) and *Outlaw* (1994). She has also curated several film programmes for film festivals and arts institutions in the UK and Turkey.

Laura U. Marks is the author of *The Skin of the Film: Intercultural Cinema, Embodiment, and the Senses* (Duke, 2000), *Touch: Sensuous Theory and Multisensory Media* (Minnesota, 2002), *Enfoldment and Infinity: An Islamic Genealogy of New Media Art* (MIT, 2010) and many essays. She is currently working on a book on experimental cinema in the Arab world. Dr. Marks has curated programs of experimental media art for venues around the world. She is the Dena Wosk University Professor in the School for the Contemporary Arts at Simon Fraser University, Vancouver, Canada.

Heather McIntosh is Assistant Professor of Communication Arts at Notre Dame of Maryland University. Her research interests focus on documentary, media industries, and social movements. She is a co-editor of a forthcoming volume about the intersections of gender violence and documentary, and she writes about documentary as a blogger for PBS's POV series. She received her PhD in Mass Communications from Pennsylvania State University.

Viviane Saglier is a PhD student in Film & Moving Image Studies at Concordia University in Montreal. Prior to that, she studied at the Sorbonne and the Ecole du Louvre in Paris. She has contributed to several film festivals in Europe, France, and Quebec.

Sally Shafto is a film historian living in Morocco, where she has taught at the Polydisciplinary Faculty of Ouarzazate. She writes for the film journals *Framework* and *Senses of Cinema*. Before moving to Morocco, she ran the 29th edition of the Big Muddy Film Festival at Southern Illinois University. She did a post-doctorate at Princeton University. In Paris she taught in a film school, translated for *Cahiers du cinéma* and collaborated with the Centre Pompidou. In 2007, she published her monograph *The Zanzibar Films and the Dandies of May 1968* (Paris Expérimental).

Amber Shields is a PhD student at the University of St Andrews where she is researching representations of collective trauma in fantasy films. Prior to this she worked in film and international education. She received her MPhil in Screen Media and Cultures from the University of Cambridge and her BA in Latin American Studies from Carleton College.

Matt Sienkiewicz is Assistant Professor of Communication and International Studies at Boston College. His research focuses on Western interactions with Middle Eastern media, and on representation in American screen comedy. His publications include articles in *Popular Communication*, *Middle East Journal of Culture and Communication*, *International Journal of Cultural Studies*, and *Columbia Journalism Review*. He is co-editor of *Saturday Night Live and American TV*, available from Indiana University Press.

Stefanie Van de Peer is Teaching Fellow in Global Cinema at the University of Stirling in Scotland. Her research focuses on women's filmmaking in the Middle East. She has published scholarly articles about women and film in Morocco, Tunisia, Egypt, Syria and Lebanon. She co-edited *Art and Trauma in Africa* (I.B. Tauris, 2013) with Lizelle Bisschoff and co-directed the Africa in Motion Film Festival until 2011. She has programmed films for the Middle Eastern Film Festival in Edinburgh, REEL Festival in Damascus and Beirut, and the Boston Palestine Film Festival. Her monograph *The Pioneering Women of Arab Documentary* is forthcoming with Edinburgh University Press.

Koen Van Eynde has a Master's degree in Arabic Language and Islamic History from the University of Leuven in Belgium. He has worked as an Arabic teacher in Egypt at the Netherlands-Flemish Institute in Cairo since 2009. He is currently also working on his PhD research at the University of Leuven. The subject of his thesis is gender representations in Egyptian cinema, focusing on men and masculinities.

Alia Yunis is a filmmaker, author and journalist. She teaches Film Production and Film Festival Management at Zayed University in Abu Dhabi and is cofounder of the UAE National Film Library and Archive, the first such archive in the Gulf region. Her 2009 novel, *The Night Counter* (Random House), received critical acclaim. Last year, she produced the short documentary *Dreams in Their Eyes*, which has played at several international film festivals, winning several prizes. Her work has appeared in several anthologies and magazines, including the *Los Angeles Times*, *Saveur* and *Aramco World*.

Introduction

Dina Iordanova and Stefanie Van de Peer

Even as contributions started arriving in the summer of 2013 and we began putting this volume together, the radio was once again broadcasting worrying news – yet another global travel warning was being issued because of fears of 'an unspecified Al Qaeda attack', yet another set of diplomatic missions was being closed down, yet another round of anxiety was reinforcing the divisions and apprehensions that had taken hold of the world since 2001.[1] Rather than being beckoned closer, the region at the centre of our interest was, once again, being shut out.

So, what were we doing, working on a book about film festivals in a region that the media overwhelmingly depicts as a land governed by uncontrollably violent upheavals and treacherous pursuits? What was making us delve into a world that, according to the prevailing narrative, was to be feared and shunned as an antagonistic foe rather than, as we were doing, embraced and explored as a fully-fledged cultural partner? Was our behaviour out of touch and anachronistic? Why were we acting in a manner that could come across, to some, as stubbornly oblivious to socio-political realities?

In fact, and precisely because of this given context, we felt that our decision to dedicate our new Film Festival Yearbook to the Middle East and adjacent territories, was more than timely. Like many of the contributors to this volume, we had been ambivalent about the motivation behind George W. Bush's hasty proclamation of a supposed 'Axis of Evil' in 2001 and, prior to that, about the validity of Samuel Huntington's thesis of an inevitable 'clash of civilisations' that had served as its conceptual ground (Huntington 1996). Like most of the contributors to this volume, we did not believe in drifting apart but, rather, desired that efforts be made to encourage a coming together… through films and festivals. And, once again, like most of the contributors to this volume, we were bound by an enduring commitment to making the 'small gesture' of watching foreign films, as we knew that in these films, behind the demonisation and fear-mongering, exist whole worlds and peoples, and that it is up to *all* of us to decide to come to know and understand each other better.

We share an interest in the political importance and implications of non-Western film cultures and of those developments 'at the periphery' that prove to be of defining importance nowadays. And so we feel that we came along nicely as an editing team, with Stefanie Van de Peer's expertise in Women's Cinema from the Arab region complementing and informing Dina Iordanova's substantial and formulating experience in Film Festival Studies. It also mattered (and helped) that a growing circle of acquaintances and friends were becoming involved with some of the more influential festivals in the region, and that our own travels began taking us to the region on a regular basis.

There was also the fact that each of us was relating to the 2011 'Arab Spring' and the series of events it triggered in a personal and idiosyncratic way, informed by our own past experiences. In her writing, Stefanie Van de Peer has observed how the waves of Western interest in the Middle East – in 1981, 2001 and 2011 – have typically been spurred on by 'alarming' events (the Iranian hostage crisis, 9/11, the Arab Spring, respectively), and how this interest reflects negative media approaches towards the Middle East (Van de Peer, 2012). These media attitudes, we were now realising, had catalysed activist and / or idealist festival programmers into venturing behind the headlines in attempts to represent the embattled region in a different, more balanced light. This was familiar territory for Dina Iordanova, who has observed and recounted similar situations in the past, in her writings concerning the breakup of Yugoslavia (2001) and the end of the Cold War. We both thought that with this project we could encourage attention on the Middle East to not only touch on the politics and economics of the region, but to recognise the importance of cultural events and their influence on those politics and economics, both regionally and globally. We both believe that films and film festivals not only reflect (or fall victim to) political developments, but also instigate and shape them.

The Middle East to which the title of this book refers is a diverse, varied, multiple and contested area. It is not a geographical region that can be regarded as 'one' or as 'united'. And indeed, we acknowledge that in our coverage – which includes material dealing with Turkey and Iran, and which explores the festival scene in North Africa (the Maghreb) – we somewhat stretch the concept. We believe it to be a justifiable approach in that it allows us to test the scope of a regional consciousness across culturally associated lands that are not usually referenced by a single term.

Geographies remain determined, in many respects, by colonial legacies, and these, in turn, determine the view of the region from outside. Ultimately, the designation 'Middle East' seems little more than a geographical notion, an attempt to divide the world into manageable, bite-size, physical chunks. This patently European colonialist terminology ("East of where?") has been critiqued by such eminences as Edward Said (1981) and Bernard Lewis (1993), and balanced by Marwan Kraidi through theoretical approaches such as 'critical transculturalism' and 'hybridity' (2005). While we acknowledge the shortcomings and biases inherent in 'Middle East', we nevertheless needed a concept to work with, and alternatives such as MENA (Middle East and North Africa), 'the Arab world', or 'the Muslim World' were equally dubious or limiting, and failed to encompass the diversity that we encounter and would like to reflect on. The events that have been problematically termed the 'Arab Spring' may have initiated a new wave of media interest in the Middle East, but we feel that it is by looking closely at circuits and networks, like those that take shape within the film festival landscape, that we can learn to truly comprehend and appreciate regional and transnational efforts to allow film to contribute to the dialogism between culturally diverse regions of the globe.

Thus, our settling on 'Middle East' was inevitably a compromise; we were committing to the concept chiefly for convenience, whilst being mindful (and hopeful) that the complexity of the cultural and geographical specifics of the area we cover in this book would be properly addressed through our coverage and the commissioning process. Questions like 'Do we include Turkey?' or 'How about Iran, the film culture of which gave rise to the very term "festival film"?' made us rethink our initial focus on Arab cinema and prompted us to expand our examination substantially. More questions challenged the concept: 'How does Morocco fit into the Middle East?' And, of course, the question 'How will we manage to cover both Israeli and Palestinian festivals?' presented a challenge. Not only for our conceptualisation of the book and its title, but also in the commissioning of chapters, especially in light of the cultural boycott of Israel which determined some academics' and practitioners' involvement or otherwise in the project.[2]

Again, the choice to call this book Film Festivals *and* the Middle East (as opposed to *in* the Middle East or *around* the Middle East or in the *MENA*) was also made in full awareness of its limitations and divisive potential. We chose *and* in the title in order to enable the inclusion of diasporic communities, to write about exilic filmmakers and to problematise whether film festivals need to take place *in* a place to be relevant for study *of* that place. The nature of prepositions is that they link nouns and verbs – and the *and* in our title signifies the diversity and, hopefully, also the openness of the chapters included here. Until we come to a more useful term for this huge geographical space, we have little choice but to use 'Middle East', and we hope the contents of the book exhibit the hybridity and diversity we acknowledge and celebrate as defining features of the region.

By investigating the respective film cultures and film festivals of this wider area, we hope to reveal how a culturally-informed geopolitical scope can ultimately shape a distinct and evolving take on the world. Indeed, the way in which 'parallel modernities' (Larkin 1997) manifest themselves in the context of various cultural activities has been at the centre of our interest for many years. Exploration of the history and politics of film festivals located in non-Western territories, and which are thus often influenced by distinctive ideologies and agendas, permits us to not only register differences, but also see the logic that shapes these variances. These are festivals that bring forward cinematic texts from lesser-known aesthetic and conceptual traditions and display them in unique contexts. The cinemas and the narratives featured here reflect the political and cultural dynamics of an area that alternates between the vibrant and the volatile.

The Veteran Festivals

Our previous research into film festivals in East Asia (Iordanova and Cheung 2011), in addition to the research that went into this current project, reveals a picture that parts ways with the view of the film festival as a phenomenon with largely 'European roots' that only picked up to become a widespread phenomenon in the 1980s (De Valck 2007:14 & 19-20). Contrary to this Eurocentric view, we have reasons to believe that film festivals have been thriving in a variety of non-Western countries since the mid-1950s and particularly during the 1960s and 1970s. A range of important festivals has been around for much longer than many of those in Europe, the U.S. and Australia.

As is true in other parts of the world, film festivals have existed in the Middle East for much longer than is commonly believed. The sequential table we have included at the end of this book chronicles the first appearances of select festivals. Here we reproduce a short extract, which reveals that the film festival has been a feature of the Turkish, Iranian and Tunisian film cultures since the early 1960s.

In Turkey, the International Antalya Golden Orange Film Festival was inaugurated in 1963, and the film festival in Adana in 1969 (see Akser in this volume). In Tunisia, the first festival was inaugurated in 1964, dedicated to the thriving amateur filmmaking society in Kélibia. The important Journées Cinématographique de Carthage, a.k.a. JCC (www.jccarthage.com), was set up in 1966 and, for a long time, was the most important and the biggest event in the region (not the same thing, of course), dedicated to showcasing Arab as well as African films, and positioning itself as the defining place to exercise and experience Pan-Africanism and Pan-Arabism in cinema.[3] In Iran, the Roshd International Educational Film Festival dates back to 1963. The Tehran Film Festival,

Est.	Festival	Location
1963	Roshd International Educational Film Festival	Tehran, Iran
1963	International Antalya Golden Orange Film Festival	Antalya, Turkey
1964	International Amateur Film festival in Kélibia / Festival International du Film Amateur de Kélibia (FIFAK)	Kélibia, Tunisia
1966	Days of Cinema in Carthage / Journées Cinématographiques de Carthage	Tunis, Tunisia
1969	International Golden Boll Film Festival	Adana, Turkey
1972-1977	Tehran International Film Festival	Tehran, Iran
1975	Karraka Film Festival in La Goulette / Festival Karraka De La Goulette	La Goulette, Tunisia
1976	Cairo International Film Festival	Cairo, Egypt
1977	African Film Festival of Khouribga	Khourigba, Morocco
1979	Alexandria International Film Festival	Alexandria, Egypt
1979	Damascus International Film Festival	Damascus, Syria
1982	Fajr International Film Festival	Tehran, Iran
1982	International Children's Film Festival	Isfahan (15 times) Tehran (6 times) Hamedan (4 times) and Kerman (1 time), Iran
1982	Festival National du Film de Tanger	Tangiers, Morocco
1982	Istanbul International Film Festival	Istanbul, Turkey
1983	Haifa International Film Festival	Haifa, Israel
1984	Jerusalem Film Festival	West Jerusalem, Israel

Table 1: Select Festivals in the Region, Chronological (1963-1984)

which is covered in a chapter in this volume, ran between 1972 and 1976, and even the relatively recent Fajr festival dates back to 1982. The festivals in Cairo and Alexandria in Egypt were started in the 1970s, as was the event in Damascus. And, also having launched in 1982, the festivals in Istanbul and Tangiers predate those in Haifa and Jerusalem.

These festivals came about and had their heydays under geopolitical configurations very different to those of today. Their emergence and early days are largely shaped by distinct narratives of the world-at-large: a humankind divided along Cold War lines; a range of tenuous alliances, some of which would be fully reversed later on; a string of successful anti-colonial movements (accompanied by communicable anti-colonial rhetoric); robust non-aligned movements; and local wars with far-fetching global consequences. In such contexts, the motivations and visions underlying cultural exchanges and the concrete steps towards cultural diplomacy that many of these early festivals constituted, followed patterns that, in order to be properly understood, would need a closer and significantly more extended scrutiny than we can offer here.

It was a different world. Yet the professionalism of these festivals was as close to the way that the European standard-setters operated as it could get. The Tehran festival, for example, was inaugurated by Queen Farah in 1972 and clearly played a key role in cultural diplomacy efforts, being explictly run 'with the ambition of becoming the Cannes of Asia' (see Farahmand in this volume). Even if short-lived, this festival had secured and enjoyed an A-Category accreditation (the prestigious FIAPF accreditation moved to the festival in Cairo in 1986).[4] Many of the films that came through Tehran, as Farahmand observes, were later considered as constituents of the Iranian New Wave. The Fajr festival (since 1982), a decidedly post-revolutionary new venture, yet still a de facto successor to Tehran (1972-1976), maintained a professional standard by publishing a daily bulletin and inviting international programmers (as illustrated by Chris Berry's and Anne Demy-Geroe's contributions). Even after being marked by an idiosyncratic approach to public relations and tainted by recent censorship controversies, Fajr remains the main destination for all those engaged with Iranian cinema. One cannot possibly disregard the fact that it was through Fajr that Iranian cinema, the cradle of prototypical 'festival films' (as per the definition supplied by Bill Nichols in 1994), found its way through to the West. The festivals in Cairo, Istanbul and Jerusalem, are considered equally important as source events for primary material entering the global circuit.

When exploring these older festivals, the JCC in Carthage needs to be given particular attention, not only because it is old and well-respected, but also because it played an important role in cultivating notions of African and Arab cinema that are still of importance.[5] The JCC's website proudly states that

> [f]rom the early days of the festival, its activism offered southern countries alternatives to the monopoly of distribution companies and movie operators. It gave them the opportunity to develop and distribute their own images.
> (JCC Website Archives)

Over the years, winners have included politically important filmmakers, such as Ousmane Sembène from Senegal, Youssef Chahine from Egypt, Med Hondo from Mauritania, Merzak Allouache from Algeria, Souleymane Cissé from Mali, Moufida Tlatli from Tunisia, Haile Gerima from Ethiopia and many other influential African and Arab producers.[6]

Even if it is somewhat peripheral to what is usually regarded as the Middle East, being regarded as more closely linked to North Africa, the Carthage festival and those events that took place in Algeria have played an important role in shaping the self-consciousness of African and of Third Cinema in general. Taking place biennially, the JCC has been alternating with FESPACO in Burkina Faso over more than four decades; the North-South coordination between FESPACO and JCC has been productive and creative.[7] Both festivals focus on African cinema at large (including North Africa); JCC adds Arab filmmaking and FESPACO African diaspora filmmaking from around the world to their respective programmes. The historical Pan-Africanism of both FESPACO and JCC have the potential to speak to similar audiences. Not least important is that FESPACO and JCC were part of the same Pan-Africanist injection into the Pan-African Federation of Film-Makers (FEPACI).

Created in 1969, FEPACI had been taking shape since the mid-fifties, when African intellectuals began to organise themselves against colonialist domination and ongoing cultural dependence. In 1952, then, a group called African Cinema was started, informally, by Paul Vieyra (a.k.a. Paulin Soumanou Vieyra, 1925-1987). In 1959, at the Rome Congress, artists had called for a

> resolution to develop art in Africa. The resolution stressed the need for African ownership of the means of expression, control of production and strategic proprietorship of public platforms that disseminated the African story and its imagery.
> (Tapsoba)

Growing anti-colonialist sentiment urged them to seek to create

> a new turn and tone, a new lexicon and vocabulary of
> intellectual thought [that] was found in the speech against
> colonialism delivered in the 1950s by Aimé Césaire's 'The
> Discourse on Colonialism'. Ideas expressed by African
> and Caribbean intellectuals about the role of the colonial
> enterprise in the disruption of African societies and the
> negation of their indigenous cultures became more succinct
> and radical. (Tapsoba)

In 1966, in Dakar, the resolution was implemented. At this congress, the African Cinema Group was officially established (and in 1969 was re-named FEPACI) and 26 films from 16 African countries were screened. Also in 1966, JCC was born.

Newly-emancipated Algeria, while not covered in our up-close studies of specific festivals, had an important role to play in the Pan-African movement of cineastes. The first FEPACI conference was held in Algiers in 1969, and it was pervaded by the spirit of Third Cinema. African film directors proposed to take a cultural stance against the dominance of European funding and exhibition power over African films. In 1973, still in Algiers, a committee penned the 'Resolutions of the Third World Film-Makers' Meeting', discussing the role of cinema in the Third World as an opposition to imperialism and neo-colonialism. The committee consisted of filmmakers, journalists and observers such as Fernando Birri, Flora Gomes, Jorge Silva, Mohamed Abdelwahad and Bensalah Mohamed (Bakari and Cham 1996). In their 'Resolution', they defy colonialism and the persistence of European power in African countries, and depict the role of cinema as a social act within an historical reality. The role of the filmmaker, they wrote, is

> extended to other fields of action such as: articulating,
> fostering and making the new films understandable to
> the masses of people by associating himself [sic] with the
> promoters of people's cinemas, clubs and itinerant film
> groups in their dynamic action aimed at disalienation
> and sensitisation in favour of a cinema which satisfies and
> interests the masses. (In Bakari and Cham 1996: 24)

One of their chief goals for the distribution of Third Cinema was the fostering of festivals, film markets and film days at the Third World level, implying a collaborative effort between Third World nations and their festivals.[8]

In 1975, the conference was again held in Algiers and established FEPACI as a grouping driven by 'political militancy' and led by film pioneers. The Algiers Charter was composed. Once again, this document expresses displeasure with the ongoing domination of colonial power. Directors and other film professionals such as Ousmane Sembène, Med Hondo and Tahar Cheriaa took part and expressed the need for festivals to take place on the African continent so that the very audiences for whom African films were intended had the opportunity to see them. This extremely successful conference endorsed the biennial FESPACO, which had been instrumental, in partnership with the biennial JCC in Tunis, in shaping FEPACI. This was an approach conceptualised by critic and JCC founder Tahar Cheriaa, who was present. Pan-Africanism was thus successful in establishing at least two truly influential and lasting film festivals on the African continent: one North of the Sahara, in Tunis, and another South of the Sahara, in Burkina Faso's Ouagadougou.

In contrast, the project of Pan-Arabism thrived only temporarily, during Egyptian president Gamal Abdel Nasser's tenure (1956-1970), and has, over the past decades, greatly lost its significance. Nevertheless, it is an ideal to which many politicians still refer and many cultural producers still aspire. Although Nasser was a fan of Egyptian cinema, he never made efforts to establish a film festival in Egypt. The Cairo festival was not inaugurated until 1976, six years after his death, and occurred within the nationalist spirit of politics instituted under Anwar Sadat (1970-1981). In fact, most film festivals set up in the Arab world in the 1970s and 1980s seem to have had as their main goals the celebration of a national identity and the showcasing of a national cinema (or the affluence that more often than not accompanied these showcases, at least).

While the International Film Festival in Cairo remains the only film festival in the Middle East to have gained A-list accreditation from FIAPF, it no longer enjoys such prestige. It remains in the limelight, illuminated by its attention to elegance and wealth, by showcasing local stars and brands, and by maintaining long-standing competition strands. Nevertheless, as Jean-Michel Frodon argues in this volume, it has been rapidly losing ground in its critical standing. The JCC's significance in the region also appears to be dwindling slowly. [9] It seems reasonable to suggest that such a loss of influence and its relative isolation is a consequence of cultural and political / economic factors, and maybe even accompanies the increasing isolation of North Africa from the Middle East and sub-Saharan Africa.

Looking back at the five decades over which film festivals have existed in this region, we can assert that veteran festivals like the JCC, Cairo, Fajr, Damascus, Istanbul, Jerusalem and others, have played an important role in shaping regional and global film cultures. Still, Carthage and Cairo have undeniably lost in power and prowess, something observed in this volume by Alberto Elena. The same diminution in influence is true for other festivals that have managed at some time to be the focal point of film culture in the region – Fajr, for example, remains of key importance for those who follow the great cinema of Iran, but it is growing more and more idiosyncratic and is rarely covered as much as the newer festivals that have arisen in the twenty-first century.

Why is it that many of these older festivals have seemed to falter, become isolated or lost influence since the late 1990s and early 2000s? Could it be the region's volatile politics and seemingly irreconcilable ideological fault lines that make open dialogue so difficult? Could it be the increasing Islamisation of the region? Or perhaps the proliferation of new players with new money to spend?

New Kids on the Block

Scores of new festivals have sprung up around the world since the turn of the century. None of these newcomers, however, has enjoyed the buzz that has accompanied the four newcomers based in the region under our scrutiny. The festivals in Marrakech (since 2001), Dubai (since 2004), Abu Dhabi (since 2007) and Doha (since 2009), have achieved unprecedented international attention and visibility (the latter three events are aptly summed up by Jean-Michel Frodon as representing an 'Emirates model' in his piece here). These four festivals are rumoured to be among some of the most lavishly financed film festivals on the global circuit, although we have not been able to confirm their budgets. And while abundance of funding may be a matter of perception, these are undoubtedly among the most glamorous festivals around. As they are known to actively enable a vast number of journalists to attend, they have also been covered extremely well in the trade press right from the start.[10]

These new kids on the block, then, are known chiefly for two things: lavish funding and glamour. Although no numbers are readily available showing how much these festivals cost to produce or how much their programmers and directors earn, the consensus is indeed that they are particularly wealthy and, above all, generous to their guests. Whilst initially they benefited from the engagement of Western or international programmers, more recently there has been a tendency to prefer local professionals (previously, locals had been chiefly responsible for the programming of local strands, such as emerging Arab Filmmakers or Emirati Filmmakers).

Glamour, whilst also present at the older festivals, is undoubtedly a defining feature of these new events.[11] Guests, including jury members, executives from competing film festivals, members of the press, as well as sponsors and funders, are all usually given an extraordinary experience. This typically takes the shape of VIP seating, indulgent flights and hotel rooms, escorts and transport in luxury-brand cars, as well as ample opportunities to meet the press for (self-)promotion. There are events sponsored by cosmetics, drinks and catering companies, opportunities to network in a Wonderland of lavish parties, and so on. In short – these are festivals that bedazzle their guests with a show of glitz and glamour.

Still, all these elements – the parties, the networking, the luxury – have little to do with the films themselves, so we could hastily declare them irrelevant by-products. But is this Vanity Fair really so far removed from the purpose of the film festival? Can we not acknowledge that alongside film screenings and film industry events, glamour and its related system of events constitute an inextricable component of film festivals, a shaping factor which must be recognised and discussed as such? Is it not time to acknowledge that many of the stakeholders behind certain festivals are committed not only because of their interest in cinematic art, but because they see the film festival as yet another (and good) opportunity for promotion or fundraising or pure celebration?

And isn't it particularly telling that the successes of the four festivals mentioned here show how the real sites for glamour in the early twenty-first century have moved away from the West, and are now located at film festivals across Asia and the wider Middle East? Indeed, it is in places such as Marrakech or Doha that the background is more suitable and the ground more fertile for unabashed showiness than upon the familiar (and somewhat tread-worn) red carpets of an 'old', largely post-monarchic Europe.

The new festivals enjoy solid centralised support from both the ruling elites and corporations. The Dubai IFF (www.dubaifilmfest.com), for example, is financed and sponsored by the Dubai Government, by the Investment Corporation of Dubai and by companies such as Dubai Holding, Emirates Airlines and Jumeirah Hotels. It is artistically directed by Masoud Amralla Al Ali, and supported by a team of internationally renowned professionals (see the Dubai festival website). The festival in Abu Dhabi operated under a governmental umbrella until 2012, when the management was transferred to TwoFour54, 'an organization whose primary goal is to foster Emirati talent in all media' (Yunis, in this volume). It was formerly run by Peter Scarlet from the U.S., who was replaced, also in 2012, by Ali Al Jarbi. It is currently sponsored by Dolphin Energy, Mercedes-Benz and Etihad Airways. The festival in Doha operates as part of the Doha Film Institute, and was led by British-Australian executive Amanda Palmer from its inception in 2009; for the first few years it ran in close collaboration with the New York-based Tribeca Film Festival (tribecafilm.com/festival). Since 2013, however, the event has also been undergoing profound transformations: it is no longer associated with Tribeca, has entered into close collaboration with the festival in Sarajevo (*www.sff.ba*), and was split into two new festivals (one of which, at the time of writing, is still to materialise).[12]

Writing in *Variety* in 2013, Nick Vivarelli observed that the emancipation of prestigious festivals originally set up with the assistance and expertise of Western festival professionals, and their subsequent (and recent) transfer to the control of local investment and expertise, appears to be a marked trend in the United Arab Emirates (UAE) and Qatar. This tendency, which is sure to develop further in the years to come, also seems to be reflected in their programming, as regional film directors now come more into focus. Indeed, such freeing-up of their organisations and the transfer of programming and managerial powers to native executives and decision-makers is to be observed not only in this region, but is characteristic of film festival trends worldwide.[13]

The emancipation may have been planned from the outset, but still, it reflects a trend in regional opening up. Perhaps there is even the spirit of a new Pan-Arabism in which festivals become sites of cultural exchange, and where the globalisation of the Arab region is re-centred on screening Arab films in Middle Eastern settings. Like film festivals elsewhere, these new festivals also function as bridges between industry and politics, as cultural nodes in a transnational infrastructure, as clusters of creativity and commerce, and as ideological spaces where the transnational is set against the national (Iordanova 2011a: 15-22). We do not mean to imply here that the involvement of Western programmers was part of a larger scheme of colonisation of these festivals – after all, these filmic figures were invited by local policy makers in order to legitimise, establish and grow the festivals in line with the leading knowledge and expertise available. But we do believe that the developments reflect a tendency in the film industry at large, where postcolonial filmmaking needs to establish its independence from European and / or American domination; something which it is increasingly managing to accomplish. The fact that the Middle Eastern film industry is not only growing financially and quantitatively, but also becoming more popular with local audiences and qualitatively appreciated abroad, is another factor underlying these decisions.[14]

Yet, the three festivals in the Gulf are too close together in space and time to be vying for the same audiences. This can be construed as the main reason for trying to break out of their similarities. Doha's increasing focus on grassroots film initiatives, Dubai's decidedly international focus (with a jury headed by Western superstars) and Abu Dhabi's strength in showcasing the wider Arab world's best cinema, are enabling the events to become more diverse and less competitive, and to assert their independence. Yet, even if, as in this volume, Jean-Michel Frodon talks of a 'bidding war', there is also evidence that the three festivals are simultaneously trying to maintain an appearance of interdependency and mutuality: by inviting one another, by promoting each other's work on their respective websites and by collaborating on reciprocally interesting development initiatives.

Going back to the question of why glamour is such an inherent part of these new festivals, it must be admitted that there are no straightforward answers. Of course, it is a matter of showing off: a festival is, after all, the showcase of a nation, its customs and opulence. It is a festivity, an opportunity to celebrate. It is also a way of impressing the guests, and of establishing new and potentially durable relationships.[15]

Indeed, when we think of these and the other new festivals that have stressed the glamour element, we feel it is important to assert that there is as much need for recognition and study of the film festival as a site for glamour as there is for its examination as a factor in tourism and cultural planning for host cities. The 'party', which André Bazin declared to be one of the key aspects of the festival's ritualistic order as early as 1955, may have become more modest and contained at a number of festivals, but it is not over, and has indeed grown in stature (and fetches higher sponsorship figures) at other events; the importance of an attendant glamour has increased correspondingly.[16] Such non-cinematic sidebars as red carpet arrivals, galas, prestige parties and so on, are what make a festival festive. And, no matter if we like it or not, at some places notions of brand-awareness and displays of glamour are sometimes more important than the films. Today, the red carpet and the party appear to be two vital aspects of the film festival, and whilst many festivals in the West may be tending to dispense with the red carpet, many new festivals that flourish in other parts of the world have gone in the opposite direction by emphasising and cultivating it. Photo calls, celebrity appearances, pageants of clothes, jewellery and sex appeal may be auxiliary experiences, PR add-ons, as it were, yet they can be just as important to a festival's standing and future as the architecture of the film programme.

In a way, it is all part of the 'gift' economy described by Marcel Mauss (1954). The festival guests may be celebrated at the event, yet one expects that they will further promote the importance of the festival, of the city and of its executives, beyond the limited time and space of the festival itself; that they will reciprocate at a later point and give something in return. It is all about setting up relationships that will develop and pay off later on.[17]

'Full service' festivals?

With Islam as the state religion in a number of the countries in the region, the status of cinema requires special attention. Because Islam declares that Allah is the only image-maker – the only creative and shaping being with divine inspiration – representational and pictorial art was eschewed. The relationship between film and religion in Muslim societies is therefore an uneasy one.

Traditionally, Islamic visual culture focused on portraying meaning and essence rather than physical form. Decorative arts such as calligraphy, ceramics, architecture and other crafts, were far more acceptable than film or painting due to an underlying concern that the depiction of human form comes too close to idolatry. Thus, traditional Islamic art relied chiefly on abstractions (Naddaf 1991: 110; see also Gruber and Haugbolle 2013), and artists faced religious insecurities about representational arts. This resulted, on the one hand, in great achievements in all anti-mimetic, non-figurative arts and, on the other, in on-going uncertainty in all areas based on representation and realism, including film. General shortages in infrastructure, funding and interest, only added to the already fraught relationship Muslims had with film. In addition, local cinema is often regarded by local power elites, both religious and political, as 'too Western'. In countries such as Saudi Arabia, for example, cinema is still associated with U.S. 'decadence', and its intent to create pleasure and entertain is typically seen as sinful.[18]

For its part, the West is sometimes too preoccupied with the awkward position of film in Muslim society. One constantly discusses examples that show how artists in the Middle East suffer a greater degree of censorship than in the West. And whilst we cannot ignore the fact that filmmakers in the Middle East do, indeed, face limitations, it is important to keep in mind that censorship regimes differ from country to country. In Saudi Arabia, for example, it is much more acute than in Morocco, even though officially the Centre Cinématographique Marocain (CCM) is still on the lookout for films that insult the Monarchy and Islam, the state religion.[19]

Yet in spite of all ideological constraints, cinema flourishes in most countries of the region, and remarkable cinematic traditions have developed in Iran, Turkey, Egypt, Israel and many of the other territories. During the Yeşilçam era, for example, Turkish cinema produced over 250 films a year. Egypt was one of the biggest film producing countries in the region, with hundreds of films being released during the Golden Age period of the 1950s and 1960s. In Iran, a variety of films was made in both the pre-Revolutionary (between 25 and 65 films per annum) and the post-Revolutionary periods (around 30 per annum).

Nowadays, following a global trend, output numbers are substantially down, yet overall film production appears alive and well across the region, despite the decline in the number of theatres (which also replicates a world-wide situation). New undertakings in Morocco and the Gulf are acknowledged internationally, such as the Atlas film studio space and facilities near Ouarzazate, which attracts large international productions (and there are similar developments in the Emirates). Hyde Park Entertainment's Indian-born CEO, Ashok Amritraj, is particularly active in the region, and speaks of potential and dynamism and of plans to capitalise on linkages with the Indian film industry. 'Suddenly today,' he remarks, 'Asia and the Middle East are growing so much quicker than America is; these are really important now to Hollywood' (Mitchell, 2013).

In such a context, the festivals serve to maintain and, frequently, in the case of the Middle East, to develop the film culture locally. The festivals' existence or arrival results in the cultivation of consciousness of the political and social importance of cinema and makes cinema an integral part of the culture of the region. Recent developments in the Middle East bring to mind the comment (made with reference to Korean cinema) that a more wholesome film culture could be likened to a 'full service' petrol station model (Berry 2003).

Fostering local film culture both politically and financially is, then, a major consideration. Festivals boost film culture in a variety of ways, but mainly through encouraging and enabling film production and by building audiences. Film festivals like those in Istanbul (which holds the Meetings on the Bridge workshops, discussed here by Azize Tan), Tunis (discussed by Mohamed Mediouni), and Fajr (discussed by Anne Demy-Geroe), are known to work pro-actively towards encouraging a variety of filmmaking interactions known to foster the growth of a film culture of the type these festivals have sought. More recently, there have been important developments related to the Gulf and to other countries that traditionally do not have elaborate film cultures – funding there has been channelled not only towards the encouragement of domestic industries, but has benefited a wider range of Arabic-speaking filmmakers. And indeed, those countries with new festivals have seen remarkable growth both in audiences and in output. When it comes to fostering local film culture, people such as Prince Al Waleed bin Talal in Saudi Arabia have given exemplary support.[20] Wealthier film festivals, such as those in Doha and Abu Dhabi, where workshops and production funds lead to new initiatives in the filmmaking business, have been increasingly committed to boosting local production.[21] The Doha Film Institute maintains an education and training arm, the Gulf Film Development (GFD), which is:

> a division [...] established to support filmmakers in Qatar and the GCC region, to identify, monitor and develop the region's creative and technical talents, and to contribute to a vibrant, self-sustaining filmmaking community. Its objective is to build a strong foundation for Qatar's emerging film industry through a series of workshops and labs that provide training in each aspect of the film production process. Facilitated by seasoned local and international experts, GFD sessions are conducted in consultation and partnership with local educational institutions and visiting professionals. (DFI website)

The Doha Film Institute also runs numerous workshops for aspiring filmmakers, with a focus on developing practical skills, writing and editing, and thus on laying the groundwork for their next initiative, the Film Labs, in which filmmakers learn to bring their ideas to the screen. The last step in this educational programme consists of the Professional Programme, which offers 'ongoing creative, professional development, financial, production and networking assistance to help ensure projects are launched with the best possible support' (DFI website).

Abu Dhabi boasts the SANAD Fund, established in 2010 and dedicated to development and post-production. As the festival website states, 'SANAD provides talented filmmakers from the Arab world with meaningful support from within the region towards the development or completion' (Abu Dhabi website). They offer up to U.S.$20,000 per project for development assistance and up to U.S.$60,000 per project for post-production support. The resulting films are then screened at the Abu Dhabi Film Festival. Veteran filmmakers, such as Lebanese Jocelyne Saab and Iraqi Maysoon Pachachi, as well as new, exciting directors, such as Moroccan Hicham Lasri, are recognised by the Fund. Films such as *Mé Nmoutéch* (*Hidden Beauties*, Nouri Bouzid, Tunisia, 2012), *Al-khoroug lel-nahar* (*Coming Forth by Day*, Hala Lotfy, Egypt, 2012) and *Alam Laysa Lana* (*A World Not Ours*, Mahdi Fleifel, Lebanon / UK / Denmark / UAE, 2012) have all benefited from SANAD and gone on to circumnavigate the world's film festival circuit. The Fund not only focuses on developing new, up-and-coming film directors, but also on fostering established filmmakers' new projects. The increasing attention on local filmmaking at the festivals in the Gulf, as described by Vivarelli in *Variety*, can be seen to extend beyond exhibition into production (Vivarelli 2013).

Instead of investing in production, the festival in Dubai focuses on distribution via what is quickly developing into a successful film market. It maintains the IWC Schaffhausen (Swiss) Filmmaker Award, which grants U.S.$100,000 to a budding Gulf-based filmmaker to aid in production; a direct linkage of the festival to the film market. Their latest initiative is Dubai Docs, a spin-off which aims:

1. To help selected producer/director teams from the region realise their documentary projects with the assistance of decision-makers from the region, Europe and the United States
2. To introduce the international professionals attending DIFF to creative documentary filmmaking in the Arab world. (Dubai Film Festival website)

With the Dubai Docs initiative, Dubai prioritises increased visibility via prize-giving and the development of a resultant interest in local, experimental and documentary films through its event. In other words, where Abu Dhabi and Doha invest in production and development initiatives to draw attention to Gulf-based and Arab filmmaking talent, Dubai, with its film market, actually exercises the role of a de facto distributor for Middle Eastern films. This investment certainly results in an increased exhibition of locally-made films, although it must be acknowledged that censorship (and self-censorship) plays a part in tempering artistic production across the Middle East. Alia Yunis, in her piece in this volume, discusses these festivals' contributions toward the development of local audiences in the Gulf, but the support extends further to include women filmmakers and Palestinian-themed projects.[22]

A Look at Some of the Circuits

The festivals in Cannes, Venice, Toronto, Rotterdam and Berlin, have traditionally paid close attention to cinema from the region, and a host of other festivals have started paying attention, too, since the so-called 'Arab Spring.'[23] And while this recognition of Middle Eastern cinema at international film festivals worldwide is certainly a positive development, it can also (and more cynically) be regarded as a trend that reflects an overall media-fed curiosity about the Middle East. Unlike those Western festivals that may showcase Asian cinema, for example, there is no one festival in the Middle East that would be charged with a central distribution role, and the cinema of Iran, Turkey, Israel, or the Arab world, is programmed by the big players via specialists from the region. The numerous specialised film festivals mainly cater to the diaspora, so those in France predominantly focus on the Maghreb (or the Mediterranean), while those in Germany look at Turkey and its diasporic filmmaking.

Over the years, Cannes seems to have done a good job in presenting Middle Eastern films. Algerian director Mohammed Lakhdar-Hamina was acclaimed for his *Le Vent des Aurès* (*The Wind of the Aurès*) in 1967, before winning a Palme d'Or in 1975 for *Chronique des Années de Braise* (*Chronicle of the Years of Embers*). The Cannes In Competition selection has featured Middle Eastern films since 1946 when *Dunia* by Egypt's Muhammad Karim was screened. In the 1940s and 1950s, the Middle East in Cannes was represented chiefly, if not entirely, by Egypt (a notable exception is a Lebanese film by Georges Nasser (*Ila Ayn*, 1957). Youssef Chahine and Salah Abu Sayf featured in the official selection more than once.[24] This is entirely in line with the productivity and popularity of Egyptian cinema's Golden Age in the Middle East and further afield during the 1950s.

A detailed recounting of the presence of films from the region at festivals would be far too expansive a task for this introduction to undertake. (The topic of Iranian cinema at global festivals would merit a separate investigation of its own.) And so, here we will look at only three select examples of transnational festival circuits so as to reveal how certain political trends are taken up globally via the festival circuit. And how this facilitates the movement of a body of cinematic works and enables them to reach out to dedicated interest groups.[25]

The first example concerns the active international posture assumed by new documentary festivals. Documentary is flourishing through initiatives like Dubai Docs, discussed in the previous section, and the Al Jazeera International Documentary Festival (AJIDF) (http://festival.aljazeera.net), each of which is set on building global networks.[26] Having entered into partnerships with Asia's most significant film festival in Busan, through their Asian Network of Documentary Fund, and with the documentary distributorship Taskovski Films (http://www.taskovskifilms.com), the AJDIF (and its parent organisation Al Jazeera) engage in the support and dissemination of new documentary filmmaking from around the world.[27] The partnerships entered into by these new events are significant, as they suggest that those players who were formerly regarded as peripheral are now gaining in strength, and joining forces to put forward alternative narratives into the global public sphere.

A second area of interest comes with the way in which festivals network so as to showcase the work of women directors working in the Middle East and adjacent territories. This came across clearly in the context of the 2013 Bird's Eye View Film Festival (BEV; http://www.birds-eye-view.co.uk) at London's National Film Theatre. Having previously and consistently focused on women's films and thematic programmes, but never on a specific region, in 2013 BEV dedicated its entire programme to Arab Women Filmmakers.[28] This decision was remarkable, in light of the oft-remarked oppression of women in the Middle East. But, as has been shown elsewhere (e.g. Martin 2012, Dönmez-Colin 2004), and particularly in Dönmez-Colin's contribution to this volume, Middle Eastern women filmmakers have been extraordinarily productive. Lina Khatib has observed that in recent years, female directors from the region have been more productive and received greater recognition than their male counterparts (2008: 44). Thus, the 2013 BEV festival was a timely and exceptional success. Elhum Shakerifar, a documentary producer based in London and working on films with a human rights interest in the Middle East, was hired to program the Arab focus of the festival. She confirms that

> the wave of emerging female filmmakers from the Arab world in the past few years has been noticeable outside of the region's political backdrops – Arab female filmmakers have had work screened in the world's most prestigious festivals from Cannes, to Toronto, Berlin and Venice – in the past two years. It was this wave that we wanted to highlight. I think that the key to this new wave is the creation of new funding streams to support the work of filmmakers across the board from the MENA region – it just so happens that the frontrunners are female directors [...] Certainly, the revolutions across the region brought additional interest to the films that were being there. The political backdrops certainly gave the press something additional to focus on when discussing the work of Arab female filmmakers. (Personal correspondence, October 2013)

Undoubtedly, the attention garnered by the Arab Spring has finally given curators and programmers at a number of film festivals in Europe the incentive to focus on the region, and to give its cinemas the coverage they deserve. After all, film is often co-opted by and adapted for use in Western media contexts. So, even though some of the films may not exactly be reflections of a sudden impetus towards critical filmmaking, they do serve as proof of a defiance that has evolved during decades of oppression, even if the attention of the West is only captured in the context of the current revolutions. Although this is a situation that may not be based on any profound understanding of the issues, it still benefits the continued productivity of Middle Eastern filmmakers, and especially among them a growing number of women.

Having been made famous by the increased festival attention to women-filmmakers from the region, the first Saudi Arabian woman-filmmaker, Haifaa Al Mansour, recently saw her first feature length film, *Wadjda* (2012) celebrated on the circuit. Funded by Prince Al Waleed bin Tawal's film production company, Al Mansour has said in an interview that 'in Saudi there are no movie theatres, there is no film industry to speak of and, therefore, little money for investment' (Grey 2013). The precarious position of cinema in Saudi Arabia, then, not only did not prevent the film from participating at more than 30 festivals around the world, but perhaps even contributed to its numerous awards and nominations on the global festival circuit.

Our third and final example concerns the role of festivals in enabling the emergence of Palestinian cinema. More and more festivals realise that, in the absence of a recognised state, Palestinian artists may need outspoken support in order to participate fully in the global cultural arena. From early on, with attention and awards for films ranging from Michel Khleifi's *Urs Al Jalil* (*Wedding in Galilee*, Belgium / France / Israel, 1987) to *5 Broken Cameras* (Emat Burnat and Guy Davidi, 2011, Palestine / Israel / France / Netherlands), until, more recently, by giving explicit attention to such directors as Elia Suleiman, Annemarie Jacir and Hani Abu-Assad, major festivals such as Cannes, Berlinale, Venice, Toronto and Busan, have ensured that films from Palestine can gain adequate global exposure.[29]

Rasha Salti makes the important observation that Palestine has become a metaphor in the Arab imagination for the region at large. While the Nakba in 1948 and the Naqsa in 1967 were traumas on a national level for expelled Palestinians, they were also experienced as traumas by the whole region. Salti writes:

> The question of Palestine, the lived experience of struggle for its liberation and bearing witness to the historic injustice, have occupied a foundational position in the universe of modern Arab consciousness. (Salti 2006: 30)

As a metaphor, then, Palestine signifies not only those injustices experienced or witnessed specifically in the Palestinian Territories, but becomes representative of a wide range of matters related to colonial oppression and human suffering throughout the Middle East. Palestine is a source of inspiration for many stories and films now coming from the region. Protracted occupation and conflict serves as inspiration for important Syrian films such as Tewfik Saleh's classic *Al Makhdu'un*

(*The Dupes*, 1971), based on Palestinian Ghassan Kanafani's acclaimed novella *Rijāl fīsh-Shams* (*Men Under the Sun*, 1963), and Mohammad Malas's Golden Tanit-winner *Al Layl* (*The Night*, 1992), which explores the Arab-Israeli conflict through the lens of an Arab family. Renowned Syrian documentaries such as Omar Amiralay's *A Plate of Sardines* (1998, France) and Mohammad Malas' poignant *Al Manam* (*The Dream*, 1987, Syria) illustrate how strongly these Syrian filmmakers have been influenced by, if not directly involved with, the Palestinian cause.

Writing in 2013, *Financial Times'* cultural critic Peter Aspden decried the limitations suffered by Palestinan participants at festivals who have to endure huge difficulties to attend those events abroad that their art requires (such as the Shubback Festival of Contemporary Arab Culture at the ICA in London) (Aspden 2013). And it seems that many festival services like FestivalScope.com make a special effort to enabling the growth of Palestinian cinema and also to ensuring globally-made films that critically problematise Palestinian rights do gain global exposure; films such as *Schildkrötenwut* (*The Turtle's Rage*, Pary El-Qalkili, Germany, 2012), *A World Not Ours* (Mahdi Fleifel, UK / Lebanon / Denmark / UEA, 2012), *Nichnasti pa'am lagan* (*Once I Entered a Garden*, Avi Mograbi, Israel, 2012), or projects like *Art / Violence* (Udi Aloni, Mariam Abu Khaled and Batoul Taleb, Palestine / U.S. / Israel, 2013).

As it becomes clear from the discussions in the piece by Sienkiewicz and McIntosh and from the interview with Isaac Zablocki, a sizable network of Israeli and Jewish film festivals operate both across North America and globally. The number of festivals around the globe that feature Palestinian films, does not come anywhere near it (see the table in this volume).[30] It is such imbalances that new developments, particularly those from within the well-funded festivals in the Gulf region, seek to compensate: actions often take the shape of active support for production, distribution and exhibition of Palestinian films.

The People of the Circuit

It has been argued that the festival circuit exists only as long as there are those 'sole traders' who keep hopping between individual festivals to keep the circuit revolving and evolving (Iordanova 2009: 32-35). No festival exists without people behind it, and, as a mark of respect, at least some of the people who have been prominently engaged on the circuit in the region ought to be explicitly identified and named here.

At JCC, North Africa's quintessential festival, the role of founder Tahar Cheriaa who gave the festival a Third Cinema orientation is undoubtedly of great importance; but so, too, is the exemplary leadership of producers Tarak Ben Amar and Dora Bouchoucha (the latter is one of the rare female film producers in the region). As Mahmoud Kassem's detailed chronicle indicates, however, it is the role of Sa'ad Wahba that has been of decisive importance for the success of various festivals in Egypt. In Morocco, more recently, the tireless work of critic Nour-Eddine Saïl, the Director of Centre Cinématographique Marocain (CCM), has been of critical prominence. In Dubai, Abdulhamid Juma has been at the helm from the onset and has served as Chairman since 2006. In the case of the new festivals, the role of royal sponsors has been of notable substance, particularly by Sheikha Al Mayassa bint Hamad bin Khalifa Al-Thani in Qatar and Prince Moulay Rachid in Morocco.

Women have played and continue to play an extremely important role in the growth of festivals, and not just women's film festivals. Lia Van Leer, for example, has been a high profile presence on the A-festival circuit for many years and is the founder and President of the Jerusalem Film Festival. In Istanbul, the festival there has grown under the leadership of two women – Hülya Uçansu and, more recently, Azize Tan. Dimitris Eipides, now director of the festival in Thessaloniki and a regional programmer for Toronto IFF in the past, has been credited with orchestrating the breakthrough of Iranian cinema to global audiences. Rasha Salti, a programmer of international repute (currently with the Toronto IFF) has curated numerous original panoramas of film from the region and is probably the festival figure with most clout when the topic of discussion turns to the Middle East.

Even if they do represent the cinema of 'a country with no industry' (Aftab 2013), Palestinians have been active in showcasing their plight in a variety of imaginative ways. Filmmaker Rashid Mashawara is known to have been engaged in film festival-type screenings in refugee camps in the 1990s and Khaled Ziada started the London Palestinian Film Festival a decade ago.

Well-known foreign directors and critics have been closely associated with festivals in the region in the past and continue to be so today. British critic David Robinson, for example, served on the inaugural jury at the Cairo festival in 1976 (alongside Egyptian veteran director Shadi Abdel-Salam) and American director Elia Kazan, originally an Armenian from Turkey, led demonstrations against censorship at the festival in Istanbul in 1984. More recently, the Greek-French director and high-profile public figure Costa-Gavras protested the closure of Istanbul's Emek cinema, the main venue for the city's film festival, in April 2013. [31]

In the past decade a number of Western festival professionals were increasingly involved with the new film festivals that sprang up across the region; their expertise was actively sought, for varying periods of commitment and particularly by new festivals, like that at Marrakech or those in the Gulf. Over the years, well-known specialists, such as the late Sheila Whitaker (1946-2013), former BFI London Film Festival Director, and Peter Scarlet of the San Francisco and Tribeca festivals, over the years became involved in the Gulf. Others followed, including Bruno Barde's Parisian consultancy firm Système Publique, which is largely responsible for programming Marrakech, as well as Paris-based Melita Toscan du Plantier, who stepped in to become the public face of Marrakech after the passing of her husband and director of the first festival, Daniel Toscan du Plantier, in 2003. Australian Amanda Palmer was a high-profile presence in the Gulf region over a number of years, as Director of both the Doha Film Institute and its attendant festival. Other luminaries had stints as consultants: Chicago's Alissa Simon, Durban and Sydney's Nasheen Moody and Simon Field (formerly of Rotterdam's festival) at Dubai, Ludmila Cvikova at Doha, and so on.

Structure, Contributors and Contributions

As with other *Film Festival Yearbooks*, the contributors to this book represent a productive mixture of academics, practitioners and professionals, as well as some who straddle two or more of these functions within the field of Film Festival Studies. Once again, we have worked to ensure we could present a true diversity of voices. The authors hail from several continents and a dozen countries. Some, like Zena Al Tahhan and Asma Ajroudi are young students whereas others, like Abbas Arnaout and Mahmoud Kassem, are veterans of the field. We take pride in being able to bring together scholars and critics, as well as film festival organisers, in order to establish a dialogue between different stakeholders and between theory and practice. Like other volumes in this series, this collection boasts writings by contributors based both in the region under discussion and in the West, and includes transnationals, migrants and those defying borders. Those chapters which had to be translated posed interesting challenges, both linguistically and culturally – references to political systems, words unknown in the English language and films we had never heard of, all opened our minds and eyes and made us more conscious of our own limited knowledge. A further diversity revealed itself in comparisons of the writing styles and approaches of established academics with those of early-career scholars. These are all dimensions that we regard as the strengths of the *Film Festival Yearbook* series from its outset, and which we feel important to foreground once again, as they demonstrate the dynamism of the field and the dialogic nature of our ongoing project.

And like the other books in this series, this one opens with a section called Contexts, boasting essays that offer general considerations and that contextualise the theme. Yet, whereas in other books we have usually followed up with an extensive section of Case Studies, this time around we opted for a different approach and decided to cluster the contributions together in sections that relate to a specific region or country. We did this specifically because, by including territories such as Turkey and Iran, as well as the Maghreb, we were straying beyond what is usually referred to as the Middle East proper. So, as we have noted earlier, we felt we needed to find a logical structure for the diverse material that was commissioned. The resulting clusters open with a group of chapters on Iranian festivals, followed by a section on Turkish cinema, both structured more or less chronologically. Next we turn to the Middle East itself (including Egypt, Lebanon and Syria, Israel and Palestine, as well as Iraq), before featuring sections on the Gulf and the Maghreb. This clustering within the wider region proved to be a productive way to work, by providing us with those bite-size chunks with which we are familiar. Our research reveals that the network of festivals, and the circuit itself, do not necessarily follow their own logic and that, in fact, these chunks of the region's geography largely correspond to self-sufficient and relatively confined cultural spheres. We are confident that the dynamic between festivals such as Marrakech and Dubai (regarding the role of sponsors and the significance of red carpet events), or between Carthage and Beirut (regarding artistic integrity and the programmer-focused image of the festival), is likely to be sensed more adequately through such an overall structuring.

Most of the books in the *Film Festival Yearbook* series contain a third section detailing Resources. It is a section in which we traditionally include interviews, tables, bibliographies and other source materials. Whilst we continue this same groundwork, which we regard as crucial and necessary (Iordanova 2011b), for this volume we have opted to integrate the interviews within those subsections dedicated to specific geographical areas. (We would like to emphasise the subjectivity of the nature of the interview and stress that statements made in interviews and interview-based case studies do not necessarily reflect our own views.) The tables have similarly been added to the chapters they correspond to. The reason for doing this was, again, simple: since the region under scrutiny in this book is so vast and diverse, we opted to keep countries and smaller regions together for consistency and clarity.

Regretfully, we could not ensure that all the material we had hoped to see created actually materialised. One of the regrettable gaps is an interview with veteran festival figure Lia Van Leer, the founder of the Jerusalem International Film Festival, which we commissioned yet never received. We also feel we do not have enough on the all-important festival in Carthage, one of the oldest, most highly-respected and well-known institutions in the region, yet we hope that this is, in part, compensated for by writing on the festival by Patricia Caillé in *Journal of African Cinemas* (2013) and by Jeffrey Ruoff in *Film International* (2008), in addition to the *Cineaste* reports by Paquet (1975) and Shohat and Stam (1995). As we recognise the importance of this festival, we hope that its pre-eminent position is properly highlighted in and by this introduction, in the interview with its current director Mohamed Mediouni and by the chapters by Alberto Elena and Jean-Michel Frodon.

In the initial Contexts section of this collection, then, Alberto Elena steers us towards a new cartography of Arab film festivals, reflecting on the waxing and waning of certain festivals in popularity or status. In a similar vein, Jean-Michel Frodon offers a new typology of the festivals in the region. The increasing visibility of women on the festival circuit is highlighted expertly by Gönul Dönmez-Colin, and illustrated by an extensive table highlighting Women's festivals in and beyond the region. Laura U. Marks focuses on the usually neglected genre of the experimental film in her chapter examining experimental art films and their exhibition in Lebanon, Syria and Egypt. Alisa Lebow offers a polemical piece that expounds on the demands that festival programmers encounter in the context of the Arab Spring. Dina Iordanova wraps up the Contexts section with a meditation on how some of the festivals in the region begin the formation of a circuit for 'parallel cinemas', Bollywood in this instance.

On to the Case Studies part, the Iranian section of which opens with Azadeh Farahmand's study on the legacy of the high-profile film festival staged in pre-revolutionary Tehran (1972-1977). In a lively personal memoir that is both entertaining and insightful, Chris Berry recounts his attendance at Fajr, Iran's foremost film festival since 1983, in the 1990s. Brisbane-based Anne Demy-Geroe takes up where Berry leaves off, continuing the story of Fajr by sharing her decade-long experience as invitee, jury member and programmer (for her own successful Iranian Film Festival Australia). Maryam Ghorbankarimi closes the Iranian ranks with a detailed historical table of film festivals in Iran.

Savas Arslan opens up the section dealing with Turkey with an historical look at the oldest festivals there. Murat Akser critically explores the rivalry of the two main festivals in the country: in Antalya and in Adana. Melis Behlil's interview with Azize Tam from the Istanbul International Film Festival offers insights into the financing model of this event and also into its specific position within the region. The tables which end this section showcase the diverse film festivals taking place in Turkey, as well as some of the main diasporic film festivals dedicated to Turkish cinema.

The section on the Middle East features an essay by Egyptian critic Mahmoud Kassem, who delineates the origins and evolution of the Cairo and Alexandria film festivals, richly illustrated by Koen Van Eynde's table. Stefanie Van de Peer then explores the complexity of festivals in conflict zones like Lebanon and Syria. We have also included a Beirut-related fragment of an article by Laura U. Marks, 'The Ethical Presenter: Or How to Have Good Arguments over Dinner', originally published in *The Moving Image* in 2004. These pieces are followed by an essay by Matt Sienkiewicz and Heather McIntosh who explore how the distribution of Israeli cinema capitalises on controversy and on the extensive circuit of diasporic Jewish festivals. Dina Iordanova reports on the Other Israel Film Festival in New York (based on her interview with founder Carole Zabar and programmers Ravit Turjeman and Isaac Zablocki) and is supplemented by a table of film festivals in Israel compiled by Viviane Saglier. Nick Denes, one of the key figures of the London Palestinian Film Festival, reflects on matters of funding and politics. Tables featuring Palestinian film festivals, both in the Occupied Territories and all over the world, and a table incorporating Iraqi film festivals, close this section on the Middle East.

The range of film festivals that have sprung up in the Persian Gulf – Doha, Abu Dhabi and Dubai – is explored in the enlightening piece by the Abu Dhabi-based Alia Yunis. She looks in detail at the festivals' approaches to audience building, and in particular at their interactions with local universities and film students. An interview with Abbas Arnaout, Director of the Al Jazeera Documentary Festival, offers insights into the unique programming of this acclaimed newcomer to the documentary circuit. A table listing festivals in the Gulf region rounds the section out.

The volume concludes with a number of pieces examining festivals in the Maghreb, the extreme West of the Middle East. Moroccan scholar Jamal Bahmad opens, with his tale of the festivals in Marrakech and Tangiers and their distinctive influence on the development of Moroccan cinema. This is followed by an extensive interview with Mohamed Mediouni, Director of the Carthage Cinema Days, conducted by our colleague in Madrid, Javier H. Estrada. Sally Shafto, a prolific writer on Maghrebi festivals over the years, contributes a unique piece on a festival that cultivate imagined communities: she investigates France's unique Arab film festival in Fameck. Stefanie Van de Peer closes this section with a table indicating the festival landscape in the Maghreb, focusing on Morocco, Algeria and Tunisia.

The Bibliography, compiled by Amber Shields, was assembled in close consultation with the Editors. In the resources available to date, the Middle East has been largely under-represented, so we hope that our collection and this bibliography will contribute significantly to the continued efforts of international scholars to examine in more detail the significance of this region to the global film festival 'treadmill' (Iordanova 2009).

* * *

Joana Hadjithomas and Khalil Joreige's remarkable documentary *The Lebanese Rocket Society* (Lebanon / France / Qatar, 2012) is one of the recent festival highlights from the Middle East.

Ostensibly the tale of an ambitious rocket project that a group of 1960s Beirut-based Armenian physicists – inspired by the space exploration achievements of bigger nations – embrace, but are then forced to abandon, the film, in fact, explores (and subtly challenges) the manipulation of collective memory and the suppression of national self-esteem. All in the name of a shaky and dubious Middle Eastern power balance. Forced into oblivion in the aftermath of the 1967 war, the 'rocket society' project is brought back to life in the film – through pictures, interviews and in an activist-type endeavour to reconstruct and publicly transport a rocket through the streets of present-day Beirut. In the course of all this, one is shrewdly posed audacious questions about 'confiscated dreams' and stifled aspirations. Why is it that, if one is Lebanese, one is not supposed to dream of space travel? Why the double standards? Why is the sky off limits for exploration?

Representing the most active generation of Middle Eastern directors, Hadjithomas and Joreige speak discontentedly about paralysed ambitions and suppressed generational pride. They embrace the self-esteem and elation that the Arab Revolutions bring. The ability to dream may once have been stifled, but it has now been re-awakened. It cannot be stopped across the region: 'Maybe the fear is more inside us…Maybe we should stop being afraid?'

Made with support from one of the new Gulf-based funds, it is the first time that the work by these established yet esoteric experimental filmmakers has travelled through the global documentary circuit for screening in places such as London, Copenhagen, Toronto, Nyon and Buenos Aires. It was only courtesy of the streaming platform Festival Scope, which provides a valuable service to festival programmers who cannot travel personally to all events, that we viewers outside the region originally had the chance to see this film.

Indeed, it is due to the very existence of festivals that those films which help us understand oblique experiences and aspirations are able to become part of our lives and minds – films such as *Un été à La Goulette*

/ *A Summer in La Goulette* (Férid Boughedir, Tunisia / France / Belgium, 1996), a tale of happy conviviality disturbed forever in that divisive 1967 summer of the Six-Day War, or Moufida Tlatli's *Samt el qusur / Silences of the Palace* (France / Tunisia, 1994), an account of subtle and painful revelations about exploitation underwritten by colonialism. The list is endless, growing and always illuminating.

Even now, many facets of Middle Eastern historical, political, social and cultural realities are chiefly available to us mainly through film festivals. We should all be grateful for that.

Works Cited

Abu Dhabi Film Festival website. On-line. Available HTTP: http://www. abudhabifilmfestival.ae/en/ (10 March 2014)

Aftab, Kaleem (2013) 'Rasha Salti on Falling in Love at Toronto International Film Festival', *The National*, September 5. On-line. Available HTTP: http://www.thenational.ae/arts-culture/film/rasha-salti-on-falling-in-love-at-toronto-international-film-festival (28 February 2014)

Aspden, Peter (2013) 'Pop Culture Diplomacy', *Financial Times*, Arts, 29-30, 15.

Bakari, Imruh and Mbye Cham (1996) *African Experiences of Cinema*. London: BFI.

Bazin, André (2009 [1955]) 'The Festival Viewed as a Religious Order', in Richard Porton (ed.) (2009) *Dekalog 03: On Film Festivals*. London: Wallflower Press, 13-20.

Berry, Chris (2003) 'Full Service Cinema: The South Korean Cinema Success Story (So Far)', Young-Key Kim Renaud, R. Richard Grinker and Kirk Larsen (eds) *Text and Context of Korean Cinema: Crossing Borders*. Sigur Centre Asia Paper No. 17, 7 – 16.

Caillé, Patricia (2013) 'A Gender Perspective on the 23rd Edition of the JCC', *Journal of African Cinemas*, 4, 2, 229-233.

De Valck, Marijke (2007) *Film Festivals: From European Geopolitics to Global Cinephilia*. Amsterdam: University of Amsterdam Press.

DFI (2012) 'Berlinale's Arab Focus – Panorama Interview', video. On-line. Available HTTP: http://www.dohafilminstitute.com/videos/berlinale-s-arab-focus-panorama-interview (16 January 2013)

Diawara, Manthia (1994) 'On Tracking World Cinema: African Cinema at Film Festivals', *Public Culture*, 6: 385-396.

Doha Film Festival website. On-line. Available HTTP: http://www. dohafilminstitute.com/filmfestival (10 March 2014)

Dubai Film Festival website. On-line. Available HTTP: http://www. dubaifilmfest.com/en/industry (10 March 2014)

Dönmez-Colin, Gönül (2004) *Women, Islam and Cinema*. London: Reaktion Books.

Grey, Tobias (2013) 'The Undercover Director', *Financial Times*. 29 March, 14.

Gruber, Christiane and Sune Haugbolle (eds.) (2013) *Visual Culture in the Modern Middle East*. Bloomington: Indiana University Press.

Huntington, Samuel P. (1996) *The Clash of Civilizations and the Remaking of World Order*, New York: Simon & Schuster.

Iordanova, Dina (2001) *Cinema of Flames: Balkan Film, Culture and the Media*. London: BFI.

___ (2009) 'The Film Festival Circuit', in Dina Iordanova with Ragan Rhyne (eds) *FFY 1: The Festival Circuit*. St Andrews: St Andrews Film Studies with College Gate Press. 23-39.

___ (2011a) 'East Asia and Film Festivals: Transnational Clusters for Creativity and Commerce', in Dina Iordanova and Ruby Cheung (eds) *FFY 3: Film Festivals and East Asia*. St Andrews: St Andrews Film Studies, 1-35.

___ (2011b) 'The Resources: Necessary Groundwork', in Dina Iordanova and Ruby Cheung (eds) *FFY 3: Film Festivals and East Asia*. St Andrews: St Andrews Film Studies, 189-196.

Iordanova, Dina and Ruby Cheung (eds) (2011) *FFY 3: Film Festivals and East Asia*. St Andrews: St Andrews Film Studies.

Joselyn, Thomas (2013) 'US Closes Diplomatic Facilities in Response to Al Qaeda Threat', *The Long War Journal*. 2 August. On-line. Available HTTP: http://www.longwarjournal.org/archives/2013/08/us_closes_diplomatic.php (4 March 2014).

Journées Cinématographiques de Carthage Official Website. On-line. Available HTTP: http://www.jccarthage.com/ (13 March 2014),

Jungen, Christian (2014) *Hollywood in Cannes: The History of a Love-Hate Relationship*. Amsterdam: Amsterdam University Press.

Khatib, Lina (2008) *Lebanese Cinema: Imagining the Civil War and Beyond*. London: I.B. Tauris.

Knee, Adam and Kong Rithdee (2011) 'Tourism and the Landscape of Thai Film Festivals', in Dina Iordanova and Ruby Cheung (eds) *FFY 3: Film Festivals and East Asia*. St Andrews: St Andrews Film Studies, 154-166.

Kraidi, Marwan M. (2005) *Hybridity: The Cultural Logic of Globalization*. Philadelphia: Temple University Press.

Kraidi, Marwan M. and Joe Khalil (2009) *Arab Television Industries*. London: BFI.

Larkin, Brian (1997) 'Indian Films and Nigerian Lovers: Media and the Creation of Parallel Modernities', *Africa: Journal of the International African Institute*, 67, 3, 406-440.

Lewis, Bernard (1993) *Islam and the West*. Oxford: Oxford University Press.

Mauss, Marcel (1954) *The Gift: Forms and Functions of Exchange in Archaic Societies*. London: W.W. Norton and Company.

Marks, Laura U. (2004) 'The Ethical Presenter or How to Have Good Arguments over Dinner', *The Moving Image*, 4, 1, 34-47.

Martin, Florence (2012) *Screens and Veils: Maghrebi Women's Cinema*. Bloomington: Indiana University Press.

Mitchell, Wendy (2013) 'Amritraj predicts Arab film boom in next 10 years', *Screen International*, 26 October. On-line. Available HTTP: http://www.screendaily.com/5062924.article (3 March 2014)

Naddaf, Sandra (1991) *Arabesque: Narrative Structure and the Aesthetics of Repetition in the 1001 Nights*. Evanston: Northwestern University Press.

Nichols, Bill (1994) 'Discovering Form, Inferring Meaning: New Cinemas and the Film Festival Circuit', *Film Quarterly* 47, 3, 16-30.

Paquet, Andre (1975) 'Toward an Arab and African Cinema: the 1974 Carthage Film Festival', trans. Renée Delforge, *Cinéaste*, 7, 1, 19-21.

Peckmezian, Mark (2014) 'This Guy Can Get You On The List,' *Business Week*, January 20-26: 63-65.

Ruoff, Jeffrey (2008) 'Ten Nights in Tunisia: Les Journées Cinématographiques de Carthage', *Film International*, 6, 4, 43-51.

Said, Edward (1997 [1981]) *Covering Islam: How the Media and the Experts Determine How We See the Rest of the World*. London: Vintage.

Salti, Rasha (2006) *Insights into Syrian Cinema: Essays and Conversations with Contemporary Filmmakers*. New York: ArteEast and Rattapallax Press.

Shohat, Ella and Robert Stam (1995) 'The Carthage Film Festival', *Cinéaste*, 21, 3, 56.

Tapsoba, Clement (no date) 'The History of African Cinema and the Origins of FEPACI', *FEPACI Archives*. On-line. Available HTTP: http://fepaci.org/congress1/archives/Origins%20Of%20Fepaci.pdf (24 January 2014)

Van De Peer, Stefanie (2012) 'The Moderation of Creative Dissidence in Syria: Reem Ali's Documentary Zabad', *Journal for Cultural Research*, 16, 2&3, 297-317.

Vivarelli, Nick (2013) 'Tribeca, Doha Film Institute End Partnership', *Variety*, 30 April 2013. On-line. Available HTTP: http://variety.com/2013/film/international/tribeca-doha-film-institute-end-partnership-1200427812/ (24 January 2014)

Notes

[1] See Joselyn (2013). Based on intercepted electronic communications between senior al-Qaeda figures, it was believed that the potential for an attack was particularly strong in the Middle East and North Africa. The temporary closure of embassies expanded to many of the countries where film festivals covered in our volume take place (e.g. Abu Dhabi, Iraq, Egypt and Dubai).

[2] Some of the potential contributors we approached turned us down when they learned that we were planning to include material related to Israeli film culture and festivals, as they thought the boycott ought to be applied in a manner that would see the exclusion of Israel from any collection dedicated to the Middle East. We fully acknowledge the complexity of the region and the role of Israel and its festivals in the Middle East and around the rest of the world. Our decision to include chapters on Israeli film festivals, both within and outside of Israel, was made in full awareness of the boycott and so we feel that the chapters we commissioned and the interviews we conducted show our own and the authors' consciousness regarding the current deadlock. We hope to enhance the understanding of the significance and complexity of film festivals in the political and the cultural arena, anywhere around the world.

[3] Whilst we do not fully endorse Javier Estrada's claim that the JCC 'is the longest running festival outside of Europe' (interview with Mediouni in this volume), we concede that it is important for this festival's long pedigree to be taken into serious consideration by the film festivals study community.

[4] We hope that in the not-too-distant future we will see someone from within the Film Festival Studies community undertake an investigation into the history of all these A-Category accreditations. When it comes to festivals beyond the West, they appear to involve particularly curious (and instructive) twists and turns.

[5] The JCC in Carthage has not been around as long as Cannes, but as it remains the most established and well-respected film festival in the Middle East, it is valuable to compare its winners with the selections of Middle Eastern films at Cannes. Cannes has a much broader scope; Carthage focuses on African and Arab films. It is unlikely that we can deduct that Carthage, because it takes place at a later point in the year, looks at Cannes for its selection. Certainly, Cannes does not select from Carthage, as it prefers world premieres for its Official Selection. Nevertheless, there does seem to be a sense of a circuit, or at least some form of 'festival film' (or maybe more accurately 'festival director') that is popular on the circuit.

A full list of JCC Tanit d'Or winners since inception:

1966: *La Noire De...* (*Black Girl*, Ousmane Sembène, Senegal)

1970: *Al Ikhtiyar* (*The Choice*, Youssef Chahine, Egypt)

1972: *Al-makhdu'un* (*The Dupes*, Tewfik Saleh, Egypt/Syria) & *Sambizanga* (Sarah Maldoror, Guadeloupe, France)

1974: *Kafr kasem* (Borhane Alaouié, Algeria) & *Les 'bicots-Nègres' vos voisins* (Med Hondo, Mauritania)

1976: *Les Ambassadeurs* (*The Ambassadors*, Naceur Ktari, Tunisia)

1978: *Mughamarat batal* (*The Adventures of a Hero*, Merzak Allouache, Algeria)

1980: *Aziza* (Abdellatif Ben Ammar, Tunisia)

1982: *Finye* (Souleymane Cissé, Mali)

1984: *Dreams of the City* (Mohamed Malas, Syria)

1986: *Rih essed* (*Man of Ashes*, Nouri Bouzid, Tunisia)

1988: *Wedding in Galilee* (Michel Khleifi, Palestine)

1992: *Al Layl* (*The Night*, Mohamed Malas, Syria)

1994: *Samt Al Kussur* (*The Silences of the Palace*, Moufida Tlatli, Tunisia)

1996: *Salut cousin* (*Hello Cousin*, Merzak Allouache, Algeria)

1998: *Vivre au paradis* (*Living in Paradise*, Bourlem Guerdjou, Algeria)

2000: *Dolé* (Imunga Ivanga, Gabon)

2002: *Le prix du pardon* (*The Price of Forgiveness*, Mansour Sora Wade, Senegal)

2004: *A Casablanca, les anges ne volent pas* (*In Casablanca, Angels do not Fly*, Mohamed Asli, Morocco)

2006: *Making-Of* (Nouri Bouzid, Tunisia)

2008: *Teza* (Haile Gerima, Ethiopia)

2010: *Microphone* (Ahmed Abdallah, Egypt)

2012: *Al Juma Al Akheira* (*The Last Friday*, Yahya Alabdallah, UAE/Jordan)

The festival's first ever winner was Senegalese Ousmane Sembène in 1966, with *La Noire De...* (Black Girl), which was screened earlier that year in the 'Semaine Internationale de la Critique' at Cannes. The first similarity is visible in 1970. Chahine first won a Palme d'Or for *The Land* and later that same year a Tanit d'Or in Carthage for *The Choice*. In 1980 *Aziza* was selected for the 'Section Parallèle Director' at Cannes and then won the Tanit d'Or in Carthage. The same happened in 1982: *Finye* was screened at the 'Un Certain Regard' selection in Cannes and then won in Carthage. So, while the festivals do not exactly copy one another, they do screen films by the same directors (hence, again, the term 'festival director' might be more productive than 'festival film').

[6] The oldest Western writing we were able to locate dealing with JCC is the 1975 piece by André Paquet for *The Cineaste*; two decades later the magazine included coverage of the festival by Ella Shohat and Robert Stam (1995) who had just published their politically influential study *Unthinking Eurocentrism* (1994). Writing in *Public Culture*, African film specialist Manthia Diawara acknowledges the importance of the JCC, yet spends more time discussing a festival of African cinema that takes place at the Lincoln Center in New York City than the Tunisian event (Diawara 1994).

[7] Critics have argued that the JCC has been alternating with the festival in Damascus, but Mohamed Mediouni, current director of JCC, opposes this simplistic evaluation (see the interview in this volume), not only because the inaugural date of Damascus is contested, but also because DIFF, which also runs biennially, is a much smaller event of significantly lesser reach.

[8] This is further illustration of the view on 'parallel cinemas' that Iordanova develops in her contribution to this publication.

[9] This losing streak of Carthage is, in our view, not only explicable by trends like the growing Islamisation of Tunisian politics, the rise to power of the new festival in Marrakech, as well as the new festivals in the Gulf, but also by the diminishing importance of Tunisian cinema itself. In the Maghreb, Tunisia is fast losing its prominence to Morocco. Since the late 1990s, after Tunisia's Golden Age in the 1980s, Moroccan cinema has grown exponentially in productivity and quality, and is recognised both nationally and internationally. Filmmakers such as Layla Marrakchi, Nabil Ayouch, Faouzi Bensaïdi and Hicham Lasri have really put Moroccan cinema on the map, while the Centre Cinématographique Marrocain

is centralising and developing the industry. This has enabled organisations such as the CCM to establish Morocco as a prime place for filmmaking, both by Moroccan local and diasporic filmmakers and, as a location, by international production groups. This productivity and entrepreneurial spirit, and the resulting financial growth of the Moroccan film industry, has ensured attention is being paid to Moroccan cinema, and has enabled increasingly successful film festivals to be set up for the showcasing of Moroccan masterpieces. The Marrakech International Film Festival and the Tangier Festival of National Cinema are two flourishing results of these new tendencies in the Maghreb.

10 Christian Jungen (2014) has shown that the coverage of a film festival is directly linked to the number of journalists whose attendance the festival is able to fund. As far as programmers are concerned, they do not find it as easy to attend as invitations, following the prestige principle, are chiefly sent to executives rather than the artistic directors or region programmers of other global film festivals (Iordanova, personal communication with programmers of various Asian festivals, 2013).

11 In the 1980s, as evidenced by Mahmoud Kassem in this volume, some of the older festivals in the region – like the one in Alexandria (Egypt) – were similarly associated with a lavish offer of food and lodgings, and were reputed as favoured exotic vacation destinations on the festival circuit.

12 Ajyal Film Festival (since 2013) focuses on children and young people, whereas Qumra – announced for 2015 – will focus on international and regional films. The Qumra festival was initially announced for an inaugural edition in March 2014, but then it cancelled because the organisation wanted to focus its efforts on developing local, grassroots audiences and initiatives to showcase at the festival. Both Doha festivals are now run by the Doha Film Institute and executively directed by young Qatari banker Abdulaziz Al Khater.

13 In our past work we had the opportunity to investigate a non-Western festival that never took the step to emancipate and switch to local expertise. The case in point is the extravagantly staged (and notorious) event in Bangkok which was also funded lavishly but which, unlike the events in the Gulf, was entirely run by Western-based executives. An analysis of the disastrous consequences of such management is to be found in the piece by Adam Knee and Thai critic Kong Rithdee (2011).

14 Unlike its counterparts in the Gulf, the festival in Marrakech is still being programmed and run out of Paris at the time of writing. This has been a contentious issue with the local film community in Morocco from the outset (Iordanova, personal communications, 2013). For more information, see the contribution of Jamal Bahmad in this volume.

15 In an interview that Stefanie Van de Peer conducted with Michel Khleifi (Brussels, 2013), the celebrated Palestinian filmmaker and darling of many film festivals pointed out that the dominance of glitz and glamour is precisely why he has developed an aversion to film festivals. 'The original meaning of the term film festival,' he said, 'is to celebrate filmmaking, and I don't see that any more. Instead, I see clusters of people trying to impress one another with a show of wealth and status, and I am not interested in that.'

16 Even a festival like Sundance, associated with the more modest version of filmmaking undertaken by indies, was said to be hosting about 400 parties in the context of its 2014 edition. In such a busy atmosphere, where marketing, fashion and the 'party-circuit circus' are assigned such priority, films inevitably

lose in importance – something which is acknowledged in Peckmezian's piece with an apposite commentary line: 'Yes, Sundance has movies, too' (Peckmezian 2014: 64).

[17] It may well be that careful deliberation over the dates of festivals is evidence of this 'gift' exchange and reciprocity, and of course it enhances the interdependent relationships between festivals. The Doha Tribeca Film Festival used to take place in October, and then moved to November. The Abu Dhabi film festival takes place in October and has done since its inauguration. The Dubai film festival takes place in December. For a very small region, this seems to be a very busy and cluttered period of festival junkets towards the end of the year; and in a relatively small square mileage: October, November and December have each been devoted to a festival in the Gulf. The carefully deliberated move of Doha to split the festival up – and to organise a children's festival in November – has freed up some space for festival hoppers to spend October, December and then March in the UAE and Qatar instead of three months in a row.

[18] Nevertheless, television increasingly shows films – mostly from the Middle East (and with an emphasis on the ever-popular Egyptian melodramas). For more on the matter of television in the Arab world see Kraidi and Khalil (2009). One film festival only was established in 2013: the Television & Film Festival organised by the King Abdul Aziz Cultural Centre.

[19] According to one of our informers, who opted to stay anonymous, in the Gulf no one pursues topics that could be construed as controversial. 'People don't rock the boat or present any original opinions or criticism of anything because the reality is that the governments (tightly run monarchies), are central to everything. The citizens here are generally happy – the government is very good to them – but in return, no one pushes the envelope in journalism or the arts […] This is Shangri-la as long as you just stay floating on the top and don't try to dive in […] People here are just always scared to talk about even the most banal things. This sensitivity has only increased with the so-called Arab Spring, because of which the government has become much stricter about who can and cannot work here' (personal communication, 2013). The controversy that surrounded Caveh Zahedi's project The Sheikh and I (2012, U.S. / UAE), which was originally commissioned by the Sharjah Biennale but then censored, only confirms this point.

[20] Al Waleed is one of the richest men in the Middle East, and benefactor for many Middle Eastern (particularly Palestinian) causes, as well as worldwide causes such as the Tsunami victims. He plays the most important role in cinema in Saudi Arabia via his donations and investments in infrastructure and production. And he is the CEO of the King Abdul Aziz Cultural Centre, the venue that organised the first Saudi Film Festival.

[21] As the Doha Film Institute's website states: 'DFI's initiatives include funding for MENA and international film and television productions, year-round film screenings, education and training, and an annual film festival' (http://www. dohafilminstitute.com/education).

[22] When it comes to fostering film culture at large in the Middle East, Metropolis cinema in Beirut, Lebanon, holds an annual European Film Festival (http://www. metropoliscinema.net/2013/20th-european-film-festival), and so does the ECU festival in Amman, capital city of Jordan (http://www.ecufilmfestival.com/en/). There is even a European Film Festival in Jeddah, Saudi Arabia, that started in 2007 at the Italian Cultural Club. The event in Beirut is organised by one of the

most dynamic cinemas in the entire region. In Jeddah it is organised by the consul of Italy in Saudi, and consuls from other countries settled in Saudi are invited to the festival when films from their home country are screened. The festival in Amman is organised by the French ECU – The European Independent Film Festival, a travelling film festival based in Paris. These three examples illustrate a different incentive in their establishment: the Saudi festival promotes the art and culture of the European countries represented by the consuls in Saudi; the festival in Amman celebrates European independent film in a French context; and the event in Beirut is a symptom of Metropolis Cinema's dynamic local programming team. The presence of European cinema in the Middle East is therefore diverse and hybrid and individual.

23 Rotterdam, Berlin and Venice have shown a significant shift in their showcasing of Middle Eastern films since 2011. Rotterdam and Berlinale opted in 2012 to focus one of their strands on films from the Middle East. In Rotterdam the programme was called Power Cut Middle East and programmed by Peter Van Hoof, usually an expert in experimental cinema, and Bianca Taal, who specialises in feature length films from Greece, Turkey, Israel, Iran and the Arab world. At the Berlinale, Wieland Speck, director of the festival's Panorama section, says they did 'not look for Arab films' but they 'found them'. Speck touches on the increased recognition of quality films from the Middle East worldwide.

24 In fact, Abu Sayf shows up three times, and Chahine four times: we might then speak of 'festival directors', maybe more so than 'festival films'. From the 1960s onwards, Algeria is the Middle Eastern country to be found most frequently on Cannes' short list, dominated completely by Mohammed Lakhdar-Hamina, whose films feature four times. This is perhaps due to France's vacillating position towards its former colony at that time.

25 Ideally we would have also liked to include here a discussion of the expansive variety of diasporic festivals that present the cinema of the respective countries in the region to the West. But this is a huge topic that we thought would be best left for dedicated investigation: pieces by Sally Shafto on the Fameck festival in France and by Iordanova on The Other Israel in New York, as well as tables provide some idea of the expanse of such festivals.

26 This festival's funding model – festival attached to a TV network and entirely financed by it – is one of the more original examples of financing that we came across in the process of putting this volume together. The other, equally interesting example, is the festival in Istanbul, which is privately owned by a corporate foundation (see the interview with Tan).

27 The project involves a group of ten Asian documentary filmmakers who participate in a training workshop which takes place during the Busan festival in October. Six selected projects are awarded U.S.$50,000 and are then shown on the AJE channel.

28 In existence since 2007, past editions included retrospectives such as Bloody Women (2011), Blonde Crazy (2010), and Screen Seductresses (2009). The festival had screened Middle Eastern films only occasionally: in 2009 it organised a debate on the topic of Afghan Women On the Screen; in 2010 it screened Palestinian film Amreeka by Cherien Dabis; and in 2011, Women of Hamas (Suha Arraf, Palestine / Israel / Germany, 2010) was screened.

29 These include, among others, Elia Suleiman's Chronicle of a Disappearance (1996, Palestine / Israel / U.S./Germany/France) and Yadon ilaheyya (Divine Inter-vention, 2002, France / Morocco / Germany / Palestine), Annemarie Jacir's Milh

Hadha Al Bahr (*Salt of This Sea*, 2008, Palestine / Belgium / France / Spain / Switzerland) and *Lamma shoftak* (*When I Saw You*, 2012, Palestine / Jordan / Greece / UAE) and Hani Abu-Assad's *Paradise Now* (2005, Palestine / France / Germany / Netherlands / Israel) and *Omar* (2013, Palestine).

30   This is an outcome of the global specifically Jewish diaspora; there is perhaps nothing like this available to other diasporas. Moreover, equating Israeli and Jewish is endemic, as well as Palestine and Palestinian (Denes, in this volume). Yet both equations are problematic. Sienkiewicz and McIntosh talk of 'unique and systematic ways in which the [Jewish] festival system plays an important role in globalizing cinema production of a relatively small nation', whereas their interviewee Ruth Diskin notes that 'conflict and controversy make up a significant proportion of her business' (in this volume).

31   Many Turkish film critics, festival programmers and filmmakers were involved in the protests, an event which preceded the widely publicised stand-off at Gezi Park. Director Zeki Demirkubuz is known to have been the most vocal proponent of the protest from among the Turkish filmmaking community.

Part 1: Contexts

Towards a New Cartography of Arab Film Festivals

Alberto Elena

November 2008. The Cairo International Film Festival (CIFF) (www.ciff. org.eg), in its 32nd edition, takes an unexpected step. Under the aegis of Egypt's Minister of Culture, Farouk Hosny, and along with a new programme section devoted to the African continent's film production, a symposium is held under the provocative title *African Cinema... Goodbye Isolation*. The event brings together a number of filmmakers, critics, scholars and representatives of the film industry from different countries. Chaired by the South African producer, writer and media activist Firdoze Bulbulia, a panel of nine discusses how to end, once and for all, the isolation, if not ghettoisation (Diawara 1994: 385-396), of African cinema as a whole. The composition of the round table is rather atypical and goes a long way towards exemplifying the new winds that are blowing on the continent. The presence of two French experts – Serge Toubiana, then the Director of the Cinémathèque Française, and Olivier Barlet, President of *Africultures* – is unsurprising. But the remaining panellists break all expectations: three Nigerians (each with a very different profile), a South African filmmaker, two film festival directors from Cameroon and Côte d'Ivoire, but just one representative of the Arab cinemas, the Egyptian film writer Ahmad Shawki.

How should such an unusual initiative be read in the context of a festival that up to now had been quite unconcerned with a Pan-African dimension and had never stood out as an important festival node for Arab cinemas? Undoubtedly, the intense competition characterising the festival circuit (especially among the A-Category festivals, such as CIFF) makes it necessary to continually redefine strategies, to try out new formulas and modalities. But in this case the decisive and very significant move by CIFF towards a new Pan-African emphasis, must be viewed as a manoeuvre of greater importance, in consonance with major transformations taking place in the region's production over recent years (both in sub-Saharan Africa as well as the Middle East and North Africa). In an apparent response to a commitment made by the Festival's directors during its previous edition, CIFF was finally offering a home to some cinemas that many felt had traditionally, and undeservedly, been omitted from its programming. But this was far from being simply a tactic to garner contributions from the flourishing Nigerian and South African cinemas, which up till then *had* been systematically excluded or marginalised by other events focused on Pan-African film, such as FESPACO (www.fespaco.bf) and the Journées Cinématographiques de Carthage (JCC) (www.jccarthage.com). The operation undertaken by CIFF was a full-blown offensive to topple the old strategies linked to the French-speaking world and establish a new cinematographic alliance, with Cairo as its epicentre. The Arab world's oldest and most glamorous festival was trying to chart a new course. The idea was to take the traditional, and at times prestigious, Carthage-Dakar-Ouagadougou axis (which, it must be remembered, depends strongly on French funding and technical assistance), and replace it with a new, and presumably more autonomous triumvirate formed by Cairo-Lagos-Johannesburg.[32]

Starting Points

Founded in 1976 and still the only A-Category festival in the entire Arab world (and on the African continent), the CIFF was instituted with the firm intention of playing a central role in the region. However, the programming demands of FIAPF (Fédération Internationale des Associations de Producteurs de Films / International Federation of Film Producers Associations) with their inescapable quota of premieres, may have been more of a liability than anything else, and the festival's programming has often been questionable. It is certainly not the case that Arab cinema at the time was lacking in forums and platforms: since 1966 the JCC had brought together the finest and most distinguished of new Arab cinema, along with a certain amount of sub-Saharan production, in a kind of reciprocal exchange with its twin initiative FESPACO in Ouagadougou, Burkina Faso (then still called Upper Volta). This rivalry with the CIFF would become increasingly evident, especially with the inauguration in 1979 of the Damascus International Film Festival (DIFF) (www.damascusfest.com), which was held every two years in alternation with the biennial Carthage competition. While the JCC reserved its official competition for Arab and African films only, in Damascus they opted, from the outset, to broaden the festival's range and create a space for Asian and Latin American productions as well. By contrast, the Egypt-centric perspective of the CIFF was usually complemented by the greatest and most effective doses of glamour that the festival could muster.

The agenda set by the JCC – a festival during which, in 1970, the Fédération Panafricaine des Cinéastes (FEPACI) was founded – was unquestionably political, being based on the consciousness of supranational Arab identity linked to a shared geographical space and linguistic practice. But, as Dina Iordanova aptly notes, 'festivals that evolve around identity affiliations carry along an array of narratives which they put forward with variable degrees of success, depending on the festival's political clout and access to funding' (2010: 22). The 'verbal architecture' (Dayan 2000) of a festival such as the JCC emphasises from the outset its commitment to promoting and disseminating Arab (and African) cinema as a counter to the hegemony of Hollywood (or, on the regional scale, of Egyptian commercial cinema). It also turned out to be an excellent tool, along with FESPACO and the 1969 Pan-Africain Cultural Festival in Algiers, for configuring new circuits of dissemination and circulation linked not just to the new Pan-African rhetoric, but also to the solidarity and revolutionary demands of what was still known as the Third World. A very illustrative passage appears in a *Cineaste* review of the JCC's 1974 edition by André Paquet:

> The 'cultural' consciousness of a few years ago has now been succeeded by a clearer, more resolutely revolutionary political consciousness. Having first affirmed their cultural authenticity, the Arab and African cinemas were then obliged to go beyond the stage of 'independence', to shake off their 'heritage' and become the mouthpiece for a continent now at the forefront of the revolutionary process. (1975: 19)

It cannot be denied that in terms of impact, the JCC initially fulfilled its objective. This is illustrated by both the ample coverage given to the event by part of the international specialised press, and also by the fact that the festival became the main springboard for launching Arab film production on the world stage. The lucid observations made by Abé Mark Nornes in *FFY3: Film Festivals and East Asia* that the importance of 'various Asian film festivals has typically been judged by a utilitarian measure: a festival matters to the degree that it serves the programmers of Europe [and] North America' (2011: 38).

It could be said that Carthage was, in a way, a victim of its own success and that it should have ceded its central exhibition and distribution role to festivals of greater magnitude, such as Cannes (www.festival-cannes.fr), Venice (www.labiennale.org) or Berlin (www.berlinale.de), each of which, at a certain point, began to find places for the international premieres of new Arab films (Ruoff 2008: 49). It was, therefore, neither the competition with CIFF nor the alternation with DIFF that eventually caused the JCC to fall into a long-lasting crisis. Rather, it was, on the one hand, the rechanneling of the major Arab films towards more central, resounding nodes in the context of the international festival circuit, and, on the other hand, the decline – 'failure' being, perhaps, too strong a word – of the Pan-African, Third World and revolutionary rhetoric that had been its defining feature during its first decade.

It is appropriate here to recall Gideon Bachmann's sceptical appraisal of JCC only one year earlier. Even in the context of the markedly negative tone of the review, his conclusion can be seen as somewhat portentous: 'Festivals that pretend that there is more in common than there is, risk showing up only the difference' (Bachmann 1973: 51). The traditional and ever-present divide between 'Arab Africa' and 'Black Africa' was looking more and more like a true parting of the ways, very similar to what was going on at FESPACO, an event always operating under the umbrella of FEPACI (Pan-African Federation of Filmmakers), always fuelled by technical and financial assistance from France and with which the JCC was closely linked.[33] The Pan-African rhetoric would remain solid, although fewer and fewer really had faith in its potential. Revolutionary ardour would also slowly diminish; at least until an unexpected revisitation took place whose magnitude and true significance are still to be reckoned: the recent Arab Spring uprisings. But by that time the landscape was very different.

New Nodes

In the Northern autumn of 2011, in the wake of the so-called Egyptian Revolution, the CIFF could not be held, ostensibly because of 'budget limitations and political instability'.[34] The latent crisis was a badly-kept secret and the 2012 edition turned out to be highly problematic despite certain attempts at renewal, which took the form, primarily, of changes in the directing and programming team. And then there was DIFF, which at no point had much impact outside of the Arab world and which held its last edition in 2010. For the JCC, grown increasingly weak in terms of international projection and its traditional role as a forum for Pan-Arab (or Pan-African) debate, the 2010 edition revealed a strong sense of crisis in the air. Some attributed this it to a lack of autonomy in the directing team – which had certainly made its share of mistakes and was closely controlled by the government – as well as to the growing competition of new festivals, such as those popping up in the Persian Gulf or the very glamorous (and French-supported) Festival International du Film de Marrakech (FIFM) (www.festivalmarrakech.info).[35] Again, changes would be made in the directorial team for the 2012 edition in the hope of straightening things out in a context that remained adversarial and in which critical voices in Tunisia and other countries could still be heard. As the outspoken Director of Centre Cinématographique Marocain (CCM) Nour-Eddine Saïl would say in his inaugural address to the symposium *Les cinémas du Maghreb et leurs publics dans un contexte arabo-africain*, held during the 2010 JCC, if there was one thing that had not changed over the years, it was precisely the awareness of the need for a new orientation:

> I remember having attended workshops like this one, in the very same city, on the occasion of the very same festival, back in the 1980s and 90s... The themes change but in essence we have never escaped the same iterative and sometimes redundant interrogation: 'What is happening with our cinemas?' [...] The issue that has always brought us together in Carthage - in fact it is this festival's specialty – has always been: 'Where are we? What are we doing?' And I have to say that we are more or less in the same place. (2012: 18)

For Saïl then, this is a scenario in which many of the variables have changed and so requires those long-familiar questions to be addressed in new ways. The case of Morocco is very revealing in this sense. The policies that the Centre Cinématographique Marocain (CCM) has had in place for about a decade – independent of the aforementioned FIFM – have, among other positive effects, revitalised the Moroccan film festival scene. Essential to this have been the consolidation of the Festival National du Film (www.ccm.ma/fnf14) and the sponsorship of the Mediterranean Short Film Festival of Tangier (www.ccm.ma/11fcmmt). This latter event has become a forum for new talents and a significant platform for the renewal of Moroccan film (Elena 2007). Elsewhere, along very different lines, but still embodying the virtues and vitality of some of the new festivals in a context of great artistic and cultural effervescence, the Cinema Days of Beirut (Ayam Beirut Al Cinema'iya) (www.beirutdc. org) constitutes quite an atypical experience in the Arab world. Set in motion by a private cultural association – Beirut DC – and linked to the regular activity of two art house cinemas in the city's centrally-located Ashrafieh district, the festival, held biennially since 2000, has gradually become one of the primary sites for the screening of independent Arab film and video creation, niches that often go unfilled these days.[36]

Some of the other new festivals do not have the benefit of a long-standing cinéphile tradition such as that which exists in Lebanon (and a few other countries in the region, especially Tunisia), although of course they do have their own unique and decisive assets, mainly in the areas of budget and political support at the local level. So, the new festivals appearing in the Gulf countries since the mid-2000s have rung in a new era in the history of Arab film festivals and have made a significant mark on the traditional festival map. Foremost among these festivals are: the Dubai International Film Festival (www.dubaifilmfest.com), inaugurated in 2004 and the true pioneer in the region; the Abu Dhabi Film Festival (ADFF) (www.abudhabifilmfestival.ae), founded in 2007 as the Middle East International Film Festival, but shortly thereafter assuming its current name; and the Doha Tribeca Film Festival (www.dohafilminstitute.com), active since 2009. These events are held in countries where there are still very few commercial cinemas and where the spectacle of film has yet to attain the public dimensions it has in other places. As such, they have had to assume hitherto unfamiliar cultural and political agendas compared to other, more fortunate festivals in the Arab world.

The ADFF's website explicitly states its intention to help 'create a vibrant film culture throughout the region'. And so this and the other new festivals have had to design careful verbal architectures that allow them, on the one hand, to reach out to local audiences largely unaccustomed to the experience of 'going to the cinema' and, on the other, to make a place for themselves on the rather variegated festival circuit. Undoubtedly, these new festivals in the Gulf countries (with their hefty budgets the envy of those near and far) all 'aspire to the status of a global event, both through the implementation of their programming strategies and through the establishment of an international reach and reputation' (Stringer 2001: 139). At the same time they are calculated – and not in the least bit masked – operations aimed at helping the Gulf region 'elbow its way onto the cultural stage as [it] has already succeeded at doing in the business world' (Malamud 2011). Just as Thomas Elsaesser (2005) rightly interprets the development of the European festival network as occurring within the framework of the growth and competition of secondary global cities in a new post-Fordist economy. Just so, the dazzling success of the film festivals in the Gulf was achieved in an atmosphere of fierce competition rather than collaboration, and must be viewed as a new articulation of decisive nodes in more general transnational infrastructures (Iordanova 2011).

It would not be fair, therefore, to make hasty judgments about the role that the new Gulf festivals are destined to play on the international circuit, or even in the more specific context of the Arab world. For some, 'Dubai and Abu Dhabi [...] have yet to establish themselves as influential stops on the international film festival circuit' and are '[l]acking programming vision' (Ruoff 2012: 6). It may be that, in effect, the bond with local audiences is still too fragile, that the markets associated with these festivals have not yet really gained momentum, that these events have still to become tourist attractions, or that the recent changes in the directing teams, replacing qualified foreign professionals with local figures linked to the business world, are weaknesses in an experience that, at this point, is still too recent to assess. However, it cannot really be claimed that these festivals lack 'programming vision' or that they have not acquired, for better or worse, an unquestionably key role at the regional level, thereby eclipsing to a large extent some of the traditional nodes such as the JCC and CIFF.

A final element must be taken into consideration. If we acknowledge Yousry Nasrallah's (2013) stark statement that the film industry of the Arab countries 'is in a state of total catastrophe' and that production, more than ever before, depends on transnational financing – with its well-known pros and cons – then the fact that the Gulf festivals have become a new regional financing agent through different funds and subsidies, takes on considerable relevance. The opinion expressed by Jordanian filmmaker Mahmoud Al Massad is doubtlessly shared by many others: 'I wish to have a film funded by an Arab body. Personally, I am tired of looking for European funds and trying to convince them why it's important to fund an Arab film.' Although they are obviously insufficient, Enjaaz, SANAD and the MENA grants, among other funds sponsored by the region's festivals, make a big difference both for young Arab filmmakers and for those more veteran filmmakers somewhat displaced (for a variety of reasons that need not be discussed here) from their respective national industries. As an example, no better or worse than others, a glance at the list of beneficiaries of the Doha Film Institute Middle East and North Africa (MENA) grants in 2012 reveals the names of Yasmine Kassari, Ibrahim El Batout, Dima El Horr, Shawkat Amin Korki, Ghassan Salhab, Jillali Ferhati, Mahmoud ben Mahmoud, Merzak Allouache and Hakim Belabbes (Doha Film Institute 2012). This is a list which illustrates – albeit with prospects very different from those that made Carthage, Damascus and even Cairo, the central nodes of a regional network of festivals and without daring to predict what the future may hold – that Arab film's epicentre of activity seems to have moved to the Gulf.[37]

A Broader Network

In addition to the numerous and sometimes very dynamic minor festivals held in various Arab countries, consideration must also be given to the extensive network of film festivals dedicated to Arab cinema in other parts of the world. It must be remembered that the large parallel screening circuit that film festivals have managed to develop has become more than just the door through which certain films access normalised commercial screenings. Indeed, it is a film's very transit through the circuit that '*is* the real exhibition' (Iordanova 2009: 25). In this sense, the circulation of a good part of Arab cinema is nowadays limited to its presence in festivals, both in the Arab world itself and elsewhere. Europe has traditionally set the pace in this area and the list of Arab film festivals there is very long: the Rotterdam Arab Film Festival (Netherlands) (www.arabfilmfestival.nl), the Alfilm-Arab Film Festival Berlin (Germany) (www.alfilm.de), Festival du Film Arabe de Fameck (France) (www-cinemarabe.org), the Liverpool Arab Film Festival (UK) (www-fact.co-uk/projects/arab-film.festival), the Malmö Arab Film Festival (Sweden) (www.malmoarabfilmfestival.se), the International Arab Film Festival Zurich (Switzerland) (www-iaffz.com), the Mostra de Cinema Àrab i Mediterrani de Catalunya (Spain) (www.mostracinearab.com). And the list goes on. None of these has perhaps managed to occupy the empty place left by the legendary Biennale des Cinémas Arabes de Paris (1992-2006), which was a true showcase and meeting place for Arab cinematographies and their representatives; something not even its detractors – disagreeing mostly about programming policies – dared to question. The Marseillian association AFLAM, working towards a better cross-cultural understanding of Arab cinema in France,[38] collaborated with the Parisian Biennale for some years and, in an attempt to somehow recover the spirit of that event, it recently held the 1st edition of the Rencontres Internationales des Cinémas Arabes (2013) in Marseilles (www.lesrencontresdaflam.fr). The event was conceived 'as a real meeting place where exchange and expansion can occur' rather than 'as yet another festival dedicated to presenting films from certain countries and giving out prizes' (Rencontres 2013).

Only time will tell if AFLAM's Rencontres can fill the space left by the Parisian Biennale. What we can be sure of is that Europe is no longer alone in its role as a showcase for Arab film. In the U.S., there are many festivals devoted to Arab film, almost all of recent creation; the veteran San Francisco Arab Film Festival (arabfilmfestival.org) is a notable exception. In Australia, the vibrant Sydney Arab Film Festival (arabfilmfestival.com.au) continues to grow in influence. Arab film even occupies an important place in India with Osian's Cinefan of Indian, Asian and Arab Cinema (cinefan.osians.com). So, there is a vast 'secondary' circuit (no pejorative connotations intended) that places Arab film into contact with potential audiences that it would otherwise probably never have. The notion of ghettoisation, formulated by the Malian critic and scholar Manthia Diawara and mentioned in passing above, is based on some well-founded arguments and continues to have numerous supporters. But it is just as true that the two decades since the theory was initially developed have not passed in vain, and that today the situation is very different from when Diawara was writing.

Lindiwe Dovey (2010: 67) recognises how those contemporary African film festivals held outside of Africa have become 'vital to building an international audience for alternative African Cinema.'[39] The case of Arab film is not very different. A new cartography seems to be taking shape, a redrawing of the festival map that contains a role for Arab film festivals outside the region. This will be of prime importance for promoting and maintaining the dynamism of those of the region's cinemas that are burdened by serious industrial problems, that are perpetually undershown to audiences and that, unfortunately, are still far from receiving the attention they deserve.

Works Cited

Abu Dhabi Film Festival Website. On-line. Available HTTP: http://www. abudhabifilmfestival.ae/en/about (17 September 2013).

Al Massad, M. 'Film Funds for Arab Filmmakers', *Euromed Audiovisual*, 19 October 2012. On-line. Available HTTP: http://euromedaudiovisuel. net/p.aspx?mid=21&l=en&did=991 (17 September 2013).

Bachmann, Gideon (1973) 'In Search of Self-Definition: Arab and African Films at the Carthage Film Festival (Tunis)', *Film Quarterly*, 26, 3, Spring, 48-51.

Barlet, Olivier (2012) 'Le cinéma tunisien à la lumière du printemps árabe', in Patricia Caillé and Florence Martin (eds), *Les cinémas du Maghreb et leurs publics*. Paris: Africultures / L'Harmattan, 270-280.

Buch-Jepsen, Niels (2003) 'Fespaco and the Transformations of Pan-African Film Promotion', *Senses of Cinema*, 26, May. On-line. Available HTTP: http://sensesofcinema.com/2003/festival-reports/ fespaco/ (17 September 2013).

Dayan, Daniel (2000) 'Looking for Sundance: The Social Construction of a Film Festival', in Ib Bondebjerg (ed.), *Moving Images. Culture and the Mind*. Luton: University of Luton Press, 43-52.

Diawara, Manthia (1994) 'On Tracking World Cinema: African Cinema at Film Festivals', *Public Culture*, 6, 2, 385-396.

Doha Film Institute (2012) *Film Financing. MENA Grants 2012*. Doha: Doha Film Institute.

Dovey, Lindiwe (2010) 'Director's Cut: In Defence of African Film Festivals outside Africa', in Dina Iordanova and Ruby Cheung (eds) *FFY 2: Film Festivals and Imagined Communities*. St Andrews: St Andrews Film Studies, 45-73.

El Adl, Omar (2012) 'The Trouble with the Cairo International Film Festival', *Daily News Egypt*, 17 September. On-line. Available HTTP: http://www.dailynewsegypt.com/2012/09/17/the-trouble-with-the-cairo-international-film-festival (17 September 2013).

Elena, Alberto (ed.) (2007) *Las mil y una imágenes del cine marroquí / Les mille et une images du cinéma marocain*. Madrid / Las Palmas: T&B Editores, Festival Internacional de Cine de las Palmas de Gran Canaria.

Elena, Alberto, and María Luisa Ortega (2011) 'Cine árabe: tensiones y reverberaciones', *Awraq* [new series], 4, 79-96.

Elsaesser, Thomas (2005) 'Film Festival Networks: The New Topographies of Cinema In Europe', in Thomas Elsaesser, *European Cinema: Face to Face with Hollywood*. Amsterdam: Amsterdam University Press, 82-107.

Iordanova, Dina (2009) 'The Film Festival Circuit', in Dina Iordanova and Ragan Rhyne (eds), *FFY 1: The Festival Circuit*. St Andrews: St Andrews Film Studies, 23-39.

Iordanova, Dina (2010) 'Mediating Diaspora: Film Festivals and "Imagined Communities"', in Dina Iordanova and Ruby Cheung (eds), *FFY 2: Film Festivals and Imagined Communities*. St Andrews: St Andrews Film Studies, 12-44.

Iordanova, Dina (2011) 'East Asia and Film Festivals: Transnational Clusters for Creativity and Commerce', in Dina Iordanova and Ruby Cheung (eds), *FFY 3: Film Festivals and East Asia*. St Andrews: St Andrews Film Studies, 1-33.

Jaafar, Ali (2012) 'Arab Cinema is in Crisis - It Needs Dramatic Resolution', *The Guardian*, 10 October. On-line. Available HTTP: http://www.theguardian.com/ commentisfree/2012/oct/10/arab-cinema-crisis (17 September 2013).

Malamud, Randy (2011) 'In Dubai, a Cinematic Door to the Mideast', *The Chronicle of Higher Education*, 57, 2, 27 February. On-line. Available HTTP: http://chronicle.com/article/In-Dubai-a-Cinematic-Door-to/126487/ (17 September 2013).

Nasrallah, Yousry (2013) 'A Filmmaker is a Filmmaker, Whether there's an Industry or Not', *Euromed Audiovisual*, 21 June. On-line. Available HTTP: http://euromedaudiovisuel.net/p.aspx?t=interviews&mid=91&l=en&did=1497 (17 September 2013).

Nornes, Abé Mark (2011) 'Asian Film Festivals, Translation and the International Film

Festival Short Circuit', in Dina Iordanova and Ruby Cheung (eds), *Film Festival Yearbook 3: Film Festivals and East Asia*. St Andrews: St Andrews Film Studies, 37-39.

Paquet, André (1975) 'Toward and Arab and African Cinema: The 1974 Carthage Film Festival', *Cineaste*, 7, 1, Fall, 19-21.

Rencontres Internationales des Cinémas Arabes (2013) *Comuniqué et Dossier de Presse*, June. On-line. Available HTTP: http://www.

lesrencontresdaflam.fr/communique-et-dossier-de-presse/ (17 September 2013).

Ruoff, Jeffrey (2008) 'Ten Nights in Tunisia: Les Journées Cinématographiques de Carthage', *Film International*, 6, 4, 43-51.

Ruoff, Jeffrey (2012) 'Introduction: Programming Film Festivals', in Jeffrey Ruoff (ed.), *Coming Soon to a Festival Near You: Programming Film Festivals*. St Andrews: St Andrews Film Studies, 1-21.

Saïl, Nour-Eddine (2012) 'Journées Cinématographiques de Carthage 2010: allocution d'ouverture du colloque', in Patricia Caillé and Florence Martin (eds), *Les cinémas du Maghreb et leurs publics*. Paris: Africultures / L'Harmattan, 18-26.

Saul, Mahir, and Ralph A. Austen (eds) (2010) *Viewing African Cinema in the Twenty-First Century: Art Films and the Nollywood Video Revolution*. Athens: Ohio University Press.

Slocum, J. David (2009) 'Film and/as Culture: The Use of Cultural Discourses at Two African Film Festivals', in Dina Iordanova and Ragan Rhyne (eds), *FFY 1: The Festival Circuit*. St Andrews: St Andrews Film Studies, 144-145.

Stringer, Julian (2001) 'Global Cities and the International Film Festival Economy', in Mark Shiel and Tony Fitzmaurice (eds), *Cinema and the City: Film and Urban Societies in a Global Context*. Oxford: Blackwell, 134-144.

Yunis, Alia (2013), 'Reshaping Middle Eastern Film Production: The 'Gulfization' of Arab Cinema in Changing Economic and Political Times', paper delivered at the IAMCR 2013 Conference Dublin, 25-29 June 2013. On-line. Available HTTP: http://www.iamcr2013dublin.org/content/reshaping-middle-eastern-film-production-%E2%80%9Cgulfization%E2%80%9D-arab-cinema-changing-economic-and-pol (17 September 2013).

Notes

[1] Finally heeding the changes occurring in the region's film industries, FESPACO itself tried to shift orientation in the 2007 edition. This was recognition of the vitality of not only recent Moroccan production, but also that of Africa's English-speaking countries, led by South Africa and Nigeria, which have historically been marginalised for political reasons (anti-apartheid sentiment in the former) or supposedly technical reasons (the use of video format in the latter). See Slocum (2009: 144-145) and for a more general overview Saul and Austen (2010).

[2] An insightful report on the 2003 edition, pointed out the serious problems that FESPACO faced as a result of its persistent dependence on Europe and its 'increasingly thin claim to panafricanism'. In addition there came widespread feeling that among its most urgent needs was to adapt to the 'continent's [new] politico-cultural landscape' (Niels Buch-Jepsen, 2003).

[3]   The explanation first appeared on the festival website and spread quickly throughout the local and international press. See, for example, El Adl (2012).

[4]   The diagnostic was formulated by Hassen Alileche in the journal *Écrans de Tunisie*, 14, October 2010, 28-21; cited by Barlet (2012: 271).

[5]   The very particular case of documentary film festivals cannot be examined here for reasons of space and scope. However, see Elena and Ortega (2011: 90-91).

[6]   A very different problem, as Ali Jaafar (2012) points out, is that this abundance of funds sometimes has a perverse effect: '[W]hen that funding is too readily available for filmmakers whose scripts are not properly developed, whose stories are not interesting enough, whose characters are not engaging and who have no idea of the concept of dramatic resolution', it becomes too easy for these filmmakers to devote themselves to the creation of mediocre films with no real potential for impact. Or, as Alia Yunis (2013) maintains, it may be that the price of such generous financing inevitably involves the imposition of numerous restrictions, resulting in the growing 'gulfization' of Arab cinema that encourages the production of 'safe films', while other more problematic or controversial projects are neutralised or untouched.

[7]   AFLAM (http://www.aflam.fr) is an association created in 2000 for the common interest of the people of Marseilles and Arab cultures through the image and film. AFLAM aims to provide visibility and space for Marseille's (and the region-at-large's) little known Arab cinema, in order to promote a better understanding of Arab culture and encourage the exchange of films throughout the Maghreb, the Middle East and the Arab diaspora generally.

[8]   Dovey (2010) also underlines, very appropriately, the contribution that the festivals make to changing people's views on Africa, launching the careers of young directors and furnishing filmmakers with some financial returns for their labour.

The Film Festival Archipelago
in the Arab World

Jean-Michel Frodon

Film festivals are significant markers of complex social dynamics; they have become vehicles of local as much as of international transformations. There are now thousands of film festivals all over the world. If almost every day a new festival is launched somewhere on the planet, it is because political and economic leaders, as well as artists and cultural industry professionals, have understood that this type of event is likely to have a range of positive social, economic and cultural impacts upon, for example, tourism, diplomacy, territorial planning and political and religious propaganda.

This general overview, now extensively documented (Stringer 2001; De Valck 2007; Iordanova 2009; Ruoff 2012), fits particularly well in the Arab world. It so happens that the two countries where the 'Arab Spring' started at the turn of 2010-2011 are also the birthplaces of what have been regarded for decades as the main film festivals in the Arab world: Journées Cinématographiques de Carthage (JCC, Carthage's Cinema Days), inaugurated in 1966 near Tunis, and the Cairo International Film Festival (CIFF), which began in 1976. The former festival was crucial for the discovery of Arab and African cinemas by European and North American film buffs, and even more instrumental in fostering and firing the passions of a whole generation of intellectuals, critics, academics and civil servants from these regions, all dedicated to cinema (Barlet 2012). The latter was instrumental in the development of Egyptian cinema (by far the dominant Arab cinema since the 1950s) tracing a shift from a limited genre selection of romance-cum-song-type films to more complex scripts and directorial efforts, eventually combining overt entertainment with elements of artistic excellence tempered by acknowledgement of the social realities within which the films were created (Wassef 1995; Thoraval 1996).

However, both festivals fell into decline during the last decade of the twentieth century. This decay went hand-in-hand with the manifesting obsolescence of those political systems, social organisations and cultural ambitions that marked the previous historical periods in their home countries, and were associated with the leading charismatic figures of Habib Bourguiba in Tunisia and Gamal Nasser in Egypt. The downfall of previous models that had been the basis of the modern establishment of these nations, mirrors the general background of the 2011 'Arab Spring' uprisings. It was festival managements, driven by corruption and oligarchy, as well as a general lack of moral authority to develop a space for international visibility and recognition, which defined the fate of these festivals. Thus, the festivals can be seen as symptomatic of the general socio-political and cultural malaise.

The 1990s witnessed the sudden blossoming of new film festivals in the Arab world, a trend that is still active – and growing. There are now well over 100 film festivals in the region. These new festivals are extremely diverse in size, purpose, location and effect; so much so that it is difficult to compare them. Their specificities are directly related to their geopolitical and economical contexts. Their individualities are accentuated by various policies implemented by the selective involvement of various European countries' cultural services. With a primary interest in promoting their own national cinema(s), these international partners (including the European Union itself) also bring with them different types of support (in the shape of various types of public funding for production, distribution, travel grants and print traffic, as well as support for dedicated festivals), which opens up access for local audiences to contemporary or heritage works that they would otherwise not have been able to see.

I would like to propose here a classification of the Arab world's most significant film festivals that divides the events into three main categories. First, there are those festivals that partake in a kind of one-upmanship between the Persian Gulf monarchies, each seeking to outdo the other in glamour, prestige and regional and international influence through soft-power, not to mention the local leaders' vanity, without any consideration for wider economical benefits or cultural improvement for the community. I call these the Emirates Model.

Second are those festivals that work according to a specific development strategy, where great efforts for the development of cinema have been launched, based largely on filmmaking infrastructures from and partnerships entered into with Western entertainment industries. This can be illustrated in Morocco, for example, by the special role given to the Marrakech International Film Festival (MIFF), which stands apart in the context of a festival dynamic that has no equivalent in the Arab world – or almost any other region. Morocco is a nation of festivals, and great importance is attached to augmenting and reinforcing the country's cultural significance, both regionally and internationally.

The third category is reflected in the accelerated rise of an alternative network of festivals, where artistic projects and critical political agendas meet in constructive ways. The variety of places, purposes, political and economical situations, levels of freedom of speech and diverse cultural infrastructures, bring to minds a sense of dispersion, which is partly true and partly misleading.

A deeper investigation of these categories will be helpful here.

The Emirates Model

Since the first decade of the new millennium, three major events have been competing for the most visible spot on the Arab festival calendar. First to appear was the Dubai International Film Festival (DIFF) established in 2004; next came the Abu Dhabi Film Festival (ADFF) in 2007; and finally the Doha Film Festival (DFF), which appeared in 2009. (Other festivals exist, of course, though their influence is negligible beyond their immediate audiences. Thus we see: the Al Jazeera International Documentary Festival (http://festival.aljazeera.net), also in Doha, which started in 2005; the much less visible Muscat International Film Festival in Oman (www.m-iff.com), and the Sharjah Biennale (www.sharjahart.org/biennial), launched in 1993 and dedicated to contemporary art, but with an ever-increasing interest in video and cinema production.) The three leading festivals have similar characteristics. All were born in an area where cinema was almost non-existent: according to Armes (2012), previously only a total of seven features had been shot in the United Arab Emirates (UAE), one in Oman, one in Qatar and one in Kuwait. However, the growth in the consumption of Western products (including cultural products) by increasing expatriate populations, brought an interest in new audio-visual technologies and a strong demand for stories, images and sounds from the émigrés' native countries. This largely diasporic dimension to cinema came with a relative reduction of censorship.

The three main events – DIFF, ADFF and DFF – were products of the wills of high-level political leaders. Their emergence was accompanied by investments in infrastructure; they were supposed to be elements of the politics of prestige, intended to increase the international visibility of the Emirates. With some difficulty, they attempted to enhance cultural values, an approach that was reflected also in their increased collaboration with major Western museums, such as the Museum of Modern Art, the Guggenheim or the Louvre, or with Western Universities. All these initiatives went hand-in-hand with an input of prestige and glamour at the festivals, thanks to the presence of imported Hollywood stars, courted with exorbitant royalties for their attendance, private jets and fairy tale conditions in incredible palaces. All three festivals put special efforts into building strong ties with U.S. cinema institutions. The ADFF hired Peter Scarlet, former head of the San Francisco Film Festival and then the New York-based Tribeca Film Festival, as Artistic Director. The DIFF answered by signing an agreement with (the New York-based) Lincoln Center Film Society. In its turn, the DFF dealt with the Tribeca organisation, which gradually took charge of the entire Doha programming strategy. In the latter case, the U.S. connection was largely due to the fact that the leading figure at the origin of DFF, Sheikha Al Mayassa bint Hamad bin Khalifa Al Thani, the daughter of the Emir of Qatar, was educated at Duke University in the U.S. It is she who has been the driving force behind the expansion of cinema in her homeland.

After a few years of escalating bids in terms of budgets, star names (whether they actually attended or not was another matter) and attempts at other public relations extravaganzas, the balance sheets showed disappointing results. Most of the collaborations with big U.S. directors have been terminated; all appointments and collaborations have been short-lived. Beyond the specifics of each situation, generally speaking, it appears that neither the U.S. nor the Arab side have found this alliance fruitful; or even endurable. To varying degrees, it has been the lack of freedom in programming, the expectation of massive financial income and support to the home organisation and difficulties in engendering personal relationships in light of the players' very different cultural backgrounds that have brought collaboration to a close.

All three festivals pledged their dedication to the development of opportunities for filmmaking in the 'region'. As it turned out, this apparent oasis in the desert was merely a mirage. Just what the notion of 'region' might refer to specifically, remained vague. Was it the Gulf area? The wider Middle East? The Arab world at large? Or an even larger area, which would span as wide as to include Turkey, Iran and Central Asia? Or the whole of the Muslim world (whatever that may mean)? Moreover, the launch of a national, or even regional film industry, is hard to guide from the top, at least not without a suitable production environment in place, and most certainly not within such an unstable geopolitical and sociological context. Several attempts quickly reached the limits for artistic openness, notably in Sharjah where artists challenged the lack of artistic freedom permitted (usually related to freedom of speech, and sensitive issues such as sex, religion or those in power) – which led to the eviction of the Venice Biennial's Artistic Director, Jack Persekian, in April 2011.

So far, the local effects of the huge investments, especially in terms of film production, have proved extremely weak. However, the creation of the Doha Film Institute in 2010, followed closely by the inauguration of the Dubai Studio City and the Arab Film Studio in Abu Dhabi, is testament to a more permanent and cultural industry-oriented approach to cinema. With most of the early prestigious alliances with major American bodies having now been discontinued, the Gulf festivals have started to reshape their mode of operation. They are now building connections with more modest festivals. For instance, in a move away from Hollywood, DFF has built an alliance with the Sarajevo Film Festival (www.sff.ba) and DIFF with the Rencontres de Toulouse Festival (www.cinelatino.com), as both festivals seek to inscribe themselves into the wider global network of festivals and to exchange part of their immense financial resources[1] for the expertise and connections that auteurs, directors and sales agents closer to the 'real' festival world, away from Hollywood can bring. The reshaping of the glamorous DFF (as announced at Cannes in 2013) into two separate events, also reveals this process. The first event, the Ajyal Youth Film Festival, programmed in late November, is dedicated to children's films, educational films and family audiences, showing Arab stories. The other, the Qumra Doha Film Festival, in March, is dedicated to art house films from all over the world.

One of the most difficult issues these festivals face is the absence, or at least the extreme disinterest, of local audiences.[2] This is a situation that generates a challenging question: is it possible – in the era of globalisation and virtualisation, and even with massive financial means – to sustain an 'out of this world' cinema, without any roots in a local history, a local culture and a local social practice?

The Marrakech Model and Morocco

The turn of the last century in Morocco saw the crowning of the 'modernist' king Mohammed VI, and with it the launching of an ambitious project of national cinema development. The chief organiser of this process has been, so far, the former film critic Nour-Eddine Saïl, who was nominated in 2003 as head of the Centre Cinématographique Marocain (CCM), the state body dedicated to cinema. This national development is largely based on an economic approach to film production, and consists mainly of both the development of local film production and of powerful initiatives to attract big-budget productions from abroad, by courting not just American studios, but also European, and even Asian projects. This policy generated a significant improvement in technical infrastructure, including an accumulation of shooting facilities and up-to-date postproduction technologies. A significant effort has also been made in terms of professional education, with the prestigious international school École supérieure des arts visuels being set up in Marrakech in 2006. Over this same period, the country experienced the tragic decay of its theatrical circuit and the disappearance of many silver screens, underlining a crucial oversight in the national production strategy: the relationship between films and their local audiences.

Marrakech, the number one tourist destination in Morocco, became the birthplace of the Marrakech International Film Festival (MIFF) (www.festivalmarrakech.info) in 2001. This was chiefly the result of the converging interests of the Throne towards creating an internationally open modernity. Also influential was the presence of European intellectuals, mostly French and those connected with the show business world, for whom the city, with its luxury hotels and exotic ambience, had become a regular holiday destination. Before his death in 2003, French producer Daniel Toscan du Plantier masterminded MIFF together with the King's closest advisor, André Azoulay. Designed as an international and prestigious event, MIFF spent a lot of money and expended much effort on attracting glamorous stars and renowned directors, in an attempt to compete with Cannes, Berlin and Venice. It has constantly tried, with limited success, to maintain such a competitive stance, and to do so without losing its connection to the very active local cinema world. Although it did succeed in attracting the world's media attention (which was its number one goal), the festival has been systematically denounced by Moroccan film directors, film museums, film archives, and other cultural activists. This criticism reached a peak in 2011, when the Association of Moroccan Cinema Critics (ACCM, Association des critiques de cinéma au Maroc) boycotted the festival in response to what they felt was the festival organisers' subordination of their roles to that of the foreign critics and journalists in attendance.

The situation at MIFF is coloured by the diversity and complexity of its relationship with cinema. In the wake of an official quantitative strategy towards production (based on the premise that quality will emerge from quantity, a hypothesis which has still to be confirmed by reality), Morocco has experienced a very significant blossoming of its cinema culture. It is the Arab country in which by far the most film festivals can be found (more than twenty), with a wider diversity of topical approaches and in more geographical locations.[3] A few well-established independent institutions, most significantly the Tangiers Cinémathèque, provide a solid basis for this pluralistic and dynamic cinema world.

The festival phenomenon in Morocco, then, appears to be polarised by two diverging tendencies. There is a prestigious international event which aims to belong to the international circuit of major film festivals while it simultaneously acts as the self-appointed driving force behind other local events (though these events are openly lukewarm to MIFF's leadership). And then there is a galaxy of local initiatives, loosely connected, though occasionally in competition with each other, and all rooted in strong ties with the local film culture. Many of these events are related to political or social issues, with thematic film festivals dedicated to issues such as women's films, the Amazigh (Berber) language and culture, or those intending to connect Morocco with its Mediterranean or African neighbours. In a global, economically dynamic context, and with a relatively relaxed censorship, Morocco clearly appears as the most promising place in the Arab world for a culturally significant evolution based on cinema.

The Archipelago and the Network

Between these two major nodes on the festival circuit – the Emirates to the East and Morocco to the West – several other noticeable elements influencing festivals in various parts of the Arab world can be identified. The use of cinema to support minorities is perhaps most visible (chiefly in Algeria, but also in Morocco to a lesser degree) in relation to the cultural arena surrounding the indigenous Berber or Amazigh ethnic group, and manifests in the Festival International du Film Arab à Oran / Annual Oran Arab Film Festival (www.fofa-dz.org, Algeria), the Festival Culturel National Annuel du Film Amazigh / the Annual National Cultural Festival of Amazigh Film (www.film-amazigh.net/fr/index.php, Algeria) and the Azrou Summer Moroccan Short Film Encounter (www.cineazrou. org). Also in Algeria, the short film festival in Bejaïa, inaugurated in 2003, has become a permanent place for film teaching and experimentation; it is the most visible peak of permanent activity in cinema in Algeria (Pasquier 2012). Nevertheless, that country remains deeply affected by the wounds of the 'black years',[4] a trauma which, at least in the short term, prevents the country from developing, or restoring what was once, during the 1960s and 1970s, its leading role in the cinema of the Maghreb and beyond (*Cahiers du cinéma* 2003).

In Tunisia, where there once existed a rich cinéphile culture (see the cinéclubs described by Khélil (2007)) and where cinema lay at the centre of some of the most significant post-revolution conflicts,[5] the most important film festival initiatives are now based around new technologies, the same technologies that played such an important role in the eviction of former president Zine Ben Abedine Ben Ali. Here, one can find the Festival film minute D9i9A, a 'minute films' festival in La Manouba (www.facebook.com/d9i9a.sitin), dedicated to films shot on mobile phones; the International Amateur Film Festival in Kélibia / Festival International du Film Amateur de Kélibia (FIFAK, www.ftca.org. tn), which relies on light digital image technology; and the Tunisian Mobile Film Festival (www.tmff.tn), which operates entirely online, without a territorial implementation. Still, in Tunisia, the main issue remains the possible re-invigoration in Carthage of the JCC, which has suffered a fall in quality and respect. It needs to be reinstated as the essential meeting point for films from the Arab world and from Sub-Saharan Africa, as the 'place to be' for both Tunisian film lovers and for professionals (buyers, media) from the rest of the world. The future of film festivals and cinemas in Tunisia is currently very unclear and dependent entirely upon unpredictable political decisions.[6] It is dependent, too, upon the financial situation of local cinema, which is itself largely reliant on the future moves of the dominant producer and businessman in the country, Tarak Ben Amar.

Early in the new millennium, prior to the uprising in Tahrir Square, Egypt seemed very weak in comparison to the mighty presence it held on the international stage from the 1950s to 1980s. Certainly the Cairo International Film Festival is in decline, but the Alexandria Film Festival (alexandriafilm.org) and, more recently, the Luxor Film Festival (luxorfilfest.com/en), display improvements the general festival situation. A strong new generation of filmmakers and cultural activists is emerging, but the political situation generates a high level of uncertainty about the future of film production and exhibition.

Uncertainties exist in two other countries recently struck by violent events and changes of regime: Iran and Libya. The three film festivals in Baghdad (the International Kelar Short Film Festival (no website), the Baghdad International Film Festival (www.baghdadfilmfest.com) and the Baghdad Eye Human Rights Film Festival (www.baghdadeye.org)), and the event in Tripoli, serve chiefly as markers and exhibits focussing on claims of change and affirmations of normality that are still to be confirmed in reality. The very existence of these events gives hope, though, even before one knows what is being screened and to whom.

One might make similar comments about festivals in Palestine, with the major difference being that, even if there is only one properly identified festival – the International Al Kasaba Festival in Ramallah (www. alkasaba.org/festival2010/#) – cinema is very present in various ways in the Palestinian Territories. It should also be noted that a significant amount of Palestinian or Israeli-Palestinian films are screened at Israeli festivals, mostly in Jerusalem, which hosts the Jerusalem Film Festival (www.jff.org.il), and in Haifa, which has its own Haifa International Film Festival (www.haifaff.co.il).

Lebanon boasts by far the most important artistic scene in the Arab world and, historically, is one of the leading countries in feature film production (Armes 2012). Lebanon, and more specifically Beirut (the only place where significant cinema-related activities are to be found), hosts two rival international film festivals, the Beirut International Film Festival (www.beirutfilmfestival.org) and Ayam Cinema Days of Beirut (www.ayambeirut.wordpress.com), in addition to a festival dedicated to Lebanese cinema (Né à Beirut – www.neabeyrouth.org). There is also the Forbidden Films Festival (part of the Beirut International Film Festival) that takes place at a local cinema complex, the Metropolis, and bears a name which indicates a challenge to the tight censorship that prevails in the area; a rare thing to do in the region. Beirut also hosts the important Turkish Film Festival at the Metropolis, an event that is of particular interest to both amateur film filmmakers and professionals. This permanent provision of a home for cinema at Metropolis casts the place as a kind of permanent festival, and the complex actually hosts several thematic or nation-based programmes (for example, the popular Beirut Animated (www.metropoliscinema.net/2013/beirut-animated-3rd-edition)), often complete with brochures and other printed material. Lebanon, and again Beirut in particular, enjoys a relatively open, progressive society and the presence of enthusiastic and talented artists and cultural activists with many international connections. Still, the constant political uncertainty prevents the country, or the city, from taking on the role of leading role festival node for the whole region.

Conclusion

Dispersal and heterogeneity appear to underline the festival phenomenon in the Arab world. And this is true, but not completely. Taken individually, only a few of the above-mentioned festivals wield any significant power in terms of audience building, establishment of a film culture, promotion of their country or city on the international scene, or recognition of emerging local talents. The region's unfulfilled potential to produce important films and filmmakers was revealed more than a decade ago when the proliferation of festivals commenced. Just what the future holds in the way of delivering on this promise is still to be determined.

The most visible signs of a great deal of activity in the cultural field, and especially in cinema, are to be found in the activities of the many ciné-clubs, magazines, dedicated websites, schools, training courses, film archives and so on. Film festivals function according to a particular process involving the accumulation of operational strengths, even though they generally function separately, and often in competition with one another. There is a 'critical mass' effect, fed by the constant circulation of films, people, money, ideas and collective images, generated by the informal Arab cinema festival circuit, whose influence stretches beyond the individual motivations of each of its component festivals.

More and more, festivals in the Arab world come closer to the European or Asian models for such events. Broadly speaking, they connect the showing (and often the sale) of existing films with providing an impetus towards the creation of new films. By maintaining funds dedicated specifically to production, co-production or sponsorship, as well as through the organisation of workshops and encounters with producers, script writers or people in charge of public services related to cinema, these festivals now support the actual making of films – not only their circulation. In this sense, the Arab festivals play, and will continue to play a significant role in the rise of new generations of filmmakers in the region, even if the example of the first years of the Emirate festivals has proved that a constant flow of large sums of money alone is not enough to accomplish a healthy film culture. Festivals participate in the training of experts in not just film, but also events organisation, in the economy of the specific cultural field or in the media related to these art forms and topics. Because these events exist in a single place for only a limited timeframe, all those involved are constantly circulating, meeting each other, discussing, exchanging and meeting again at the next festival 'instalment'. The result is the construction of a common sphere of influence, a shared synergistic festival circuit that exists and functions above and beyond the singular interests of the individual festivals.

Festivals play a significant role across the broad spectrum of society, both through what they actually do, and through what they claim to be doing. In a region where freedom of speech remains subject to tight political, religious and conservative social control, festivals and the films they screen films are able to trigger a certain amount of constructive change, even if such change is difficult to achieve and fragile in its effects. History has shown that it is too simplistic to expect that, for instance, a rigorous religious regime will necessarily destroy or limit cinema. As evidence, we have the example of Iran, where the period between the end of the Iran-Iraq War and the election of Mahmoud Ahmadinejad as President, proved conclusively that cinema has the power to bring about change (Devictor 2004). In this context, the specific role of a festival as a zone of relatively light social control, exerting sensitive effects on the general situation, shows its transformative possibilities, especially if the festival is able to attract celebrated actors or directors who may be convinced to advocate for freedom of speech, and thus for film. Experience has shown that festivals can have a decisive role in this process. In 1984, the guests of the International Istanbul Film Festival (www.film.iksv.org/en), led by Elia Kazan, took to the streets to demonstrate against the banning of four of the films selected by the festival. Changes ensued: it was ruled that films shown during the festival no longer had to be submitted to the censorship bureau.

Nevertheless, it is unlikely that a single festival would have an important region-wide effect. And it is clear that any event designed to attract celebrity-gossip media will have no cultural significance. (Indeed, one can argue that such a festival's effects could only be counter-productive.) Still, if a festival does find a way to become part of a network of actions and practices, or even generates a network itself, such as the one in Bejaïa (Algeria), its significance and influence could be multiplied (*Cahiers du cinéma* 2008). Examples of this from other parts of the world include Burkina Faso's FESPACO, Argentina's Bafici (*www.bafici.gov.ar*), Brazil's Sao Paulo Film Festival (http://36.mostra.org/en) and Korea's Busan International Film Festival (www.biff.kr). All are testaments to the major impacts that well-conceived events may have, not only in establishing or reinforcing a national cinema, but also in supporting and increasing a vast amount of cultural, institutional and educational practices that reach far beyond cinema. And then there are the very significant revenues on offer.

Though naturally inscribed in local and national agendas, film festivals trigger effects that extend beyond these areas, and participate in the blossoming of a multi-faceted progressive social vitality that includes and spans generational phenomena, financial currents, expertise exchanges and inter-connectedness between geographic zones. They drive, too, networks of influence between art forms: between cinema and the visual arts; between cinema and television; between cinema and video games; and, of course, between cinema and the internet.

All these reasons, and more, make the 'archipelago' of cinema festivals in the Arab world a particularly efficient vantage point from which to explore the current changes happening in the region. This vast and complex local process is intertwined with the rise and diversification of festivals dedicated to Arab cinema, or to films from any specified Arab country, occurring in the rest of the world.

Works Cited

Armes, Roy (2010) *Arab Filmmakers of the Middle East: A Dictionary.* Bloomington: Indiana University Press.

Barlet, Olivier (2012) *Les Cinémas d'Afrique des années 2000, perspectives critiques.* Paris: L'Harmattan.

Cahiers du cinéma (2003) 'Où va le cinéma algérien?'. Paris: Cahiers du cinéma. Hors série. February-March.

Cahiers du cinéma (2008) 'Festivals dans le monde'. Paris: Cahiers du cinéma. Numéro Spécial Atlas.

De Valck, Marijke (2007) *Film Festivals: from European Geopolitics to Global Cinephilia.* Amsterdam: Amsterdam University Press.

Devictor, Agnès (2004) *Politique du cinéma iranien, de l'âyatollâh Khomeyni au président Khâtami.* Paris: CNRS Editions.

Iordanova, Dina and Ragan Rhyne (eds) (2009) *FFY 1: The Festival Circuit.* St Andrews: St Andrews Film Studies.

Khélil, Hédi (2007) *Abécédaire du cinéma tunisien*. Tunis: Simpact.

Pasquier, Marion (2012) '10èmes Rencontres cinématographiques de Béjaïa', *Critikat*. On-line. Available: HTTP: http://www.critikat.com (August 2013).

Ruoff, Jeffrey (ed.) (2012) *Coming Soon to a Festival Near You: Programming Film Festivals*. St Andrews: St Andrews Film Studies.

Stringer, Julian (2001) 'Global Cities and the International Film Festival Economy', in Mark Shiel and Tony Fitzmaurice (eds) *Cinema and the City: Film and Urban Societies in a Global Context*. London: Blackwell. 134-144.

Thoraval, Yves (1996) *Regards sur le cinéma égyptien*. Paris: L'Harmattan.

Wassef, Magda (ed.) (1995) *100 ans de cinéma égyptien*. Paris: Plume.

Notes

[1]   Although there are no official data available about the exact budgets of these festivals, it is common knowledge that their financial situation is a privileged one.

[2]   The concept of 'local audiences' is in fact a difficult one in a nation where 90% of the inhabitants are not actually local but expatriate.

[3]   A non-exhaustive overview of the Moroccan film festival landscape shows three festivals in Agadir (cinema and migration, documentaries, Amazigh), one in Casablanca (student films), one in Errachidia (university cinema), one in Fes (general festival), two in Khourigba (documentary, African films), two in Meknes (TV films, yuth cinema), two in Oujda (shorts, documentaries), one in Rabat (auteur films), one in Salé (women's films), two in Tangier (Moroccan films, Mediterranean shorts), one in Tetouan (Mediterranean films), one in Zagora (Trans-Sahara films). In 2013, at least one new festival dedicated to international cinema was announced, in Saïdia. [Editor's note: Please see the tables at the back of the book for details on these festivals.]

[4]   Editor's note: the 'Black Years' or *La décennie noire is a period in 1990s Algerian history when a civil war raged between Islamists and the Algerian army.]*

[5]   Examples of such conflicts include: on 9 April 2011, Nouri Bouzid, the most well-known Tunisian director, was brutally attacked on the street and wounded; on 26 June 2011, the cinémafricart, the leading independent art house cinema in Tunis, was attacked and partially destroyed by an Islamist mob and has been closed ever since; on 7 October 2011, Islamist activists attacked the private television Nessma TV building with the intention to burn it down after the braodacasting of Marjane Satrapi's film *Persepolis*. The director of the TV channel was later condemned by Tunisian justice. Nadia El Fani, director of the documentary *Laïcité Inch'Allah* (2011) has received thousands of death threats.

Women's Film Festivals in the Middle East: Challenges and Rewards

Gönül Dönmez-Colin

Film festivals, whether held in the fashionable seaside towns of countries with accomplished film industries, or in the vacation spots of nations lacking such infrastructure, have become an integral part of the film industry, often playing a defining role in the very creation, production and distribution of films. Although most film festivals aim at a universal, unbiased point of view in terms of their selection and exposition of the films, a prevailing feeling of under-representation has played a major role in the establishment of festivals dedicated to one particular segment of society that feels 'othered' by the majority or mainstream. At the same time, certain issues need more space and time if they are to be properly addressed and a louder voice if they are to be heard. Lesbian and gay film festivals, queer film festivals, ethnic film festivals (such as Kurdish film festivals) and women's film festivals are usually born of such concerns. They are the venues where the subaltern may speak. For the sceptics, such festivals have a tendency to endorse by their very nature the 'othering of the othered'; marginalisation of the already marginalised. However, when the issue in question involves a certain region, such as the Middle East, and more specifically, women's filmmaking in that region, the issue becomes even more complex.

Middle Eastern cinema, with its rich history, has been undermined and underrepresented for decades by the more powerful industries elsewhere. Middle Eastern women filmmakers, in addition to all the trials and tribulations of being a woman filmmaker that their colleagues face around the world, have been endeavouring to practice their trade in defiance of several culture-specific obstacles, including imprisonment (Iran) and death threats (Afghanistan). In such a context, even attempting to organise women's film festivals in the Middle East is a commendable feat. Any support / solidarity from other regions or countries – and support has been manifest in the number of international film events (women's film-festivals, special screenings, panoramas or homages held in major festivals) dedicated to the films of women from the Middle East – is encouraging and productive for the determined, outstanding, but often silenced filmic voices of the women in the region.

Flying Broom (Uçan Süpürge) International Film Festival (FBIFF) (www.festivalucansupurge.org) was inaugurated in 1998 in the Turkish capital of Ankara. It was the first women's film festival in Turkey, and

LIVERPOOL JOHN MOORES UNIVERSITY
LEARNING SERVICES

is the only women's film festival in the Middle East to run consecutive editions. It was instituted to function as the most important activity of the Flying Broom Organisation (FBO), which was founded in 1996 with the aims of establishing a network among women's NGOs and functioning as an information and documentation centre. Since that time, the organisation has raised many funds from both national and international sources, for projects with the scope to improve women's status and capacity. Supported by a large circle of volunteers from women's NGOs, media, universities, individual activists and many others, it has contributed to the processes of democratisation and the development of a civil society in Turkey decreed by the international gender equality norms and principles formulated at Beijing (1995) and other international conferences and summits. At the same time, it supports newly established women's organisations, believing that the empowerment of women's organisations is the first step towards the empowerment of women.

One such organisation is the 'Local Women Reporters Network', begun in March 2003. Women reporters from different provinces in Turkey are chosen to document the lives of women in their area as active sources of information, to enable the creation of an effective women's alternative media group. They receive support from the FBO in applying information technologies to the quest for a more egalitarian, democratic and fair society. The FBO is also actively involved in the denunciation of child marriages, a regional social malaise threatening the lives of women. The 'Child Brides: Victims of Destructive Traditions and a Social Patriarchal Heritage' event was held in 54 cities throughout Turkey (between 15 April 2010 and 15 October 2011) to highlight the issue of early and forced marriages, to reshape public opinion, and to set persons, institutions and organisations into motion to arrive at alternative solutions. (A research project entitled 'Early Marriages' was conducted in 2006, and a short film, *Child Brides* was made by the organisation in 2008.) During the event itself, film screenings and seminars (by psychologists, lawyers, doctors and sociologists) were held, followed by interviews with women of all ages. A documentary of the events was made which placed a special emphasis on the negative impacts of early and forced marriages on the psychological and physical welfare of women.

Since its first edition, FBIFF has screened feature films, short films and documentaries, has organised panel discussions and exhibitions, and is producing documentaries and publishing books. Short film and short film screenplay competitions have been taking place since its second year. In its sixth year in 2003, an international section, 'Each Has a Different Colour', was added to the programme and a FIPRESCI

(International Film Critics Federation) jury was established to award a film from this section. The festival promotes itself as the only women's film festival in the world to award such a prize. Other prizes, including an honorary award for a filmmaker or performer and the Bilge Olgaç Achievement Awards for women who contribute to different sectors of cinema (named for Turkey's most accomplished woman filmmaker), were established the same year. The Flying Broom Young Witch Award has been presented to promising young performers since 2009. The first year's recipient was Elit İşcan for her remarkable role in Reha Erdem's *Hayat var* (*My Only Sunshine*, 2008).

The long term aims of the festival are to encourage dialogue related to gender and women's issues by using the language of cinema; to introduce films by women from around the world to local festival audiences; to make contributions to the history of cinema in Turkey and the world through research conducted within the framework of the festival; and to promote the cinemas of individual countries and artists, thereby enhancing institutional efforts to improve the status of women. Neighbouring Middle Eastern countries – Iran, Syria, Palestine, Lebanon and Egypt – receive special attention. Such luminaries of women's cinema as Rakhshan Bani-Etemad, Tahmineh Milani and Mania Akbari, have been regular guests over the years, taking part in valuable exchanges on cinematic experiences during their seminars. Students from the 11 universities in the capital of Ankara, as well as the middle and upper-middle class followers of cultural activities, constitute the majority of the audience. The documentaries in the programme are shown without charge on the campuses of the three major universities in Ankara.

A challenging overall theme is decided upon each year (Peace and Women; The Contribution of Men to Women's Unhappiness; Be Yourself, Think and Create), so that for example, in its 12th edition in 2009, the festival focused on the notorious 12 September 1980 *coup d'état*. An interactive exhibition, 'On 12 September', displayed handwritten letters, sound recordings, cartoons, graphic designs, photos, drawings, paintings and videos by women, and invited visitors to write their own letters, with the goal being to remember — and to make others remember – Turkish cinema's landmark films from the 1980s. *Mine* (1985) and *Ölü bir deniz* (*A Dead Sea*, 1989) by the late Atıf Yılmaz celebrating the liberation of the female body in the atmosphere of the belated arrival of feminism in Turkey – also formed part of the programme.

The theme for the 2010 edition was very provocative: 'She is bad, and you?' The 'badness' is that supposed moral wickedness attributed to women both in real life and in cinema. A parallel section, 'The Other History' was organised, focusing on films exposing the victims of ethnic and religious othering. *Nahide'nin türküsü* (*The Song of Nahide*, Berke Baş, 2009), about the director's grandmother who was forced to hide her Armenian identity, and the powerful drama *İki tutam saç - Dersim'in kayıp kızları* (*The Disappeared Daughters of Dersim*, Nezahat Gündoğdu, 2010), about Kurdish girls given to military families for adoption after the massacre of their birth families in Dersim (today's Tunceli), expose the dark side of Turkey's history.

The 16th edition in 2013 chose the overall theme of 'Despite: Solidarity, Resistance, Action'. The 'Each Has a Different Colour' section included a range of international films, such as *Bejbi Blues* (*Baby Blues*, Katarzyna Rosłaniec, Poland, 2012), *Ginger & Rosa* (Sally Potter, UK / Denmark / Canada / Croatia, 2013) and *Lamma shoftak* (*When I Saw You*, Annemarie Jacir, Palestine / Jordan, 2012). The special section of 'Despite: Solidarity, Resistance, Action', screened *Albom Mishpachti* (*Family Album*, Lihi Binyamin, Israel, 2012), *Yema* (*Mother*, Djamila Sahraoui, Algeria / France, 2012) and, from Turkey, Kurdish filmmaker Mizgin Müjde Arslan's autobiographical *Ben uçtum, sen kaldın* (*I Flew, You Stayed*, 2012). The 'Family: the Scene of Incidents' section, presented a confronting Kurdish short film from Iran about female mutilation, *An Alley Behind Our House* (Shilan Sadi, 2012), and *Kızıl Çarşaf* (*The Scarlet Sheet*), by Kudret Güneş, about a Kurdish exile living in France, foregrounding the virginity issue. The section devoted to feature films from Turkey showcased, among other films, *Araf* (*Somewhere in Between*, Yeşim Ustaoğlu, 2012) and *Gözetleme kulesi* (*Watchtower*, Pelin Esmer, 2012), two exceptional works that expose women's limited choices in androcentric societies. Both approach the issue of unwanted pregnancies, each with a pessimistic ending showing the women making compromises to ensure their own safety and security in an unaccepting society. Mai Zetterling was presented as 'The Witch from the North', while Monika Treut was the special guest with her provocative films in the section 'Attention! Monika Treut!'

The Flying Broom Film Festival is often reproached in conservative and Islamist circles for screening films that go against the moral and religious values of the country. One Anatolian newspaper was particularly enraged at the screenings of *Baise-moi!* (*Rape Me!* France, 2000) by Virginie Despentes and Coralie Trinh Thi, and of *Parfait amour* (*Perfect Love*, France, 1996) by Catherine Breillat. The festival was accused of exhibiting pornography in the name of art. Such debilitating ideological negativism, and the reliance of the festival on the Ministry of Culture and Tourism as its sole sponsor in the capital (where a private sector hardly exists), has been a major handicap to its smooth operation. Another comes with the disposition of some of the established women filmmakers/producers, who, although supportive of the festival, prefer to compete with men on equal terms, arguing that women's film festivals have a stigma attached to their specificity. Despite such drawbacks, FBIFF is slated to take place between 8 and 15 May 2014, to celebrate its 17th anniversary in the capital Ankara.

Based in Istanbul, the International FilmMor (Purplefilm) Women's Film Festival on Wheels (www.FilmMor.org) is organised by women for women, and is dedicated to all the violated, silenced or ignored. In the wake of several campaigns by women against male oppression, in 1990 the Mor Çatı (Purple Roof) Women's Shelter was founded by Melek Özman, an independent feminist filmmaker, to protest against domestic violence. Ever since, the Shelter, run by volunteers, has been receiving victims of violence and giving them support by providing psychological, social or legal aid. In 2003, Özman founded the FilmMor Women's Cooperative and established the festival to increase the involvement of women in cinema and in the media. The major goals of each organisation are the enhancement of communication, of production areas and opportunities, and of the power of women to express themselves in this field. They aim to disseminate non-sexist representations and experiences of women, thus contributing to a life free of sexism, violence and discrimination in cinema, media and, ultimately, society as a whole. Taking place annually in Istanbul during the second week of March, and travelling to other cities depending on the demands of local organisations, the festival underscores the importance of representing women as 'non-passive, non-traditional and non-sexist', focusing on resistance, action and the dreams of women. The Atölyemor: Women's Cinema Workshops were organised in Istanbul in 2004, 2005, 2007 and 2010 and in the South-Eastern, largely Kurdish city of Diyarbakır in 2006, involving film analyses and criticism, and producing films by women, on women and for women that examine the different life stages and experiences of womanhood. The Atölyemor: Editing and Camera Workshop was created in 2009 and has produced such projects as *Klitoris nedir?* (*What is Clitoris?* 2003); *Kadınlara yönelik siddete son* (*Stop Violence against Women*, 2007) and *Namus İçin neler cektik?* (*What is Honour?* 2008) by Melek Özman.

FilmMor celebrated its 11th anniversary in 2013 with thematic sections, retrospectives, workshops and discussions. And with the motto of 'Women need solidarity, not competition' (there are only two competitive sections in the festival's programming: the Purple Camera for Promising Woman Filmmaker and the Golden Okra Awards, the latter awarded for uncovering manifestations of misogyny),[2] the festival reached audiences in Istanbul, İzmir, Sinop and Bitlis. The various other sections of the festival include Women's Cinema, Our Body is Ours, A Purse of Her Own and Sexuality. The Special Section, Women Make Movies, was a collaboration between FilmMor and Women Make Movies (www.wmm. com), a multicultural, multiracial, non-profit media arts organisation based in New York, which has facilitated the production, promotion, distribution and exhibition of independent films and videotapes by and about women since 1972.

The cinema section of the Istanbul Modern Museum, a favourite venue for Istanbul cinéphiles, played host to FilmMor in 2013, with retrospectives of two distinguished women filmmakers: Yeşim Ustaoğlu from Turkey and Doris Dörrie from Germany. Ustaoğlu's award-winning *Araf* (*Somewhere in Between*, 2012) and Dörrei's *Männer* (*Men*, 1985), about a womaniser faced with the adultery of his wife, received particular attention. Another featured filmmaker, Mizgin Müjde Arslan, is a staunch believer in the political nature of all films by and about women, and has tackled a number of taboo subjects, entering cinema as a Kurdish woman determined to tell her story. Her first feature-length documentary *Kirasê mirinê: hewîtî / Ölüm elbisesi: Kumalık* (*A Fatal Dress: Polygamy*, 2009), was shown in the programme and focuses on the desperate lives of rural women under the atrocious practices of polygamy, child marriages and physical abuse.

Women filmmakers in Turkey have not been able to shake the status quo even though they have the full support of women's film festivals at home and abroad. Those who have entered the profession in the new millennium are more confrontational than their male counterparts in exposing social and political conflicts. They bring new dimensions to the male social imaginary in crisis (Laborie 1992), and to the revalorisation of rural life as an imaginary refuge that is observed in large number of films made by male filmmakers. Women's social imaginary (Marini 1991) is no longer absent in films because women are no longer absent from positions of power in Turkish cinema. The country's most successful producer, known for the award-winning films by Nuri Bilge Ceylan, is a woman: Zeynep Özbatur Atakan, the recipient of the European co-production prize – Prix Eurimages (2010). She founded her production company, Zeyno Film, in 2007. The company is also involved in training young professionals. A retrospective of fiction, documentaries and shorts, 'Rebel Yell: A New Generation of Turkish Women Filmmakers', was organised by the Toronto International Film Festival Cinémathèque (www.tiff.net/cinematheque) (22-29 August 2013) and curated by Rasha Salti, and presented some of the best examples of this new vitality. Films screened included Şimdiki zaman (*Present Tense*, Belma Söylemez, 2012), about unemployment and alienation in an arbitrarily developing city; *Atlıkarınca* (*Merry-Go-Round*, İlksen Başarır, 2011) on the taboo of incest;

Köprüdekiler (*Men on the Bridge*, Aslı Özge, 2009) about urban underdogs; and *Oyun* (*The Play*, 2005), Pelin Esmer's award-winning documentary about nine peasant women creating and performing a play called, *The Outcries of Women*. The programme was a pleasant surprise for Canadian audiences, whose chances, apart from occasional festival screenings, of encountering courageous works by Turkish women filmmakers are very slim.

In the case of a closed country like Iran, our knowledge of women's issues is very limited and generally based on second-hand information through the Western or Western-oriented media. Film festivals, or organised film events often serve to bridge the gap, introducing indigenous movies that recount first-hand stories. Some of these films are sponsored by the regime, others are censored or banned in their home country, yet somehow manage to cross the borders and reach larger audiences through one of the most efficient and productive phenomena of the film industry – the film festival. While Tahmine Milani, Rakhshan Bani-Etemad *et al.* have succeeded in exhibiting their films both in Tehran and on the international scene, Merziyeh Meshkini, Mariam Shahriar, Negar Azarbayjani, Niki Karimi, Mania Akbari and several other talented women, have also found the freedom of expression denied to them at home in the medium of the film festival abroad. For example, London cinéphiles had a rare opportunity in the Northern summer of 2013 to watch all of Akbari's films at the British Film Institute Southbank (www. bfi.org.uk) and this was followed by another retrospective in September at the Oldenburg Film Festival in Germany (www.filmfest-oldenburg.de).

The Parvin E'tesami Film Festival (PEFF) (www.parvineff. ir), dedicated to the Iranian poetess Parvin E'tesami (1907-1941), who published her first collection in 1935, has been taking place in Tehran since 2007, exhibiting short fiction, documentary, animation and experimental films. Information is scarce regarding this event, particularly in the English language, though it seems to take place without the committed involvement and support of the distinguished women filmmakers and actors of the country. According to the Assistant Executive Manager Mahdiyeh Araqhi whom I met during my visit to the 32nd Fajr International Film Festival in February 2014, the festival screened only films by Iranian women in its first year. Orders from the government decreed that men's films would have to be included if the festival wished 'to hold a truly feminist point of view', and so the festival began to accept works by Iranian men if they focused on the issues of women. Organised since 2011 by the Iranian Supporting House for Artist Women, the seventh edition took place over 19-22 February 2013, showcasing 100 short films from around the world and focusing on the theme of

'Women's Roles in the Family Economy'. An Iranian section comprised subcategories such as Golden Lotus, Silver Lotus, New Vision and The Parvin E'tesami section. The distinguished jury included Amir Esfandiari, the Chief Executive of Co-productions at the Farabi Cinema Foundation (the main representative of the Iranian cinema abroad) and the Director of International Affairs (1997-2012) of the Fajr International Film Festival, as well as veteran filmmaker Dariush Mehrjui and the researcher and producer Ali Moallem – all men… Turkey, Lebanon, Armenia, Tajikistan, Yemen, India, Romania, Poland, Netherlands, Ireland, UK, Morocco and Australia were just some of the participating countries in an official international competition that included 30 films.

Between 40 and 50 national and international films compete each year for several awards: the Iranian section, Best Fiction Film, Best Documentary, Best Animation, Best Experimental Film, a Special Jury Award and the Best Screenplay; all receive the Golden Lotus trophy, the Diploma of Honour and a cash prize. The Silver Lotus Award of a trophy, Diploma of Honour and a cash prize are given to the Best Female Director, Scriptwriter, Researcher, Cinematographer, Sound Recordist, Editor, Costume Designer, Composer and Make-up Artist. Several other awards are presented to films shown in the Special, New Visions and Parvin E'tesami sections. In the International Competition section, the Parvin Golden Trophy, a Diploma of Honour and a cash prize are given to the Best Fiction, Best Documentary, Best Experimental and Best Animation films. The festival 'Grand Prize' of the Parvin Golden Trophy, Diploma of Honour and a cash prize of €5,000 (U.S.$6,800), is awarded to the Best Foreign Filmmaker in the International Competition. Screenings are free of charge and are attended by around 3,000 spectators, mostly university students, both men and women. The festival is not sponsored by the government, but by private foundations and by UNICEF. However, the government imposes its choice of themes – issues of honour or stories about the prophet Mohammad – and selected films are subject to government scrutiny. Controversial political and social issues pertaining to Iranian women are deliberately avoided. The major goal of the festival is to contribute to the visibility of the women filmmakers by exposing their talents. Unfortunately, the festival's future seems rather bleak given that the 2014 edition has already been cancelled.

If the PEFF is Iran's best-kept cinema secret, another women's film festival in neighbouring Afghanistan rivals it in striving for recognition. Lying geographically outside the somewhat artificial and Eurocentric definition of Middle East, but still politically very much part of it, Afghanistan is connected to cinema in the Western mind not through its indigenous films but through foreign productions, mostly Iranian;

Samira Makhmalbaf's *Panj é asr* (*Five In the Afternoon*, 2003) and Hana Makhmalbaf's *Buda as sharm foru rikht* (*Buddha Collapsed out of Shame*, 2007) spring to mind. Even in the face of such an oppressive force as the Taliban, one of the most important recent socially progressive movements in the country has been the increased appearance of women behind the camera. Roya Sadat, an autodidact from Herat, made her directorial debut as a 24-year-old with *Se noughta* (*Three Dots*, 2005) about a single mother of three, to considerable international acclaim. Her principal actress, a young woman wearing the headscarf, was the only person to accept the role – despite the threat of Taliban reprisal – and then, only because she needed the money to feed her children. The first Herat International Women's Film Festival (www.royafilmhouse.org/ IWFF/1st-international-women-s-film-festival-herat) was held in Herat (6-9 March 2013) with the support of 40 human rights and women's organisations and media partners. The festival was initiated by the Armanshahr Foundation / Open Asia (an NGO active in Afghanistan since 2005) and Roya Film House (Roya Sadat's company; she is now the leading woman filmmaker of Afghanistan). In the tunnel-like structure of the historical Herat Citadel (the Citadel of Alexander), 36 films from 20 countries focusing on women and the marginalised were screened as the Afghan National Police stood guard. The province of Herat (which has the highest number of self-immolations by women in Afghanistan protesting the denial of their right to education, and women trapped in forced marriages and domestic violence) has, in the last decade, also produced the highest number of women filmmakers. This despite a total lack of training facilities and limited possibilities of transnational projects. *Violence Against Women: Ten Years On* (2012), a documentary by newcomer Alka Sadat, Sadat's sister, which focuses on the clandestine practices of the Taliban, especially in the rural areas, received the Afghan Peace Prize. *Laila* (2012), another documentary, directed by Batool Moradi, exposes the traumas of war by recounting the stories of women patients in a mental institution in Kabul. Addiction to alcohol or drugs, a recurring motif in Afghan films, is the main theme of Aqeela Rezai's drama *The Road Above* (2010) and of Zabiullah Fahim's *Flavour of Powder* (2012).

Immigration is another recurring theme in Afghan cinema. A number of transnational productions exploring women's predicaments as exiles and refugees were screened. A co-production with Slovakia, Ľahký vánok / Zápisky z deníku jednej emigrantky (*Light Breeze: Memories of an Immigrant Girl*, Sahraa Karimi, 2009) depicts the sentiments of exile by the use of poetry and diaristic reflections. A film from Iran, *Where Do I Belong* (Mahvash Sheikholeslami, 2008) recounts the dilemmas of Iranian girls married to Afghan men living in Iran and Afghanistan. In addition to those from Afghanistan and Iran, films from India, Venezuela, Tajikistan, Japan, Bangladesh, Pakistan, Australia, Hong Kong, China, Turkey, France, Canada and Thailand were also included. The festival was supported by the Ministry of Culture and Information, human rights organisations and local NGOs, and by patronage from Afghanistan's internationally acclaimed filmmakers, Atiq Rahimi and Seddiq Barmak. Additional assistance came from as the Asian Women's Film Festival of India (www.iawrt.org) and the DIDOR Tajikistan International Film Festival (www.didoriff.com), among others.

Against the odds and in light of pressing and oppressive political and economic issues in the region, particularly the on-going wars, civil and otherwise, local festivals showcasing the works of women are marginal events, but they do take place. One such commendable event is the annual Women's Film Festival (www.shashat.org) in Palestine which began in 2005 and holds its opening screenings in four cities: Ramallah, Bethlehem, Nablus and Jerusalem. Select films go on a Palestinian tour, in partnership with ten universities, lasting from September to December with over 100 screenings across the West Bank and Gaza. Professional filmmaking workshops, public panels, debates and school screenings of Arabic subtitled works are organised. The festival is part of a broader 'I am a Woman from Palestine' project which highlights concerns for women in general, and Palestinian women in particular, through a series of public screenings, discussions, television programmes and filmmaking workshops in the West Bank and Gaza. The two-year project was initially funded by the European Union with additional support from the Heinrich Boll Foundation, the Goteborg Film Fund and the Ford Foundation.

An independent initiative run by a group of women filmmakers and curators in Egypt is the *Baina Sinemay'at* (Among Women Filmmakers) Cairo International Women's Film Festival (www.cairowomenfilmfest.com). The festival was created in 2008 by its current director Amal Ramsis as the Arab-Ibero-American Women's Film Festival to present awarded films and high-quality cinema made by women but which had no possibility of being shown at commercial theatres. The first annual international women's film festival in the Arab world, it has travelled to Lebanon, Syria, Jordan, Morocco, Palestine, Spain, Bolivia, Argentina, Cuba, Colombia, Costa Rica, Peru, Mexico, El Salvador, Paraguay, Germany and Slovenia. Due to its success during its first five years in attracting large audiences and creating new cinematographic debates about social and political issues, it was upgraded to the level of international women's film festival in its sixth edition (16-22 November 2013). The festival is a meeting ground for women filmmakers from across the Arab world and other parts of the globe. Fiction, documentary and short films from places as far apart as Colombia and Japan, Palestine and Georgia and Brazil and the Netherlands, were programmed for 2013. It targets participants and audiences from among women filmmakers, activists, NGOs and study centres about women's issues; from among ordinary citizens who normally do not have access to such films; from among university students (especially of media and film education); from national and international broadcasters, producers and distributors; and from commissioning editors, international festival coordinators and the programmers of other women's film festivals. Its aims are to encourage a higher production of films made by women filmmakers and to encourage filmic debate. In this way, Egyptian audiences are invited to learn more about different forms of cinematographic expression and about the hidden worlds of women, and partake in the exchange of experiences and knowledge between women filmmakers, producers and programmers. The festival seeks to be a platform for a new wave of women filmmakers trying to create their own cinematographic languages. The festival travels to different countries of the Arab world and to Latin America and each year, and focuses thematically on one particular country, screening for free around four films so as to offer the Egyptian public (which votes for the Best Film) a cinematographic panorama of that nation through the eyes of women filmmakers. In 2013, the Country in Focus was the Netherlands and the focus of the Tribute to a Cineaste section, dedicated to pioneers filmmakers, was Egyptian-Lebanese filmmaker Nabiha Lotfi.

The International Women's Film Week Festival in Amman, Jordan, is a UN Women's initiative, organised in partnership with the Aat Network (a platform for engaging with human rights and gender issues through the arts), embassies in Jordan and the Royal Film Commission Jordan (RFC). It is held in collaboration with the Arab Film Festival (www.arabfilmfestival.org) as an annual event, organised in March to coincide with International Women's Day. The festival aims to raise awareness of gender issues and human rights, to stimulate critical engagement and foster an activist audience. In 2013, 20 films from around the world were screened. The Jordanian short film *Horizon* (2013), directed by Zain Duraie (a disciple of Annemarie Jacir) about an illiterate housewife's struggles to have her children educated despite her husband's resistance, was one of the festival favourites. Jacir's own *Lamma shoftak* (*When I Saw You*) about a Palestinian boy separated from his father during the 1967 Arab-Israeli War and placed in a refugee camp in Jordan, was also screened, along with a number of films dealing with Palestinian women refugees, such as *Ein el Hilweh* (*Kingdom of Women*, 2010) by Lebanese-Palestinian Dahna Abourahme.

Israeli cinema has gained new vitality in the new century, although it is still male-dominated. It was considered an important achievement when a film directed by a woman, Rama Burshtein's *Lemale et ha'halal* (*Fill the Void*, 2012) about the forced levirate marriage of a young Hasidic Jewish woman to an older widower, represented Israel at the Oscars® for consideration in the Foreign Language category. The Women in the Picture Association was founded in 2004 with the goal of promoting women's films, and particularly women in the Israeli film industry, through the medium of a film festival. The International Women's Film Festival Israel (www.en.iwff.net), which celebrated its 10th anniversary in Rehovot (21-27 October 2013), is one of the Association's initiatives. A competitive event, the 2012 festival screened around 60 films, over half of which were by Israeli women. The films travel to other cities after the event. The Lethal Lesbian Festival in Tel Aviv started in 2008 and is dedicated entirely to lesbian content, promoting lesbian Israeli women filmmakers in any genre, from comedy and drama to video art and documentaries (http://awiderbridge.org/lethal-lesbians-film-festival).

The exposure of exceptional works by Middle Eastern women to audiences in the West is rewarding for both the filmmakers and their audiences, not only from an academic point of view, but as a way to bridge the gap between different cultures. Such a re-examination of prejudices and prejudgments resulted in 'Rebel Yell: A New Generation of Turkish Women Filmmakers' mentioned above.

In 2006, during the 15th Brisbane International Film Festival (www.biff.com.au) in Australia, I curated the program 'Unveiling Islam: Women and Cinema in Iran and Turkey', a visual rendition of my book *Women, Islam and Cinemas* (2004). Films from both of these countries were screened with parallel presentations by film scholars. Two distinguished Iranians, actor/activist/filmmaker Fatemeh Motamed-Arya and filmmaker/producer Tahmineh Milani, gave presentations on the place and role of women in cinema. These seminars were attended by a large number of expatriates and locals. *Khaneh siah ast* (*The House is Black*, 1963), a twenty-two-minute documentary by Forugh Farrokhzad (the rebel-poet credited with establishing the foundations of the Iranian New Wave (*moj-e no*), a movement that flourished in the 1960s and 1970s) and Tahmineh Milani's fifth feature, *Do zan* (*Two Women*, 1998) from Iran and *Yol* (*The Way*, Şerif Gören, 1982), winner of the Palme d'Or at Cannes and scripted by the legendary Yılmaz Güney and *Masumiyet* (*Innocence*, Zeki Demirkubuz) from Turkey, were just some of the films that attracted audience interest.

The Bird's Eye View Film Festival's (www.birds-eye-view.co.uk) Celebrating Arab Women event (3-10 April 2013) at the British Film

Institute in London, screened the internationally successful *Wadjda* (Haifaa Al Mansour, Saudi Arabia / Germany, 2013), the first feature film from Saudi Arabia; *When I Saw You* (Annemarie Jacir), *Habibi (Darling, Something's Wrong with your Head*, Susan Youssef, Palestine, USA, Netherlands / UAE, 2011) and *Al-Khoroug lel-nahar Coming Forth by Day* (Hala Lotfy, Egypt / UAE, 2012), among other exceptional works. It was a unique opportunity to familiarise Londoners with the new trends in women's cinema in the Arab world, and to reflect on the lives and aspirations of people from different cultures.

In addition to events held in the large metropolises of the world and distinguished women's film festivals in the West (Créteil (http://www.filmsdefemmes.com) in France, Cologne / Dortmund (http://www.frauenfilmfestival.eu) in Germany, etc.), noteworthy efforts have been made in those non-Western parts of the world not necessarily privileged to host prestigious festivals. The Asian Women's Film Festival, the Indian chapter of International Association of Women in Radio and Television (www.iawrt.org), that took place in New Delhi (5-8 March 2013) was an outstanding opportunity for cinéphiles in India's capital to gain their own 'bird's eye view' of women's cinema in Iran. Akbari's *20 angosht (20 Fingers,* 2004), which examines marital rape, adultery and homosexuality, and Azarbayjani's *Aynehaye rooberoo (Facing Mirrors,* 2011) on trans-sexuality surprised Indian audiences, whose films are not free of censorship, and who did not expect Iranian films to touch upon such taboo issues. (Both films had already had successful screenings at the Kerala International Film Festival (www.iffk.in) and the Samsung Women's International Film Festival in Chennai (www.inkocentre.org) in programmes I curated.)

Film festivals have become major venues for serious filmmakers to exhibit their work. Working in the sector carries with it the challenges of financial issues, overt and covert forms of censorship, and distribution difficulties. These difficulties are not necessarily gender-based, except in those Arab countries where the industry hardly exists and to make a film is a major challenge, even for male filmmakers. Accomplished women are an essential part of the international festival circuit today and are rerecognised on an equal basis in terms of participation, awarding and funding. This last issue is very important given that the possibilities of funding at home are inadequate or non-existent. Women's film festivals in the Middle East are generally born out of dedication to women's issues, both across society and in cinema; two arenas largely regulated by men. The obvious obstacle of being unable to schedule recent films coupled with the reluctance of directors / producers whose first choice is the more prestigious global events, means festivals often pursue other goals than offering premières. In some instances they serve as the 'memory' of a film culture, unearthing the achievements of neglected or misrepresented women in cinema. They can shine a light on an actor who has contributed to cinema significantly while remaining in the shadow of the stars, or on a dubbing artist whose face no one has ever seen. But most importantly, women's film festivals in the Middle East, while vital in supporting individual women filmmakers and women's filmmaking generally, also deliberately shoulder the responsibility of raising public awareness about gender issues.

Works Cited

Laborie, Pierre (1992) 'Vichy et les Français', Jean-Pierre Azéma and François Bédarida (eds), *Le Régime de Vichy et les Français | The Regime of Vichy and the French*. Paris: Fayard.

Marini, Marcelle (1991) 'La place des femmes dans la production culturelle' |'The Place of Women in Cultural Production', Georges Duby *et al.* (eds) *Histoire des femmes, 5*. Paris: Plon.

Notes

[1]   I wish to thank to Amal Ramsis, the Director of Among Women Film-makers / Baina Sinemay'at: the Cairo International Women´s Film Festival; Mahdiyeh Araqhi, the Assistant Executive Manager at the Parvin E'tasami Film Festival; Necati Sönmez, the Director of Documentarist-Istanbul Documentary Days; Niki Karimi, the Iranian actor/filmmaker; Halime Güner, the President of Flying Broom International Women's Film Festival and Özlem Kınal, the Co-ordinator of Flying Broom. All were very generous in sharing their expertise and providing valuable information.

[2]   The Golden Okra Award is a prize awarded with the intention of shaming the sexist attitudes that still pervade the world of cinema. It is presented to criticise the male dominance of the cinema sector and its inherent sexism.

Women's Film Festivals

Est.	Name	Dates	Website
1998	Flying Broom International Women's Film Festival, Ankara, Turkey	May	http://festival.ucansupurge.org/english/
2003	FilmMor Women's Film Festival on Wheels, Istanbul, Turkey	March	http://www.filmmor.org/default.asp?sayfa=11
2004	International Women's Film Festival, Tel Aviv, Israel	October	http://www.iwff.net/
2004	International Women's Film Festival of Salé / Festival International du Film de Femmes Salé, Morocco	July	http://www.fiffs.ma/
2005	Shashat Women's Film Festival, Palestine	Sept – December	http://www.shashat.org/new/etemplate.php?id=642
2008	Among Women Filmmakers / Baina Sinemay'at: the Cairo International Women's Film Festival, Egypt	November	www.cairowomenfilmfest.com
2011	Arab Women's Film Festival, The Hague, The Netherlands	March	http://www.arabwomensfilmfestival.nl/
2013	Bursa Women's Short Film Festival, Turkey	March	https://www.facebook.com/pages/1st-Bursa-Womens-Short-Film-Festival/523685727660643
2013	International Women Film Festival Heart, Afghanistan		http://www.aiwff.org/

Compiled by Stefanie Van de Peer
Table is comprehansive, not exhaustive

Arab Media Art:
Experiments in Exhibition

Laura U. Marks

This chapter examines how experimental cinema and media art from the Arab world circulates within and beyond it. Where and how do experiments in Arab cinema get seen? There are few festivals in the world devoted to works that experiment with conventions of form and modes of production. Since most festivals are trying to reach broad audiences and to exhibit a majority of movies that can go on to attain theatrical or television distribution, they minimise the space allowed for 'difficult' films. In the Arab world, such works are more often shown by non-profit art organisations, especially those that support production and exhibition. Therefore, this chapter will focus on those venues more than on the actual festivals. These observations point to a tension between experimentation and institutions and, in turn, between state and international institutions, around which the following discussion will turn.

Experimental works do show up in festivals both within and beyond the Arab world. When festivals and individual screenings do explore the experimental side of Arab cinema and media art, it is often due to the commitment of a small number of programmers. I started to list these people, but realised that such a list would only annoy some people and ingratiate myself with others, all the while failing to disentangle the festival / theatre and biennale / gallery scenes. A subtle power dynamic comes into play when one tries to account for the relative influence of film programmers and art curators, and while this would be fruitful to examine, it leads too far away from the stated purpose of this chapter. So the one programmer I must mention in this context is Rasha Salti, whose programming at CinemaEast in New York, the Abu Dhabi Film Festival, the Toronto Film Festival, and the incomparably rich series 'Mapping Subjectivity: Experimentation in Arab Cinema 1960-Now' at the Museum of Modern Art between 2010 and 2012, has long privileged experimentation.

Institutional Experimentation: An Oxymoron?

To talk effectively about festivals that programme Arab experimental cinema, I need first to define experimentation, and then to demonstrate the tension that arises between experimentation and institutions, including film festivals. If the words 'experimental cinema' make us think of a genre of formalist and structuralist works on 16mm film from the 1960s, we must stretch our minds to accommodate a vaster notion. Experimental cinema, or, more broadly, experimental media art, includes films and videos that experiment formally with the medium, from film formats to low-end video formats to HD to mobile and on-line platforms (I consider 'cinema' to denote all moving-image recorded media). It includes experiments, drawn from critiques of cinema and TV, with narrative and the construction of meaning: Rasha Salti (2013) points out that experimentation in Arab cinema often involves responding to the canon of Arab cinema in particular. It experiments with the relationship between fiction and documentary, in questions about presence, index and performance. Indeed some of the richest experimentation works with performativity, treating cinema as an event, from the pro-filmic act to the act of reception. Experimentation also regards content: experimental narrative, essay films, experimental documentary and certain political work. Most experimental cinema is practicing philosophy: dealing with epistemology, what we can know; ontology, what is real or true; and phenomenology, what our perceptions can tell us about the world, to name but a few of its foundational concepts. A negative definition of experiment entails whatever does not fit into standards for commercially viable fiction and documentary; it is any 'short' that is not a calling-card film. Yet the best narrative feature films contain experimental moments.

The works with which this chapter is concerned are experimental in two senses: they carry out experiments or try things out; and they are experiential, or based on experience. As Sophie Chamas writes in the context of the Abu Dhabi Film Festival, experimental Arab films 'refuse to show or tell, and instead, put the viewer's body through an ordeal, sucking her into the screen, dissolving the distance between film and viewer' (Chamas 2012). In both ways, experiment and experience, experimentation cuts through convention and gets close to something newly emerging, to life itself. This double sense of experiment and experience is more akin to the Arabic word *tajriba*, like the French *experience*, than it is to the English *experiment*: one can speak in Arab of *sînemâ tajribî* with that double sense of experiment and experience (though it tends to connote experimental cinema of the 1960s and 70s, as Sherif El Azma tells me – which takes us right back to the restricted definition I mentioned at the outset!).

Must Experiments Come from Grassroots Organisations?

Most of Arab cinema is already experimenting, even if its formal audio-visual means are simple and its narrative structure is conventional. This is because Arab filmmakers, video makers and artists, struggle to a greater or lesser extent to avoid clichés and received notions and to manoeuver deftly around imposed criteria. Creativity arises from acutely local circumstances; singularities. But relevance is imposed from without. Institutions of all sorts impose criteria of relevance: artists and filmmakers are demanded in turn to represent the nation favourably, to criticise religion, to uphold religion, to self-Orientalise, to critique Orientalism, to explain the Arab world to the West, to tell stories that everyone can relate to, to be expressive, to be authentic, to be conceptual, etc., etc. Festivals and other kinds of exhibitions often impose criteria of relevance quite aggressively.

Looking at the various kinds of infrastructures for this work, how can we tell which of them best support and sustain an experimental and creative practice? The cinematic infrastructure (training, funding, production, exhibition and distribution) in many parts of the Arab world does sometimes emerge from within established institutions, including those of the state. Yet it also involves working relationships and collectives that spring up when there is no institutional support. Some of these assemblages stabilise into institutions, others dissolve or re-form after their work is complete. This gives them a mobility and sensibility that more conventional structures lack.

Initial observation suggests that short-term, lightly-institutionalised projects produce the most vital results. A related hypothesis is that top-down institutional structures are bad for creativity. Before investigating these hypotheses we need to distinguish between two kinds of institutions: those of Arab states and those of international organisations. State support comes with complex constraints. International support usually comes with strings attached in the form of the donors' criteria. For organisations that emerge without state support, the more complex the organisation is, the more it relies on international funding. Both kinds of institutions, state and international, enable and constrain experimental production.

It must be acknowledged that even to focus on experimental film or video art in the Arab world brings with it a whiff of cultural imperialism, at least until very recent years. Experimental media art has long been a minor form, as opposed to more conventional cinema, and late to arrive at official recognition. As Jessica Winegar points out in the case of Egypt, state cultural organisations, including universities and exhibitions, were slow to include video, installation and other media that arose after modernism as aspects of culture. She writes that although the Egyptian Ministry of Culture began to encourage new forms in the 1990s, they sped to recognition in Egypt through private-sector exhibitions in the early 2000s. New forms, including video, were introduced by Western-trained artists and Western, or Western-trained, curators (Winegar 2006: 282-286). In Egypt, video appeared in private galleries and foreign-funded NGOs before it made it onto the curricula and into the exhibitions of state organisations in the course of the 2000s. The new media not only appear 'foreign' to the majority of Egyptian artists, they also (sometimes) propel their practitioners into the international art circuit. Egyptian artists are thus torn, Winegar argues, between two institutions: the state and the global neoliberal economy.

> Young artists thus became the subjects of two operations of power – one emanating from the Egyptian state apparatus and one from Western curators. Just as state officials 'created' young artists to prove Egypt's cultural progress, Western curators 'created' young artists to prove theirs. While the state gave prizes to certain kinds of art and emphasised surveillance, Western curators chose the same kinds of art and used a combination of neoliberal and neocolonial discourses to justify those choices. (Winegar 2006: 294)

Winegar does not distinguish between non-commercial and commercial private-sector institutions; for example, she refers to the director of a non-profit arts organisation as its owner. However, this constitutes a fundamental division in the North American art world. Artist-run centres (in Canada) and non-profit arts organisations (in the U.S.) tend to represent more experimental, less marketable art, which sometimes migrates to the commercial sector. These institutions, especially in Canada (like their counterparts in Europe) receive government funding: thus state support actually nurtures experimentation.[1] The issue seems to be cultural capital more than making money from art sales *per sé*: art NGOs in Egypt (or Lebanon, Morocco and Palestine) deliver artists to the international art scene, which raises their visibility and cultural capital. Eventually, in some cases, it raises the prices they can charge for their work. How this occurs for moving-image media, which remains less saleable than painting and sculpture, is another question. Yet art NGOs in the Arab world receive the majority of their funding from European and North American governments, other NGOs and corporate foundations whose stated aims are not to raise a generation of international commercial artists but to foster dialogue, support minority voices, etc. – aims that are ideological but not market-driven in themselves.

In light of these double pressures, from the state and the international art market, it appears that those local organisations that are relatively free of either kind of support are best at nurturing creativity.

But institutionalised creativity should not be considered an oxymoron. Instead, I propose to examine each organisation and event individually in terms of what creative connections it has been able to generate. To idealise the pure, authentic and grassroots, can often enact a kind of Orientalism that desires Arab artists and filmmakers to be practicing while simultaneously remaining innocent of the world-at-large. Such a view ignores the ways international and institutional pressures contribute to how a work takes shape creatively. Thus, rather than reject institutional influence, whether state or private, out of hand, I suggest we look at how creative practice individuates under the influence of these structures. Does it generate more interesting connections? Does it become more complex? Similarly, I do not want to fetishise the local or project authenticity onto it; rather, a criterion of *creative individuation* (inspired by the concept of Gilbert Simondon, 1993) should help identify those institutions, loose groupings and single events that give rise to creative ripples.

Where are the Festivals for Experimental Arab Media Art?

Experimental works are not well-represented in film festivals in the Arab world; you are more likely to come across them in a Western country. As Samirah Alkassim notes, regarding what she calls the Arab avant-garde, 'most of these filmmakers have difficulty showing their work in their countries of origin. One has to be attending a film festival in Rotterdam, a biennale in Sao Paulo, an art gallery in Paris, or' – and here Alkassim points to a difficulty in distribution that people sometimes forget – 'has to have enough bandwidth to download a compressed video file if the work is stored on the Internet' (Alkassim 2006: 132).

As the very existence of this volume, *Film Festivals and the Middle East*, attests, there are a great number of Western festivals of Arab cinema, and some of them regularly screen experimental works.[2] Yet foreign festivals, exhibitions and individual screenings, often impose criteria of relevance in opportunistic and short-sighted ways. To give a single example: Raed Yassin's brilliant short video *The New Film* (Lebanon, 2009), premiered at Photo Cairo in December 2008,[3] remarks on the staying power of Egypt's military regime by rapidly editing together scores of scenes from popular Egyptian cinema. In each, the now-ousted Egyptian leader Hosni Mubarak's portrait presides over a scene of people in an office negotiating with, flattering and abusing each other by turn. Mubarak is timeless, Yassin's video suggests, anchored by the power of the Egyptian military. During the rash of screenings after the Tahrir Revolution in 2011, Yassin says, exhibitors lost all interest in *The*

New Film, considering that it represented a past era.[4] Just how wrong they were indicates the problems with reactive curating. Nevertheless, we can remain open-minded in looking for foreign support as 'affinitive transnationalism' to employ Mette Hjort's terminology (Hjort 2010).[5]

In Arab countries, experimental works are more often shown at events staged by private, non-profit art organisations, especially those that support production and exhibition: organisations that generate festivals from the work they support themselves. I will detail some of these. The following case studies look at moving-image media produced in the tension between state and private infrastructures for film and visual culture and between experimentation and institutionalisation.

Negligible State and Heavy Private Infrastructure: Lebanon

Given the lack of cultural infrastructure after the Lebanese civil war and the lack of a Lebanese film industry, an experimenting, non-commercial model of Lebanese cinema had to invent itself. Lebanese filmmakers' inventiveness has been boundless and has inspired others across the Arab world and beyond. It seems that it is the very dearth of top-down structures that made this creativity possible (Khatib 2008).[6]

In Beirut, an independent documentary movement formed during the civil war, around the work of politically committed documentarists such as Borhan Alawiye, as well as Mohamed Soueid, who had been a television documentarist during the war, the Palestinian Mai Masri, the Lebanese Jean Chamoun, who made high-quality documentaries for French television, and others. In 1999 a group of film and video makers founded Beirut DC (Beirut Development and Cinema), in recognition that a creative, politically-committed cinema could only take shape independently of the state, television and foreign NGOs. Their manifesto stated in part,

> Beirut DC has the aim of giving picture and voice to everyone and above all to the marginalized people and to allow them to freely express themselves so that they may define themselves, their reality and their problems and to broadcast these to the large public with the hope of being able to induce some change. ('Beirut DC dossier' 2002)

The current mission statement is just a bit different, saying in part:

In a region where individuality is generally restricted, Beirut DC encourages its partners and collaborators to produce films that are relevant to their society, that seek to question pre-established forms and beliefs, and aim to induce change and new, personal approaches. (Beirut DC website)

Beirut DC founded a production centre for local film and video makers that continues to be extremely active. The works vary widely, but in general privilege social justice, personal approaches to historical memory and the representation of experiences ignored by commercial media. Their festival, Beirut Cinema Days (http://ayambeirut.wordpress. com), showcases these productions and other works from throughout the region: a stunning variety of work with a strong emphasis on short and experimental films and videos. Though Beirut DC's organisers initially wished it to be free of the influence of foreign NGOs, it now receives support from the Ford Foundation, ARTE, the Goethe Institut, the Dubai Film Festival, the Heinrich Böll Foundation and the Swedish International Development Agency, as well as from the Lebanese Ministry for Culture (Beirut DC website).

In 2001, to address the paucity of experimental video production in the Arab world, Akram Zaatari and Mahmoud Hojeij invited artists from throughout the region to Lebanon to take part in a workshop called 'Transit Visa: on Video and Cities' (Zaatari and Hojeij 2001). They prepared the guest list with the goal of mixing perspectives from artists both experienced with and new to video: participants included Ammar el Beik and Lubna Haddad from Syria, Sherif El Azma and Hassan Khan from Egypt, Hassan Abou Hammad and Mais Darwazeh from Jordan, Ziad Antar and Farah Dakhlallah from Lebanon, and the rather out of place Ghazel from Iran. During the carefully-planned week, Zaatari and Hojeij dispensed creative assignments. To help focus on lived relationships with one's city they asked participants to bring a sample of local news, documentation of their bedroom, house and street, and documentation of their favourite part of their city. One assignment asked participants to mark on their bodies the names of cities important to them; another, to relate their earliest memory. The artists met with Lebanese filmmakers, artists, curators and critics, viewed work by local film- and video makers, and made short videos. Despite Jalal Toufic's dismissal of all the resulting videos as clichés (Toufic 2001), some of them are lasting gems. 'Transit Visa' gave a powerful jumpstart to most of the participants' careers.[7]

Also in 2001, a group of friends – Pierre Sarraf, Wadih Safieddine, Nadim Tabet, and Danielle Arbid – started the film and video series Né à Beyrouth (Born in Beirut; www.neabeyrouth.org), which focuses somewhat more on narrative works. Housed at the stylish gallery Espace SD in Jeitawi, and programmed and promoted in French, Né à Beyrouth had connotations of Christian East Beirut: relatively wealthy, privileged and Francophone. Karine Wehbé, one of Espace SD's founders, says

> Our situation was ambiguous, people thought we were rich kids and that the space belonged to us. People actually thought that Wadih was the owner of the space, but we were completely broke! [...] There was also a certain animosity concerning our project because we were francophone, therefore all of Espace's communication was in French. People were criticising us because of that. (2010: 14)

Yet from its East-side perch, Né à Beyrouth has created a lot of activity, organising the Lebanese Film Festival (www.lebanesefilmfestival. org) continuously and producing works. Reorganised as a production company, Né à Beyrouth is able to support independent filmmaking by producing advertising, corporate films and music videos. It recently co-produced, with the organisation UMAM Documentation and Research from a deeply Shi'a neighbourhood way across town, Wissam Charaf's documentary *It's All in Lebanon* (2011), a political study of the Lebanese video-clip industry as produced by rival sectarian television stations. Short works rarely get distributed, so it was great that a short-lived distribution company, Incognito, produced a DVD of selected Né à Beyrouth works from 2001 to 2005 for distribution (Wilson-Goldie 2006). Now Né à Beyrouth broadcasts selections from the festival weekly on Lebanon's MTC (Azouri 2012). Ashkal Alwan, the Lebanese Association for the Plastic Arts, grew out of a series of multimedia art events that Christine Tohme began organising in 1995 in response to emerging local issues. Ashkal Alwan grew to dominate the Lebanese art scene and some of the artists it has supported shot to international fame. Tohme has worked to raise money for the organisation without sacrificing its integrity. For example, as Mark Westmoreland relates, Tohme told a public gathering that she refused funding from the Ford Foundation when it required her to sign a statement that Ashkal Alwan would not support terrorism. 'Does this mean I can't support Iraqi or Iranian artists? I refused to sign it' (Westmoreland 2008: 170). Instead Ashkal Alwan relies on funders like the Danish Prince Claus Fund that do not attach strings.

Ashkal Alwan began the series 'Video Works' in 2006, inviting artists to submit proposals for videos that the organisation would fund and premiere. Many fine works have come out of this process. Often their aesthetics are more like what we find in 'gallery video' than in experimental film or video art, insofar as one can still distinguish these: an emphasis on performance for the camera, conceptual explorations and interrogations of the archive of Lebanese and Arab television and cinema.

Another intercessor in the Beirut cinema scene, the Docudays festival (www.docudays.com), operating annually with a few missed years since 1999, screens Lebanese, Arab and international documentaries, usually selecting works that are more conventional in style. And recently, a collective of filmmakers at Metropolis Cinema-Sofil, including Joana Hadjithomas and Hania Mroué, started a theatrical screening series, showing for example the bubbly Lebanese commercial cinema of the brief industrial period in the 1970s in a summer 2012 series.

All this creative production and exhibition activity in Lebanon continues despite the near-complete lack of involvement by the state, and with the support of numerous Western organisations.

Heavy State Infrastructure, Minor Private Infrastructure: Syria

In countries with an entrenched official art culture – represented by a Ministry of Culture, staid higher-education arts curricula and, in some cases, state-sponsored cinema education and production – media arts that experiment have arisen in ventures independent from the state. In Syria, from 1964 to the civil war, the National Film Organization (NFO) completely dominated cinema production. The NFO had to approve the script and the final film, and could also prevent a completed film from being exhibited. Those filmmakers who managed to work for the NFO worked free from the need to make commercially profitable films and received salaries and sufficient funding to pay collaborators and crew. Within the tightest of government constraints, two generations of Syrian filmmakers developed long-term relationships of creative support and complicity (Dickinson 2012, Salti 2006). But the frustrations of slow production and censorship forced Omar Amiralay, the only documentary filmmaker of his generation, into exile in France.

In 2005, Amiralay returned to Damascus, disillusioned by the short-sightedness of the French media for which he worked (Al Abdallah Yakoub, n.d.). Amiralay, together with Lebanese-American experimental filmmaker Hisham Bizri, Hala Galal, Jesper Højbjerg, Jakob Høgel, and Anders Østergaard, founded the Arab Institute of Film (AIF), with the goal of producing independent documentaries, funded by the Danish organisation International Media Support. Its goals included 'to foster a thoughtful and critical reflection about the principles of innovative aesthetic practices, social foundations, and cultural expressions in Arab cinema' (Bizri 2005). The ambitious plan was to train 75-100 students per year, beginning in 2005, and for the workshop to become an MFA-granting institution by 2010; it would make its start in Amman and move to Sidon, Lebanon. Faculty included Arab, Danish and American instructors (Bizri 2005).

Though it did not achieve these goals, AIF fostered the production of some very powerful films: alumni include Reem Ali and Rami Farah of Syria and Maggie Kabariti and Sandra Madi of Jordan, among others (Ciecko 2009). And 2008, the year AIF ended, was also the year that Amiralay founded the DoxBox documentary cinema festival (www.doxbox.org/, URL broken) to exhibit some of the works produced there, though some, such as Reem Ali's *Zabad* (*Foam*, 2006) were censored. Amiralay died in February 2011. In 2012, as civil war raged in Syria, DoxBox's organisers cancelled the Damascus screening and instead planned a worldwide one-day screening on March 15, the anniversary of the start of the Syrian uprising – in practice, March 14-16 (Van de Peer 2012). The programme of Syrian documentaries comprised classic works by Amiralay and Oussama Mohammad, independent documentaries by Nidal Al Dibs and Meyar Al Roumi, and works made under the auspices of AIF. The preliminary list of participating venues that screened DoxBox's programme gives a good snapshot of organisations able to respond to the demand:

Arab Countries:
1. Cinémathèque de Tanger (Tangiers, Morocco)
2. Jesuit Cultural Center (Alexandria, Egypt)
3. Sudan Film Factory (Khartoum, Sudan)
4. Cimathèque, in collaboration with Mosireen (Cairo, Egypt)
5. ESAV - École Supérieure d'AudioVisuel (Marrakech, Morocco)

United States & Canada:
1. Spectacle Theater (New York)
2. Temple University (Philadelphia)
3. Simon Fraser University (Vancouver)
4. University of Pennsylvania (Philadelphia)

Europe:
1. Frontline Club (London, UK)
2. Filmhouse Cinema (Edinburgh, Scotland)
3. FIDMarseilles (Marseilles, France)
4. DOK Leipzig (Germany)
5. CPH DOX (Denmark)
   (DOXBOX Press release 2012)

I organised a screening at my own institution, Simon Fraser University in Vancouver. It was very moving to watch these works in company with other groups around the world. Interestingly (perhaps due to the connections of my Iranian-Canadian research assistant), it was attended mostly by Syrian-Canadians and Iranian-Canadians, who noticed numerous points in common between their former governments. Audience members were struck by the emotional detail through which Oussama Mohammad's *Khutwa khutwa* (*Step by Step*, Syria, 1978) documents the origins of Alawite loyalty to and dependence on the Ba'ath regime.[8]

In 2008, AIF relocated to Beirut and took the name Screen Institute Beirut (SIB), also supported by International Media Support. Screen Institute Beirut's Film Fund started in 2009 and it is developing a training academy, thus bundling training and funding together. Its goals differ from both Beirut DC and AIF, in that a desire to support free and creative expression in documentary is tempered by the need for professionalisation. Television producers appear prominently on SIB's board of directors. The organisation's website states that its aims include to support young professionals to 'produce films that would otherwise not be realized', to provide training in the region and to support networking. 'Applicants are encouraged to develop films based on stories that relate to their own realities', that is, not imposed perspectives. Yet SIB also emphasises that it wishes to support minorities, disadvantaged groups and women, suggesting an NGO-driven agenda. The foundation of teaching philosophy is 'the focus on the cinematic story', which suggests that certain experimental approaches are not encouraged (SIB website).

A sample of films that SIB has supported includes Wissam Charaf's *It's All in Lebanon* (Lebanon, 2012); Khaled Jarrar's *Mutasalilun* (*Infiltrators*, Palestine / UAE, 2012), a document of the ways Palestinians devise to sneak past Israeli checkpoints, which screened at the Dubai International Film Festival (DIFF); and *My Love Awaits Me by the Sea* by Mais Darwazeh (Lebanon, 2012), who got her start in video production through Zaatari and Hojeij's 'Transit Visa' project and went on to make several experimental shorts before getting an MFA in film in the UK.

Substantial State and Private Infrastructure: Egypt

Egypt also offers instructive examples of the (sometimes) productive tensions between state and private culture. Given the continuity of the Egyptian film industry, which focuses on popular commercial production (especially, Alkassim argues, since the Saudi market has come to direct Egyptian commercial production), it makes sense to look elsewhere for experiments; in particular, for the purposes of this chapter, experiments that lead to exhibition. Lina Khatib points out that in recent years, Egyptian filmmakers are looking to Lebanese short films for inspiration, because the Egyptian industrial model is slow to change compared to lightweight, seat-of-the-pants Lebanese production models (Khatib, 48).

One artist whom Akram Zaatari and Mahmoud Hojeij invited to participate in the 2001 Transit Visa project in Beirut was Egyptian Sherif El Azma, who had completed his Master of Fine Arts (MFA) in filmmaking in the UK and returned to Cairo, where he felt completely isolated. El Azma relates how, when he was beginning to pursue his experimental practice, he could not have survived without the example and encouragement of experimental makers in Lebanon. 'I don't know if I'd have been able to go on without Beirut, Akram and all'. In the early 2000s, El Azma's work could not find a place in Egypt, between the 'monolith' of Egyptian industrial, narrative cinema and the visual art world.

> Cinema could not accept experimental film, and the art scene was where you show Super-8 [...] There was no space between video art and cinema in Egypt. It is all subject-based or genre-based. Videos opened up another space. (El Azma)

Most Egyptian experiments with moving-image media have taken place in the (sometimes) productive tensions that arise between state-supported training and exhibition and the private sector. Kaelen Wilson-Goldie characterised this state-private bifurcation in 2009:

> Photo Cairo 4 and the Cairo Biennale epitomise the enduring polarisation of the Egyptian art scene. The biennale, renowned for its curatorial confusion and shambolic organisation, represents the official, government-sponsored public art sector of a state where the Ministry of Culture receives the second highest federal budget allocation after the Ministry of Defence. Photo Cairo – young, edgy and conceptually precise – represents an unofficial, fiercely independent alternative art scene that has, over the past decade, earned widespread international recognition for being critical, credible and almost claustrophobically tight-knit. (Wilson-Goldie 2009)

Wilson-Goldie's description recalls the conflict between state and private organisations in Egypt detailed above – with a definite preference, when compared to Winegar, for non-state institutions. The fulcrum of this tension has been the Townhouse Gallery. Founded by Canadian curator William Wells in 1998 in a neighbourhood of auto detailing shops, Townhouse became a hub of critical and experimental activity.

In 2000 and 2001, Townhouse, Espace's Karim Francis and Mashrabia Gallery organised the Nitaq Festival (since 1999). This festival launched a first generation of Egyptian video artists and experimental filmmakers, including Hassan Khan, Sherif El Azma (who won Best Work at the festival for his video *Interview with a Housewife* (Egypt, 2000)), and others who would later work in film and video, such as Doa Aly, Khaled Hafez and Wael Shawky (Al Nitaq 2001: 15-21). Nitaq ended abruptly in 2001, but from its initial impetus evolved Photo Cairo (since 2002), organised initially by Townhouse, then taken over by the non-profit Contemporary Image Centre, a biannual series that exhibits video and installation as well as still photography.

In 2009, the state-run Cairo Biennale took some risks, hiring as Artistic Director the young sculptor Ehab El Labban, who exerted more control over the loose selection process, perhaps in response to the fact that non-state exhibitions like Photo Cairo were eclipsing the Biennale (Wilson-Goldie). Also in 2009, as Omnia El Shakry recounts, the Twentieth Youth Salon, organised in Cairo by the Ministry of Culture, controversially selected a jury of young artists with connections to the international art scene, and appointed two members of the jury, Hassan Khan and Wael Shawky, to curate the exhibition (El Shakry 2009: 5). These may be examples of established, state institutions appropriating the creative energy of emergent artists and intellectuals; or they may give evidence that old institutions are capable of transformation.

Egyptian artist-produced workshops all sprang from a critique of university art teaching. The curriculum at the Fine Arts colleges emphasises form over concept, tends to be imitative and still emphasises modernist styles. Video is still often perceived as a Western art form (Hendawy 2011). This might seem an odd observation, since most of the Fine Arts curriculum is based in modernist painting and sculpture techniques and styles of Western origin (Karnouk 1995; Winegar 2006). However, video, like installation and performance, is associated with conceptual and, later, research-based practices that are not part of the modernist academic curriculum. Elnoshokaty generously recognises the virtues of the traditional curriculum, which trains artists in more hands-on skills in a variety of media than do Western conceptually driven arts curricula:

> Even though this system had its negative consequences it also paved the way for talented students to try all branches of art (painting, sculpture, design, ceramics, printmaking, wood work, metal work, tapestry, folkloric crafts as well as various theoretical subjects: History of art, Art appreciation

and criticism, various fields of psychology, teaching methods, curriculum design, etc.) A whole generation of young artists learned to experiment with different media as well as having gained extensive knowledge of art history, theory and the different trends and schools of art from ancient civilizations to post-modernism. (Elnoshokaty 2013)

Nevertheless, the state arts colleges were not preparing artists in media art. Thus, starting in the late 2000s, a handful of artists working mainly in film and media art began to organise independent study programmes. These initiators, including Elnoshokaty, El Azma and Wael Shawky, all received their Masters of Fine Arts in the West and exhibit internationally. Thus they conform to Winegar's characterisation of Western-trained artists importing Western values, but a more innocent view sees them simply as artists who wished to share their knowledge in a forum more flexible than the state institutions were able to provide. Their low-budget ventures combined training, production and exhibition: in each case, the organisers brought together a group of young artists and provided them with some skills both in video production and in a research-based or conceptual practice; they concluded with exhibitions.

For example, in 2011 El Azma initiated a project that echoes the 'Transit Visa' workshop he took part in ten years earlier. For 'Video by the Kilo', El Azma invited five Alexandrian artists who had not previously worked in video to take part in a five-month workshop at the Alexandria Contemporary Art Forum (ACAF). The finished works were shown at ACAF and some of the artists continue to work in video. El Azma pointedly chose artists whose work showed awareness of form and was free from fashionable conceptualism – people who could develop formally strong and emotionally intense work from a period of intense process (rather as El Azma does himself), instead of 'overeducated bilingual conceptual Egyptians' as he puts it (El Azma 2012).

These independent workshops helped nurture an environment for experimental media, which has since grown deeper roots. Elnoshokaty now teaches a contemporary curriculum at the American University in Cairo, in a department headed by American art theorist Bruce Ferguson: the students, mostly from high-income families, thus get a jump on experimental production methods.

As mentioned, in Egypt experiments in theatrical cinema lagged behind those in video in part because the commercial film industry is so strong. But changes are afoot in theatrical exhibition. In 2012, filmmakers Khaled Abdallah and Tamer El Said founded the Cimathèque, an alternative production and screening space. Though the ambitiously-planned screening room and archive are still under construction and pending funding, the space already houses a couple of independent production companies and organises screenings, including DoxBox Global Day.

Finally, to mention an actual festival, there is the Cairo Experimental Video Festival (medrar.org/5thcvf), which was inaugurated in 2009. It is organised by the non-profit artists' group Medrar, with funding from the Egyptian Young Arab Theatre Fund, the U.S.-based Foundation for Arts Initiatives (which supports several Arab cultural organisations, and whose board includes William Wells of Townhouse), and the Abbara Program of the Arab regional organisation Cultural Resource, a body funded by international NGOs whose mandate is 'to support the independent cultural sector in Egypt, Tunisia, and other Arab countries undergoing democratic transitions' (Mawred website). The 2013 festival featured about 150 artists from dozens of countries. Here is a festival of international experimental video works, with strong representation from Egypt and the Arab world, supported by a combination of Egyptian government funding and foreign NGOs. Mostly exhibited in single-channel form, these are not works that could survive in the commercial art world.

Conclusion

The above examples indicate that experimental media production and exhibition in the Arab world take place in a tension between state support, foreign support and, in fact, no support. We could look at other examples of festivals and one-off screenings with strong representation of experimental film and video: the Cinémathèque de Tanger would be interesting to consider as a local institution that is able to respond to local needs (such as the needs of Moroccan documentary and experimental filmmakers to exhibit their work in their own country) by making judicious use of foreign support.

In conclusion, I note that recently the exhibition of experimental works has shifted from the festival-distributor circuit to the biennale-gallery circuit. One of the reasons for this shift is the artists' hope that they will gain more visibility and make more money on the gallery scene than in the festival circuit. Yet artists from the Arab world also face difficulties getting paid for their work, raising the question of fees to artists and artists' rights generally. And mention must also be made of the sheer difficulties that organising and attending screenings of experimental films and videos pose, difficulties that cause attention to turn to other means of exhibition and distribution. These issues of appropriate venue, payment to artists and distribution, add further complexity to the question of how experimentation can best thrive in an atmosphere of competing institutions.

Works Cited

Al Abdallah Yakoub, Hala (n.d.) 'Interview with Omar Amiralay', *Arte East*. On-line. Available HTTP: http://www.arteeast.org/content/files/userfiles/file/Interview%20with%20Omar%20Amiralay%20by%20Hala%20Al%20Abdallah%20Yakoub.pdf (26 September 2013).

'Al Nitaq Festival of Art in Downtown Cairo (2001) 15-24 March', *Al Ahram*, 15, 21.

Alkassim, Samirah (2006) 'Experimental Video in Cairo', *Nebula*, 3, 1, 132-151.

Arsanios, Mirene, Wehbé, Karine, and Safieddine, Wael (2010) 'How Espace SD started', in Mirene Arsanios (ed.) 'How to Make (Nice) Things Happen', *98 weeks*, 0, 14.

Azoury, Philippe (2006) 'L'ébullition libanaise: A l'occasion du festival Côté court de Pantin, rencontre à Beyrouth avec de jeunes cinéastes tant inquiets qu'ardents', *Quotidien*, 29 March. On-line. Available HTTP: http://next.liberation.fr/cinema/2006/03/29/l-ebullition-libanaise_34607 (26 September 2013).

Beirut DC Website (2002) 'Beirut DC Dossier'. No longer online.

Beirut DC Website (2013) 'Partners'. *Beirut DC*. On-line. Available HTTP: http://www.beirutdc.org/beirutdc/partners/default.aspx (26 September 2013).

Bizri, Hisham (2005) 'Al Ma'ahad al-'Arabi lil-Film [Arab Institute of Film]'. Beirut: Arab Institute of Film.

Chamas, Sophie (2012) 'Experimental Arab Cinema: Film as Sensory Experience', *Abu Dhabi Film Festival Magazine*, 20 March 2012. On-line. Available HTTP: http://www.abudhabifilmfestival.ae/en/year-round/magazine/2012/02/20/experimental-arab-cinema-film-sensory-experience (26 September 2013).

Ciecko, Anne (2009) 'Digital Territories and Sites of Independence: Jordan's Film Scenes', *Afterimage*, 36, 5.

Dickinson, Kay (2012) 'The State of Labor and Labor for the State: Syrian and Egyptian Cinema beyond the 2011 Uprisings', *Framework*, 53, 1, 99-116.

DoxBox, ArteEast, and Network of Arab Arthouse Screens Press Release (2012) 'International Film Community Stands in Solidarity with Syria by Screening a Special *DOX BOX Global Day* Program', 2 March.

El Azma, Sherif (2013) Interviews with the author, 10 June 2012 and 29 April 2013.

El Shakry, Omnia (2009) 'Artistic Sovereignty in the Shadow of Post-Socialism: Egypt's 20th Annual Youth Salon', *e-flux Journal*, 7, 5.

Elnoshokaty, Shady (2013) 'Experimental Media Workshop, Helwan University, 2007-2009', *Media Art Workshop*. On-line. Available HTTP: http://mediaartworkshop.com/about.html (26 September 2013).

Hendawy, Fatma (2011) 'MASS Alexandria: Toward a contemporary art educational program', *Egypt Independent*, 17 May.

Hjort, Mette (2010) 'On the Plurality of Cinematic Transnationalism', in Nataša Ďurovičová and Kathleen Newman (eds) *World Cinemas, Transnational Perspectives*. London: Routledge. 12-33.

Karnouk, Liliane (1995) *Modern Egyptian Art*. Cairo: American University in Cairo Press.

Khatib, Lina (2008) *Lebanese Cinema: Imagining the Civil War and Beyond*. London: I.B. Tauris.

Mawred (2012) 'About Us', *Mawred*. On-line. Available HTTP: http://mawred.org/about-us/ (29 October 2013).

Salti, Rasha (2006) 'Critical Nationals: The Paradoxes of Syrian Cinema', in *Insights into Syrian Cinema: Essays and Conversations with Contemporary Filmmakers*. New York: ArteEast & Rattapallax, 21-44.

Salti, Rasha, and Fawz Kabra (2013) 'Curating Film'. *Ibraaz*, January. On-line. Available HTTP: http://www.ibraaz.org/usr/library/documents/essay-documents/curating-film.pdf (26 September 2013).

SIB 'Screen Academy'. On-line. Available HTTP: http://www.screeninstitutebeirut.org/ (26 September 2013).

Simondon, Gilbert (1993) 'The Genesis of the Individual' in *Incorporations*, ed. Jonathan Crary and Sanford Kwinter. New York: Zone Books, 296-319.

Toufic, Jalal (2001) 'Quick! A Stereotype!', in Zaatari, Akram and Hojeij, Mahmoud (eds) *Transit Visa: On Video and Cities*. Beirut: Transit Visa.

Van de Peer, S (2012) 'The Film Festival in Exile – DoxBox Global Day Celebrates Omar Amiralay' *Guardian*, 14 March 2012. On-line. Available HTTP: http://www.theguardian.com/film/filmblog/2012/mar/14/dox-box-global-day-omar-amiralay (26 September 2013).

Wilson-Goldie, Kaelen (2006) 'Beirut DVD market latest platform for local films: Directors, festivals work with new company Incognito to bring their work to the masses', *The Daily Star*, 8 March.

Wilson-Goldie, Kaelen (2009) 'Underdogs on top', *The National* (UAE), 23 January.

Winegar, Jessica (2006) *Creative Reckonings: The Politics of Art and Culture in Contemporary Egypt*. Palo Alto, CA: Stanford University Press.

Zaatari, Akram and Hojeij, Mahmoud (2001) (eds) *Transit Visa: On Video and Cities*. Beirut: Transit Visa.

Notes

1   An ongoing argument in Canada says that art here is less daring because artists enjoy the cushion of state funding. This is inaccurate on several fronts, but I will not detail them here.

2   To mention just a few: the Biennale des Cinémas Arabes at the Institut du Monde Arabe, Paris, changed to Imag'IMA: Les Rencontres des cinemas arabes, 1992-2006 ((http://www.imarabe.org/page-sous-section/biennale-des-cinemas-arabes-0); the Arab Screen Independent Film Festival, London, begun in 1999 (http://en.asiff3.com/about-asiff); the Rotterdam Arab Film Festival, since 2001 (http://www.arabcamera.nl/en), and also the Rotterdam Film Festival (http://www.filmfestivalrotterdam.com/en); the screenings organized by ArteEast since 2003 (http://www.arteeast.org/category/programs); and the Abu Dhabi Film Festival (http://www.abudhabifilmfestival.ae/en), an Arab festival that includes a greater than average amount of experimental works, thanks to the vision of curator Rasha Salti.

3   This festival of photography and video has taken place since 2002

4   Conversation with Raed Yassin, September 15, 2013.

5   Kay Dickinson refers to Hjort's argument in light of former Soviet support for Syrian cinema in 'The State of Labor and Labor for the State: Syrian and Egyptian Cinema beyond the 2011 Uprisings', *Framework*, 53(1): 99-116.

6   Lina Khatib (2008) argues that Lebanese cinema's lack of infrastructure has become an advantage since more filmmakers work in digital formats.

7   These include Hassan Khan and Sherif El Azma, of course. Mais Darwazeh from Jordan, who was a designer when she attended Transit Visa, continued to make experimental documentary works after making video for the first time in Transit Visa. After earning an MA in documentary production in 2007 she continued to work on more ambitious projects. The Syrian filmmaker Ammar Al Beik makes works that circulate both in theatrical and gallery settings; Ziad Antar has a successful career in the gallery circuit.

8   [Editor's note: One of the editors of this book, Stefanie Van de Peer, co-organised the screenings in Edinburgh and London, and attests to the sentiments of solidarity and activism among UK audiences.]

Filming Revolution: Approaches to Programming the 'Arab Spring'

Alisa Lebow

In the spring of 2012, I had the opportunity to curate a programme for the Istanbul Film Festival related to films emerging from the revolutionary movements in the Middle East. Every major international film festival had included some version of this programme in its line up since Cannes in May 2011, often taking an active role in hastening the production of the material to be screened. This pressure to produce had mixed results and put undue strain on the producers. The revolutions that began in early 2011 were on-going phenomena, unfolding at a rate that defied easy narration or packaging. The filmmakers were often also activists, engaged in the tireless struggle that social and political change requires, and rather than simply demanding exportable products from them it seemed there could be a possibility of productive engagement with films and filmmakers of past struggles, creating a space of reflection where questions could be asked of the process, strategies could be evaluated and contemporary filmmakers could have the opportunity to regenerate. Needless to say, this was not the usual festival programme.

What are Film Festivals For?

Major international film festivals, as far as I'm aware, are not the places where revolutions happen. Nor are they, generally speaking, the sites of insurrectionary struggles. One does not necessarily expect to go to a much-vaunted film festival to hear inflammatory rhetoric from the filmmakers during their Q&A sessions, or radical political oratory from the programmers or directors. You do not attend a film festival in lieu of marching on the streets, and you are not likely to confuse your active cinéphilia with any other form of activism.[1] Film festivals, and in particular the mainstream, high profile events bearing the names of their host cities, are essentially places where the art of film and the business of film meet. They are often national showcases of largesse and good taste, simultaneously supporting cultural tourism, cultivating international reputations and promoting cinema as a viable cultural industry.

The A-list festivals, so designated both by official FIAPF recognition and by consensual public awe, are the gatekeepers of refined cinematic judgment and the standard bearers of good cinematic taste. It is a rare film that makes it into the upper echelons of the film festival circuit, and many, if not most, now find their way via high-level backroom business relations and deals.[2] In other words, by now, festivals like Cannes and Venice keep their cache by tightening the cordon of access, showcasing only a tiny elite of films by filmmakers designated as A-listers and / or those with distributors willing and able to pay for the added cultural capital of having their commercial film (whose release is often the very next day after the festival première) bask in the red carpeted pageantry of the Croisette or the Lido. There are, of course, exceptions, and more frequently, parallel events that attempt to be somewhat more inclusive, such as the Quinzaine des Réalisateurs (Director's Fortnight, www. quinzaine-realisateurs.com) at Cannes or the Forum at Berlin, yet even those, by now, are quite restricted. Thousands of aspiring filmmakers every year try to find their way past these velvet cordons, but most will be lucky to receive even a polite rejection. Many ambitiously apply, excruciatingly few are chosen.[3]

If you have ever been to one of these festivals, you'll know that it does not take long to figure out that there are even hierarchies of spectatorship, complete with colour coded-access cards depending on your accreditation status (non-industry, industry, market, student, minor press, major press, filmmaker, jury-member, VIP), a stratification stringently observed and policed. With no excuses made to justify the hyper-exclusivity, it is all carefully designed to maintain the mystique of an elite. Everything is organised to keep (the wrong) people out: out of the competition screenings, out of the elusive parties, out of whatever draws moths to light at that moment, so that it can continue an allure that feeds directly into its cultural capital. The logic of elitism prevails, wherein exclusion breeds desire. Cannes, Venice, Locarno (www.pardolive.ch), Berlin – they are all magnetic force fields unto themselves: filmmakers and industry professionals, not to mention film lovers of all varieties, flock to them in droves. Overall, and with very few known exceptions, for aspiring filmmakers from around the world, the motto could be, 'you call us, we won't call you'. Further, there is a well-established preference for films from the West, with the rest of the world's films receiving token attention at best. Rare is the year when there are more than a handful films from any given region outside of North America and Western Europe.

Knowing all this, it is all the more unfathomable that in 2011, festival programmers from virtually all of the A-list festivals (and quite a few of the Bs and Cs as well) seemed to be calling everyone they ever knew in Tunisia and Egypt, soliciting virtually anything that could be cobbled together in the few short intervening months between the toppling of a dictator and their opening night. Stories have emerged of phone calls to known producers in Tunis and Cairo literally asking for anything they have got.[4] Consider this rapid-fire turn around: Ben Ali flees Tunisia in January 2011 and *La khaoufa baada Al Yaoum* (*No More Fear*, Mourad Ben Cheikh, Tunisia), the first film about the Tunisian revolution, premieres at Cannes only four months later, in May of the same year. Mubarak resigns on 11 February 2011, and *Tahrir: Liberation Square* (Stefano Savona, Italy / France) premières at the Locarno Film Festival that August. *Tahrir 2011: The Good, The Bad, The Politician* (Tamer Ezzat, Ayten Amin and Amr Salama) premières just a few weeks later in Venice. Admirable as it may be that filmmakers in the midst of such upheaval managed to come up with the goods, it is still slightly mystifying to think of these festivals soliciting feature length work at the snap of their fingers. For one thing, these festivals should understand that a good film is not made in an instant. For another, since when did they shift into pursuer mode? When Cannes summons, refusal is simply not an option. Yet surely if the majors wanted something beyond rekindling their festival's sheen with the sparkle of the revolutionary moment, they could have instead assisted filmmakers to make well-considered, generously-funded projects, carefully produced over time rather than urging them to hastily cobble something together.

In the festival season of 2011-12 all of the major film festivals and most of the minor ones, featured one or several films from the 'Arab Spring'. There was a rush to represent events that is deserving of some explanation, or at least further consideration. What compelled all of these 'call us, we won't call you' festivals to pick up the phone and solicit films about current political events from a region that is, at best, usually under-represented in their programmes? Why, suddenly, did these festivals draw their heads out of their rarefied shells, to want to represent events that the global media was already covering seemingly exhaustively? How can we account for this momentary aberration? I honestly do not have the answers, but I find the phenomenon intriguing.

Festivals Demand Images

If neither spectators nor programmers believe or expect these film festivals to be the place of revolutionary sentiment, let alone foment, what is it that their programmers sought in their rush to represent the wave of revolutionary events that spread from Tunisia across Northern Africa and into the Levant that year? What did they hope to achieve and what was the impetus for this seemingly unprecedented demand for images? If we concede that most non-specialist festivals are happy to leave the business of geopolitics at the well-guarded entrance to the festival (even if it always finds its way in through the backdoor, as it were),[5] why would Cannes, Venice, Locarno – and later, Toronto and Berlin – all, without exception, as if following a script, want to include films on this theme, with the first three seeming to have actively solicited titles, in some sense 'producing' the work by demand? Why, all of a sudden, this absolute fascination with a region not normally given any priority in these venues? What was the attraction to the politics or the possibility evinced by these highly-mediated political events that moved programmers and directors of these festivals to radically reverse the dynamics of exchange?

Admittedly, images from Sidi Bouzid in Tunisia and Tahrir Square in Egypt were nearly ubiquitous, and many of those, such as faces painted in the colours of the Egyptian flag, had already become iconic. Worldwide news coverage was abundant and self-representation in the form of YouTube, Facebook and Twitter posts, had virtually gone viral. Subtitled or not, images of people chanting 'Ash-sha'b yurīd isqā' an-ni'ām' ('The people demand the fall of the regime') were etched in the imaginary of the time, the hope that this notion of 'the people' invoked went some way to dispelling the cynicism induced by the neo-liberalism that had marked the current era up to that point. (The only revolution many of this generation expected to see in our lifetimes was the 'internet revolution'.) Regime change, not orchestrated by the CIA, imperialist adventurism or some other nefarious plot, suddenly seemed possible, and the power of the people surging into the streets, occupying the proverbial square (from Tahrir to Puerta del Sol, Syntagma, Zuccotti, St Pauls, and eventually Taksim), seemed to actually yield real political effects. It is yet to be seen what those effects will ultimately be and how things will pan out, with myriad stakeholders, international forces and transnational manipulations finally weighing in. But the images that were filling the screens, large and small, told a story that many disgruntled, hopeless, apathetic spectators wanted to hear. Never mind the back story, the one in front of the literally thousands of cameras, from mobile phones to DSLRs, was infinitely compelling: at its best, seditiously inspiring insurrectionary dreams against brutal dictatorships and autocratic regimes; at its slightly less salutary, satisfying an armchair fantasy that required neither ideological commitment nor, for most of us, even the slightest sacrifice of comfort or privilege. For a brief time (before NATO stepped into Libya, before Syria descended into all-out civil war, before the Egyptian military staged their coup), filmgoers and news watchers alike, especially those out of the range of gas canisters, rubber bullets or worse, could indulge in a fantasy that twenty-first century revolution was a matter of tweets and posts, and could be mediated instantaneously to great political effect.

The films that found their way to the festival circuit early in the struggle clearly had an international audience in mind, even if, in some cases, they were so absorbed in the local circumstances that they partially failed to translate. One of the 'hit' films of the time was the three part *Tahrir 2011: The Good, The Bad, and the Politician*, as it was one of the few films emerging from this hothouse that managed to decipherably strike all of the notes – the heady highs of the protests, the shadowy, darker strains of the secret service and the police, and the giddy, yet arch, humorous trills, in this case launched against the much-hated figure of the despot Mubarak – that these events in all of their different manifestations, seemed to inspire. *Tahrir 2011* was perhaps the most accomplished work of the moment. With three filmmakers tasked individually with the three separate sections of the film, we might ascribe its success to this division of labour, so no one filmmaker had to find a way to express all of the registers on his or her own. However, the limitations of this film are shared by all of the others emerging breathlessly at the time: a lack of context and analysis. While these are not demands one usually makes on creative practice – for obvious reasons a film of this nature, especially of the documentary variety, is called upon to take account of these structuring narratives – it was clearly too soon to make sense of the developing contexts.

Other films, such as Stefano Savona's *Tahrir: Liberation Square*, depended on the trope of individual characters – a young man and a young woman, both active in the uprising – as guides to help personalise and make sense of the chaos of Tahrir. The strength of this film is precisely that of all observational documentary: the sense it imparts of 'being there', having access to the 'behind the scenes' of the protests and clashes, staying on when the journalists have long since left the scene. The trouble with this film, which I showed in my Istanbul Film Festival programme and believe has many merits, is that the two narrators or 'guides' feel forced and slightly artificial, with the filmmaker downplaying the fact that their role was set up before the filming ever started. The film attempts to present a seamless 'access' to the events via these coincidental, unacknowledged narrators. One suspects that the filmmaker, an outsider himself, felt that a European audience would need these Egyptian guides for decipherability's sake, following recent narrative conventions in documentary that demand a protagonist and a coherent story complete with emotional cathexis. He delivers on this, which on the one hand is admirable, given how little set up time he had, but on the other feels slightly patronising, as if there's no other way to make sense of the material, Egyptians being otherwise inscrutable to the outside world.

Programming Revolution at the Istanbul IFF 2012

Like so many others, I was drawn to these and other representations of the same events, so I am not dismissing the attraction to these films out of hand. To an extent I even salute the desire to show and see them outside of their original context. These are, by any measure, momentous events, happenings that we are lucky to have seen in our lifetime and that are clearly deserving of attention. I only question the ways in which we pay that attention and the unreasonable demand on image-makers to produce, without the time, space and support necessary to effectively narrate those events. Nonetheless, the demand was there, coming from all corners, and it had the momentum of, well, revolution.

Aware of these developments and the move by all major film festivals to represent the events in feature length filmic form, and as a first-time programmer for the Istanbul Film Festival (IFF film.iksv.org/en), I proposed something that might fulfil this seemingly inevitable demand while nonetheless resisting its more troubling tendencies. In late 2011, in conversation with IFF director, Azize Tan,[6] I developed a film programme that would attempt to avoid reproducing that which was happening at an alarming rate at international film festivals, creating a qualitatively different space, a space of reflection, not only for film goers, but for the filmmakers themselves. To be fair, the idea was not mine. It was the brainchild of a seasoned programmer, Rasha Salti,[7] who was acutely aware and not uncritical of the prevailing trend. Rasha has extensive prior relationships with filmmakers and artists from the region, and witnessed first hand the kinds of impossible demands being placed on those people 'on the ground'. In the midst of such historically momentous events, she felt strongly that filmmakers and artists in Egypt, in Tunisia, in Syria, could benefit greatly from dialogue with those who had struggled similarly in the past, with wise interlocutors who could give them ideas, energy, courage, support to carry on. Instead, the incessant demand to produce for a foreign audience just drained people, and some of those who were best positioned to produce may not have even been the ones the world should be hearing from.[8] There was clearly the need to step back and reflect. Yet how, given that there was also the overpowering demand?

We came up with the idea of curating a set of historical films to screen alongside contemporary works, and to invite a host of people, not only filmmakers in the throes of representing these contemporary events, but historians, archivists, and filmmakers of prior events, all coming together to reflect on the theme of 'filming revolution'. It also made sense to capitalise on Istanbul's unique geographic positioning, between the current uprisings to its East and the rich revolutionary history to its West. Together with Azize Tan, we decided it would not only strengthen the programme but would have more relevance to the festival's audience to define the regional remit beyond the so called 'Arab Spring' countries, allowing us to consider not only North Africa and the Levant, but also Eastern Europe, a region that clearly had something to teach in terms of filmic representations of revolution. In practice, of course, there are limitations to how many films and how many participants one can invite, but the great privilege of being affiliated with a festival that has a budget (however limited) meant that I could include nine films and invite seven participants for the roundtable discussion.

Some of the questions we were asking, both in the curation and in the public programme itself were about how one approaches historical events as they unfold and what the motivations might be behind the impetus to document. We asked: what can be seen in the moment of insurrection, and what is obscured, what is lost in the urge to produce quickly and what might be gained? We tried to think about how one can gain perspective in order to understand and make sense of the images one records. In the Benjaminian sense, what do these moments reveal of past insurrectionary hopes? Is it enough to create heroic narratives of struggle, or is it possible to convey the ambivalence, ambiguity, uncertainty, that inevitably accompanies the elation of the moment? The programme began by looking to the dynamic films of past revolutions and revolutionary movements in the region, so as to bring them into fruitful dialogue with those of the present moment, films like *La battaglia di Algeri* (*The Battle of Algiers*, Gillo Pontecorvo, 1966, Italy) and the lesser known *Leila wa al ziap* (*Leila and the Wolves*, Heiny Srour, 1984, Palestine).[9]

It seems there is much that can be learned. For instance, how have filmmakers in the past conveyed the tensions, traumas, lessons and victories of revolution? What aesthetic strategies have they come up with to represent these struggles? *Battle of Algiers*, the best-known film in the programme, chooses to pursue a heroic narrative in combination with a documentary style to compound its realist effects. *Leila and the*

Wolves takes a more experimental approach, attempting a revolutionary structure that would break the hegemony of dominant narrative traditions and more conscientiously communicate an alternative political vision. Meanwhile it highlights women's participation in the Palestinian liberation struggle, something that tends to be obscured in later retellings. Due to the necessarily limited space, we could only select four historical films about revolutionary movements to screen alongside films from the current movements, especially from Egypt and Tunisia. A more ambitious programme, which ideally I would still like to do, would have included landmark films such as Eisenstein's *Oktyabr* (*October: Ten Days that Shook the World*, Soviet Union, 1928) and such deconstructive (and instructive) works as Andrei Ujica and Harun Farocki's *Videogramme einer Revolution* (*Videograms of a Revolution*, Germany / Romania, 1992). I would even like to expand beyond the region, to include films from Latin America among other important contributions.

Questions that we were asking of both historical and contemporary films is: what can film reveal of revolution? Can revolutionary moments be documented in all of their complexity or does film as a medium necessarily reduce the elements to the demands of a neatly relatable narrative? How are these events depicted and whose version prevails? Is documenting revolution the same thing as making revolutionary cinema? What would a revolutionary cinema of these events entail? Our questions were often of an aesthetic nature, but they necessarily involved an interrogation of narrative and the role of cinema in the writing of history. In this way, we managed to have a dialogue about process, about intent and about craft, instead of just attempting to satisfy a perceived demand for more undigested images.

A more recent film we screened, *Orange Winter* (Andrei Zagdansky, U.S., 2007), tells the impressive and under-reported story of the peaceful struggle that won a transition of power in the Ukraine in 2004-2005. The film intercuts events of the Orange revolution with a simultaneous staging in Kiev of the opera *Boris Godunov*, and effectively tells a parallel tale of the consequences of illegitimate power and ambition. Elements such as allegory, which elevate the documentary beyond mere reportage, were yet another tool lacking in most of the representations being churned out in rapid succession, and something that needed to be considered moving forward. Allegory, metaphor and allusion all transform mere documentation into creative commentary, something that came up over and over again in our public discussions during the programme. Participants all agreed that such layers take time to develop, suggesting yet again that the hastily prepared festival films may have needed more time to gestate.

We very much wanted to include a film from the Iranian 'Green' movement that emerged during and after the 2009 elections in that country, but finding a suitable film in Ahmadinejad's post-election political climate proved a challenge. The footage existed, but filmmakers were apparently reluctant to edit it into a film and send it out of the country to be screened in foreign film festivals. As is well known, the situation was tense and filmmakers feared retribution. So as not to be in the position of commissioning films that are not yet ready to be made, in the end we chose a very interesting film made by an anonymous Iranian filmmaker based in Paris, who has literally pieced together the puzzle of events in Tehran leading up to, during, and in the aftermath of the 2009 elections, based on the clips s/he could find on YouTube. The result is the intriguing *Fragments d'une révolution* (*Fragments of a Revolution*, France, 2011), a great example of 'filming revolution' via Web 2.0. We know well the hype surrounding the impact of social media on these waves of insurrection. Much has been made of it; to the point that one feels the need to contest the emphasis. Revolutions happened well before Web 2.0 was invented with revolutionaries using whatever the most effective communication and organising tools they had to hand. In this generation, we have the internet and the mobile phone, so inevitably, these have been harnessed to the cause. Interestingly though, these tools have enabled a type of 'remote' compilation filmmaking that was previously much more cumbersome to achieve. Yet the precursors should be recognised, all the way back to Esfir Shub's *Padenie dinastii Romanovykh* (*The Fall of the Romanov Dynasty*, Soviet Union, 1927), and again more recently, thinking of *Videograms of a Revolution*. Our programme maintained the importance of looking back to understand the debts to past endeavours as much as understanding the unique contributions of today's filmmakers.

Another recent yet 'historical' account that we included in the programme was the Egyptian short documentary *Democracy 76: State of Emergency* (2006) by Wael Omar, a filmmaker who incidentally made the difficult – and quite public – decision *not* to film during the days of Tahrir (Sevcenko 2011). *Democracy 76* sets the stage for the events that occurred five years later in Tahrir in 2011, suggesting in very clear terms, that revolutions do not happen in a vacuum, they are the culmination of years of struggle. Even a cursory search into recent documentary production prior to the big headlining events of 2011 was enough to suggest that film had been used (and not only in Egypt, mind you) as a mechanism to convey a mood, an inclination, a tendency toward political dissent and resistance, that was palpable to those attentive to the signs.

For the contemporary aspect of the programme, we invited two films from Tunisia, two about Egypt and one about the Iranian Green movement of 2009. Seeing the two films from Tunisia, *Rouge Parole* (Elyes Baccar, Tunisia / Switzerland / Qatar, 2011) and *La Khaoufa Baada Al'Yaoum* (*No More Fear*, Murad ben Cheikh, 2011) back-to-back, gives a multidimensional view of the events leading up to and following the fall of the Ben Ali regime. *Rouge Parole* layers its narrative with the creative contribution of artists and photographers, while *No More Fear*, not unlike Stefano Savona's *Tahrir-Liberation Square* (Italy, 2011), takes the viewer to the streets of Tunisia as the events unfold. The Tunisian revolution is credited with having set in motion something of a domino effect in the region, yet it remains the least known of all, perhaps because it was quickly overshadowed by events in Egypt, Libya, Yemen, Syria, Bahrain and elsewhere. But these films remind us of where it all started and take distinct but compatible approaches to its representation.

As mentioned earlier, the film we chose to depict the events in Cairo, *Tahrir-Liberation Square*, is ostensibly an observational film by outsider Stefano Savona, the viewing of which makes one feel the terrifying force of Mubarak's thugs and the powerful counterforce of 'the people' resisting with every means at hand, including digging up sidewalk cobblestones as ammunition. Savona flew into Cairo within days of the first protests in January, and confines his lens to events unfolding within the occupied traffic circle in the heart of central Cairo, known to the world as Tahrir Square. Savona's camera films exclusively from the perspective of the protesters, as they chant slogans, recite poetry, argue politics, and unswervingly demand the fall of the regime. Swarms of protesters from all walks of life come into view, moving as if with one unifying thought – to bring down the Mubarak regime. Knowing the end of the 18-day drama takes nothing away from the breath-taking power, suspense and momentum of the film. What the film, in this micro-view, cannot achieve is either analysis or creative commentary. Instead, it is an elegant and accomplished reportage.

As *Leila and the Wolves* foretells, women's participation in contemporary revolutionary movements is all too easily erased, despite unprecedented contributions to all aspects of the struggle. To round out the view of the situation in Egypt, we screened Hanan Abdalla's stunning film *In the Shadow of a Man* (Egypt, 2012), about changing roles of women in Egypt and the ways in which the revolution has or has not impacted on women's individual lives. Premièred in Berlin in February 2012, it was the latest film to emerge from the continuous wave of productions detailing and documenting the revolutions of our time.[10]

Programming a Space for Reflection

With this program of both historical and contemporary representations of revolutionary movements, along with a roundtable discussion with filmmakers, historians and activists, the Istanbul Film Festival allowed us to create a space of reflection, a brief respite to stop and think about what it means to film revolution in our day. As such, it also proved that festivals can be much more than showcases of soft power and high-brow commercialism. They can actually be places where activism meets active cinéphilia, producing ways of thinking about representation that might even transform our ways of watching and making film.

I am aware that there is something of the having one's cake and eating it too in this arrangement. While attempting to get it right, we nonetheless also yielded to the festival mania sweeping the circuit. Yet, given that some form of this programme would likely have been presented at this festival, like all others, we were at least able to devise a programme that would be of interest and possibly even of some relevance to the filmmakers themselves. The festival could also take a principled stance vis-à-vis this material, attempting to be accountable to the filmmakers instead of making demands of them. It aimed, in effect, to give something back, though we surely received more than we gave.

I will end with an anecdote that, for me, resonates beyond the exhausting but invigorating week-long programme. We had invited Syrian film producer and festival organiser Orwa Nyrabia, who was to bring some clips of recent work from Syria to show and discuss in an informal lecture set-up. Nothing had been curated or settled in advance. As it happened, he arrived with just the clothes on his back, his suitcase – along with the DVDs he planned to show – mysteriously failing to arrive with him at the airport. It was a time of transition in the Syrian struggle from non-violent resistance to more militant forms of combat and we were lucky that Nyrabia was even able to come. Between YouTube grabs and the two or three Syrian documentaries I luckily happened to have with me (*A Flood in Baath Country*, Omar Amiralay 2003, and *Tournesols / Sunflower*, Anonymous, 2011), and of course Nyrabia's impressive commentary, we managed to pull off a dynamic screening. In the discussion there were questions from the audience regarding strategies of filming in the midst of the violence to which Nyrabia provided what answers he could and then, almost without a pause, he gave this ominous exhortation: 'Pay close attention, you may need this information yourselves one of these days...'

Little over a year after those words produced a stifled gasp in the IFF audience, the Gezi Park protests exploded in Istanbul. The conviction that we had in devising the programme with productive dialogue in mind was only confirmed by this incredibly prophetic exchange. Revolutions may not happen in the darkened theatres of film festivals, but if carefully planned (and guided by wise festival directors), the effects of these programmes on filmmakers and festival-goers alike, can nonetheless be transformative.

Works Cited

Elwaki, Mai (2011) 'Director Defends Egypt's Revolutionary Contribution to Cannes Film Festival', in *Egypt* Independent. On-line. Available HTTP: http://www.egyptindependent. com/news/director-defends-egypts-revolutionary-contribution-cannes-film-festival (18 October 2013).

Iordanova, Dina and Leshu Torchin (eds) (2012) *FFY4: Film Festivals and Activism*. St Andrews: St Andrews Film Studies.

Rastegar, Roya (2012) 'Difference, Aesthetics and the Curatorial Crisis of Film Festivals', *Screen* (Autumn) 53 (3): 310-317.

Sevcenco, Melanie (2011) 'Freelance Revolutionary: Wael Omar', *Al Jazeera*, April 2011. On-line. Available HTTP: http://www.aljazeera. com/indepth/features/2011/04/201141213138200558.html. (18 October 2013).

Torchin, Leshu (2012) 'Traffic Jam Revisited: Film Festivals, Activism, and Human Trafficking', in Dina Iordanova and Leshu Torchin (eds) (2012) *FFY4: Film Festivals and Activism*. St Andrews: St Andrews Film Studies. 95-106.

Wieczorek, Dieter (2012) '31st Istanbul International Film Festival, 2012: World Actualities in a Narrow Look', *FIPRESCI* 2012. On-line. Available HTTP: http://www.fipresci.org/festivals/archive/2012/ istanbul/dwieczorek.htm.

Notes

[1] There are, of course, festivals that do hope to foment activism, such as the numerous human rights festivals around the world. But in this article my focus is on the major film festivals. I will not be discussing specialist film festivals at all. For that, see *FFY4: Film Festivals and Activism* edited by Dina Iordanova and Leshu Torchin (2012).

[2] Roya Rastegar refers to such practices when discussing her research into curatorial practices at film festivals, see Rastegar, 'Difference, aesthetics and the curatorial crisis of film festivals' *Screen* (Autumn 2012) 53, 3: 314.

3   Rastegar notes, for instance, that in one year the Sundance Film Festival received over 4000 submissions and selected only 112 films for their programme. The ratio of acceptance then, is less than 5%. See Rastegar, 311.

4   While most of these stories emerge informally, there are hints of these pressures to be found in articles such as 'Director defends Egypt's revolutionary contribution to Cannes film festival' published in the *Egypt Independent* on 13 May 2011. While it is clear that Cannes did not commission the film in question, *18 Days*, the Cannes programmer hopped on it as soon as plans were announced to make it. The article is available on-line. HTTP: http://www.egyptindependent. com/news/director-defends-egypts-revolutionary-contribution-cannes-film-festival

5   I am aware that Leshu Torchin makes the claim that 'Since 2005, mainstream film festivals have gained momentum as sites for advancing political agendas', however I believe this is something of an overstatement, not to mention that it is unclear which political agendas might be advanced. Further, Torchin is specifically concerned in her article with the question of human trafficking initiatives, and not revolutionary struggle. See Torchin, 'Traffic Jam Revisited: Film Festivals, Activism, and Human Trafficking', pp. 95-106. There is also a distinction to be made between certain campaigns taken up as a cause célèbre, and a more radical orientation towards societal and political transformation.

6   [Editor's note: An interview with Azize Tan is included in this collection: Behlil, Melis (2014) '"Meetings on the Bridge": An Interview with Azize Tan, Director of the International Istanbul Film Festival'.]

7   Rasha Salti is a Beirut-based writer, curator, programmer and thinker, who has programmed festivals and film series such as CinemaEast in NY and 'Mapping Subjectivity: Experimentation in Arab Cinema from the 1960s till Now' (http://www.moma.org/visit/calendar/films/1115) and art events such as the 10th Sharjah Biennial in 2011 (http://www.sharjahart.org/biennial/sharjah-biennial-10/welcome). She is currently the Africa and Middle East programmer for the Toronto International Film Festival (http://tiff.net/thefestival/filmprogramming/programmers/rasha?from=rasha).

8   This, for instance, is precisely the claim made about the screening of *18 Days* in Cannes 2011, as the film was made in part by filmmakers who had made promotional films for Mubarak's previous re-election campaign. See above article, 'Director defends Egypt's revolutionary contribution to Cannes film festival', *Egypt Independent*. On-line. Available HTTP: http://www.egyptindependent.com/news/director-defends-egypts-revolutionary-contribution-cannes-film-festival.

9   For a description of the programme see: Pera Museum Blog (2012) '31st Istanbul Film Festival', *Pera Museum*. On-line. Available HTTP: http://blog.peramuzesi.org.tr/en/pera-film/31-uluslararasi-istanbul-film-festivali/ (18 October 2013). For an English language review of the programme that indicates the cultural work it was attempting, see: Wieczorek, Dieter (2012) '31st Istanbul International Film Festival 2012: World Actualities in a Narrow Look', *Fipresci*. On-line. Available HTTP: http://www.fipresci.org/festivals/archive/2012/istanbul/dwieczorek.htm (18 October 2013).

10   The interesting backstory to this film is that it was actually commissioned by UN Women and largely shot before the revolution took off, and yet when the events of Tahrir began to unfold, the filmmaker wisely found a way to integrate it, not as the main story, but in relation to the well-developed characters' lives that the film traces.

Film Festivals as Conduits for Parallel Cinemas: Bollywood[1]

Dina Iordanova

'I know you are a scholar of cinema, but I will tell you a secret about motion films. They do not happen in the projector or on the screen in front of you. They are happening in your head [...] There is a lot in common between the magical darkness inside our skulls in which dreams fester and memories ripen, and the magical darkness of film theatres.'

Tabish Khair, *Filming*, 107

In recent years, I have frequently opted to use Emirates for long haul flights to Asia. Invariably, this has meant a stop over at Dubai International Airport, and this, in turn, has meant exposure to the regional English language press: a pile of glossy tabloid-format dailies with titles such as *Gulf Today*, *Gulf News*, *Gulf Times* (Qatar), as well as the *Time Out Dubai* weekly, and whatever else the airlines would provide. They all feature solid film sections, always fascinating reads, as they present a completely different and enthralling cinematic coverage from the usual Hollywood-cum-European-plus-occasional-Asian cinema talk found in British newspapers.[2] In contrast to media in the West, where the few surviving professional film critics are chiefly paid to talk up new Hollywood releases, in the Gulf the coverage appears to be centred largely on recent Bollywood output and stars; Hollywood is present, but as a secondary concern.[3]

The in-flight film choices available on Emirates reflect the same configuration: indeed there is a wide selection of American and European (as well as Chinese, Japanese, Korean and Arabic language films), but the richest choice is inevitably that devoted to Bollywood. Sometimes I want the flight to last longer, as it is a unique opportunity to catch up on everything important in recent Indian cinema I may have missed.

The impression that I am left with is that the newly-evolving discourse and film culture across the Gulf region, as well as in some other parts of the Arab world, gradually shapes the region as an important node in the channel for Indian cinema's spread to the rest of the world. Assuming a transmission role for Indian film provides the festivals with huge credibility on the Indian subcontinent and in Asia at large, a cultural positioning that will pay dividends in the long run and one on which the West is missing out.

In personal exchanges, friends such as cineaste Mark Cousins and writer Tabish Khair, whose views on this matter I hold in high regard, have remarked that no large Western film festival has managed to embrace Indian cinema in a way that would make it an enduring channel for what could be a hugely important and profitable cultural exchange between the massive film culture of the subcontinent and the West.[4] Many festivals in the West have, in the course of the past decade, showcased the occasional film (or short series of films) of the new Indian cinema. Indeed, there is some evidence that Cannes is preparing to flirt with Bollywood.[5] Yet no single Western festival plays the perpetual role of a conduit similar to that which we have seen evolve in conjunction with the festivals in Vancouver, Rotterdam or Venice (or the specialised Far East Fest in Udine), and that have, at various times, been recognised as channels for new cinematic material originating from East Asia. The gap between Indian cinema and the West remains wide; the transmitting power of Western film festivals does not seem to be part of this global parallel circuit. Instead, it is the new festivals in the Gulf and the event in Marrakech that seem to be conscious of the gap and that are making efforts to step in by ensuring an enduring and comprehensive Bollywood presence.[6]

Qatar, for example, where the popular Bollywood Nights disco events at Doha's Pearl Lounge Marriot draw large party crowds, holds Bollywood in high esteem. The gala premiere of the documentary *Bollywood: The Greatest Love Story Ever Told* (Rakeysh Omprakash Mehra and Jeff Zimbalist, India, 2011) at the Doha Film Institute was one of the most glamorous events covered in non-Western media (see, for example, the *India Times* article 'Doha Tribeca Film Festival: Photo Gallery'). During the final Doha Tribeca Film Festival in 2012, Bollywood celebrities were chauffeured around in limousines provided by the official festival sponsor, BMW. In that year, the festival hosted a tribute to Yash Chopra, the larger-than-life Indian producer and director who had just passed away and whose last film as director, *Jab Tak Hai Jaan/J.T.H.J.* (2012) premiered at the festival to a standing ovation (Kem 2012). The festival opened with diasporic Indian director Mira Nair's *The Reluctant Fundamentalist* (USA / UK / Qatar, 2012) and featured director Ashutosh Gowariker as jury member. The festival hosted a discussion moderated by established film critic Rajeev Masand, entitled 'Going Global: Can Bollywood Films Really Crossover?' with director and editor Shimit Amin, actor Anupam Kher and the Vice-President of International Promotions for Yash Raj Films, Avtar Panesar. Considered a serious industry event, it was covered in respected non-Western publications such as *Arabian Business* (Sambidge 2012) as well as across Indian broadsheets.

For the past few years, the festival in Abu Dhabi has regularly held panel discussions on topics related to the U.S.$2-billion-a-year Indian film industry's global position. In 2012, actress Shabana Azmi, known from her work with directors such as Shyam Benegal, Satyajit Ray and Mirnal Sen, and regarded as 'a forthright spokeswoman for the power of film', presided over the Narrative Competition jury of the festival (Radhakrishnan 2012). In 2013, actor Irfan Khan (of Ang Lee's *Life of Pi*) was a high-profile presence at the festival. Most importantly, in 2013, the festival held an extensive '100 Years of Indian Cinema' panorama, screening a carefully-curated selection of classics, including Guru Dutt's existential drama *Pyaasa* (1957, India) and M.S. Sathyu's post-partition drama *Garam Hava* (*Scorching Winds*, India, 1974).

Dubai is no different. In 2009, it welcomed superstar Shah Rukh Khan. In 2011, it ran a programme entitled 'Celebration of Indian Cinema', which featured a combination of world and international premieres, as well as several first-ever regional screenings of films in Hindi, Tamil, Malayalam and Bengali (True Celebration 2011). Prolific composer A. R. Rahman received a Lifetime Achievement Award. In 2012, Shah Rukh Khan was in attendance again, and actress Freida Pinto served on the jury. In November 2013, the Asiavision Movie Awards held at Dubai Festival City saw awards distributed to Bollywood grandees John Abraham, Rani Mukherji and Preity Zinta (alongside other noted personalities from Tamil 'Tollywood').

In November 2012, another 'new' high-profile player, the festival in Marrakech, structured its 12th edition around a Tribute to Hindi Cinema, to mark the centenary of film art in India. The event was opened by veteran star Sharmila Tagore, known for his work in classic films by Satyajit Ray. The extravaganza involved a Lifetime Achievement Award for superstar Amitabh Bachchan (presented by French screen legend Catherine Deneuve) and the Moroccan Royal Honour Wissame Al Kafaa Al Fikria (Award of Intellectual Merit)[7] for Shah Rukh Khan (handed over by Morocco's Prince Moulay Rachid).[8] Khan, who is described as a 'demigod' and has been labelled 'King Khan' ('Bollywood' 2012), was escorted by more bodyguards than an American president and performed at a huge open air concert at the famous Jamaa El Fnaa Square: a particularly telling gesture as the actor is known to suffer back problems and rarely engages in live appearances.

The lavish spectacular dedicated to the centenary featured a parade of all the great and good of Indian cinema today (parts can be seen on YouTube under the title 'hommage pour la cinema indienne au festival Marrakech 2012'). Amitabh Bachchan hosted a gala alongside Catherine Deneuve – an interesting combination of two megastars, each adored in their own respective home 'territory' but, interestingly, virtually unknown in the other's. Yet, while Deneuve's star power is largely implied, an image based on past glories and relying on the adoration of those who remember her performances from earlier times, Amitabh's career is still in great shape and he makes for a striking presence even for those who do not know his larger-than-life legendary status.

Parallel Cinemas

The bringing together of these two stars representing different but parallel worlds in the galaxy of cinema, informs my view that world cinema can be subdivided into several bigger industrial complexes / systems. These systems bring along their respective outputs, distribution circuits, celebrity cultures, fan bases and so on, and function relatively independently of each other. I call them 'parallel cinemas'. The key elements of a 'parallel cinema' go beyond specific films and include, in my view, a critical mass of production, a distinctive distribution system (often linked to specific exhibition patterns), a unique star system and developed practices of style / glamour. The existence of a system of international outlets engaged with the creation and circulation of narratives talking up the figures of this cinema to a transnational audience (star gossip, reporting on events and developments beyond the specific films) is also important.[9]

Each of these parallel cinemas has a global circulation channel but their paths do not cross very much. These include Hollywood, the most developed, successful and visible circuit, followed by that for of Indian cinema (often referenced as 'Bollywood' but not only limited to that), the Nigerian cinema circuit ('Nollywood') and the French cinema circuit ('Francophonie' subsuming). We also have relatively independent circuits in terms of distribution and audiences for Arab and East Asian cinema, and for Latin American and European cinema, but they do not function as such pronounced entities.

Whilst still relying on their specific conduits for the vast majority of their circulation, in recent times these self-contained systems have started appropriating the festival circuit as well. I believe that in the case of the 'new' festivals in the Middle East (the three big Gulf events, as well as the festival in Marrakech), Bollywood seems to be gradually finding a valuable outlet.

My interest here lies in exploring how a group of festivals can form a circuit that serves as a conduit for one of these parallel cinemas; for Indian cinema, in this instance.[10] Up until now, other than by exploring the circulation of East Asian cinema (Iordanova 2011), it has been difficult to discern a clear festival pipeline for other parallel cinemas. In fact, some of these 'parallel cinemas' can be described as such precisely because they have managed to develop a global distribution circuit outside festival networks (whereas Latin America, Europe and East Asia, have more heavily relied on circulation *through* the festival circuit). However, I speculate that we will soon see festivals become more and more consciously engaged with turning themselves into circuits for diffusing parallel cinema. The 'new' festivals in the Arab world becoming a sort of outlet for Bollywood product may be one of the first manifestations of what I expect is likely to become a trend. I expect to see more of this conscious assumption of a 'conduit' role soon. It is likely that the circuit will embrace further parallel cinemas (with festivals likely to pay more systematic attention to Nollywood in particular). I do not think French cinema will experience a similar cycle – both because there are dedicated French film festivals operating around the globe (Iordanova 2010: 31-32; also exchange with Martin 2010: 20), and also because the festival in Cannes, even if it is an international showcase by default, is also widely regarded as a vehicle for the French film industry, thus serving as an already established hub for a French festival circuit.

Another important message that comes from the scrutiny of these processes is that of growing self-sufficiency in this circuit of events: they form a dynamic and rich cultural sphere that effectively brackets out the West and does not need the stamp of approval from the big festivals in Europe; or even from Hollywood. In this respect, these festivals in Doha, Dubai, Abu Dhabi and Marrakech, seem to be stepping in to fill a cultural void in the global dynamics of cinema in a way that is balanced with dignity but also with glamour.

Works Cited

'Abu Dhabi Film Festival 2013 to Screen Bollywood Classics *Pyaasa* and *Garam Hava*', (2013), *Bollywood Life*, 16 October. On-line. Available HTTP: http://www.bollywoodlife.com/editors-pick/abu-dhabi-film-festival-2013-to-screen-bollywood-classics-pyaasa-and-garam-hava/ (10 November 2013).

'Bollywood "demigod" Khan Casts Spell on Moroccans', *Marrakech Film Festival Website*. On-line. Available HTTP: http://en.festivalmarrakech.info/Bollywood-demigod-Khan-casts-spell-on-Moroccans_a562.html (10 November 2013).

'Doha Tribeca Film Festival: Photo Gallery' (2011) *India Times*, On-line. Available HTTP: http://photogallery.indiatimes.com/movies/film-festivals/doha-tribeca-film-festival/articleshow/10506713.cms (10 November 2013).

Iordanova, Dina and Dimitris Eleftheriotis (eds) (2006) 'Indian Cinema Abroad: Transnational Historiography of Cinematic Exchanges', Special issue of *South Asian Popular Culture,* October, 4, 2.

Iordanova, Dina (2010) 'Mediating Diaspora: Film Festivals and "Imagined Communities"', Dina Iordanova and Ruby Cheung (eds) *FFY2 2: Film Festivals and Imagined Communities.* St Andrews:
St Andrews Film Studies. 12-44.

Iordanova, Dina (2011) 'East Asia and Film Festivals: Transnational Clusters for Creativity and Commerce', Dina Iordanova and Ruby Cheung (eds) *FFY 3: Film Festivals and East Asia.* St Andrews:
St Andrews Film Studies. 1-33.

Kem, Stuart (2012) 'Doha Tribeca Film Festival to Host Tribute to Bollywood Filmmaker Yash Chopra', 8 November, *Hollywood Reporter.* On-line. Available HTTP: http://www.hollywoodreporter.com/news/doha-tribeca-film-festival-host-387677 (10 November 2013).

Khair, Tabish (2007) *Filming: A Love Story.* London: Picador.

Larkin, Brian (2008 [2003]) 'Itineraries of Indian Cinema: African Videos, Bollywood, and Global Media', Dudrah, Rajinder and Jigna Desai (eds) *Bollywood Reader.* Maidenhead: Open University Press. 229-243.

Radhakrishnan, Manjusha (2012) 'ADFF: Meet jury president Shabana Azmi', 14 October, *Gulf News.* On-line. Available HTTP:

http://gulfnews.com/arts-entertainment/film/movie-news/adff-meet-jury-president-shabana-azmi-1.1088915 (10 November 2013).

Saadi, Meyrem (2014) 'A Festival is Not Only About Money: Interview with Melita Toscan du Plantier', *Tel Quel* (Morocco) 597, 6–12. Translated by Sally Shafto for *Framework: The Journal of Cinema and Media,* 55, 1. On-line. Available HTTP: http://www.frameworkonline.com/festivals/FIFM2014/MelitaToscanInterview.html (10 February 2014).

Sambidge, Andy (2012) 'Doha Film Fest Pays Tribute to Bollywood Legend', 9 November, *Arabian Business,* On-line. Available HTTP: http://www.arabianbusiness.com/doha-film-fest-pays-tribute-bollywood-legend-479016.html (10 November 2013).

'True Celebration of Indian Cinema at Dubai Fest' (2011) *Press Trust of India,* November 23. On-line. Available HTTP: http://movies.ndtv.com/bollywood/true-celebration-of-indian-cinema-at-dubai-fest-152439 (10 November 2013).

Notes

1   I am grateful to auntie Bhanu, Melis Behlil, Renu Bhojwani, Mark Cousins, Rajinder Dudrah, Lalitha Gopalan, Dennis Hanlon, Eva Jørholt, Tabish Khair, Shuchi Kothari, Sally Shafto, Prasun Sonwalkar, Rosie Thomas and Daya Thussu, for the opportunity to engage in many pleasurable chats and indulge in our passion for Bollywood over the years.

2   The immense popularity of Bollywood in the Arab world is nothing new; it has been outlined most articulately in the work of Brian Larkin (2008[2003]). It is also explored in the special issue of *South Asian Popular Culture* that Dimitris Eleftheriotis and I put together in 2006, with the intention being to begin correcting and expanding the record on the global presence of Indian cinema. It contained contributions and testimonies from Hamid Naficy, Rada Sesic and Asuman Suner, among others.

3   In the Gulf, in particular, the interest in Bollywood is additionally sustained by the presence of a large workforce from the subcontinent. As Alia Yunis notes in her piece in this volume, a number of theatres are specialised in exclusively playing Bollywood films. In addition, Bollywood films play on TV and are to be found everywhere on DVD (and, one can assume, receive attention from those who prefer downloading from the Internet). Similarly, Sally Shafto comments on Morocco: 'If Marrakech has succeeded in showcasing Bollywood, it is because the desire for that cinema already exists in Moroccan society. Indian and Bollywood films are shown on at least two Moroccan television channels: the first channel and the movie channel. That's why the MIFF can open a Bollywood film on the Jamaâ El Fnaa and have an enthusiastic audience of several thousand people. The films are apparently generally shown in VO with subtitles' (Shafto, personal communication, 15 December 2013).

4   Personal exchanges with Mark Cousins in Edinburgh (October 2012) and with Tabish Khair in Copenhagen (October 2013).

5   Highlighting the previous year's *The Gangs of Wasseypur* (Anurag Kashyap, India, 2012), in 2013 Cannes marked the centenary of Indian cinema by receiving a large delegation and featuring a gala linked to the screening of the omnibus film *Bombay Talkies* (2013, India, Zoya Akhtar, Dibakar Banerjee, Karan Johar and Anurag Kashyap). The Toronto International Film Festival featured Mumbai as the subject of its 2012 City to City sidebar. And in September 2013 the centennial was celebrated with a fundraising gala designed by Toronto's own Deepa Mehta (a member of the festival's governing board, who reportedly mooted the idea).

6   For a discussion of the specific contextual role of these festivals, see the essay by Jean-Michel Frodon as well as the text by Alberto Elena in this volume. Indian media magazines, such as *Stardust*, and sites, such as Bollywood Life (http://www.bollywoodlife.com) give extensive coverage to these matters, plenty of material is posted on youtube.

7   The same edition of the Marrakech festival bestowed a Lifetime Achievement Award upon famous Chinese director Zhang Yimou. It is noteworthy, however, that by comparison with Hindi cinema, it is unlikely that a similar tribute to Chinese cinema could have been programmed. The Chinese film industry is not yet comparable in status to the 'parallel cinema' of Indian – it still does not have all the attributes in place, and its star and glamour systems are still in the making.

[8]   A recent interview with Melita Toscan du Plantier (2014 [2013]) reveals that the turn to Bollywood may have been precipitated, to some extent, by Westerners. She reveals that in the aftermath of the April 2011 terrorist attack in Marrakech, American stars were not really permitted to come to the festival as 'their insurance agents who indiscriminately lump Morocco in with Afghanistan and Pakistan barred them from coming. As a result, that year we invited some Indian stars, and fortunately for us, Shah Rukh Khan was able to come. It was one of the highlights of the FIFM to date' (in Saadi, 2014). In 2012, Shah Rukh Khan returned to Marrakech for a second visit.

[9]   I am grateful to Marc Siegel for bringing the importance of 'gossip' to my attention in a personal exchange in Frankfurt (January 2014). In the case of Bollywood, it is particularly important to note that 'Bollywood's presence is further enhanced by the many Bollywood stars with homes in Dubai or who vacation there with much media attention', as Alia Yunis remarks in an endnote to her piece in this volume.

[10]   I must mention the comment by Prasun Sonwalkar from *Hindustani Times*, who alerted me to the fact that 'in the Indian context, "parallel cinema" is used to refer to 'art' films, the kind of films that are excellent but do not do well commercially (exponents of this are people like Nasiruddin Shah, Smita Patil, Shyam Benegal, Mrinal Sen). So using "parallel cinema" in the way you mean it may be confusing to Indian readers' (Personal correspondence, 13 January 2014).

Part 2: Case Studies

Iran

A Forgotten Legacy:
The Tehran International Film Festival
(1972-1977)

Azadeh Farahmand

Film festivals have, on occasion, been associated with dramatic moments in film history, especially in relation to film movements.[1] For example, the inauguration of the French New Wave has been linked to the screening of Francois Truffaut's *Les quatre cent coups* (*The Four Hundred Blows*, France, 1959) at the 1959 Cannes Film Festival; and the birth of the New German Cinema has been located in the inscription of the Oberhausen Manifesto during the 1962 festival (www.kurzfilmtage.de). Yet, in these narratives, the festival setting comes across as the mere décor of film history rather than its mise-en-scène. The implied sense of festivity and popular involvement in the very concept of the festival could be an underlying reason for film scholarship's exclusion of film festivals from serious investigation, a trend that has changed in recent years.

My own interest in this general topic, and specifically in the relationship of film festivals to the canonisation of national cinemas and new waves, was triggered by the international acclaim that Iranian films started to receive in the 1990s, attention that would not have been possible without the international forum provided by festivals. It was just a few years later that a historical context began to emerge, linking the new post-1979 cinema of Iran to an *older* new cinema from before the Revolution. This became partly possible because the theocratic government, which controlled the discourse on national cinema and the traffic of local film prints in an outside of Iran, began to support and, in fact, promote this connection – previously, anything produced during the monarchy (especially movies) was considered suspect, and any link with this chastised past was denied.

One of the early moments of this bridging between the two new cinemas materialised in 1999 when 'the largest festival of Iranian films' (according to the event's flyer) took place in London over June and July. 'Life and Art: New Iranian Cinema' screened over 50 films. This elaborate screening was held at the National Film Theatre (NFT), London, and was co-sponsored by the British Film Institute in association with the Iran Heritage Foundation. In addition to recent productions from the 1980s and 1990s, the series included *Haji Agha Actor-e Cinema* (*Mr Haji, The*

Movie Actor, Ovaness Ohanians, 1932/1934), an early Iranian silent feature whose film print has fortunately survived,[2] as well as films of the 1960s and 1970s commonly associated with the Iranian New Wave.[3] Film prints were brought together from various personal collections and international archives, including Iran's own National Film Archive, an organisation that up until then had not been quite open to loaning out its pre-Revolution collection. I attended several of these screenings as a participant in the international conference focused on Iranian cinema that was held in conjunction with the screenings.[4]

This encounter with the mosaic of films – including some rarely-seen gems, all showcased through the high-quality cinematic experience provided by NFT – was an eye-opener, and prompted me to try to better understand the very context that encouraged an alternative wave of filmmaking in Iran before the Revolution.[5] This path brought me to the thriving film culture and festival scene of the 1960s and 1970s in Iran, specially the Tehran International Film Festival, of which I had only recently heard, and knew nearly nothing about.

The Tehran International Film Festival (TIFF) was financed by the Ministry of Arts and Culture (MCA), inaugurated by Queen Farah in 1972 and closed its 6th and final annual edition in December of 1977 before the storms of Revolution swept the country. The lavish financing behind it, and the meticulous efforts of its organisers, created an annual event unprecedented in scope and quality in the region. Other film festivals in Iran had been established prior to TIFF, such as the International Children's Festival, which operated from 1966 to 1977 yet, despite its international reach, was limited in the genre of films it showcased (focusing on themes pertaining to, and suitable for, children). This festival was organised by the Centre for Intellectual Growth and Development of Young Adults, a semi-government organisation established in 1964 by Queen Farah's close friend Lili Jahan Ara, initially to provide nurturing and educational environments for children through libraries and educational activities. After the festival's third edition, the realisation that quality films from Iran were lacking in the festival line-up prompted the Centre to expand its activities and establish a film-training workshop. It was a workshop that grew to become one of the most influential environments for cultivating new filmmakers, some of whom later produced critically acclaimed shorts, animations, educational documentaries and narrative features that screened around the world. Filmmakers trained at the Centre include Abbas Kiarostami, Amir Naderi, Bahram Beizai and Sohrab Shahid-Saless, all directors whose filmmaking careers, especially at their beginnings, reflect the focus on children that characterises their background.

Another noteworthy festival of this era was the Sepas Film Festival (the word *sepas* means gratitude in Farsi). It started in 1969, focused primarily on local productions, and held annual events through 1974. Other festivals had existed prior to this: the earliest, dating back to 1950 was organised by Farrokh Ghaffari and showcased British films; and the first festival of Iranian films was launched by Siamak Pourzand in 1954 (Omid 1995: 965 and 967). Nonetheless, Sepas is noteworthy for its successive runs, popularity and the passion of its organisers. It was launched by the popular film magazine, *Film o Honar* (*Film and Art*) and through the efforts of Ali Mortazavi, a veteran film magazine editor who had initially intended to use the festival to increase the magazine's readership. Starting out, Sepas based its festival prizes on popular votes cast by the magazine's readers, a policy that resulted in rewarding movies most popular at the box office. However, from its second year, Sepas instituted a jury so as to balance mainstream appeal with critical merits in rewarding the movies. With aspirations to become an Academy Awards for Iran, the national festival rewarded its winners with a trophy in the shape of two hands, one male one female. Because of its humble beginnings and private financing, Sepas did not have the glitz and glamour of government-financed events. However, precisely because of its independence from government channels, it enjoyed enormous popularity through attendance and in media coverage. According to Jamal Omid, the closing ceremony of Sepas' fourth edition was telecast live on the Iranian National Television and watched by an outstanding 13 million viewers in 1972 (974-5).

One unique characteristic of TIFF that distinguished it from its local predecessors and contemporaries was its accreditation as an A-list festival by the International Federation of Film Producers Association (FIAPF), a rare honour that only four other festivals – Venice, Cannes, Berlin and San Sebastian – had achieved by that time. This made TIFF the first major festival in the Middle East. The A-list status is no longer used in official FIAPF rhetoric and is now equivalent to the class of non-specialised competitive international festivals that also host an international film market.[6]

Having turned 80 in 2013, FIAPF has long served as a regulatory and mediating agency among festivals, being involved in various roles, such as quality assurance of its member festivals' functions, and in negotiating festival dates for a more proportionate dispersal of competitive events throughout the calendar year. Although in recent decades its impact has been unclear and its relevance questioned, its decisions have influenced many trends, past and present, on the festival circuit. For example, from the outset it required that international competitions in its accredited festivals be judged by an international jury, a practice that continues. Further, in its member selections FIAPF has sought to ensure that accredited festivals remain unique in their countries and regions of origin, unthreatened by any other competitive international film festival of equal calibre in the immediate vicinity. This strategic outlook encouraged FIAPF's elevation of TIFF into its highest and most esteemed category.

Attaining FIAPF accreditation was a key goal for Hajir Dariush, a filmmaker and graduate of the Institut des Hautes Etudes Cinématographiques in Paris, who was approached by the MCA to help organise a new festival for the government. The MCA did not want to create yet another festival of local films, a mission that had already been successfully carried out by Sepas. Instead, it aimed to invest its efforts in a festival that was international in scope. Dariush, who had served as the Secretary General (aka Director) of the International Children Festival, a FIAPF-accredited 'specialized' festival, convinced them that this plan would only be worthwhile if the festival earned a FIAPF A-list status (Omid 1995: 978). Dariush negotiated and achieved this desired goal for the festival he helped launch.

For the MCA, a festival of such stature would not only be unique and unrivalled in the region, but would also add to the international visibility of Iran as a promoter of arts and cultural products, a goal aligned with the aim of a monarchy that had grown in influence and confidence in the early 1970s. Additionally, this annual film event would align the MCA and its head, Minister Mehrdad Pahlbod (the Shah's brother in-law), with a high-profile affair, while its key rival, the National Iranian Radio and Television (NIRTV), headed by Reza Ghotbi (the Queen's cousin), had put together the Shiraz Arts Festival, an elaborate international art event that staged a wide – and wild – range of performance arts from around the world.[7] The Shiraz Arts Festival included a non-competitive film sidebar, and in the spirit of rivalry between the two government organisations, it occasionally screened films banned by its conservative rival MCA during its sidebar screenings.

A Crossroad of East and West: The Tehran International Film Festival

The first edition of TIFF was inaugurated in 1972 and festivals were held annually until 1977. Hajir Dariush did not accept the role of organising the festival's first edition; that task went to another prominent figure in Iranian cinema, Farrokh Ghaffari.[8] Dariush became the festival's Secretary General as of the second edition. The first festival was held in the Northern spring, but due to its close scheduling with the Cannes Film Festival, TIFF's subsequent editions were held the winter. Omid told me that this move may have helped with obtaining better quality films sent to the festival (2013 phone interview).[9] A leading historian of Iranian cinema, Omid not only foresaw publication of the festival's daily bulletin, but was also part of the organising board and selection committee of the festival. As of TIFF's fifth edition, he also acted as the consultant to the Secretary General.

In the first year of the festival, Minister Pahlbod welcomed the guests gathered at the opening, and Queen Farah sat among the attendees. The Empress continued to be a presence at the festival thus enhancing its profile and glamorous image. In addition to an International Competition, the festival also included sidebar programmes, such as special foci on select national cinemas and auteurs. The festival's 'Information Section' consisted of recent films shown out of competition that, according to the first bulletin of the festival, were among the 'award-winners and highly acclaimed features from various countries' (1971). This sidebar programme was renamed 'Festival of Festivals' as of TIFF's 3rd edition. In compliance with FIAPF's requirements, the festival also hosted a film market that featured films from around the world.

From the outset, TIFF was launched with careful planning and professional publicity. A bilingual festival catalogue (in English and Farsi), along with daily bulletins, announced the line-ups and venues, introduced the attending personalities (such as the festival jury, prominent guests, filmmakers, etc.) and included articles, news updates, interviews or briefings on and around festival events (such as panels, retrospectives, press conferences, the film market and parties). Other year-round journals and periodicals dedicated special issues to the festival and reported on its events. The most prominent of these magazines, *Cinema*, was affiliated with TIFF and issued the daily bilingual bulletins under the supervision of Bahram Reypour and with Jamal Omid as the Managing Editor. The festival also invited international journalists, another requirement of FIAPF, which secured its coverage in the Western media and trade journals such as *Variety*, *Sunday Times*, *American Cinematographer* and the *Daily Telegraph*, among others. The event's international echo and its attempts to maintain political neutrality helped position it as a significant destination within the international festival circuit and as a hub of 'cultural diplomacy' and exchange.[10] In addition, it enhanced Iran's market strength for foreign and especially American film studios. According to a *Variety* piece written in 1973, when a large U.S. delegation, headed by the influential MPAA President Jack Valenti, went to the second festival, Iran was recognised as 'the biggest market in the Middle East and Central Asia for the American Companies'. Quoting Valenti, the piece projected TIFF's immediate future on par with the Cannes Film Festival:

As for the Teheran festival, the MPAA head said he was impressed with the national commitment to develop it as a major international film gathering in terms of a large-scale investment to fund it and energetic manpower to staff it. 'Given this national commitment', Valenti said, 'the Teheran Festival in the next two to three years could rank alongside Cannes.' (Werba 1973)

The festival invited an impressive range of internationally-renowned and high-profile film personalities to participate in the festival. Among the jury at the first festival in 1972 were Satyajit Ray (India), Paulo Emilio Sales Gomes (Brazil), Grigoriy Chukhray (USSR), and Michael Kutza (U.S.).[11] As of 1973, TIFF established several international affiliates who would assist in locating and inviting notable films and filmmakers from around the world (Omid: 2013 phone interview). In addition to Michael Kutza, founder and director of the International Chicago International Film Festival, these included Peter Cowie, British film historian and general editor of the annual *International Film Guide*, and Pierre-Henri Deleau, founder and director of la Quinzaine des Réalisateurs de Cannes (Directors' Fortnight at Cannes).

The festival grew significantly in its second year, with the number of participating countries increasing from 26 to 35. Among the 1973 jury were Sergei Bondarchuk (USSR), Leopoldo Torre Nilsson (Argentina), Mrinal Sen (India), James Mason (UK) and Frank Capra (U.S.), who was also subject of a retrospective that year. Prominent guests throughout the life span of the festival also included Francesco Rosi and Peter Sellers (1973), Shadi Abdel Salam, William Wyler, and Toni Curtis (1974), Michelangelo Antonioni and Ellen Burstyn (1975), Otto Preminger, Emmanuelle Riva, and Lino Ventura (1976), Susumu Hani, Sergio Leone and Nikita Michalkov (1977), among many others.

The international celebrities whose attendance embellished the festival and raised its profile, enjoyed extravagant guest services. Lavish royal treatment added buzz, helped elevate the image of Iran as a prosperous and flourishing country and introduced many of its scenic sites and tourist destinations to festival guests. Hearsay has it that a plentiful supply of caviar and the most delicious sturgeon dishes were on the menu during the festival's parties. Omid underscores the generosity of the festival in receiving its guests. Typically, three to five individuals affiliated with each official film entry were invited as festival guests. Unlike Cannes, which at that time covered the expenses of its invitees for up to five days, TIFF fully feted its guests for the entire duration of the festival, which lasted between 11 and 15 days throughout its years of

Image 1: Press conference with the jury committee of 1974 TIFF. From right to left: Rouben Mamoulian, Manouchehr Anvar, Kamran Shirdel, Gillo Pontecorvo, Gabriel Figueroa, Alain Robbe-Grillet, Miklós Jancsó. The two individuals on the far left are unidentified. Anvar and Shirdel were not part of the jury committee, but provided translations to and from English (Anvar) and Italian (Shirdel). Photograph courtesy of Kamran Shirdel.

Image 2: Q&A with Francesco Rosi during the 1973 TIFF. Rosi's *Lucky Luciano* (1973) was recipient of the Grand Prix during TIFF's second edition. From left to right: Kamran Shirdel, Francesco Rosi, Manouchehr Anvar. Photograph courtesy of Kamran Shirdel.

operation. The number of international invitees reached its peak in the 5th edition, when TIFF handled over 400 guests (2013 phone interview).

The Iranian Centre for International Conferences (ICIC) ensured that travel and accommodation for the more than 300 foreign guests invited annually went smoothly. It handled ticket services, transportation and hostesses – chosen from 4,000 revolving staff members who spoke the languages of their guests. According to the director of ICIC, VIP guests received personal cars while others enjoyed arranged transport services that ran from their hotel to festival sites and back.[12] Giving everyone their own car would have exacerbated Tehran's hectic traffic, which was already a liability. Omid recalls that during the initial planning phase, organisers had considered Ramsar (a city in the lush green northern part of Iran) or Isfahan (architecturally one of the most fascinating cities of Iran) as alternative locations. Tehran, the capital, was ultimately agreed upon, though its notorious traffic remained one of the on-going complaints (2013 phone interview).

The rhetoric generated by the festival helped establish its place as a crossroads of East and West. The festival distanced itself from a Third World identity and, instead, situated itself as a mediating bridge. Organisers referred to the broad philosophical tenets of the festival. During the third year of the festival, Dariush described some of its goals:

> First, this festival belongs to humanitarian and humanist cinema; and therefore it aims to encourage and support this kind of cinema [....] Second, with its persistence, this festival will promote the kind of cinema that contains humane, cultural and artistic values as evidence that this cinema would not exclusively belong to the West. In its programming, this festival aims to create a balance between the cinemas of the industrially-advanced countries and the New Cinemas of – what we often mistakenly or randomly call – 'the Third World', such as Asia, Africa and Latin America. (Dariush 1974, my translation)

The open image conveyed by the festival, and further perpetuated by international guests and journalists, underscored the organisation's humane mission within the context of the country's claim to long traditions of mysticism, philosophy and an indigenous artistic heritage that included poetry, music and miniature painting. The welcoming message of the fourth festival addressed the 'Honoured Guest' as such:

> A millennium before the age of cinema, the Persian poets and philosophers were already thinking four-dimensionally.

When they posited 'love', they didn't mean a nineteenth century romantic notion. They meant the miracle of life captured in the discipline of art [....] In an age when both poetry and philosophy have been discredited as communications media, the Persians of today are attempting to express the heart, mind, guts, and spirit of life in terms of the new art. Art detached from life is mere window dressing. The Tehran International Film Festival celebrates the art that captures life through the alchemy of 'love'. (Bulletin 1 1975)

By 1974, TIFF boasted 54 participating counties, with 177 films included in the festival and 210 in the film market. In 1975, again 54 countries participated, but this time with 237 films in the festival and 239 in the market. By 1976, the number of participating countries reached 74, with 302 films in the festival and 350 in the market. During its sixth and final year in 1977, the festival had scaled back considerably (likely due to concerns about the previous year's extensive reach and the ambitious Secretary General Dariush stepping aside) returning to earlier participation levels with 30 countries attending, 150 films in the festival and 103 in the market (Omid 1995: 980-982).

Like other contemporaneous festivals of its calibre, TIFF showcased auteur films and national cinemas. The entire oeuvre of Pier Paolo Pasolini was screened in 1972; René Clair and Frank Capra in 1973; William Wyler and Milkós Jancsó in 1974; Charles Chaplin, François Truffaut and Michelangelo Antonioni in 1975; Buster Keaton, Douglas Fairbanks and Federico Fellini in 1976; King Vidor in 1977. In several cases, the filmmaker whose retrospective was being held attended as a VIP festival guest and participated in Q&A during screenings or press conferences. The festival showcased panoramas of African Cinema (1973), Cinema of Asia (1974), and Latin American Cinema (1975). In 1973, a panel of African filmmakers was invited to discuss the state of the film industry in Africa and encourage better distribution and exhibition mechanisms within the African continent and beyond.[13] Among the panel participants were Ousmane Sembène (Senegal), Omar Khlifi (Tunisia), Oumarou Ganda (Niger) and Youssef Chahine (Egypt). Not surprisingly, Iranian cinema was placed firmly in the spotlight by TIFF, further underscoring new Iranian filmmaking talent and reinforcing the presence of a national new wave that had already emerged before the festival.

Image 3: TIFF year 4 with Antonioni. Q&A with Michelangelo Antonioni during the fourth TIFF (1975). Following showing a repertoire of his films, Antonioni received an honorary plaque from the Queen in this year's festival. From left to right: Kamran Shirdel, Michelangelo Antonioni. Photograph courtesy of Kamran Shirdel.

The Tehran International Film Festival and its Impact on the National Cinema

Dariush Mehrjui's *Gaav* (*The Cow*, 1969) along with Masud Kimiai's *Qeysar* (*Caesar*, 1969) and Naser Taghvai's *Aramesh dar Hozur-e Deegaran* (*Tranquility in the Presence of Others*, 1969/1973) are considered by many as the trio of films that launched the Iranian New Wave.[14] Of the three, it was *The Cow* and its director that received the most significant international recognition. Adapted from a short novel written by psychiatrist and left-leaning author Gholam-Hossein Sa'edi, *The Cow* was commissioned and financed by the MCA and then banned by that very same Ministry. The film print was taken out of the country and shown at the 1971 Venice Film Festival, where it received the FIPRESCI award. It was after this honour at Venice that the MCA began to embrace the film at home. The film travelled to Chicago, and then to the Berlin Festival in 1972 where it screened at the Forum of New Films.

Every year, Iranian films were featured in competition with films from other countries. Under FIAPF rules, the festival was allowed to select up to four films from the host country for competition (in total across the Feature and Short categories), while it could receive up to three from any other country. In its 3rd edition in 1974, TIFF put together a special section called 'New Iranian Cinema' that featured 22 films. This spotlight included Farrokh Ghaffari's *Shab-e Ghuzi* (*Night of the Hunchback*, 1964), Davoud Molapoor's *Shohar-e Ahu Khanom* (*Ahu's Husband*, 1968), Khosrow Haritash's *Adamak* (1971), Nosrat Karimi's *Doroshkechi* (*The Carriage Driver*, 1971), Kimiai's *Dash akol* (1971), Arby Ovanessian's *Cheshmeh* (*The Spring*, 1972), Bahram Beizai's *Ragbar* (*Downpour*, 1972), Mehrjui's *The Cow* and *Postchi* (*The Postman*, 1972), Taghvai's *Tranquility in the Presence of Others;* Parviz Kimiavi's *Mogholha* (*The Mongols*, 1973) and Sohrab Shahid Saless's *Yek etefagh-e sadeh* (*A Simple Event*, 1973).

The festival helped group alternative filmmaking efforts into a unified front. In fact, local critics had begun distinguishing *two* trends of alternative cinema in the country. One trend, referenced as 'Cinema-ye Roushanfekri' ('Intellectual cinema') or at times 'Cinema-ye Moallef' ('Auteur cinema') contained purely intellectual and artistic sensibilities with no regard for the box office. These films typically drew from modern literary sources and many had government funding, as a result of which there was little pressure on the filmmakers for return of investment. Films of this calibre included *The Cow* and *Tranquility in the Presence of Others*, both of which happened to come from the same literary source (novels written by Dr Sa'edi), and did in fact experience soft returns at the box office. The other trend, called 'Jebhe-ye Sevvom' ('Third Front'), neither complied with mainstream formulas, nor did it embrace an intellectual engagement. This class of films, which was for the most part funded by private investors, broke away from mainstream clichés and yet exhibited box office potential. The archetypal example was *Caesar*, an unconventional story of revenge and family honour that created an unprecedented anti-hero of its protagonist and enjoyed tremendous ticket sales. Its lead actor, Behrouz Vossoughi, and supporting actor, Nasser Malekmotei, watched their careers and earning soar to astronomical heights. The film earned a near-cult status and its tickets were sold on the black market. Likely because of its colossal popularity, *Caesar* drew mixed reactions from film critics, many of whom hailed it as the forefront of an alternative cinematic movement in Iran, though a few dismissed it as lacking artistic merit.[15] Interestingly, *Caesar* was left out of TIFF's spotlights, while *Dash akol*, another feature by director Masud Kimiai, based on a novel by the modernist author Sadegh Hedayat, was included in the 1974 panorama of New Iranian Cinema.[16]

This distinction was masked by the festival, which showcased the films as generally part of the broad category of New Iranian cinema. During this edition of the festival, references to a new wave in Iranian filmmaking appeared in writings surrounding the event. The films and filmmakers featured in the 1974 panorama were the subject of articles and reviews by international critics. In a contemporary piece written about this section of the festival, Peter Wilson commented:

> Those interested in Iranian cinema have yearned for years for just such a retrospective as 'Iran's New Filmmakers', to be screened during the festival [... H]ere at last is a chance to grasp the trends of Iranian cinema as a whole, to see some of its most outstanding achievements, and to judge both its recent past and hopes for the future. (Wilson 1974)

Interestingly, this early article attempts to carve out a space for the Iranian New Wave by exploring the possibility of defining it against a past national tradition, in a manner similar to the way in which other new waves have been defined since:

> There are no real equivalents in Iran to the German Expressionism of the 30s and 40s, the 'Classic' French directors of the 40s and 50s [....] Despite the sporadic ventures from the Qajar period onward [...] no 'Bombay talkies' industry took root here [....] As for the 'New Wave', it is just the beginning – one of the major purposes of this retrospective should be to determine whether or not such a movement actually exists, and if so, what it consists of. (Wilson 1974)

The year 1974 was remarkable in another sense: Iranian entries won the highest festival honours in both the Short and Competitive categories. This included Kamran Shirdel's *Un shab ke barun umad* (*The Night It Rained*, 1967), a stylised and sarcastic documentary which was also originally commissioned and then banned by the MCA, before being publicly screened for the first time at TIFF. Bahman Farmanara's *Shazdeh Ehtejab* (*Prince Ehtejab*, 1974), based on a novel by Houshang Golshiri was the winner of the Grand Prix in the Feature category, having competed against a host of 21 other features that included Bahram Beizai's *Gharibeh o meh* (*The Stranger and the Fog*, 1976) and Masud Kimiai's *Gavaznha* (*The Deer*, 1976).[17]

The festival's fourth edition offered a section called 'Iran's Future Filmmakers' screening documentary, animated, experimental and narrative short films. Omid explains that this section was planned in response to international journalists who voiced increasing interest in learning about the cinema of TIFF's host country. Dariush took note of this, and followed the 1975 sidebar program with another in the following year called 'Magic Lantern', showcasing films from earlier years of production in Iran (2013 phone interview). By 1975, the conception of a new wave in Iranian cinema had become more acceptable, summoning forth discussions of the industry and the cultural contexts from which it arose. In an article about the state of the growing cinema culture and industry in Iran, Edna Palian and Terry Graham recount various contributing factors to the growth of creative activities and non-commercial endeavours in Iran. Following a brief discussion about the 'inseparability of great poetry and profound music' that is reflected in 'the visual expression of the Iranian art', Palian and Graham point out the various government and semi-government organisations such as MCA, NIRTV, the Centre for Intellectual Growth and Development of Children and Young Adults as well as the Independent New Film Cooperative and the NIRTV-supported organisation Free Cinema that played important roles in producing 'what has been called "the New Iranian Cinema"' (1975). [18]

It is remarkable that almost all of the Iranian films screened in the competitive or sidebar segments of the Tehran festival during its six-year span of operation were later regarded as constituents of the Iranian New Wave canon. This core list also included: Sohrab Shahid Saless's *Tabiat-e bijan* (*Still Life*, 1974); Bahram Beizai's *Kalagh* (*The Crow*, 1976); Ali Hatami's *SootehdDelan* (*Desiderium*, 1978); and Abbas Kiarostami's *Gozāresh* (*Report*, 1977). For Jamshid Akrami, a well-known Iranian film critic and former magazine editor who had contributed to the TIFF's daily bulletins and had a chance to work closely with the festival's organisers, TIFF was a 'disproportionately large event in the Iranian art scene' that helped the Iranian New Wave to flourish. Currently a Professor of Film in the Communication Department of William Paterson University, Akrami kindly partook in an email interview about the international platform and prestige that TIFF provided to Iranian films prior to the 1979 Revolution:

> At a time when Iranian films had just begun to register a modest footprint on the international film map, TIFF created the impetus that helped spur further growth of the Iranian cinema. The Grand Prix TIFF awarded to the Iranian film *Prince Ehtejab* was the highest festival honour an Iranian film had received then. Some cynics might have seen this as some sort of favouritism towards the host country, but when you look at the names of international luminaries who made up the festival jury in 1974, you realise artists such [...] Miklós Jancsó, Alain Robbe-Grillet, and Rouben Mamoulian would never sell their votes [....] The festival definitely helped the flourishing of the Iranian New Wave. It celebrated many of the New Wave filmmakers' achievements by providing the first international exposure for their films. (Akrami 2013 email interview)

It is interesting that few Iranian historians tackle the question of whether or not Iran did actually experience a cinematic new wave. Jamal Omid's monumental manuscript on Iranian cinema history is a case in point, as it does not acknowledge the existence of an Iranian New Wave, or at least that Iran did not have a New Wave in 'the same organised and defined' fashion seen in other countries. Certainly, there were filmmaking attempts outside of the terrain of the commercial cinema, but these did not last for more than a few years, and filmmakers did not exhibit consistent tendencies, and so, for Omid the label is not properly warranted (2013). Hamid Naficy, whose four-volume history of Iranian cinema was published in English in 2011/2012, takes a more moderate approach, suggesting that 'the new wave was not so much a filmmaking movement as a filmmaking moment' (Naficy 2011: 353). Akrami, however, takes a diametrically-opposed stance, seeing 'the Iranian New Wave as one of the most significant film movements of the 70s' even though it did not receive adequate recognition. These films, he asserts, are marked by an 'acute awareness of the social conditions' and a strong commitment to explore the social, a characteristic they 'had in common with the Italian Neorealism movement of two decades earlier' (Akrami 2013 email interview).

Disagreements like this are less a reflection on the particular cinemas in question than a testament to the fluidity and constructedness of terminologies, the conditions through which they arise and the community which uses and legitimises them. Films associated with the Iranian New Wave emerged before TIFF. However, a film movement is hardly conceivable without a cultivating environment and a forum to package and display the group of films it produces, and to underscore their common sensibilities – regardless of their differences, contradictory contexts and lifespans.

Concluding Remarks

The Tehran International Film Festival is a noteworthy event in the history of international film festivals that launched and thrived at a time when top-tier destinations had previously only been located in Europe. Over a short span of six years and with the ambition of becoming the Cannes of Asia, TIFF manifested as a festival crossroads for films from around the world, blessed by a FIAPF stamp of approval that brought recognition and a reputation comparable to just a few contemporaneous top international festivals. Its location in the Middle East, its organisation by a prosperous royal establishment and its claim to the rich cultural traditions of Persia and the colourful palette of the local landscape, gave it a unique – if not mythic – stature that set it apart from European festivals of its time.

The festival emerged in Iran at a time when an alternative film culture was brewing, marked by a growing number of film publications, increasing film training centres, the government stepping into commissioning films and a wave of young filmmakers tapping into literary sources and making films outside the mould of mainstream norms. Many of these young filmmakers (such as Ghaffari, Mehrjui, Kimiavi, Dariush, Shirdel) were educated abroad, in Europe and North Amrica, where they had been exposed to European art cinemas, followed new cinematic trends worldwide and projected similar sentiments onto their own and their colleagues' works in their home country.

Mentions of TIFF have, for the most part, been absent from the contemporary discourses about Iranian cinema and discussions that have introduced Iranian films beyond the country's borders since the 1979 Revolution. Its affiliation with the monarchy, combined with the subsequent regime's initially suspicious attitudes towards cinema as a medium of mass corruption, brought an end to its operation, and resulted in a historical denial of its legacy.[19]

The Fajr Film Festival (www.fajrfilmfestival.com), now the main annual film event in Iran, started out in 1982 and has since been held annually during the 10-day period that commemorates the victory of the Islamic Republic each winter. Veteran TIFF programmers Jamal Omid and the late Bahram Reypour started planning Fajr's programming, bringing the wealth of their experience to the newly-defined entity and using their familiarity with FIAPF to help secure a B-list status for Fajr. Fajr's FIAPF membership began in its fifth year when the festival moved from a national focus to include international entries – but still far from the scope and reach that TIFF had attained. Omid served as a the Director of Planning and Executive Committee of Fajr for 22 years, and in the late 1990s recommended to the late Seifollah Dad (Deputy Minister of Culture and Islamic Guidance for Cinema Affairs from 1997 to 2001) that Fajr's membership in FIAPF be dropped – a trend they soon realised was being picked up by other festivals in light of the diminishing significance of FIAPF as a regulator of the relationship between its members and film producers (Omid 2013 phone interview).

Despite its forsaken legacy, TIFF was an undeniably large-scale world event that not only facilitated cultural and artistic exchange, but also boosted the confidence of young Iranian filmmakers by providing a respected home-grown and international forum to showcase their films. Many of these socially-conscious filmmakers and the products of their cinematic heritage eventually re-emerged following the regime change in Iran. By bringing noteworthy films, filmmakers and international stars from around the world, to its annual extravaganza, TIFF not only positioned Iran as a patron of cinematic creativity with plenty of national and international buzz, but also helped familiarise its local patrons with current trends of filmmaking and cinematic debates both in and outside of Iran. It provided local critics and filmmakers with a new range of viewers – with different tastes and expectations from the local mainstream cinema-going public – and helped cultivate the environment for, and solidify the perception of an alternative cinematic (some would call it new) wave in Iran.

Works Cited

'Welcome Honored Guest – with all our hearts to an old idea', *Bulletin 1: The Fourth Tehran International Film Festival* (1975). Tehran: Ministry of Culture and Arts.

Akrami, Jamshid (2013) Email interview with the author (3 October).

Bulletin 1: The First Tehran International Film Festival (1972). Tehran: Ministry of Culture and Arts.

Dariush, Hajir (1974) 'Mosahebeh ba Hajir Dariush dar Moured e Sevom-in Jashnvarehye Jahani e Film e Tehran' (Hajir Dariush on the Third Tehran International Film Festival). *Bulletin 10: The Third Tehran International Film Festival*. Tehran: Ministry of Culture and Arts.

Gluck, Robert (2007) 'The Shiraz Art Festival: Western Avant-Garde Arts in 1970s Iran', *Leonardo*, 40, 20-28.

Miller, Lloyd (1975) 'Behind the Scenes – Some of the People Who Helped Making it an Excellent Event', *Bulletin 11, The Fourth Tehran International Film Festival*. Tehran: Ministry of Culture and Arts.

Naficy, Hamid (2011) *A Social History of Iranian Cinema*, Vol. 2. Durham: Duke University Press.

Omid, Jamal (1995) *Tarikh-e Cinema-ye Iran 1270-1357* (History of Iranian Cinema 1891-1978). Tehran: Rouzaneh.

___ (2013) Phone interviews with the author (19 August, 18 October).

Palian, Edna and Terry Graham (1975) 'The Film Industry in Iran - Part 1: A Rapidly Growing Industry Feeding on a Rich Cultural Background', *Bulletin 9: The Fourth Tehran International Film Festival*. Tehran: Ministry of Culture and Arts.

Werba, Hank (1973) 'U.S. Pix O'seas Gains Offset Domestic Slump, Valenti Says; 1973 Take Over 50% Of Total' *Daily Variety* (20 December).

Wilson, Peter (1974) 'Iran's New Film-makers' *Bulletin 1: The Third Tehran International Film Festival*. Tehran: Ministry of Culture and Arts.

Notes

[1]   I wish to extend my sincere gratitude to Jamal Omid who generously made himself available for phone conversations and email correspondence to address my successive queries on the International Tehran Film Festival. His first-hand experiences, wealth of knowledge, humility and unique 'researcher spirit', were truly inspiring and instrumental in developing this article. I am thankful to Hamid Naficy for making this connection possible. I am also indebted to Kamran Shirdel, whose short films (made in the 1960s and referenced later in this article) provided one of the early triggers in my own intellectual journey, and for this piece he provided images that are printed in this chapter. I am also grateful to Jamshid Akrami, one of the first Iranian movie critics I began to read, and who graciously responded to my email queries on the topic.

[2]   Ohanians directed the first silent feature film in Iran, a comedy called *Abi o Rabi* (*Abi and Rabi*, 1930). The film had its first public screening in 1931, and generated good income and positive reviews. However, the following year, the only copy of the print was destroyed in a fire. Ohanians proceeded to his next project, *Mr Haji*, in 1932, though when it was screened for the first time in 1934, it was overshadowed by the release of the first Iranian talkie, *Dokhtar e Lor* (*The Lor Girl*, Ardeshir Irani and Abdolhossein Sepanta, 1934) which became a box office sensation.

[3]   Included in the film series were *Siavash dar Takht Jamsheed* (*Siavash in Persepolis*, Fereydoun Rahnema, 1965), *Shab-e Ghouzi* (*Night of the Hunchback*,1965), *Gaav* (*The Cow*, Dariush Mehrjui, 1969), *Aramesh dar Hozur-e Deegaran* (*Tranquility in the Presence of Others*, Naser Taghvai, 1969/1973), *Cheshmeh* (*The Spring*, Arby Ovanessian, 1972), *Mogholha* (*The Mongols*, Parviz Kimiavi, 1973), *Shazdeh Ehtejab* (*Prince Ehtejab*, Bahman Farmanara, 1974), *Gozaresh* (*Report*, Abbas Kiarostami, 1977), and three shorts by Kamran Shirdel, namely, *Nedamatgah: Zendan-e Zanan* (*Women's Prison*, 1966), *Qaleh* (*The Red Light District*, 1967), and *Un Shab ke Barun Umad…Ya Hamaseh ye Rustazadeh ye Gorgani* (*The Night It Rained…or the Epic of a Gorgan Village Boy*, 1967).

[4]   The conference, 'Iranian Cinema: The Culture of Representation and the Representation of Culture', was held on July 19, 1999 at the School of Oriental and African Studies in London. Participants included Hamid Naficy (Rice University) and myself (UCLA) from the U.S., Agnes Devictor (Iran Contemporain) from France, Shahla Lahiji (Roushangaran Publishing) and Ali Reza Shojanoori (Sima Film, and formerly at Farabi Cinema Foundation) from Iran, and Richard Tapper and Ziba Mir-Hosseini (SOAS, and part of the organising committee) from the UK. British feminist film theorist and professor Laura Mulvey offered closing remarks.

[5]   Up to that point, my own familiarity with Iranian films was primarily limited to those I had watched growing up in Iran after the 1979 Revolution, and those I saw during festivals in the U.S., my place of residence since the late 1980s. Nearly all Iranian films screened in the U.S. up till then were productions made after the Revolution, and those available on video were usually poor quality versions of older mainstream titles, pejoratively called 'Filmfarsi.'

[6]   As of 2013, FIAPF has a total of 50 members, of which only 14 festivals belong to this non-specialised competitive (previously called 'A') category. These include Berlin, Cairo, Cannes, India, Karlovy Vary, Locarno, Mar del Plata, Montreal, Moscow, Tokyo, San Sebastian, Shanghai, Warsaw and Venice.

7   For a look back at the eclectic and controversial state of Shiraz Arts Festival in its performance arts programming, see, Robert Gluck (2007).

8   Ghaffari should not only be considered as a precursor of alternative filmmaking in Iran, by means of his *Jonub e Shahr* (*South of the City*, 1958) and *Night of the Hunchback*, but also the founder of the first cine-club in Iran, one the first professional movie critics and a proponent of instituting film archive, ambitions he developed during his education in Paris and employment at the *Cinémathèque Française, as an assistant to the director,* Henri Langlois. Ghaffari who also wrote on the history of Iranian cinema, moved to Paris where he wrote film critiques for *Positif*; he died there in 2006.

9   Because of FIAPF's rules, the competition films needed to be world premieres. Distancing itself on the calendar year from other A-list festivals that could have been the preferred destination because they were more established, TIFF would be the only available international forum for films finished in the winter. These films, according to Omid, could debut nationally in January of the following year subsequent to their December world premiere in Tehran.

10   The phrase 'cultural diplomacy' is borrowed from *FFY2: Film Festivals and Imagined Communities*. Of note, even though all films screened in Iran were frequently subject to censorship – a practice that existed ever since the arrival of cinema into the country and notoriously escalated after the 1979 revolution – TIFF screened all films in their original form, absolutely free of censorship, a policy it had to uphold in compliance with FIAPF.

11   The invitation ot Kutza (Director of the International Chicago Film Festival) to serve as an international jury member in the first edition of the Tehran festival followed the Chicago festival's embrace of Dariush Mehrjui's *The Cow (Gaav)* in the previous year. In the 1971 festival, *The Cow* was nominated for the Best Feature and Ezatolah Entezami received the Best Actor prize for his lead role, subsequent to the movie's world premiere at the 1971 Venice International Film Festival few months prior.

12   In response to criticism as to why they did not offer cars to 'all' the invited guests, the ICIC director responds, 'if we were to give each guest a personal car, we would be adding over 300 cars to the already congested streets'. See Lloyd Miller 1975.

13   It is worth noting an underlying assumption in this grouping that implies 'authorship' as more relevant to industrially advanced countries, whereas 'national cinema' is the more appropriate framework to showcase cinemas of the less industrially accomplished nations. In the former case, the mature individual auteur rises above the rest and controls his vision and art, whereas, in the latter case, the yet-to-mature nation stages a collective expression. Following the simplistic binary of East and West, this premise implies that the West is endowed with individuality and freedom, whereas the East represents a collective, and its films reflect a broader cultural, historical or political context.

14   Although *Tranquility in the Presence* of others was made in 1969, it was not shown until 1973, when it was screened for the first time at Shiraz Festival of Arts, again another maneuver by NIRTV, which tended to screen films banned by the MCA in an ongoing show of rivalry.

15   For the cacophony of critical voices on *Caesar*, see Omid (1995), 527-537.

16   During our conversation, Omid reiterated that 'Third Front' movies were not considered art films by critics, yet were praised for their innovative attempts to break away from formulaic moulds while still connecting with their audience.

He named filmmakers such as Masud Kimiai, Bahram Beizai, Amir Naderi, Jalal Moghadam, Ali Hatami and Davoud Molapoor, as belonging to this front. Filmmakers whose films fell within the tenet of Intellectual Cinema included Farrokh Ghaffari, Ebrahim Golestan, Fereydoun Rahnema, Parviz Kimiavi, Sohrab Shahid Saless, Bahman Farmanara and Arby Ovanessian. Omid added that Dariush Mehrjui 'confused everyone' because he oscillated between the two modes. *The Cow*, his 'masterpiece' was the archetype of 'Intellectual Cinema' and a far cry from this failed first attempt *Almaas 33* (*Diamond 33*, 1966). Yet, his third film, *Agha-ye Hallou* (*Mr Gullible*, 1971) brought Mehrjui closer to a popular appeal, aligning him more with the 'Third Front' filmmakers.

[17] Grand Prix winners received a gold-plated statuette of a 'winged goat', a familiar icon reminiscent of ancient Persian statuary.

[18] This article also picked up where the discussion left off in the previous year's debates (e.g. Peter Wilson's piece referenced above) on identifying an inaugural moment for Iranian New Wave, and carving out the 'old' context against which the 'new' arose. Palian and Graham's piece foregrounded, for example, the resignation of sixteen 'prestigious' directors, actors, and cinematographers from the Iranian Film Artists' Syndicate in 1973, a turning point that was 'regarded as a blow to the commercial control of talent'. In their 'manifesto' these artists condemned the quick-profit making approach to filmmaking that produced 'a cinema "which was not on a par with other forms of intellectual and cultural activities in Iran, was not heir to Iran's artistic traditions, did not reflect Iranian realities, and could not cope with the engaging sophistication of the general public."'

[19] TIFF's central claim as a mediating bridge between East and West was fundamentally opposed by the new regime's political isolationism and adversity to countries like the U.S. and the Soviet Union, which had materialised as the dominant motto after the 1979 Revolution: 'Neither East, Nor West.'

Fajr International Film Festival in the 1990s: The Past Is Another Country

Chris Berry

'The past is another country; they do things differently there.' So runs the famous opening line of L. P. Hartley's novel *The Go-Between* (1953). For me, the other country was the Islamic Republic of Iran, and I was in the middle of 12 years of living in Australia when I became the go-between for the Fajr International Film Festival (FIFF) in Tehran and the Melbourne International Film Festival (miff.com.au) (MIFF). I was on the board of the Melbourne festival, and I was invited to Fajr, first in 1996 and again in 1997. However, my memory is very unreliable, so an alternative title for this piece might be 'Through a Glass, Darkly'. But even though so much has been forgotten, and I cannot recall which year certain events happened or even vouch for the accuracy of those memories I have retained, my two trips to Fajr made a powerful impression on me.

Fajr as 'Soft Power'

Writing my impressions up has made me think again about the complex relationship of the film festival circuit to the persistence of Orientalism and imperialism, as well as individual film festivals and what is today called 'soft power'. Although Joseph Nye first used the concept in *Bound to Lead* (1990), it did not really gain traction until his later work, actually called *Soft Power*, came out in 2004. This was well after the years covered in this essay, but of course 'soft power' has been important since the 1930s when Mussolini got the idea of promoting his image by founding the first significant film festival in Venice, and was followed by other 'showcase festivals' with 'geopolitical agendas' (de Valck 2007: 45-80; Turan 2002: 65-123). By accepting invitations to FIFF funded by the Iranian government, were guests like me implicitly endorsing a regime that, I think it is fair to say, most would not wish to be seen as supporting without reservations? Or were we helping to support those in the Iranian film world who hope for a different, less repressive society and more contacts with the outside world? And by setting up FIFF and taking part in the international film festival circuit, were the Iranian authorities resisting or re-entrenching the structures of Orientalism and imperialism that they claimed they wanted to attack? Although it may not be palatable to those who prefer clear black and white distinctions, I suspect that not only are all of the above true, but also that it may be impossible to do one without the other. Perhaps why this is so will become clearer from an account of my experiences.

Just getting from Melbourne to Tehran was a series of surprises and contradictions that challenged whatever I thought I knew about post-revolutionary Iran. And I did not think I knew much; I was and am no expert on Iran or Iranian cinema. My itinerary took me to Kuala Lumpur first. That was the Iran Air destination closest to Australia in the 1990s. Sitting at the gate, I found myself surrounded by women in the process of removing their make-up and carefully covering up. I do not recall many of them with the notorious *chador* black cloaks, which I later came to understand are more usually associated with working class women. Rather, the preferred outfit was a neck-to-toe coat and headscarf, under which all stray locks of hair were carefully tucked away. This coat, I found out, was popular among more middle-class Iranian women and known by a word borrowed from the French: *manteau*. Many had fashionable touches like buckles at the wrist or padded shoulders. But I do not remember ever seeing anything like a belt, perhaps because that would have revealed the wearer's figure.

I concluded that the jet way to the Iran Air plane was the border to Iranian territory. But having confirmed all the stereotypes of Iran circulated in the Western media, I found that on board the plane things were less predictable. All the flight attendants were male, except for the purser, who I recall was dressed in a very elegant dark blue Iran Air uniform *manteau*. She was also very visibly in charge, telling us to notify her if any of her all-male staff did not provide satisfactory service. Later on, I discovered that the same revolution that insisted women cover up also encouraged them to enter public life and work, and throughout my time in Iran I met many women who were prominent and active in the community. One thing to be said for actually travelling to places that are heavily stereotyped in the Western media is not so much that one discovers the truth – how can one be sure that one's individual experience holds true for a whole country? – but that at least the picture becomes more nuanced.

I am not completely certain why I was invited to FIFF. But readers of the *Daily Bulletin* for 22 February 1996 were told that I had arrived the previous day and that I was 'an expert on documentaries'. At the time, I was helping the Network for the Promotion of Asian Cinema (NETPAC) by selecting and trying to publicise a package of Asian documentaries, and I suspect this is how I got this undeserved reputation. Aruna Vasudev of NETPAC was also a 'delegate' in 1996 (*Daily Bulletin*, 23 February), and perhaps she mentioned my name to the organisers. A series of events followed that taught me a lot about the perils of participating in a highly politicised festival such as FIFF, held under the auspices of the 'Directorate of Film Festivals and International Associations, Ministry of Culture and Islamic Guidance', as the covers of the catalogues from the years I attended state. Given that I am quoted responding to Iranian documentaries in the *Daily Bulletin* on the 23f February, the day after I arrived, my sense that everything happened in a bit of whirlwind may also be right.

Praiseworthy View to 'Death', Named 'Martyrdom'

I was met within hours of my arrival by Mr Nader Talebzadeh, a well-spoken and imposing man in a suit, who spoke perfect English and informed me that he had studied filmmaking at Columbia. I found out later that he was on the jury – of five Iranian men, no foreigners and no women, despite the emphasis on women in public life – both years that I attended FIFF, and was also a seasoned documentary filmmaker in his own right. He told me that there were some special screenings of Iranian documentaries at a venue away from the main festival site that he wished me to see. They were not subtitled, but a translator would whisper in my ear. Not for the last time, I made the instinctive gesture of putting my hand out to shake the hand of the woman translator, but of course that was a mistake. Fortunately, everyone laughed about it. Mr Talebzadeh informed me he would see me after the screenings, and I was whisked away.

I now know that the films I was watching that day were by Sayyed Morteza Avini (1947-1993), and they have indeed stayed with me as powerful and impressive works. Many of them were made on the frontline during the brutal war between Iran and the U.S.'s then close ally, Saddam Hussein of Iraq. Known in Iran as the 'imposed war', it ran from 1980 to 1988, and was launched by Iraq. Iraq was more heavily armed, thanks to American support, and also used chemical weapons. Iran's only option was to defend itself with waves of soldiers, who died in horrifying numbers. Many were very young. As bullets pinged off walls and whistled past his camera, Avini grabbed moments of respite to interview these children. In between the interviews, a deep voice intoned narration. My translator explained that these were eulogies, because *all* the interviewees had gone on to die in the war. Furthermore, Avini himself had also died. This happened in 1993 when he stepped on an unexploded mine while making another film about the war.

Tired, jet-lagged and overwhelmed by the films, I staggered out of the cinema in the late afternoon to find a beaming Mr Talebzadeh waiting for me with a television crew. 'How do you feel?' I think he might have asked me. In the *Daily Bulletin* for 23 February, I am reported as saying,

> Here I found an opportunity to see Martyr Avini's works and get pleased of them. His works much affected me. His praiseworthy view to 'Death', named 'Martyrdom', is very effective; the narrations are also warm and striking, and it can be a new style in making documentaries.

I think this must be not only the result of translation into Farsi and then back into English, but also a certain amount of diplomatic improvement. The clue is in the phrase, 'His praiseworthy view to "Death", named "Martyrdom"'.

What I remember saying was that the films impressed me so much because they seemed to be all about death, and the effort to come to terms with death. The young soldiers were dead, and Avini was dead, too. Both the soldiers in the interviews and Avini himself seemed to be speaking to me from the place of death. Indeed the films themselves were all about putting us in touch with death. Death, death, death. OK, so it was a little heavy, but overall I thought I had handled my first live interview on Iranian television well. When the camera crew left, Mr Talebzadeh praised my efforts. However, he explained carefully to me that, of course, both the soldiers and Mr Avini were martyrs. By definition, martyrs are not dead. They are immortal. Fortunately, like the handshake error, this could all be excused on the basis that I was just a stupid foreigner. Not only in Iran or in China, but all over the world, I have been happy to assume the mantle of the stupid foreigner again and again.

In addition to my ignorance, what this episode also revealed was how much more you, and what you have to say, is of interest when you are in a place where you are a rarity, and also how vulnerable you are to being caught up in other people's political agendas when you are a long way from home. I cannot say that Mr Talebzadeh actually ambushed me, and I could have refused to be interviewed. But, given that I really did find the films powerful, that would have been churlish. I was far from the only person who ran into these situations at FIFF. Someone else I met that year and have remained friends with is Alissa Simon, who was programming films for the Art Institute of Chicago, including an annual Iranian festival that was about to have its 7th edition in 1996. Female, American and Jewish, she was indeed a rare visitor in Iran, and was often thronged by eager reporters. They wanted her to affirm how protected she felt wearing a veil, repeatedly. Most of the time, Alissa was very patient and gracious in her responses. But I do recall one occasion when she let her guard down a bit, and said, 'Most of the time, I feel hot, very hot'.

Self-defeating Programming

The Avini films were also a revelation because they were my first insight into the Iranian cinema we did not usually see overseas. The mainstream Iranian movies turned out to be as different from the films by Kiarostami, Makhmalbaf and the like that were wowing people on the international film festival circuit, as the Fifth Generation films from China (that I had helped to promote during my time living in Beijing) were from mainstream Chinese cinema. And, just as the government of the People's Republic of China likes movies that dwell on wars it has survived in an effort to inspire patriotism, so too it became clear that the government of the Islamic Republic of Iran was obsessed with the 'imposed war', and film after film recounted the terrible suffering the country went through. The festival schedule was also packed with paranoid spy thrillers about dangers from the outside world, none of which I could imagine any of the assembled foreign festival programmers selecting.

Mercifully, most of the catalogue of bad films that I sat through in Tehran has faded from my mind. However, I do remember Seifollah Dad's *Bazmande* (*The Survivor*, 1995). Dad recently died, and all the tributes mention his 'anti-Zionist classic', set in Palestine in 1948, when the Palestinians were being driven out of their homeland as the state of Israel was established. As I will explain in the following remarks, I think of the film as Iran's answer to *Throw Momma from the Train* (Danny DeVito, 1987), except this time Momma throws herself off the train, but not before she has set the detonator on a suitcase bomb and clutched her infant grandson under her arm. He is the survivor of the title, symbolising the Palestinian nation, as she dies saving him. Meanwhile, the train is full of 'Zionists' whom she happily massacres. Even before 9/11, I did not see this as a natural crowd-pleaser in most of the world outside the Middle East.

This seemingly self-defeating programming also repeats a puzzling pattern I have experienced with other authoritarian regimes. Although some local films had their premieres held back for FIFF in an effort to produce as large and excited an audience for local films as possible, my sense was that the Iranian public was most excited about their chance to see foreign films at FIFF. In this regard, the programme was impressive both years I went, including extensive retrospectives of filmmakers such as Kurosawa, focuses on film and literature from India and the UK, as well as round-ups of new films from around the world. So, if the primary purpose of the Iranian panorama section was to showcase local cinema for the assembled foreign delegates, what soft power end was served by making them sit through films they would never select and which might affirm the worst 'axis of evil' prejudices? One can only speculate. It is of course entirely conceivable that the regime was so absolutely certain that its values and beliefs were obviously right that it would never occur to it that others might have a problem with the massacre of civilians or suicide bombers.

Another possible explanation for this phenomenon has something to do with the psychology of authoritarian societies. In a society where power can intervene in arbitrary and unpredictable ways, achieving good soft power outcomes is not worth the risk of offending people higher up the power structure. You might well be aware that, say, Kiarostami films produce an image of Iranian society as caring, complex, and therefore help to counter the stereotype of fanatical and bloodthirsty zealotry. But if you also know that your bosses suspect Kiarostami's loyalty and worry about what his films might mean, maybe you do not show Kiarostami's films in the festival. And if you know your bosses think that *The Survivor* is ideologically on the button that trumps the fact that you also know it will disturb large numbers of the foreign delegates – and not in a productive way.

A Site of Contestation

While the programming of FIFF might have been in ideologically conservative hands, the festival was also a site of contestation. Just as Iran is a democracy of sorts, so too different social and cultural forces were present at and around the festival. In his urbane and cosmopolitan way, Mr Talebzadeh nevertheless represented the government line. But there were plenty of others who clearly hoped for social and political change, while leaving their position on the revolution itself necessarily ambiguous. Various unofficial invitations to private parties held by directors, producers and other film industry figures, revealed an alternative intellectual and cultural world that was both uninterested in the ideology of the revolution and very attuned to contemporary developments in the film festival world outside Iran. I do not recall alcohol being served at these events, most of which were held in private houses, but I do remember a lot of discussion about how to sidestep the regime in various ways, including the fact that members of the non-Muslim minorities in Iran and especially the Armenian minority were allowed to consume alcohol. One director told me that this meant

Armenians were the most popular people in all Iran.

I also remember meeting the director Mohsen Makhmalbaf. His position as a hero of the revolution who spent years in the Shah's jails, and as a popular public figure, gave him greater latitude than someone like Kiarostami. One day he rolled up outside the hotel where the foreign delegates were staying. This was the Esteghlal, formerly the Hilton, a classic 1960s American modernist edifice (Wharton 2001). It seemed that its Elizabeth-Taylor-is-Cleopatra style of purple velvet and gold trimmings had not been touched since the revolution, but there were no dry martinis to be had. The Esteghlal is in Tehran's Northern suburbs. Its famous views of the snow-tipped Alborz Mountains place it in the wealthiest parts of town. Iran's revolution was not a socialist upheaval, and so the country's bourgeois elite was left untouched and the wealth gap remained. Makhmalbaf, however, was a hero of the people, so it was not surprising that he turned up in the ubiquitous Iranian people's car, a Peykan. (In the land of cheap oil and no public transport, everyone drives one of these locally made vehicles. To a Brit like me, it was shockingly recognisable as a Hillman Hunter, because that's where the assembly line was imported from.) From the Eteghlal, Makhmalbaf drove a few of the foreign delegates deep into the working class suburbs of South Tehran, where we entered the real 'house of Makhmalbaf', met his family and enjoyed a meal together. As befits Makhmalbaf's own complex relationship to the Iranian revolution, he was making more than one point with the trip. On the one hand, he was demonstrating his own ability to communicate directly with foreigners and operate independently of the government and its various organs. On the other hand, he was also giving us another view of the heartland of the revolution, demonstrating by his own presence and the relaxed atmosphere of his household, where foreigners could mix freely with his wife and daughters, that the stereotype of a Tehran divided between a small ultra-Westernised elite North and a hard-line, drawbridge-up, working class and fanatically revolutionary South was not true.

Why We Go To Foreign Films

As each of my short visits to Tehran played out, encounters like these added layers to my sense of what sort of a place Iran was, replacing an abstract image with actual people I had met and places I had been to. Maybe Mr Talebzadeh was trying to push propaganda by taking me off to the 'martyr' Avini's films, but I also felt he had a genuine passion for the recently deceased Avini, and the films themselves were a powerful engagement with death or martyrdom, depending on how you saw it.

Makhmalbaf went on to leave Iran a decade later after the election in 2005 of President Mahmoud Ahmadinejad, a working class man with a revolutionary pedigree like his own but a conservative one. When we met him in the 1990s, he might have wanted to see change in his home country, but he was certainly neither anti-revolutionary nor particularly pro-Western. Similarly, I guess that the foreign 'delegates' did not entirely perform according to the hopes of either the cultural conservatives or the reformers in the Iranian film world during and after their visits. I do not remember *The Survivor* being programmed at many festivals around the world.

However, it is precisely this sense of things not going quite as planned that is so valuable about travelling to festivals overseas, especially festivals in places that are not very accessible. When you start to replace an abstract generality with innumerable concrete singularities, or at least add them on to the generalities, it becomes more difficult to reduce everything to some simplified sense of an 'evil other'. Having been to FIFF, it made no sense to me when George Bush came up with his 'Axis of Evil' nonsense, not only because the axis seemed far-fetched, but also because there was something deeply offensive about the idea of taking all those different people I had met in Iran and their complicated lives and ideas and shoving them into a box labelled 'evil'. And, although I do not want to exaggerate the potential for such small gestures, maybe this has something to do with why we go to foreign films. An Iranian film is a small piece of Iran. Even if we cannot go there, we can take the trouble to have our own encounter with Iran just by watching an Iranian film. And if it does not turn out to be what we expected – either because it is not an Islamic fundamentalist diatribe or because it is not a soft-centred 'humanistic' story – so much the better. Even though it was a soft power showcase festival in the 1990s, FIFF proved to be full of surprises for me, not only in the form of the event and the people who bent the festival to their own ends, but also in the films that the regime thought were soft power winners. Whether we are literally being transported to a film festival overseas or figuratively being transported by watching a movie, it is the surprise of finding ourselves elsewhere that is the power of both films and film festivals.

Works Cited

De Valck, Marijke (2007) *Film Festivals: From European Geopolitics to Global Cinephilia*. Amsterdam: University of Amsterdam Press.

Hartley, L. P. (1953) *The Go-Between*. London: Hamish Hamilton.

Nye, Joseph (1990) *Bound to Lead: The Changing Nature of American Power*. New York: Basic Books.

_____ (2004) *Soft Power: The Means to Success in World Politics*. New York: Public Affairs.

Turan, Kenneth (2002) *Sundance to Sarajevo: Film Festivals and the World They Made*. Berkeley: Universty of California Press

Wharton, Annabel Jane (2001) *Building the Cold War: Hilton International Hotels and Modern Architecture*. Chicago: University of Chicago Press.

On the Road for Iranian Cinema: Some Observations on a Decade or so of the Fajr International Film Festival

Anne Demy-Geroe

Introduction

While Iran has a plethora of film festivals spread over the year, many of them international in scope and hosting international juries and guests, the country's major contemporary film event is the Fajr International Film Festival (FIFF), established in 1983 and named metaphorically after the Muslim dawn prayer. The festival is by far Iran's largest, both in terms of its international content and as a showcase for contemporary Iranian cinema. Between 2000 and 2009, FIFF was an important entry point for programmers attempting to access more than the few films that make it past the gateposts of the major A-list festivals, Cannes, Berlin, Venice and Locarno. It offered a valuable meeting point for international festival representatives and Iranian filmmakers, and an opportunity to see a broad range of films, both within the programme and by way of private screenings. There were significant discoveries and contacts to be made. After the contested 2009 elections, many Iranian filmmakers boycotted FIFF and called on the international film industry to do likewise. Iran's major governmental and independent film distributors and sales agents, as well as filmmakers, maintain a presence at international festivals, attending the Cannes market at the very least. Consequently, while retaining its importance domestically, FIFF has recently lost significance for the international film community. With the 2013 change of government this may gradually change.[1]

Operating under the supervision of Iran's Ministry of Culture and Islamic Guidance (MCIG), FIFF is one of a group of cultural festivals celebrating the return of Ayatollah Khomeini on 1 February 1979. Khomeini made known his position on the importance of cinema in his first speech upon his return, after which cinema quickly assumed the form that it still has, that of an ideological project (Khomeini: 258). That FIFF should be inextricably linked with government, ideology and politics, is thus hardly surprising. As its subtitle indicates, this chapter is a personal account of my own observations of FIFF between 2002 and 2013; initially from my perspective as Artistic Director of the Brisbane International Film Festival (biff.com.au) (BIFF), and since 2010, as co-Director of the Iranian Film Festival Australia (www.iffa.net.au). My period of attendance covers most of the second term of the Reformist presidency of Mohammad Khatami and both terms of his conservative successor, Mahmoud Ahmadinejad, and I frame my experience in the political changes in the country.

Background

Following the 9/11 attacks on the World Trade Center in 2001, a broad intolerance of Muslims began to arise in Australia. In response, I decided to present, as part of the 2002 edition of BIFF, a programme showing daily life in Muslim societies. Iran was an obvious focus that did not compromise my 'quality' criterion: as its exhibition and award history evidences, Iran was then a veritable cinematic 'hotspot' on the international festival circuit. Awards had proliferated since 1995, with Jafar Panahi's Camera d'Or win of that year with *Badkonake sefid* (*The White Balloon*, Jafar Panahi, 1995) followed by a plethora of European festival awards, and the first Iranian film nominated for a Foreign Oscar. In 2000 Hamid Dabashi commented wittily:

> For reasons that have nothing to do with the dawn of the third millennium, because Iran follows its own version of the Islamic calendar, the year 2000 marks a spectacular achievement for Iranian cinema. (Dabashi: 259)

Richard Tapper noted in the same year, 'No respectable festival could be without at least one film from Iran' (Tapper 2000). Shortly after I had decided that it was crucial to travel to Iran, I received, in a synergetic coincidence, an unsolicited invitation to Iran's Fajr International Film Festival.

Taking place in early February, FIFF is neatly sandwiched between the International Film Festival Rotterdam (www.filmfestivalrotterdam. com/en) and the Berlinale. Due to the high-profile that Iranian cinema enjoyed in the festival circuit at the time, invitations were highly-sought after by programmers in the early 2000s. So, in February 2002, I arrived after midnight with a group of foreign film directors, distributors, festival directors and film critics, direct from Rotterdam. Waking a few hours later to the sound of busy traffic and the call to prayer, we walked to the art museum where the screenings were held in those years. Since then, my fascination with the political machinations that surround Iranian cinema, both in Iran and internationally, drew me back to FIFF almost annually between 2002 and 2013. On two occasions, in 2006 and 2011, I served as a juror at the festival.

The Festival: The Event and its Constituents

A crucial tool for implementing the government's policy relating to film in Iran has been the Farabi Cinema Foundation (FCF). Established in 1982, with a similar role to organisations such as the British Film Institute, the FCF has a production and screen culture brief, and is responsible for the international promotion, sales and festival screenings of Iranian cinema, as well as for the importation of foreign film titles. In 1983, the pre-Revolutionary Tehran International Film Festival was resurrected as the Fajr International Film Festival.[2] The Iranian Film Market (IFM) was introduced in 1995 and soon after became the responsibility of the International Affairs arm of the FCF. The IFM is one of several ways in which Iran buys and sells films. Government and independent sales agents, including both FCF and the Visual Media Institute (VMI), also participate in international markets. Many independent filmmakers, such as Abbas Kiarostami and Jafar Panahi, deal directly with international sales agents. The organisation of FIFF and the IFM remained with FCF until the responsibility was transferred to the government distribution company, the VMI in 2013.[3]

The government maintains a close supervision of the festival through the Deputy Minister of Culture and Islamic Guidance for Cinema and Audio-Visual Affairs (MCIG) which appoints the festival director. The film selection occurs through committees, including film directors and producers for each section of the festival.

The programme at FIFF is comprised of international features and documentaries, structured into sections that have changed with monotonous regularity over the years. Most sections have competitive elements judged by domestic juries. The International Competition is assessed by a jury that combines domestic and international members; directors such as Paul Cox and Volker Schlöndorff have served as jurors. The showcase of Iranian cinema does not encompass the totality of Iranian national cinema – as with most international film festival panoramas, popular cinema is largely excluded. Neither is it, however, fully inclusive of what would be considered appropriate domestic festival fare elsewhere; indeed, the programme has excluded much of what is generally considered New Iranian Cinema.

As FIFF is the major film event in Iran, most directors hoping for a domestic release time their films around it. The time-honoured tradition of filmmakers everywhere whereby prints (in the earlier days 35mm only) often arrive at the cinema at the last minute, is pushed to extremes in Iran; sometimes prints arrive after the audience. So translators are faced with the onerous task of translating as the films unspool; sometimes individual screenings are postponed. In 2011, *See-O-Seh Rouz* (*33 Days*, Lebanon / Iran, Jamal Shoorje, 2011) screened for the International Jury, several days after its scheduled date. When director Jamal Shoorje accepted the Humanitarian Award on stage, he expressed his surprise, claiming that the film was, even then, not finished.

Inevitably, this widespread practice of finishing films at the last minute leads to greater pressure on technicians and labs. Many of the processes involved in finishing the films require sign-off by an FCF official who consequently finds himself in the lab till the early hours of every morning throughout FIFF. A by-product is that the films screened at FIFF have not necessarily been viewed in their finished state by the full committee of official censors. This may be recognised as a loophole that enables filmmakers to bypass censorship. The domestic audience flocks to the festival screenings, aware that films may later be cut or refused a screening permit. A prominent example is *Offside* (Jafar Panahi, Iran, 2006), which screened at FIFF only, was subsequently banned and is still available only as an illegal DVD on the black market. The first industry screening of Asghar Farhadi's *Jodaeiye Nader az Simin* (*A Separation*, 2011) saw a stampede for seats in the two thousand plus auditorium, with many sitting on the floor. This was not just festival fanaticism about 'seeing it first'; in Iran no-one can predict whether a film will get an uncut release, and Ferhadi had been taken in for questioning during the shooting of the film.

The Iranian Film Market and Foreign Guests

International guests attend FIFF through and for the IFM. Until the VMI took charge in 2013, the international arm of the FCF facilitated invitations and organised guest schedules. At its peak, around 2005, the IFM attracted the major Iranian production and distribution companies (government and commercial), a number of European buyers and sellers, and representatives from larger festivals such as Locarno and Toronto. This gave the market a real sense of business being transacted. In the mid-2000s regular guests included important figures on the international festival circuit such as curator Rose Issa, Sheila Whittaker the former Director of the London International Film Festival, Barbara Scharres from the Gene Siskel Centre in Chicago, the Jalladeaus of the Festival des 3 Continents, Teresa Corvino, then deputy director of Locarno and Kathrin Kohlstedde from the Hamburg International Film Festival, as well as a *Variety* critic, initially Deborah Young, later Alissa Simon. Representatives from the Filmex (Tokyo), Karlovy Vary and Busan festivals attended regularly over the later years. Some international sales agents, such as Celluloid Dreams, established stands at the IFM at their own expense, while others attended without stands, indicating their commitment by paying their own costs.

Until 2010, a special programme of Iranian films, either subtitled or presented with simultaneous translation, was put together for the foreign guests. Over the years, the number of these screenings increased, with up to eight films a day over four or five days. However, many Iranian films chosen for screening on the international festival circuit did not appear on the FIFF schedule, which thus differed significantly from the Iranian cinema seen at other international festivals. For example, the films of Abbas Kiarostami were never screened when I visited. Sometimes such films were rejected, on other occasions they were not even entered by the filmmakers. In any given year there were specific themes related to social issues that had not previously been dealt with and might not recur, suggesting a connection between funding and subject matter. In my first year, 'Temporary Marriage' was one such theme. Farabi officials deny this link between issues and money, although one official conceded that other foreigners also asked him about this same matter. Another industry colleague has suggested that the themes often coincided with social issues being debated by politicians, suggesting that screening permits might be more relevant than funding.

Until 2009, a crucial feature of these special screenings was visitors' assessment of each film viewed, made using a simple grading system. In my first year, naively assuming that the festival would appreciate performance indicators from my own festival to justify my invitation, I submitted a report, only to later realise the purpose of those assessments. This feedback, and whether or not festival programmers attending the festival screened the films, was important to the FCF in determining the international appeal of films. Both FCF and independent distributors were keen to discuss changes that might make films more suitable for the international market. Sometimes these discussions resulted in serious re-edits, and as a representative of a smaller festival, my opinions were more important than my interest in screening the film. An informative example of international 'intervention' is *Gilaneh* (2005), a Farabi-funded film by feminist filmmaker Rakhshan Bani-Etemad, a short version of which originally screened at FIFF in 2004 as one section of a portmanteau film. The other two sections of this portmanteau dealt with the Iran-Iraq war on the frontline, while *Gilaneh* showed the impact of war on a mother. Many international programmers who saw it at FIFF that year were keen to screen just Bani-Etemad's section of the film. Instead, the following year *Gilaneh* had been expanded into a feature, which was subsequently well received domestically and internationally.

This interventionist and 'gatekeeping' role of foreign festival directors understandably did not impress older filmmakers – I was told that Majid Majidi, whose films *Baran* (2001) and *Beede-e Majnoon* (*The Willow Tree*, 2005) both screened to foreign guests, told an Iranian colleague of his displeasure at his films being subjected to the assessment process.

Whilst 'scoring' veteran filmmakers also seems inappropriate to me, the exposure to international programmers could be valuable for young filmmakers. Ali Reza Armini, who has moved into mainstream domestic releases, was excited to win his first award, the Network for the Promotion of Asian Cinema (NETPAC) Award at BIFF for his debut feature, *Namehay bad* (*Letters in the Wind*, 2002) as a direct result of its Fajr screening. A negative consequence of the system has become apparent, however. The problem of the 'festival film', a work deliberately developed to appeal to international festivals, is perhaps more evident in Iran than elsewhere. The underlying domestic problems of censorship and the lack of available local screens are exacerbated by this practice, which encourages filmmakers to respond to an international market taste.

A less desirable aspect of the IFM for the government was an unofficial 'fringe', with distributors and filmmakers seizing the opportunity for private screenings of films rejected by FIFF. For the foreign guests these screenings were an attraction and a break from the official rounds. In my first year, I saw Manijeh Hekmat announce, in tears with her distributor, that she had been threatened with arrest if she screened *Zendan-e zanan* (*Women's Prison*, 2002) privately to guests (the film was later made available, uncut, to festivals). Over the years, and in the company of other foreign guests and renowned Iranian directors and actors, I attended many screenings in elegant North Tehran apartments where *hijabs* were abandoned at the door along with winter coats, and traditional Iranian hospitality abounded. Among these screenings were Mania Akbari's *20 angosht* (*20 Fingers*, 2004) on the wall of an artist's home; Niki Karimi's directorial debut, *Yek shab* (*One Night*, 2005) at Jafar Panahi's house; and *Sad sal be in salha* (*Miss Iran*, Saman Moghadam, 2007), still banned, on a screen at the home of its star, Fatemah Motamed-Aria. There were also private screenings in hotel rooms, and many eager young filmmakers pressed videos, and later DVDs, into our hands.

Fajr Programming

The focus of the festival has been in a continual state of flux, with changes reflecting political imperatives. Until 1999, the international emphasis was on cinema from Muslim countries (for example, there were 27 films grouped under the heading, 'International Congress of Muslim

Filmmakers' in 1994, and in 1995 ten films under 'Filmmaking in Islamic Countries'), as well as countries of the Non-Aligned Movement.

There had been gradual changes following the election of Khatami and his Reformist government in 1997. For the first time, in 2000, the FIFF programme included (three) films from diasporic Iranian returnees (Naficy 2012: 434). Khatami's influence was most effective in 2001. His concept of 'Dialogue Among Civilizations', developed in response to Samuel P. Huntington's *Clash of Civilizations*, gained much support, culminating in the United Nations proclamation of 2001 as The *Year of Dialogue Among Civilizations*, and the FIFF programme for 2001 bore this statement. That year's programme also contained tributes to Ken Loach (present as a jury member), Roberto Rossellini and a focus on Shakespeare in Film. A section on Robert de Niro had special significance in the context of previous official antagonism towards the U.S. and Hollywood.

By 2002, my first year at FIFF, Khatami had been in power for five years, having been re-elected for a second term in 2001. There were two segments of particular interest – 'Cinema in Afghanistan', a nod to Muslim cinema, and 'In Pursuit of Peace', very much part of the Khatami rhetoric.

An Interfaith Award was introduced in 2003, intended 'to single out films which dramatise values that are common to Islam and Christianity' from the Iranian films in the festival and selected by an international jury (Iranian Director Wins). According to Peter Malone, then head of SIGNIS (the World Catholic Association for Communication), the hastily-instigated Award was the brainchild of Amir Esfandieri, head of International Affairs at FCF; in 2003 he and Malone were the sole jury members. In 2004, the Interfaith Jury, selected by SIGNIS, daringly awarded its prize to *Marmoulak* (*The Lizard,* Kamal Tabrizi, 2004), a comedy based on the clergy, initially released but then banned. Another section that year included Hollywood blockbusters *Kill Bill*, *Terminator 3* and *Absalon*, unthinkable inclusions on political grounds in earlier (or indeed later) editions.

More change came in 2005 with the introduction of an international section, 'Competition of Spiritual Cinema'. The introduction of the concept of spiritual cinema was quite controversial, with vociferous debates as to what this category should include. Nacim Pak-Shiraz, also present that year, has presented a detailed account of the event (Pak-Shiraz 2011: 53). Other 2005 inclusions were Theo Angelopoulos's *The Weeping Meadow* (2004) and the Tunisian-Iranian co-production, *Bab' Aziz* (Nacer Khemir, 2005). I sat on the third Spiritual Cinema Jury in 2007, with Polish director Agnieszka Holland, Hollywood producer David Guc, and Iranian filmmaker Nader Talebzadeh. The nominations included some that I would consider 'spiritual', along with films I would position otherwise – Thai ghost stories, and Neil LaBute's remake of the horror mystery *The Wicker Man* (2006).

'The Asian Cinema' award was introduced at the same time as that for 'Spiritual Cinema'. The comment of the (Asian) editors of a NETPAC publication suggests that these two awards are not necessarily distinct:

> It has been said before and perhaps it's worth saying again – the essence of the Asian aesthetic is its spirituality. The search for the eternal and the embrace of it is a way of life that's been lived for centuries. (Vasudev and Cheah 2012: 5)

That FIFF introduced the two awards simultaneously suggests that the festival disagrees, but in the 2010 programme, although the Asian section remained (under the title 'Turquoise Road'), the spiritual section had disappeared. Javad Shamaghdari, formerly a senior official in the conservative IRIB, appointed as the Deputy Minister (MCIG) in 2009, had expressed his opposition to the concept of spiritual cinema prior to his ministerial appointment.

> Have we ever produced films that had anything but spiritual outlook and values? ...Our Revolution was ma'nagara [spiritual] and our art and cultural products have also been in line with these values. (Pak-Shiraz 2011: 63)

Given the Reformist concessions to cinema, the introduction of the 'spiritual' concept seems, retrospectively, to be a placatory gesture towards the hard-liners. Instead FIFF featured, in 2010 only, a competitive 'Quest for Truth and Justice' section and a non-competitive 'Cinema of Oppression' section. The most significant addition was 'Hollywoodism' – a three-day conference sidebar to FIFF developed by Nader Talebzadeh, a constant presence in the development of the concept of Iranian spiritual cinema and now implementing the re-positioning of Hollywood as its nemesis.

During FIFF 2011, the 'Arab Spring' (or the Islamic Awakening, as it was officially described in Iran), was in full force. By 2012 (when I did not attend), FIFF's programme had already absorbed and reflected it. Held under the theme of 'Morality, Awareness, and Hope', FIFF 2012 retained the Iranian and international productions grouped as 'World Panorama' and the (re-named) 'Eastern Vista Asian Cinema'. It also added the new competitive sidebar 'Cinema of Salvation' or 'Muslim Countries Cinema'. An interesting Iranian inclusion was *Ghaladehaye tala* (*The Golden Collars*, Abolqasem Talebi, 2012), a pro-regime take on the post-2009 election unrest. It screened at 3 a.m. on a Friday morning because of concerns of oppositional protests (Sacred Defence Shines).

The Filmmaker Boycott

Politics have always intervened at FIFF. Farhadi's *Dabareye Elly* (*About Elly*, 2009), was eagerly awaited by foreign guests and the general public in 2010, but did not screen because of lead actress Golshifteh Farahani's involvement with Ridley Scott's *Body of Lies* (2008, U.S.). Eventually, the president decided that the ensemble cast should not be punished for the mistake of one, and a screening occurred several days later. By this time the foreign guests had left, although most saw it a few days later at the Berlinale.

However, this kind of domestic politics pales when compared with filmmakers' responses to the disputed 2009 election. In 2010, Iranian filmmakers mounted a campaign to boycott the festival, the first since the elections of the previous year. The Iranian filmmakers wrote to regular foreign guests asking them to join the boycott; many did. But I attended, believing it was more important to follow what was happening from close-by. Most of my Iranian colleagues respected this position, but Jafar Panahi sent me a verbal message of his displeasure (although later I was "forgiven"). In the same year Ken Loach, a juror at FIFF in 2001, was invited by the organisers to head the international jury. It was undoubtedly a political move. In 2009, Loach had pulled his film *Looking for Eric* from the Edinburgh and Melbourne International Film Festivals in response to their acceptance of Israeli cultural funding; Loach's acceptance of the invitation would have been a political score for Iran, but in a widely-reported move, he (along with Peter Brooks) declined in support of the filmmakers (Golab).

Since 2010, Iranian filmmakers have also considered their own position in terms of the festival. Many filmmakers distanced themselves from the festival by leaving the country. Some have declined to submit films, despite pressure from the organisers. It must be emphasised that this was not political pressure but, on the contrary, came from those who believed that the festival should remain apolitical. In 2010, the government responded to the boycott by resuming its intermittent tactic – concessionary festival screenings of several previously banned films. One was *In the Color of Purple* (2010, banned for 5 years) by prominent filmmaker, Ebrahim Hatamakia. This highly political film, depicting a romance between an intelligence agent and the daughter of a Mujahideen leader, had been 'withdrawn from the screening schedule of the 23rd Fajr International Film Festival 2005 by Hatamikia due to the

objections of the Intelligence Ministry' (Iran Culture Ministry lifts ban…).
The producer, Jamal Sadatian, wrote directly to the President, asking
him to remove restrictions preventing the screening of the film, which
subsequently won Best Film and, for Hatamikia, Best Director (Iran
Culture Ministry lifts ban; *Purple* wins). Tahmineh Milani's film *Pay Back*
(2010) had been banned for three years. Milani subsequently chaired the
International Jury in 2010.

In 2011 the festival moved to a new home with better facilities
in the Tehran International Trade and Convention Centre, known as
Milad Tower. But local industry sustained its boycott and the number
of international guests was in single figures. Given the difficulty of
maintaining contact and a sense of what was occurring in the industry
from afar, I considered it even more important to attend, and was asked
to join the International Jury. The funding allocation for guests seemed
to have shifted to the highly political 'Hollywoodism' seminar. Again,
many filmmakers were absent. Kiarostami, usually in attendance at
official events and private parties, was scouting internationally, while
Asghar Farhadi was at a film festival in Serbia; others, unusually, went to
concurrent international events such as Rotterdam (Katayoun Shahabi)
and Vesoul (Fatemeh Motamed Arya). Dariush Mehrjui's film *Aseman-e
Mahboub* (*Beloved Sky*, 2011) screened but, even though he was in town,
he sent a representative to receive the award. A senior official from the
International Affairs section of the FCF dolefully told a number of guests,
including me, that he no longer understood what the government
wanted.

Fajr 2013

During the 2013 edition, it seemed that the MCIG had finally re-shaped
the festival to its satisfaction. It transferred the organisation of both the
festival and the market from FCF, responsible for the previous thirty
years, to the VMI under the directorship of Mohammad Reza Abbasian.
He is a documentary filmmaker, formerly with the Islamic Republic of
Iranian Broadcasting, and allegedly holds strong connections to the
Deputy Minister.

The programme emphasised an Islamic theme with a 'Competition
of Islamic World's Filmmakers', the films for which screened in a section
entitled 'Cinema of Salvation'. The website notes:

> Given the promising awakening movements in the Islamic
> countries, this section will be held in order to recognize and
> promote the status of the filmmakers of the Islamic World.

Moreover, the 'World Panorama Competition' of 'World Cinema' promised a 'Festival Director's Special Award to the Best Film on the Islamic Awakening'. Other sections included: 'The Festival of Festivals' presenting perspectives on Chinese and Polish Cinema and 3D films; and 'Films from the Non-Aligned Movement Member Countries' acknowledging Iran's assumption of the chairmanship of the Non-Aligned Movement for the period 2012 to 2015. The anti-Hollywood 'Hollywoodism' conference, previously a sidebar, had become a fully integrated highlight of the festival, with more than 50 international guests and extensive media coverage. The 2013 screening schedule for the few other foreign guests varied significantly from the programme organised by FCF. Instead of special screenings of films likely to appeal to foreign programmers or distributors, we attended specified public screenings, with simultaneous translation. According to the local industry, many of what they regarded as the best films were not included in this selection.

The MCIG Deputy Minister, Shamaghdari, was prominently present and pleased with the festival. He gave an unprecedented political speech at the traditional welcome reception, discussing the sanctions and conflating the work of young scientists and young filmmakers. Minister Hosseini, in his festival wrap-up, noted that, 'The 31st Fajr Film Festival was much better than its previous editions both in terms of quality and quantity of the participated films' (Fajr Intl. Film Festival 2013 names winners). However, ten days later, on 20 February, Iranian television reported a high-level discussion between the Supreme Leader Khamenei, Shamaghdari and others, the gist of which was that the authorities felt that FIFF had not been sufficiently Islamic. During Cannes in May 2013, news leaked that the new FIFF director had resigned. Where this may have been heading was unclear. On 14 June 2013, new presidential elections were held, resulting in the election of the apparently moderate Hassan Rouhani. In September 2013, I learnt of the first film policy reversal – the re-opening of the House of Cinema, an umbrella organisation of the various film industry guilds, which had been regarded as in opposition to the Ahmadinejad government and was controversially closed by it. Its re-opening is a powerful sign of the positive intentions of the Rouhani government.

Conclusion

During the 12 years I have attended FIFF, the festival has changed significantly, though not consistently. As demonstrated, the impact of the two presidents-incumbent over this time, Khatami and Ahmadinejad, is conspicuously inscribed in FIFF. The Reformist President Mohammad

Khatami had opened up much of the previously narrow focus at FIFF by the time he stepped down in 2005. Initially, little appeared to change when hardliner Mahmoud Ahmadinejad came to power. After the contested election of 2009, which saw the politicisation of many filmmakers, Ahmadinejad returned for his second term, ending in June 2013. The resulting crackdown on the film industry had a severe impact on FIFF, with a returned programming emphasis on Muslim filmmaking and a (new) anti-Hollywood agenda. It also alienated both the filmmakers and international supporters. Along with other experts in the field, I await the inevitable organisational and political changes to FIFF under the new moderate President with keen interest.

Works Cited

'Iranian director wins Catholic-Muslim cinema award' (2004) *Independent Catholic News* (16 February). On-line. Available HTTP: http://www.indcatholicnews.com/news.php?viewStory=818 (24 October 2013).

'Iran Culture Ministry lifts ban on Hatamikia's *Color of Purple*' (2009) *Payvand Iran News* (10 August). On-line. Available HTTP: http://www.payvand.com/news/09/oct/1079.html (24 October 2013).

'*Purple* wins top prizes at Fajr filmfest, organizers snub reporters' (2010) *Tehran Times* (6 February). On-line. Available HTTP: http://www.tehrantimes.com/index_View.asp?code=213844 (24 October 2013).

'Sacred Defence shines at Fajr Festival' (2012) *Tehran Times* (13 February). On-line. Available HTTP: http://www.tehrantimes.com/arts-and-culture/95399-sacred-defense-film-shines-at-fajr-festival (24 October 2013).

'Fajr Intl. Film Festival 2013 names winners' (2013) *Press TV* (12 February). On-line. Available HTTP: http://www.presstv.ir/detail/288371.html (24 October 2013).

Dabashi, Hamid (2001) *Close up: Iranian Cinema Past Present and Future*. London: Verso.

Golab, P. (2010) 'Will the Fajr Boycott Work?', *Frontline* (25 January). On-line. Available HTTP: http://www.pbs.org/wgbh/pages/frontline/tehranbureau/2010/01/will-the-fajr-boycott-work.html#ixzz2dn9FJbY9 (24 October 2013).

Huntington, Samuel P. (2011) *The Clash of Civilizations and the Remaking of World Order*. New York: Simon & Schuster.

Naficy, Hamid (2012) *A Social History of Iranian Cinema. Volume 4*. Durham: Duke University Press.

Pak-Shiraz, Nacim (2011) *Shi'i Islam in Iranian Cinema: Religion and Spirituality in Film*. London: IB Tauris.

Tapper, Richard (2001) 'Screening Iran: The Cinema as National Forum', *Iran at the Crossroads, Global Dialogue*, Spring/Summer, 3, no. 2–3. On-line. Available HTTP: http://www.worlddialogue.org/content.php?id=154 (24 October 2013).

Vasudev, Aruna and Cheah, Philip (2012) 'Introduction: How the East Kept a Steady Gaze', Vasudev, Aruna and Cheah, Philip (eds), *When Strangers Meet: Visions of Asia and Europe in Film*. Singapore: ASEF.

Notes

1   Information regarding different programme components and film screenings has been drawn from the Fajr International Film Festival catalogues for the relevant years.

2   In 1972 the Ministry of Culture and Art had established the Tehran International Film Festival, which ran for six years until just before the 1979 Revolution.

3   The Visual Media Institute is a government organisation founded in 1994 to service the home video market. After 2009 it moved into international distribution, acquisition and the production of Iranian film weeks, internationally.

Film Festivals in Iran

Est.	Name	Date	Website	Location	Specialisation
1963	Roshd International Educational Film Festival	October/ November	http://festival. roshd.ir/	Tehran	Domestic and international film competition
1969 - 1974	Sepas Film Festival	May/June	-	Tehran	Domestic feature films
1972 - 1977	Tehran International Film Festival	November/ December	-	Tehran	Domestic and International competition of feature films
1982	Fajr International Film Festival	February	http://www. fajrfilmfestival. com/	Tehran	Domestic and International competition of feature films
1982	International Children's Film Festival	October	http://www.icff. ir/27th/pe/	Isfahan (15 times) Tehran (6 times) and Isfahan – it has also been held in Hamedan (4 times) and Kerman (1 time)	Domestic and International competition

Est.	Name	Date	Website	Location	Specialisation
1984	Tehran International Short Film Festival	October	www.iycs.ir/	Tehran	Domestic and International competition for short films (fiction and documentary)
2000	Tehran International Animation Festival	March	http://www.tehran-animafest.ir/	Tehran	Domestic and international animation film competition
2003	Nahal International Student Short Film Festival	May	http://nahalfilmfestival.ir/	Tehran	Sort fiction, documentary, experimental and animation films
2005 (not annually)	International Urban Film Festival	May	http://www.urbanfilmfest.org/index.en.php	Tehran	Domestic and International competition
2006	Razavi Scriptwriting Festival	August	http://www.shamstoos.ir/fa/news http://defc.ir/festival/index.php?fid=4&yearId=26	Mashhad	Scriptwriting competion – This festival is a part of the long running Imam Reza International Festival
2006	Parvin Etesami International Women Film Festival	December	http://www.parvineff.ir/	Tehran	Domestic competition of feature film

2007	Cinema Verite, Iran's International Documentary Film Festival	October	http://defc.ir/festival/indexphp?fid=1&yearId=25	Tehran	Domestic and International competition
2009	Fadjr International Festival of Visual Arts	February	http://www.ivafestival.ir/	Tehran	There is a short documentary competition included in this International visual arts festival
2010	Ammar Film Festival	January	http://ammarfilm.ir/Page.aspx?pid=20	Tehran (with screenings around the country)	Domestic competition
2011	Kish International Film Festival	May	http://www.kishfilmfest.ir/	Kish	Domestic and International competition
2011	Tasnim Quranic Short Film Festival	June	http://94.232.175.20/IYCS/Festival/Pages/Home.aspx?FestivalType=4	Mashhad	Domestic competition (Fiction, documentary and animation shorts)
2011	Hasanat National Short Film Festival	February	http://hasanatfilm.ir/	Isfahan	Short fiction, documentary and experimental competition

Est.	Name	Date	Website	Location	Specialisation
2011	Sacred Defence Nation Film Festival	March	http://www.defc.ir/festival/terms.php?fid=6&yearId=6	Tehran	Domestic competition
2012	Fist time filmmaker's Film Festival (Iranian Youth Cinema Society)	August	http://94.232.175.20/IYCS/Festival/Pages/Home.aspx?FestivalType=5	Tehran	Domestic competition of feature films by first time directors
2012	Tehran International Jasmine Film Festival	July	http://www.tivff.com/	Tehran	Vidoe film festival with both domestic and international competition
2013	Tehran Mobile Film and Photo Festival	May	http://tfpf.mobi/	Tehran	Domestic competition

Compiled by Maryam Ghorbankarimi
This table is representative, not exhaustive.

Turkey

A Glimpse at the History of Film Festivals and Competitions in Turkey

Savaş Arslan

Introduction

> In the next two issues, we will be publishing pictures of our readers who send us their images. Our readers will vote for the best two of these pictures [...] The two chosen young people will be presented to the productions handled by American and European film companies. (*Amerika*: 8)

The above quotation is from the 1929 issue of *Sinema Gazetesi* (*Cinema Newspaper*), which aimed to create two internationally famous Turkish film stars. At that time, only a handful of feature films were made in Turkey and the popular film industry of the country, which was named Yeşilçam (literally 'green pine', roughly between 1950s and 1980s), did not yet exist. This idea of having internationally famous film stars (not directors) has been a recurring theme in the film publications of the country. One film commentator, Tarık Dursun, writing in the 1980s, looked back on the early years of Yeşilçam with a critical eye, noting how attempts to create stars by the 1950s and 1960s film magazines like *Yıldız* (*Star*), worked as propaganda *for* Hollywood (Kakınç: 29). At the same time, such magazines were also responsible for the earliest film competitions in the country directed at creating an internationally renowned cinema from Turkey. Obviously, as their names indicate, film magazines like *Yıldız* or *Artist* primarily addressed the entertainment side of cinema, covering news stories on both international and national film actors. They were also behind some of the earliest cinema-related, but actor-focused competitions in the country. But these attempts became coupled with film festivals and / or best domestic film polls once a full-blown film industry in Turkey started to emerge in the 1950s. In this chapter, I focus on some of these early competitions and national film festivals in an attempt to suggest how the film industry in Turkey positioned itself through these events.

Towards the First Festival in Turkey

The earliest annual Best Domestic Film, Director, and Actor polls started in the early Yeşilçam era (1950s) once a large enough number of films had been made. This increased production had been enabled by a tax reduction in 1948, which allowed national filmmakers to shoot more films. Among the earliest organisations that initiated such polls were *Yerli Film Yapanlar Cemiyeti* (The Domestic Filmmakers Association) and *Türk Film Dostları Derneği* (The Association of Turkish Cinéphiles). While the first association organised the earliest domestic film competition in the country in 1948 (Yerli Film Yapanlar Cemiyeti Sanat Mükafatı – The Domestic Filmmakers Association Art Award), the second association, founded in 1952, organised Turkey's earliest film festival (even though it was more of a competition than a festival) in 1953 (Birinci Türk Film Festivali – The First Turkish Film Festival). According to one of the founders of the association, Burhan Arpad, Turkish filmmaking started in 1947 and the number of films made climbed remarkably in the years between 1947 and 1950. Yet, in his eyes, these popular films were merely action-packed crime films and Arabic-style melodramas, and were far from showing the quality filmmaking capable from Turkey (290-91). While Arpad demanded that the domestic filmmakers produce more social realist dramas, the high Yeşilçam era (1960s and 1970s, when often 200 to 300 films were made annually) is marked by melodrama and other popular genres. Thanks to the rise in the number of films, a cinéphile culture in the country also developed and, as may be seen in a 1959 article published in *Sinema 59*, the need for a Cine-Club in the country was openly mooted. Similarly, in the same year, the late film historian Nijat Özön, noting how a fire in Istanbul Municipal Film Depot led to the disappearance of some of the early domestic films, urged for the establishment of a Cinémathèque (1995: 302). A decade later, another film magazine, *Akademik Sinema* (*Academic Cinema*), dispatched news about the establishment of a Turkish Film Archive that was going to organise film festivals and be 'the most modern film archive unit in the world' ('Sinemada' 1969: 18).

Such good-willed proposals and intentions found a home once the Turkish Cinémathèque, modelled on (and also from time to time borrowing films from) the Cinémathèque Française, was founded in 1965. In his book, *Sinema bir Şenliktir* (*Film is a Festivity* 1990), Onat Kutlar describes how the adventure of the Turkish Cinémathèque began in two small, atmospheric rooms: 'From the film posters, the smell of melodrama, moaning and censorship was spreading into the room' (24). In the meantime, a short film competition called Hisar was criticised in a 1969 issue of the *Genç Sinema* (*Young Cinema*) magazine for failing to save Turkish cinema from the domination of the popular Yeşilçam industry:

> The competition is held at the Robert College for the
> bourgeois intellectuals, staying apart from the people,
> turning it into the missionary of imperialism at the Robert
> College colony. ('Hisar' 1969: 2)

Robert College, which was originally an American missionary school
before being turned into the Boğaziçi University (Bosporus), was the
location for the Hisar competition and the *Genç Sinema* writers criticised
the competition for receiving sponsorship from Shell Oil, urging the
need for an unrealised revolutionary film festival that was going to fight
against the monsters of imperialism and Yeşilçam.

Although the more critical and leftist writers of cinema advocated
a less populist cinema, Yeşilçam's rise was coupled with various festivals.
Among the earliest full-blown festivals was the Turkish Film Festival
of 1959, which was co-organised by the *İstanbul Gazeteciler Cemiyeti*
(Istanbul Association of Journalists) and Türk Sinema Sanatçıları Derneği
(The Turkish Film Artists Association) (Özgüç: 28). In 1961, as part of the
İzmir Fair, the first competition (Fuar Filmleri Yarışması) was organised.
Similarly, a domestic film competition at the Istanbul Municipality's Arts
Festival was inaugurated. In the same year, an article published in *Artist*
underlined how the domestic film industry had developed and had
created a need for an internationalisation of the festival in Istanbul by
turning it into the Istanbul International Film Festival (Gelenbevi: 25). For
him, such a festival would open up the domestic industry to international
markets, allowing domestic films to be exported and augmenting the
image of Istanbul as a centre of cultural attraction, even by turning the
city into a hotbed of the seventh art. Such a film festival in Istanbul did
not start until well into the 1980s, but the Türk Film Arşivi (the Turkish
Film Archive) was founded in 1967 to conserve domestic films, as well as
organise regular film shows.

Competition

In the 1960s, even the possibility of organising a film festival in Istanbul
sparked competition among different associations and governmental
bodies. This was highlighted by *Artist* magazine, which described how
the Istanbul Association of Journalists found itself in opposition to the
Filmmakers Association, since each association wanted to organise
a separate film festival ('Türk': 12). As part of the annual month-long
Art Festival organised by Istanbul Municipality in the early 1960s to
commemorate the conquest of Istanbul on May 29th, Baha Gelenbevi
and his associates at the Filmmakers Association rented out the Yeni
Melek Film Theatre to organise a festival. This was contested by the

Journalists Association, who wanted to organise the second instalment of a film festival titled 'The Second Turkish Film Festival of the Journalists' Association'. The aim of the festival was put forward as:

> The development of Turkish cinema, [...] to garner a closer interest on the Turkish cinema among the intellectuals and the audience [and] if possible, organising exhibitions about cinema and showing additional films not listed for the competition. ('Türk' 1961: 14).

This competition created bad blood among the major film producers, and Erman and Er's film companies announced their support for the Journalists Association's festival. Yet some other members of the Filmmakers Association decided not to support the festival organised by their own association; the decision to organise a festival was made only by the chairperson and one member of the Association. After all this commotion, Orhan Kuyacaklı noted that even though it was still difficult to compare the domestic film season with that in the Western cinemas, the most important event of the film season of 1961 was still the film festival (Kuyacaklı: 3).

And so the picture for the city that housed Turkey's film industry was, in a way, similar to that of its European counterparts in Cannes or Venice: Antalya, a southern resort town, emerged as the hotspot of Turkish film festivals in 1964. Initially, a competition rather than a festival or a late summer holiday for filmmakers, the Antalya Film Festival (www.altinportakal.org.tr/en) became the longest-running film festival in Turkey (despite a few short breaks). The success of the event and the way in which it attracted film stars to the town, which created a lot film fan buzz in the town, became an example for other towns in the 1960s and led to the establishment of film festivals and competitions in Izmir (www.izmirfilmfest.com), in Adana (www.goldenbollfilmfestival.com), in Gaziantep (no website) and in Balıkesir (no website).

Nijat Özön, in an article for *Devrim* (*Revolution*) magazine titled 'The Festival Impasse' notes:

> It is almost impossible to say that the festivals are established and rooted, nor useful. The reason is clear: these appeared and continued solely as vehicles of pretension or tourism, without completing the conditions necessary for a film festival. (1995: 396)

Özön also highlights the need to internationalise these festivals, create international juries, and most importantly, start film markets as parts of the festivals. Moreover, to prevent these film festivals turning into 'a fair for animal husbandry, agriculture or industry', Özön emphasises the need to balance aspects of trade and art (397). Özön's criticism of the film festivals contains another implicit argument: the quality of domestic filmmaking. For both Nijat Özön and Burhan Arpad, the quality filmmaking that ought to have been showcased at the festivals meant screening more social dramas than the action-adventures or melodramas popular among the audience. For Arpad, a quality film had to deal with realist themes, cover the issues in the society without harming national feelings and yet still present originality. In short, what both writers urged was the creation of a film festival more than an event of festivity with film stars in attendance. What these writers and other cinéphiles in the country wished for was perhaps best realised by another film festival that started in 1985. The International Istanbul Film Festival (http://film.iksv. org/en), which originally began in 1982 with a film show featuring only two documentaries and six features (organised in part by the Turkish Cinémathèque), became a staple of the film culture in Turkey.

Conclusion

As it stands, the film festivals of Turkey present a wider picture than ever, including well-established events such as Antalya (www. altinportakal.org.tr), Adana and Istanbul (http://film.iksv.org), a list to which one may add Izmir and Ankara (www.filmfestankara.org.tr), Bursa (www.ipekyolufilmfest.com), Malatya (http://malatyafilmfest.org. tr) and Eskişehir (www.eskfilmfest.com). Additionally, there are themed festivals, including Documentary, Women's Cinema, Children's Cinema, Environmental films, Films and History and Student Films, as well as various short film festivals and competitions.

Works Cited

'Amerika Sinemalar Paytahtı Holywoda Birisi Erkek Diğeri Kadın İki Genç Gönderiyoruz' | 'We Are Sending Two Young People to the American Cinema Centre Hollywood' (1929) Sinema Gazetesi 5, 8.

Arpad, Burhan (1968) 'Ekonomik Temeli Açısından Türk Filmi' | 'Turkish Cinema according to its Economic Basis', Türk Dili 196, 288-291.

'Bir 'Cine-Club' Gerek!' | 'A Cine-Club is Necessary!' (1959) Sinema 59, 2.

Gelenbevi, Baha (1961) 'Festival ve Filmciliğimiz' | 'Festival and Our Filmmaking', Artist 41, 25.

'Hisar Günlüğü' | 'Hisar Diary' (1969) Genç Sinema 8, 2-7.

Kakınç, Tarık Dursun (1985) 'Yeşilçam'da 'Star Sistemi' ya da Yıldız Yaratmacılığı Üzerine' | 'The 'Star System' in Yeşilçam or on Creating Stars', *Video/Sinema* 7, 28-29.

Kutlar, Onat (1990) *Sinema Bir Şenliktir: Sinema Yazıları | Cinema is a Festival: Film Writings*. Istanbul: Can Yayınları.

Kuyucaklı, Orhan (1961) 'Geçtiğimiz Film Sezonuna Umumi Bir Bakış' | 'A Look at the Last Film Season', *Artist* 47, 3.

Özgüç, Agah (1988) *Kronolojik Türk Sinema Tarihi: 1914-1968 | A Chronological History of Turkish Cinema*, Ankara: Kültür ve Turizm Bakanlığı.

Özön, Nijat (1995) *Karagözden Sinemaya: Türk Sineması ve Sorunları, 1. Cilt | From Karagöz to Cinema: Turkish Cinema and its Problems, Volume 1*. Ankara: Kitle.

Sayar, Vecdi (1995-96) 'Söyleşi: Sinematek ve Festival' | 'Interview: Cinémathèque and Festival', *Görüntü* 4, 45-53.

'Sinemada Devlet Yardımı' | 'State Aid in Cinema' (1969) *Akademik Sinema* 5, 17-19.

'Türk Film Festivalini Hangi Cemiyet Tertip Edecek?' | 'Which Association will Organise the Turkish Film Festival' (1961) *Artist* 40, 12-16.

Turkish Film Festivals: Political Populism, Rival Programming and Imploding Activities

Murat Akser

Introduction

In the autumn of 2012, two large and well-established film festivals in Turkey arrived at a stand-off. For the first time in Turkish film history, film directors were forced to choose between the Antalya Golden Orange Film Festival (www.altinportakal.org.tr/en) and the Adana Golden Boll Film Festival (www.goldenbollfilmfestival.com). Each festival required that the candidate films be premieres, which prevented their being entered in the rival festival. The end result was determined more by the politics around the festivals, which were heavily invested in by the municipal authorities as cultural showcases of successful city management. Indeed, political decisions influence the management, jury selection and activities of Turkish film festivals so much that they may explode or implode during the terms of different successive mayors.

Turkish film festivals date back to the 1960s. The first official film festival in Turkey took place soon after Metin Erksan's *Susuz Yaz* (*Dry Summer*, Metin Erksan, Turkey, 1963) won the Golden Bear for best film at the Berlin Film Festival in 1964. Turkish film professionals gathered at a Film Congress in 1964 and decided to take steps towards the international recognition and national preservation of Turkish cinema. One of the items on the agenda was the creation of a film festival and a cinémathèque.

Although, internationally, the best-known film festival in Turkey is the Istanbul International Film Festival (IFF) (http://film.iksv.org/en), established in 1982, it is two other, older festivals that will be the focus of attention here: those in Antalya and Adana. The prime focus of this chapter is the role of municipal authorities in managing festivals, which is best illustrated by the example of these older festivals.

In addition, the festival in Istanbul is controlled by a foundation for the arts, the *İstanbul* Kültür Sanat Vakfı (Istanbul Cultural and Arts Foundation) (İKSV) funded by private enterprise in the form of the Eczacıbaşı Group of companies which run a variety of arts-themed festivals ranging from jazz and theatre to cinema. It is a very urban film festival compared to the sunny shores that host Antalya: Istanbul's festival takes place in the usually rainy month of October (İKSV 2011). As the prime force behind IFF is private enterprise, municipal politics is less of a concern (Uçansu 2012).[1]

The oldest film festival, brainchild of the mayor Dr. Avni Tolunay (Güler 2009), was established in Antalya in 1963 and came to be known as the Antalya Golden Orange Film Festival (AGOFF). Antalya is a southwestern Anatolian coastal town in Turkey. It is located on the Mediterranean coast and boasts beaches clubs, and a relaxed atmosphere. The people are laid-back and the city's management traditionally goes to social democrats in municipal elections. The choice of Antalya as a site for a festival can be explained through comparisons to Cannes, which was the first place that sprang to mind when imagining a film festival in Turkey. The festival centre, film theatre and festival offices, were built in the late 1990s. These facilities are still in use today, along with the donated services of multiplex theatres in major shopping malls built in the 2000s. The monetary prize was merely symbolic until recently. It is a landmark event and celebrated its 50th anniversary in 2013. Local and national in scope, it has also been a site of film star gossip and boasts its share of jury selection and film award scandals.

The Adana Golden Boll Film Festival (AGBFF) operated between 1969 and 1973 and was only a local festival. Adana is a large city in Southern Turkey, near the border with Syria. The festival's creation there was symbolic as Adana is the birthplace of the internationally renowned Kurdish filmmaker Yılmaz Güney. After Güney's imprisonment and the suppression of his films, the festival was also abandoned. It was revitalised in 1992 by the city administration and has been kept going annually since then. Adana is a city known for its fertile soils and production of cotton. It has a hot climate and is known as the home of famous poets and artists, such as Yaşar Kemal. The AGBFF was traditionally held two weeks earlier than the AGOFF. Until recently (2010) both festivals accepted Turkish films without any restrictions, making it possible for a Turkish film to get an award from both festivals.

In 2012, AGBFF offered (with one condition) the greatest monetary prize ever to be awarded to a Turkish film: U.S.$500,000. The condition was that the film should have its world premiere at the Festival. The response from AGOFF was a similar ban in their festival bylaws to only admit Turkish films as world premieres. The results were that experienced directors with an artistic track record chose the Adana festival over Antalya, and that the latter became the choice for first-time directors. Film festivals' monetary awards have thus become a major prospective source of income for Turkish film producers. Many producers are able to pay any outstanding debts by getting an award. Film critics were divided on the issue, some favouring AGBFF for awarding filmmakers, while others criticised its art-for-profit attitude; AGOFF was hailed for giving opportunities to first-time filmmakers. Turkish film scholar Tülay Çelik states:

> It is necessary to emphasize that the money awards given by the festivals in Turkey constitute a very important support for the 'directors' cinema' field. It should not be ignored that, with the ability of paying the debts, even if this is not regarded as a production variable – in this context, directors paying their debts should be taken as an important component of the production process – and the elimination of the obligation to pay back the support of the Ministry of Culture, the awards become a decisive factor in the film production process of the 'directors' cinema' field in Turkey and this decisiveness is associated with the obstruction in the functioning of the production system. (Çelik 2012: 213)

There have been debates over the economic feasibility of running a festival with a huge deficit, for political reasons. The mayor of Adana has been re-elected five times since 1984. An extremely popular man among voters, he shifted his party-affiliation to the ruling power in each election. With a sudden turn of events, the incumbent mayor was dismissed by the Ministry of the Interior in 2010 and AGBFF was postponed due to this change in governance. With the support of city council members from Adalet ve Kalkınma Partisi (Justice and Development Party) (AKP) and Milliyetçi Hareket Partisi (Nationalist Action Party) (MHP), the two conservative right-wing parties, the acting mayor changed the structure of the AGBFF.

In Antalya meanwhile, the mayor belonged to Cumhuriyet Halk Partisi (Republican Peoples Party) (CHP), the left-wing opposition party known for is social-democratic attitude towards the support of the arts. The former mayor had belonged to AKP, the ruling conservative right-wing party. During this politically turbulent time, AGOFF was a place of galas, Oscar-winning actors ('Kevin Spacey to attend Turkey's Golden Orange' 2008) and red carpet events. The new mayor won the election on a platform condemning lavish spending on the festival. Following the change in the political landscape in 2009, both festivals became sites for a cultural and political stand-off. Where AGBFF programmed popular films by well-known directors, AGOFF chose Kurdish films and films dealing with women's issues.

Image 4: Glamorous stars are invited to attract public and media attention. Tuba Ünsal, Turkish film star at AGOFF 2008 Press Conference © Gokce Pehlivanoglu

Image 5: Global aspirations of a Turkish film festival as Hollywood actors are also invited. David Carradine greeting Michael Madsen at AGOFF 2008 © Gokce Pehlivanoglu.

It is the object of this chapter to conceptualise the uneasy relationship and tensions between the economic and political aspects of these two well-known Turkish film festivals. Firstly, tensions arise between central and municipal governments over financing and spending, and the political discourse resulting from this tension is currency for both central and local governments. Both levels of government see potential showcases in the film festivals: for efficiency, for electoral attention and for cultural recognition. In the Turkish case, the larger the festival, the bigger the control by central government. A smaller film festival may be deemed prestigious by the city government, but can be disadvantaged by competing festivals that get the support of the central government. Secondly, programming is influenced by the tensions between film festival cities. Each festival sees prestige in world premieres of national films. As prizes now regularly reach U.S.$250,000, each festival both attracts and divides filmmakers. Thirdly, each festival wants to offer something out of the ordinary, to the point of pushing the limits of acceptable categories that can be accepted in any film festival. Turkish film festivals want to be global / national, prestigious / commercial, art house / populist all at the same time. In fact though, these aims create conflicts and may cancel out each another's benefits. The festivals concern themselves more with exhibition than with distribution. Film markets are non-existent at both. In the end, it is the filmmakers who lose out, as they end up being excluded from the other national festival, without distribution and denied access to their potential audiences.

The Antalya Golden Orange Film Festival: From Global Glamour to Local Populism

It is 50 years this year since the inception of AGOFF. The festival was launched in 1964 and was the first of its kind in Turkey. The first major win at the Berlinale, by Metin Erksan's *Dry Summer*, ignited national support for the creation of a Turkish film festival in 1963. It was Dr. Avni Tolunay, then the Mayor of Antalya (1963-1973), who was the major force behind the foundation of the event. The municipality controlled the management of a foundation for the arts, which in turn controlled the festival budget and programming. This move created a two-way political pull mechanism. On the one hand, the festival was a showcase for the incumbent mayor to illustrate that tax money was being well spent and for the benefit of the city's inhabitants. On the other hand, the central government would see the festival as a showcase for the development of cultural capital. Problems would arise when the city and the central government did not see eye to eye; that is, whenever they came from different political parties with opposing political views.

A change of direction for AGOFF can be seen over the last three years, with an increasing tendency towards political populism. After the 2009 elections in Antalya, the ruling AKP party lost the city government to CHP. The mayor of the Antalya Metropolitan Municipality had been the rector of Antalya's Akdeniz University. Because he was vocal in condemning the political use of *hijab* in universities, he was not appointed for a second term as rector. As a reaction to this, he entered politics as a mayoral candidate. He defeated the mayor of Antalya who had served in office between 2004 and 2009. During his time, and with the support of the ruling liberal government AKP party, he invited Türkiye Sinema ve Audiovisuel Kültür Vakfı (Turkish Foundation of Cinema and Audio-visual Culture) (TÜRSAK) to change the festival into a Cannes-style event. Between 2005 and 2008, as a result of the vision of the TÜRSAK management style, the festival blossomed. The event now featured red carpet premieres, Oscar®-winning artists wining and dining with Turkish stars, a Eurasian Film Market for the promotion of Turkish films and parties intended to show the world how prestigious Antalya could be on the world stage. As one researcher comments:

> The Antalya Golden Orange Film Festival (AGOFF) [can be] investigated within the context of the scheme to transform Antalya into a city of culture led by the neo-liberal governance of the Antalya Metropolitan Municipality in the 2004-2009 municipal governance term. During this process, while the field of art and culture was being restructured with the hope of making Antalya a centre for location of runaway film shooting activities away from Hollywood, the field of tourism was also being restructured in Antalya to reach urban tourists or so-called niche tourists. The emergence of the AGOFF, its institutionalization process and, today, its restructuring process as the most important institutionalized collective cultural capital of Antalya to improve Antalya's representation in the global market for branding Antalya. (Varlı Görk 2010:1)

With the loss in the elections in 2009, AGOFF's budget fell overnight from U.S.$10 million to a mere U.S.$2 million. It was not only central government that pulled funding, but also the corporate sponsors who had backed the former AKP mayor rather than the newly-elected CHP mayor. The new mayor tried to compensate with a more populist approach. After the election in 2009, the festival management changed again. One of new mayor's first moves was to transfer the contract with TÜRSAK, the Istanbul-based management establishment of the festival,

to Antalya Kültür ve Sanat Vakfı (Antalya Culture and Arts Foundation) (AKSAV), Antalya's very own festival foundation. This foundation was established in 1995 by the Antalya municipality to oversee the various festival activities spread across the city, including film, music and television. Between 2005 and 2008, TÜRSAK operated alongside AKSAV but left the local host organisation only a symbolic share in the decision-making process. As AKSAV gained full control of the festival in 2009, the current mayor of Antalya has commented on the squeeze in festival funding:

> [T]he budgets of previous Golden Orange Film Festivals were too high, and last year's budget was 21 million Turkish Liras. [The] municipality still receives invoices of last year's spending. In last year's festival, 4.1 million Liras was spent for accommodation, 3 million Liras for inner city transportation, 2 million Liras for upstate transportation, 1.3 million Liras for The Turkish Cinema and Audiovisual Culture Foundation, or TÜRSAK's, consultancy, and 1.27 million Liras for human resources. ('Low budget, high quality at Golden Orange Film Fest' 2009)

The new festival was to be a 'People's Festival'. Now AGOFF tickets are U.S.$1 for students and the elderly, and free for all women.[2] Artists fade into the background: the people of Antalya are the focus. The galas happen in daytime, while evenings are reserved for free concerts, instead of parties for the stars. However, there has been a loss as well. The 'Filmmakers of the Future' programme that had served film production students was cancelled in 2009. The aim of the programme was to have ten students from each film department and to give them unlimited access to festival events and training sessions by industry professionals. There is now the 'People's Orange Film Project' that teams up film students from Antalya with ordinary Antalya citizens who want to make films. The teams make short films during the festival and get a special screening event. Another intervention has been the deactivation of the International Eurasian Film Market. The market used to help Turkish filmmakers access Asian markets and organised activities such as workshops about development, distribution and marketing. New festival events include tributes to former film artists.

So what function do film festivals perform for cities like Antalya? A film festival is supposed to publicise a city's image and bring prestige. Each year the organisers and the governing body of AGOFF claim that the previous festival managements' approach was too expensive, bringing the city to the brink of bankruptcy. This discourse continues and is used as a basis for the legitimisation of elections and of an incumbent mayor. During the 2012 festival, the special festival gazette featured accusations, by the Mayor, against the previous management on the misuse of festival funds. The reported figures of mismanaged funds grew bigger every day and the story was eventually taken up by national newspapers.

Adana Golden Boll Film Festival: A Rival Cacophony of Activities

Rivalry in local film festival politics can be equally observed in AGOFF's competition with AGBFF. Shortly after the elections in 2009, the independent Mayor of Adana, who had governed since 1984, was suspended by the Ministry of the Interior on charges of alleged financial mismanagement. (The charges are still to be proven; all court cases have now been dropped and the mayor is waiting to be reinstated.) The AKP, the ruling political party, appointed a new mayor for Adana and this move has directly influenced the fate of AGBFF. The removal of Adana's mayor created uncertainty and an intense struggle for power in the city administration, resulting in, first, the postponement and then the cancellation of the festival in 2010. However, the outlook of the festival changed in 2011 with the arrival of a mayor backed by the government. Money taps were opened up (local and national sponsors were attained through the Prime Minister's office). The budget of the festival now stands at 5 million Turkish Lira (U.S.$2.5 million) ('Adana's Altın Koza Film Festival Unrolls 20th Edition' 2013). This sum is much higher than at AGOFF, and many times more than AGBFF enjoyed in 2008. The new AGBFF festival has copied various activities that had been cancelled by the Antalya festival. For example, AGBFF invited film critics, actors, directors and celebrities who were excluded from AGOFF. A large Congress for the Cinema also took place in order to discuss the future of filmmaking in Turkey ('Golden Boll fest to host a congress' 2011). Additionally, AGBFF celebrated student filmmakers by creating an international student filmmakers competition.

The programming and publicity surrounding AGOFF and AGBFF bring to mind other festivals around the world. We can look at similar conflicts between the festivals in Montreal (www.ffm-montreal. org) and Toronto in Canada, or between the festival in Rome (www. romacinemafest.it/ecm/web/fcr/en) and the International Film Festival in Venice in Italy. Competition between cities can result in major financial burdens on municipalities that may run into the millions of dollars. However, in the last five years, municipal film festivals in Turkey have experienced a boom, regardless of whether it is national, international or thematic in origin; or ethnic, gender or class related. Since 2005, the increase in numbers and variations of Turkish film festivals is also worthy of note. These festivals are diverse and display varying thematic scopes: the international festivals accredited by FIAPF (Istanbul, Ankara and Antalya); independent festivals; those concerned with gender and sexual identity (Flying Broom, festival.ucansupurge.org, Filmmor www.filmmor.org), ethnic identity (Yılmaz Güney Kurdish Film Festival, yilmazguneyfilmfestivali.com/en), or regional identity (SineMardin, www.sinemardin.com.tr); professional groups (Golden Tooth Dentists Film Festival, iudissinema.com/kisa-film-yarismasi); schools (Istanbul Boys High School Film Festival, www.ielsinema.com); short films (Izmir, www.izmirkisafilm.org), documentary (Altınsafran FF www.altinsafran. org); and mobile festivals (Festival on Wheels, www.festivalonwheels. org).[3]

It is this diversity of film festivals and the competition among vying cities that are the marks of Middle Eastern film festivals. It is a rivalry and competition that can be found in places such as Dubai and Abu Dhabi. Each festival plays at being global, conforming to the global ambitions of their respective cities for their 2020 or 2030 developmental targets. And just like the festivals in Adana and Antalya, the Dubai and Abu Dhabi festivals – where the main issue is censorship – are challenged by local mores and conditions. International film festival rules require films to be screened uncut, whereas local Middle Eastern laws of decency may require these films to be edited (Guerrasio 2008). Turkish film festivals have managed to bypass censorship since 1992, whereas the Middle Eastern film festivals are challenged by local and global demands. For example, the Abu Dhabi Festival's decision not to censor films has been criticised by Islamic clerics (De Leon 2012).

The Programming: All or Nothing

For both AGOFF and AGBFF, programming is the result of an exclusionary rivalry. It starts with the selection of festival programmers: the pre-selection committee. The change, in 2011, of the bylaws of AGOFF proved to be disastrous. These new regulations stated that the films in the national competition had to have their first screenings in AGOFF. In reaction to this demand for exclusivity, the rival AGBFF shifted its festival schedule to roughly a week before Antalya and increased the monetary value of its awards, thus hoping to lure filmmakers away from AGOFF. It took a year for AGOFF to match the figure, but the festival did not change its dates. Festival devotees were divided. Whereas established figures such as Zeki Demirkubuz and Yeşim Ustaoğlu went to Adana, the younger filmmakers went to Antalya.

At the same time, both festivals tried to play at being global. In 2013, AGOFF's programming reflected some of the choices made by Venice, Cannes, Sundance and Telluride. The trend has been the same in selecting high-profile films for out-of-competition screenings (works by Michael Haneke, Kim Ki-duk and Abbas Kiarostami). Similarly, AGBFF's international programming highlighted independent productions from Europe and Asia.

The selection of jury members in AGOFF has also been the subject of impassioned debate. In 2011, the festival had an all-female jury, headed by the actress Müjde Ar. Ar was a famous actress in the 1980s and is well-known for her outspoken views on social issues. In 2012, Hülya Avşar, a former film actress from the 1980s and now a television celebrity, led the jury and made critical remarks about films throughout the festival. In one particular case, she was opposed to the particular representation of a young girl in a film and compared it to paedophilia (Güler 2012). This kind of interference and censorship by the jury has been taken to task by film critics. Just a few months prior to this, several prominent actors and directors resigned from the jury after declaring that Avşar was not fit to head a film festival jury ('Turkish actors withdraw from Golden Orange jury' 2012). Credibility and trust is thus at an all-time low for both festivals. And these festivals are not immune to scandal, either: in 2010, Emir Kusturica, invited by AGOFF, was attacked for allegedly not condemning Serbian cruelties and had to leave the festival amidst protests. The allegations against Kusturica had been generated by another attending filmmaker and festival favourite, Semih Kaplanoğlu ('Golden Orange Festival Marred by Politics as Kusturica Leaves Antalya' 2010).

The programming rivalry also disadvantaged directors in another way. Turkish film festivals claim to produce national heroes: between 2003 and 2008 AGOFF was a launching pad for new rising talent in Turkish cinema. Nuri Bilge Ceylan, Zeki Demirkubuz, Semih Kaplanoğlu and Reha Erdem, became household names after they had their first wins at Antalya. But since 2009, neither AGOFF nor AGBFF have been able to produce the international success story they had hoped: the number of films competing in each festival has been gradually decreasing and directors have been automatically disqualified from attending the rival festival. The news coverage of both events (awards ceremonies, parades, workshops and other activities), addressed the populist policies of city administrations rather than the films. Yet they could not produce international awards and could not promote the names of the award-winning filmmakers to the average citizen. The winning films, therefore, did not enjoy box-office success, either. Some did not even achieve distribution. In 2012, out of a total of 24 films screened in the combined national competitions of both AGOFF and AGBFF, only four films made it to domestic distribution. Previous winners, prior to 2009, had enjoyed both local box office success and wide international recognition. For example, *Sonbahar* (*Autumn,* Özcan Alper, Turkey, 2008), winner of the Golden Orange in 2008, won several international awards and reached many audiences nationwide.

The following table provides a summary comparison of the two festivals:

Festival	AGBFF	AGOFF
Activities	Social	Media-focused
Selection	Ideological	Art house
Management	Professional	City-bureaucratic
Market	Local	Global
Funding	Government	Self

Table 2: Comparison between AGBFF and AGOFF

Conclusion

Turkish film festivals are run as political spectacles by their respective city managements. The key issues they face are: the impact of political decision making processes on film selection, the level of exposure of city managers, as well as films and directors, and an emphasis on local political culture. Political choices influence the management style, jury selection and activities of the festivals. Political exposure is achieved by city management through its relationships with the media. To this end, film directors, juries and critics, are perceived as spectacles to be displayed in the city throughout the festival (through parades, posters, workshops).

According to Dina Iordanova film festivals are possessed of various qualities and perform various functions. Successful festivals bridge the film industry with politics and other spheres; are nodes in more general transnational infrastructures; are clusters of creativity and commerce; contain an inherent transnationalism that counterbalances nationalist tendencies; are sites for cultural exchange; provide an alternative to artistic migration (2011).

Judging by the above criteria, the two major national film festivals in Turkey are failing. By not offering markets and facilitating distribution they cannot bridge the gap between the talent and the market. By fuelling rival programming they polarise filmmakers and the public. By focusing too much on local activities, they avoid being transnational and hence forego the possibility of both market and cultural exchange. Political decision-making and the exposure of politicians takes place at the expense of the promotion of filmmakers.

The Antalya Golden Orange Film Festival faces many of the challenging tasks that other film festivals in Turkey do. Its economic contribution to the city, when coupled with its provision of cultural services to citizens, municipal government and bureaucrats, creates a prominent image for the festival in local and national politics. The culture of cinema is passed on to the public and is there to honour the artists. The foundations organising the film festivals are, in turn, controlled by city governments – their political-bureaucratic managers. Yet successive managements can easily negate previously valued contributions. This happened in Antalya when the new mayor was elected, became involved and the main sponsors withdrew. Government-support through the Ministry of Tourism and Culture also disappeared. The Minister himself, who used to visit the festival, stopped attending.

In comparison to a festival of the same age, such as the Toronto International Film Festival, establishment and management differences for Turkish festivals become obvious. Toronto is managed by an independent foundation. It has city, provincial and federal support. It has national corporate sponsorship from Bell and Visa. Its activities are not limited to a week, but continue throughout the year. It has a permanent festival centre, cinema halls, a cinémathèque, a touring festival, a publisher, Hollywood premieres, a film market, interviews, workshops, a museum and even its own guesthouse. And finally, it does not offer a monetary award. The people are the jury; their acclaim is the prize. Each film's press, public and industry screenings are repeated twice. Perhaps a model of this type of film festival should be created in Turkey.

A successful festival has to have sustainable programming and an objective jury; and the whole process should be guided by choices that are not dictated by politics and economics.

Works Cited

'Adana's Altın Koza Film Festival Unrolls 20th Edition' (2013) *Today's Zaman*. 15 September. On-line. Available HTTP: http://www.todayszaman.com/news-326416-adanas-altin-koza-film-festival-unrolls-20th-edition.html (16 June 2013).

Çelik, Tülay (2012) 'International Film Festivals: A Cinema Struggling to Exist Between New Resources and New "Dependencies"', *Journal of Academic Marketing Mysticism Online (JAMMO)*, 4, 14, 206-221. On-line. Available HTTP: http://www.

journalacademicmarketingmysticismonline.net/index.php/
JAMMO/article/view/827108008 (8 September 2013).

De Leon, Janice Ponce (2012) 'CUT! Is censorship hurting UAE cinema?',
Kipp Report. On-line. Available HTTP: http://www.kippreport.com/
fcs/cut-is-censorship-hurting-uae-cinema/ (8 September 2013).

Dönmez-Colin, Gönül (2012) 'Film Festivals in Turkey: Promoting National
Cinema While Nourishing Film Culture', in Jeffrey Ruoff (ed.) Coming
Soon to a Festival Near You: Programming Film Festivals. St Andrews:
St. Andrews Film Studies. 101-116.

'Golden Boll fest to host a congress' (2011) Hürriyet Daily News, 12
September. On-line. Available HTTP: http://www.hurriyetdailynews.
com/default.aspx?pageid=438&n=golden-boll-fest-to-host-a-
congress-2011-09-12 (1 November 2013).

'Golden Orange Festival Marred by Politics as Kusturica Leaves Antalya'
(2010) Today's Zaman. 11 October. On-line. Available HTTP: http://
www.todayszaman.com/news-224041-golden-orange-festival-
marred-by-politics-as-kusturica-leaves-antalya.html (10 November
2012).

'Golden Orange to be low-cost this year' (2013) Hürriyet Daily News, 23
September. On-line. Available HTTP: http://www.hurriyetdailynews.
com/golden-orange-to-be-low-cost-this-year.aspx?pageID=517&
nID=55059&NewsCatID=381 (4 October 2013).

Guerrasio, Jason (2008) 'Dubai International Film Festival', Filmmaker,
6 January. On-line. Available HTTP: http://filmmakermagazine.
com/972-dubai-international-film-festival-by-jason-guerrasio/ (10
November 2013).

Güler, Emrah (2009) 'Celebrating Turkish Cinema with Golden Oranges',
Southeast Europe: People and Cultures, 20 October. On-line. Available
HTTP: http://www.southeast-europe.eu/?id=983 (4 January 2013).

Güler, Emrah (2012) 'Incest: The last taboo in Turkish cinema and TV',
Hürriyet Daily News. 15 October. On-line. Available HTTP: http://
www.hurriyetdailynews.com/Default.aspx?pageID=549&nID=323
88&NewsCatID=381 (28 February 2013).

İKSV (2011) 30: 30 Years from 20 Directors. Istanbul: IKSV.

Iordanova, Dina (2011) 'East Asia and Film Festivals: Transnational Clusters
for Creativity and Commerce', in Dina Iordanova with Ruby Cheung
(eds) FFY 3: Film Festivals and East Asia, St. Andrews: St. Andrews
Film Studies. 1-33.

'Kevin Spacey to attend Turkey's Golden Orange' (2008) Hürriyet Daily
News, 10 October. On-line. Available HTTP: http://www.hurriyet.
com.tr/english/domestic/10087777.asp?scr=1 (23 April 2013).

'Low budget, high quality at Golden Orange Film Fest' (2009) *Hürriyet Daily News*, 1 July. On-line. Available HTTP: http://www.hurriyetdailynews.com/default.aspx?pageid=438&n=46.-uluslararasi-antalya-altin-portakal-film-festivali-2009-07-01 (19 May 2013).

'Turkish actors withdraw from Golden Orange jury' (2012) *Hürriyet Daily News*, 25 July. On-line. Available HTTP: http://www.hurriyetdailynews.com/turkish-actors-withdraw-from-golden-orange-jury.aspx?pageID=238&nid=26239 (27 May 2013).

Uçansu, Hülya (2012) *Bir Uzun Mesafe Festivalcisinin Anıları* (Memoirs of a Long Distance Festival Manager). İstanbul: Doğan Kitap.

Varlı Görk, Reyhan (2010) 'Nedir Şu Yeşilçam'in Meyvesi 'Altin Portakal'? Antalya'nin Yeniden Yapilandirilmasi Sürecinde Antalya Altin Portakal Film Festivalinin Metalaştirilmasi (What Is This Fruit of Pinewood [Turkish Hollywood], The "Golden Orange"? The Commodification of the Antalya Golden Orange Film Festival During the Course of Antalya's Restructuring)', *Akdeniz İ.İ.B.F. Dergisi* 20, 1-40. [Turkish].

Notes

[1]   The festival owes its history to Istanbul Film Days, previously run by the Istanbul Cinemathèque, founded by Şakir Eczacıbaşı in the 1970s. Not having its own cinema base, the festival's screening venues change depending on availability. For many years the Emek cinema in Beyoğlu was its prime location. Recently though government-supported redevelopment in this historical part of town led to the cinema's shut down. The building was demolished among protests and the festival lost valuable space for film enthusiasts. The Istanbul International Film Festival has a national and international award for best film and director.

[2]   The founding secularist party in Turkey, CHP, has shouldered the role of emancipator of women since the 1920s. Any symbolic gesture against the right-wing Islamist-based political power of AKP goes hand in hand with showcasing women at the forefront in CHP municipalities. In 2011 the jury at the Antalya Film Festival was also entirely composed of women.

[3]   [Editor's note: see the table on Turkish Film Festivals for more information on these festivals.]

'Meetings on the Bridge': An Interview with Azize Tan, Director of the International Istanbul Film Festival

Melis Behlil

The International Istanbul Film Festival (IFF), organised by the Istanbul Foundation for Culture and Arts (IKSV, İstanbul Kültür Sanat Vakfı), was first held as a cinematic sidebar of the much wider Istanbul Festival in the summer of 1982. Within two years, it became a separate event called Istanbul Cinema Days, and moved to April. In 1989, the event was renamed The International Istanbul Film Festival and accredited by FIAPF (Fédération Internationale des Associations de Producteurs de Films / International Federation of Film Producers Associations). IFF is not the oldest film festival of Turkey; that honour goes to Antalya's Golden Orange Film Festival which held its 50th edition in 2013, followed by Adana's Golden Boll Film Festival, held since 1969 with an 18-year long hiatus during the seventies and eighties. Nonetheless, IFF is the most internationally renowned of the festivals in Turkey, welcoming a large number of foreign guests and press, and showcasing a great variety of the local productions. In 2013, 247 films were screened across different sections over 16 days, and over 110,000 tickets were sold. The festival was covered by 187 members of the press, over a third of whom came from outside the country. Although there is no official market organised within the festival, 29 sales and distribution companies were accredited, 15 of which were from other countries than Turkey. This is largely a showcase for films from Turkey; in addition to the National Competition, the festival has a special section for non-competition films produced over the last year, as well as documentary and shorts selections. The consistency of IFF over more than three decades is closely linked with the independent nature of its host institution, *İstanbul* Kültür Sanat Vakfı (IKSV), as well as the fact that it has had only two directors since it was founded. Hülya Uçansu was director from the start for 25 years, and Azize Tan took over the helm from her in 2006.

The following interview with Tan focuses on the festival's positioning of itself, both among the Turkish film festivals and in the international arena. Although the interview was held within one session on 4 October 2013, it was nourished by longstanding discussions between Tan and the interviewer, Melis Behlil. Behlil, a film scholar and a film critic, has been an active audience member at the festival since its inception, and has worked as a volunteer on many of the editions.

Melis Behlil: *Let us start with your relationship to this festival. Before you became the director, you worked at IKSV for many years. How has this experience informed your current position?*

Azize Tan: I have worked at the IKSV for 20 years, since I was a student. I started with doing subtitle translations, and worked at the organisation as well. There was a big film project organised in France, entitled Europalia [www.europalia.be], where we had a big showcase of 116 Turkish films. I collaborated on that with the foundation and I began working full-time after that. I did almost everything at the film department, subtitling, cataloguing, film traffic, all different aspects. Then I started travelling to different festivals when I became the Deputy Director. I did that for two years, and became the Director in 2006. Our foundation has this tradition that people work here for a long time, know how things function, and eventually become the head of their department. I also worked for the Istanbul Biennial for three editions as the coordinator. I wish I could do both at the same time, but the workload makes it impossible.

Image 6: Azize Tan at the Istanbul International Film Festival Opening Reception © Basin Toplantisi

MB: *IFF is the most international of the film festivals in Turkey. Is this the result of a conscious strategy?*

AT: When the festival was first founded, I think it was modelled after all the prestigious, big festivals around the world. But then, you have to take into consideration the special conditions of your own country, of course. There are budget limitations and other restrictions. In 1982, the festival consisted only of a film week with six films. This was two years after the 1980 military coup, and nothing was happening in Turkey anymore. The Cinémathèque was shut down and festivals were the only site where people could access cinema, music, culture, any of these things. It was so successful that the dates were moved to separate the film festival from the larger festival. The foundations were laid solidly, but because of the budget limitations, while it was showing international films, the international crowd attending the festival was not very big. The number of films and guests were much lower than today.

By the time I became the director, the festival had been well-established and had great support from the audience. But I thought it was the right time to build a more international ground for it at that point. In fact, this coincided with the growth of Turkish cinema. We cannot deny the effect the festival has had on the new generation of filmmakers in Turkey; it was like a school, it was the only place where people could go and watch new films and learn what was going on in world cinema. In the second stage, the festival became like a promotional site for those new films being made in Turkey by the directors who grew up with the festival.

So, what we are trying to do now is twofold. One is to create an international platform to promote quality foreign films in Turkey and encourage their distribution outside of the festival. Today, like everywhere else, the festival has become an alternative means of distribution. We organise another festival in October, and we travel with this programme to other cities in the country to promote 'art cinema'.[1] At the same time, every year we increase the number of Turkish films that we are showing. In a way, we are trying to make a Turkish film showcase for the foreign guests that we are hosting at the festival. We have about 300 people coming from abroad; these are not just the directors, producers or actors of the films we are showing, but international distributors, heads of funds, festival directors and film critics. We are trying to create an international community in order to allow the Turkish film industry to communicate with the wider world of film. In 2006, we started 'Meetings on the Bridge', a production platform for Turkish film projects, to team them up with possible international collaborators. This is not a market *per sé*. This way, we are supporting Turkish films not just at the stage of distribution, but already during project development. This section is growing every year, and people are interested in the cinema of Turkey, so they come and want to buy these films. This is a good opportunity for the foreign guests as well, and the festival is gradually growing internationally.

MB: Where do you position the festival within the international arena? Does it traditionally have a European bent or do you see it as a leading festival within the Middle East?

AT: When it was first founded, the festival was almost like a 'best of' selection. We still try to show the best films of the year, because above all, this is an audience festival and I find this very important. Today, there is a big competition amongst festivals, where everybody is striving to screen premières. But I think there are too many festivals in the world right now. Every day, there is an announcement of a new festival somewhere. In that sense, we are becoming a leading festival in the region, with the help of the growing Turkish film industry. This is a great market for everyone; there is a lot of creativity. The success of Turkish television series in the Middle East and the Balkans also adds to this popularity. People are curious about what is going on here and the reasons behind it. We are trying to steer ourselves according to the present needs. Our priority is always the audience, followed closely by the promotion of Turkish films worldwide. This is also caused by the structure of the film industry here, because we do not have a film institute for promotion, and the festival takes on that function.

We are trying to become the base for the Turkish cinema industry on the international platform. This is more important to us than having premières. Similarly, we want to show our audience the best films that we can from the international scene. Ours is a very accessible festival; we have a very cinéphile audience that we have built up over the years, and we try to create a bond with them and the international filmmakers. The audience is perhaps our greatest asset, so it is crucial for us to sustain our relationship with them. Lately, with the problems of monopoly in exhibition that we have been facing in Turkey, these films are having a very hard time getting distribution. The festival plays a big role in uniting these films with an interested audience. With the existing distribution system both in the theatres and on television, some films fall through the cracks and get lost. We are trying to make them visible.

MB: How do you maintain the audience-friendly environment of the festival?

AT: One of our main goals is to broaden our audiences and reach more people. We also want to help diminish, make disappear even, this perceived gap between 'art house' films – a term I personally dislike – and more mainstream fare. Audiences have become consumers, they do not always want to spend time or energy on thinking more about films. This is something we are trying to break; we want to show them that they can also enjoy more 'difficult' films. I have nothing against popular cinema, but we want to make sure that people realise there is an alternative. It is not just about big-budget, big-star films; there are other types of films that the audiences can enjoy. We have a very intense bond with our audience. When programming the festival, one of our main objectives is to be able to show them the very best. That is why we follow directors through their careers, try to discover new talent and we try to present new currents, like Romanian cinema lately, or Iran. We try to create a very eclectic programme. In our October film week entitled Filmekimi, we create a boutique programme of award-winning films from Cannes and other major festivals, and tour with this throughout Turkey. Many films do get released, but they also get lost with a very limited number of copies since we do not have repertory theatres. They are screened for a week maybe and then disappear forever. We are also encouraging endeavours by independent distributors to build repertory cinemas. We do not want people to watch these only during the festival, but to make it something continuous. This would make the festival bigger and more sustainable as well, with a year-round audience. There are plans to build an independent art house cinema chain from 2014 on, which is something we want to help create. As a very well-established brand that people trust, we would be able to promote these films.

MB: *Financial strategies like keeping prices down must also have helped to create this close bond with the audiences. How do you sustain yourself financially?*

AT: To start with, our ticket prices are lower than regular theatre tickets. But for weekday daytime screenings, we have been selling our tickets for Turkish Lira 5.00, which is roughly about U.S.$2.50. This is very attractive both for students and for pensioners. We have a very young audience, because Turkey has a huge youth population, but there is also a middle-aged retired audience with limited means but plenty of time and a great interest in cinema. This has increased our ticket sales, and almost all our films play to full houses. Additionally, we have a membership programme as a foundation, which provides people with discounts and early access to tickets. We try to collaborate with different venues around Istanbul, as this is a huge city, and people want to be able to go to the festivals in a number of different neighbourhoods. We also collaborate with NGOs, trying to get women who have never been to movie theatres to go to a cinema to watch films. We collaborate with high schools and universities, organising master classes with filmmakers at schools. We have a great number of film departments in Turkey, more than 20 in Istanbul alone, so there is great interest.

The festival is organised by a non-profit NGO and 35-40% of our budget comes from ticket sales, so that is one more reason why our audience is so crucial for us. We also have private sponsors, and we are very lucky in the sense that our collaborations with the sponsors are long term. Our main sponsor will be the same company for the tenth year in a row, and this is vital for our sustainability. Unfortunately, we do not have any support from the municipality, even though the festival bears the name of the city and not that of a sponsor. Many other festivals around the country are organised by municipalities, but because changes in local governments have a direct bearing on the festival management, there is no sustainability in terms of artistic choices or organisations. We choose to remain fully independent, which may not be very attractive for the municipality. Although they do give us some promotional assistance through the use of billboards, etc., it is not enough. We also get some support from the Ministry [of Culture], but it changes every year and we never know exactly how much it is going to be. It usually amounts to around 11-16% of the budget, but this means that we need to raise nearly half of our budget from our sponsors. Other foundations, NGOs, consulates and cultural institutions, assist us as well, but their percentage in the budget of a huge festival like Istanbul is very limited, of course.

MB: You mentioned the popularity of television series throughout the region. Co-production partners for Turkish films have traditionally come from Western Europe: from France and Germany and from Western neighbouring countries, such as Greece and Bulgaria. Have you been receiving more interest from other Balkan countries and the Middle East as a result of series' popularity?

AT: Yes, of course, they are very interested. Every year we have a special focus on a country. We did collaborations with Germany, France and the Netherlands before, which initiated a number of Dutch co-productions. We founded a co-production fund between Germany and Turkey, with support from Berlin and Munich funds, as well as the Turkish Ministry of Culture. We were recently in Batumi, Georgia, and are trying to build relations between the two countries' film industries. Georgia initiated a new fund, so we hope this will result in new co-productions, as the geographic and cultural proximity would make this a very fruitful collaboration. We have also had meetings with representatives from the Israeli film industry in Haifa, looking for new ways to work together. We have close ties with the festival in Dubai as well, which is the centre for the Middle Eastern market. There is a lot of familiarity with the Turkish stars especially in the Middle Eastern countries, so we would like to take advantage of this. In 2014, we will have collaborations with Poland. We are trying to explore new territories, and in the meantime, we are waiting for the new cinema law to pass. This law has been in the making for two years, and when it passes, co-productions will be a lot easier. For example, it is impossible at the moment to have a co-production with Turkey as the minority, Turkish companies need to have at least 51% of the production. We are working on changing this alongside industry and state representatives.

MB: How are your relations with the state aside from budgetary concerns? Does the lack of clearly defined cultural policies by the state effect the festival?

AT: Being an independent NGO gives us a certain amount of freedom. We like to keep our channels of dialogue open with the Ministry of Culture, because we need them for our work with the industry. But of course, when you are a private body trying to act like a film institute in the absence of a formal institution, this has its handicaps. For example, as we have seen in the debates for a new cinema law, we need continuity and consistency from the part of the Ministry as well. The whole industry has been waiting for this law for two years; it has been drafted but because of elections and other interruptions, it has had to wait to be passed. At this point, we have to wait every time there is a change in the national political agenda, and we are losing precious time to develop the industry. We have a quickly growing industry, and the existing regulations are not sufficient. We try to develop solidarity with the industry in order to have a more direct and efficient relationship with the Ministry. In our international dealings, for example in the talks with Georgia, we have had a representative from the Ministry's Cinema Department. Or for the co-production fund with Germany, we are receiving EUR50,000 (U.S.$67,500) yearly, which is great. We try to keep these channels open in order to collaborate efficiently, but it is not always easy.

MB: Another difficulty the festival has been facing has been in finding appropriate venues, as there is no festival centre and the main cinema used for the festival, Emek, was demolished in May 2013 amidst protests and controversies. How do you deal with this problem?

AT: One of the main challenges for festivals worldwide is finding venues. Theatres with large capacities are being shut down all around the world. The Emek example is a rare one where large crowds mobilised in order to protect a cinema. We do not have a 'palais' for the festival, and this old theatre, with 900 seats, had been the main venue for the festival for 28 years. When it was shut down, we were first told that it was going to be restored, but then we found out that the project was to demolish the cinema, build a big cineplex and put Emek on the top floor of that. There were lots of protests, and the cinema remained unused for four years. Finally, during the festival in April 2013, there was a big incident where the police attacked the peaceful protesters with tear gas and water. The building was torn down shortly thereafter. This is a big obstacle for a growing festival like ours, because we need a home, and we are a festival with a large audience. When we lose a theatre with a large capacity, the number of audiences we can reach diminishes. Our main hub is Istiklal Street, the pedestrian zone right off Taksim Square at the centre of the city, but we are losing one cinema after another and it becomes more and more difficult for us to create a festival atmosphere where people can go from one theatre to the next. While we do not really want to go to the multiplexes, this seems to be the only remaining alternative for us. We are constantly looking for new venues that we can use.

Digitisation is another difficulty we are facing, because there is no support scheme to facilitate the cross-over to digital projection. This process is completely independent, so the big cinema chains that own most of the screens can go digital, but the others have a very hard time. We need digital projection to organise the festival, because at this point, between 90-95% of the prints we are getting are digital, there is almost no 35mm left. This is a problem, especially when we travel to the cities in Anatolia, where the small theatres cannot afford to buy digital projectors.

MB: *Despite all the difficulties, the number of festivals in the world and in Turkey is booming. Where do you see the future of the festivals going?*

AT: I strongly believe that festivals are important. They are a vital means for the promotion of cinema. And Istanbul is the perfect working model for this. But the competition among the festivals and the ambition to show premières sometimes overshadow the quality of these festivals. As I said, there are way too many festivals, for many different reasons. But in the end, their main goals should be to promote cinema and to serve the public. Of course there are big festivals with big markets, which is crucial for the industry. But you cannot have that at all the festivals. That is why we do not want to have a formal market at our festival with stalls for people to sell their goods. You have to know your own market, your own audience, and create a model that works for your own industry and for your own people. All the festivals are imitating one another with premières and markets, but I think one needs to think whether this really works for their festival. I do not see the point of showing a film that I do not like just for the sake of having a première. At this point, there is a festival for every film in the world, where it can be shown and can even receive awards, but that should not be the objective of the festivals. There are way too many films being produced, and I think that maybe the number of films should be reduced and we should all work more for the films that are accessible to the audiences, and festivals should work harder to promote those films, for a wider audience.

Notes

1   This festival, called 'Filmekimi' (Film-October) presents a strong selection from the year's big festival winners. While hugely popular with the local audiences, it has no sidebars, parallel events or international guests in attendance.

Turkish Film Festivals

Est.	Name	Location	Website	Dates	Specialisation
1963	International Antalya Golden Orange Film Festival	Antalya, Turkey	http://www.altinportakal.org.tr/en/index.html	October	National/international - competition
1969	International Golden Boll Film Festival	Adana, Turkey	http://www.altinkozafestivali.org.tr/	September	National/international - competition
1982	Istanbul International Film Festival	Istanbul, Turkey	http://film.iksv.org//en	April-May	National/international -competition
1987	International Short Film Festival	Istanbul, Turkey	http://istanbulfilm.wix.com/festival	November	National/international – competition (short)
1988	Ankara International Film Festival	Ankara, Turkey	http://www.filmfestankara.org.tr/en/index.php	March	National/international – non-competition
1989	International Izmir Film Festival	Izmir, Turkey	http://www.izmirfilmfest.com/en/index.php	July	National/international – competition
1995	Festival on Wheels	Travelling festival; various locations in Turkey	http://www.festivalonwheels.org/	November-December	European films

Est.	Name	Location	Website	Dates	Specialization
1996	Flying Broom International Women's Film Festival	Ankara, Turke	http://festival.ucansupurge.org/englishindex.php	May	Films on women
1997	SineMardin	Mardin, Turkey	http://www.sinemardin.com.tr/	May-June	National/international – non-competition
1997	International 1001 Documentary Film Festival	Istanbul, Turkey	http://www.1001belgesel.net/	November	Documentary films
1997	International Golden Safran Documentary Film Festival	Karabuk, Turkey	http://www.altinsafran.org/en/	September	Documentary films
1998	International FilmMor Women's Film Festival on Wheels	Travelling festival; Istanbul, Turkey	http://www.filmmor.org/?sayfa=11	March-April	Films on women
1998	Rendezvous Istanbul Film Festival	Istanbul, Turkey	http://www.randevuistanbul.com/	February	Films related to history

1999	International Eskişehir Film Festival	Eskişehir, Turkey	http://www.eskfilmfest.com/	May	National/international - competition
2000	Izmir Short Film Festival	Izmir, Turkey	http://www.izmirkisafilm.org/index_eng.html	November	National-competition (short)
2001	IF! International Independent Film Festival	Istanbul, Ankara, Izmir simultaneous in three cities	http://www.ifistanbul.com/en/index.asp	February-March	Independent films
2001	International Environmental Short Film Festival	Istanbul, Turkey	http://www.cevrefilm.org/	May	Short films related to environmental issues, international - competition
2004	Akbank Short Film Festival	Istanbul, Turkey	http://www.akbanksanat.com/en/kisa-film-festivali/hakkinda	March	Short films, national-competition

Turkish Film Festivals Abroad

Est.	Name	Location	Website	Dates	Specialisation
1989	Munich Turkish Film Festival	Munich, Germany	http://sinematurk-munchen.de/	March	Diasporic-competition
1992	Mannheim Turkish Film Festival	Mannheim, Germany	http://turkfilmfest-mannheim.de/	October	Diasporic-competition
1993	London Turkish Film Festival	London, UK	http://www.ltff.co.uk/	February-March	Diasporic-competition
1994	Turkey/Germany Film Festival	Nurnberg, Germany	http://www.fftd.net/festivalprofil.html	March	Diasporic-competition
1999	New York Turkish Film Festival	New York, USA	http://www.newyorkturkishfilmfestival.com/	December	Diasporic-competition
2001	Boston Turkish Film Festival	Boston, USA	http://www.bostonturkishfilmfestival.org/	March-April	Diasporic-competition
2001	Frankfurt Turkish Film Festival	Frankfurt, Germany	http://www.turkfilmfestival.de/	October-November	Diasporic-competition (short)

2010	Amsterdam Turkish Film Festiva	Amsterdam, Netherlands	http://www.atff.nl/	September	Diasporic-noncompetition
2011	Ruhr Turkish Film Festival	Multiple cities, Germany	http://www.tuerkischesfilmfestruhr.de/	September	Diasporic-noncompetition
2011	Rome Turkish Film Festival	Rome, Italy	http://www.filmfestivalturcodiroma.org/it	September	Diasporic-competition
2012	Los Angeles Turkish Film Festival	Los Angeles, USA	http://www.latff.org/	February-March	Diasporic-competition
2012	Chicago Turkish Film Festival	Chicago, USA	http://www.chicagoturkishfilmfestival.org/	September	Diasporic-noncompetition
2013	Red Tulip Film Festival	Rotterdam, Netherlands	http://www.rtff.nl/en/	June	Diasporic-competition

Compiled by Murat Akser
This table is representative, not exhaustive.

Middle East

Film Festivals in Egypt: An Overview

Mahmoud Kassem

Translated by Kholoud Hussein and Koen Van Eynde

Scene I: The Cairo International Film Festival

The First Cairo International Film Festival

Once upon a time, we, the people of Cairo, thirsted for knowledge of what lies in the 'great beyond' of the international film scene. Confined in Cairo, we looked with covetous eyes to our itinerant film critics. Funded by their newspapers, these nomadic critics would be sent on missions to various film festivals across the globe, returning with a detailed report of the pictures, actors and directors whose work had they watched and whom they had met. But that was not the only way in which 'knowledge of the great beyond' was relayed to us Cairenes. Many amateur film-enthusiasts, cinema-lovers and culture-thirsty youth, would head to Western 'cultural centres' to get a peek at the newest film, or read the latest review. Cairo was – and still is – littered with international cultural centres: American, British, French, German, Spanish, Italian, Russian and Hungarian, to name but a few. These centres, besides providing language instruction and other services, occasionally screened films from their home countries, across a range of genres and eras: the old, the iconic, the contemporary, the avant-garde.

Over time, these centres started putting on national film weeks – showing a marathon of classical or contemporary films – and, eventually, these film weeks started spilling out of the confines of their centres, and into the cinemas of Cairo. This cultural expansion proved very popular; the crowds flooding into the cinema halls bring to mind the line from French-Egyptian singer Dalida's song, 'Gigi L'Amoroso'.[1] Egyptian cinemas were showing international films – but still, this was becoming an annual, organised event. There was no true effort or inclination on the part of the Ministry of Culture to turn these haphazard showings into an organised festival. It was a circle of independent journalists who took a definitive stand and formed the Egyptian Association of Film and Cinema Writers and Critics (EAFCWC) in 1976 with the intention to start a film festival, and then led the festival until 1983. The founding members of the EAFCWC were amongst the most prominent arts and culture journalists at the time, including Kamal Al Mallakh, Abd Al Munim Sa'ad, Mary Ghadban,

Yusuf Gawhar, Iris Nazmi, and Mufid Fawzi. Meanwhile, cinema critics formed another group, the aptly-named Association of Cinema Writers and Critics (ACWC). Together, these institutes were responsible for the chain of events that eventually lead to the first Cairo Film Festival.

The first Cairo Film Festival (CFF) took place between 16 and 22 August 1976. The EAFCWC and the ACWC managed to obtain funding from the Ministry of Culture, harnessing the Prime Minister's support along the way – he participated in the ceremony of the Festival's opening day. And what a day! It was an event on an unprecedented scale, a dazzling show played before the audience of Cairo. The critics at the time cited the calibre and diversity of the participating international talent as an indicator of the Festival's success. Thirty-five nations took part, including prominent international actors of the time, such as Claudia Cardinale and Rajendra Kumar. The panel of judges boasted big names: film critics Thomas Quinn Curtis (*International Herald Tribune*, United States) and David Robinson (UK), directors Shadi Abdel-Salam (Egypt), Hajir Dariush (Iran) and Satyajit Ray (India). That year, Egypt scored a victory in the Best Actor Category, which went to a very prominent actor at the time, Imad Hamdy, for his role in *Al Mudhnibun* (*Sinners*, 1975), a film directed by Said Marzouk.

None of this would have been possible without the official governmental support harnessed by the EAFCWC and ACWC. Youssef El Sebai, who was Minister of Culture at the time, was made Honorary President of both societies. In spite of issues with some local cinemas, the Festival received support from tourism companies, hotels and the national airline. The festival screened many films from countries that did not a have a representative council or cultural centre in Cairo, such as Tunisia, Brazil and Algeria. This was the first time Cairenes had a glimpse of films produced in locations other than Hollywood or Europe.

Since the festival's first year, American broadcasting companies played a crucial role, overseeing the screening of American films with Arabic subtitles – such as Martin Scorsese's *Taxi Driver* (1976). The first festival was an excellent networking event for filmmakers from Egypt, who had a hitherto unprecedented opportunity to interact with others of their profession from all over the world. International filmmakers were invited to press-conferences, parties and the famous closing ceremony concert on the last day of the festival.

The Second Cairo International Film Festival

In the same spirit and gusto, the second Cairo international film festival took place between the 26 September and 5 October 1977. Once again organised by the EAFCWC, the festival was this time headed by Youssef El

Sebai, who by now had completely deserted his governmental position to officially replace Kamal Al Mallakh. This time, over 70 films from 25 different countries were screened, and 25 films officially entered into the competition. The timing of the second festival allowed for screenings of award-winning films from festivals that had taken place earlier in the year, such as Cannes, Venice and Berlin. Meanwhile, the panel of judges this time included the likes of Trevor Howard, Ursula Andress, Michael York, Irene Papas, Peter Ustinov and director Michael Cacoyannis. The EAFCWC was careful to invite international stars whose attendance has always been used as a measure of the success of the festival. The inclusive festival screened films from Asia, Albania and the Soviet Union. Meanwhile, Egyptians were proud to see their local star, Mahmoud Morsi, star in a film of Dutch / Tunisian production, *Soleil des Hyènes* (*The Hyena's Sun*, Ridha Behi, 1977). But perhaps the most-welcome feature for Egyptian audiences was the chance, for the first time, to watch uncensored films. In contrast to the heavily-policed cinema shows that took place during the rest of the year, uncut and uncensored films were to be screened in the festival. As a result, Egyptians who were eager to get a peek at what their society had hitherto classed as 'taboo', flooded the festival auditoriums. A radical shift in social thought and practice took place around this time at Cairo festivals: on the one hand, Egyptians had a chance to see the way other societies interacted; on the other, they gained access to explicit scenes which, outside of the sanction of the festival, were denied to them. A new type of slang terminology was developed by festival audiences, to differentiate between a 'story' film (whose main point of attraction was the plot) versus a 'scenes' film (whose main point of attraction were scenes of a sexual nature).

Some of the films shown at the second festival in 1977 later became iconic, leaving a mark on their audience, such as the British film *The Romantic Englishwoman* (1975) directed by Joseph Losey, and *The Duellists* (1977) by Ridley Scott; meanwhile, films from the U.S. shown at the festival included *Carrie* (Brian De Palma, 1976) and *The Deep* (Peter Yates, 1977) – both book adaptations. Meanwhile, Robert Altman presented his film *3 Women* (1977) – although he was less popular amongst Egyptian audiences as his films are considered slow-paced by most Egyptians. The three Egyptian films screened were *Afwah wa araneb* (*Mouths and Rabbits*, Henri Barakat, 1977), *Wa thalithhum el shaitan* (*The Devil's Company*, Kamal El Sheikh, 1977) and *Ota ala nar* (*Cat on Fire*, Samir Seif, 1977).

Because of the success of the first festival, the second festival's films were screened not only in Cairo, but also in Alexandria. And the subsequent box-office success of these films exerted pressure on the festival's board of managers: the demand was dangerously close to overwhelming the supply. Eventually, this would lead to various other cities in Cairo hosting their own international film festivals.

Subsequent Cairo International Film Festivals

The most prominent feature of subsequent festivals was their screening of a higher number of quality films. Furthermore, at the 3rd Cairo International Festival, in 1978, Italian writer Alberto Moravia gave a lecture in the Italian Cultural Centre in Cairo. In addition, *Safar sang* (*The Journey of the Stone*, Masud Kimiai, Iran, 1978) was screened alongside new films from Yugoslavia, Czechoslovakia and Sri Lanka, as well as other countries joining the festival for the first time. But controversy was introduced with the advent of the fourth festival in 1979. The festival took place just months after Egypt and Israel had signed the Camp David peace treaty. In the wake of this treaty, Egypt, for the first time, was able to invite and welcome international film stars, who had previously been 'boycotted' due to their supposed support for, or affiliation with, Israel. And so, in 1979, the 4th Cairo International Film Festival welcomed big Hollywood names Elizabeth Taylor, Kirk Douglas and French singer Enrico Macias. The fourth festival soon became the topic of controversial debate: as a political tool, it could solidify ties between Egypt and Israel on the one hand, but on the other hand it ran the risk of alienating other countries in the region as a result.

Another controversial aspect of the fourth festival was that, unlike its predecessors, the festival was not immune to the Egyptian Board of Censors. Twelve movies were withdrawn from the festival due to the amount of scenes the board had cut out – including *La dentellière* (*The Lacemaker*, Switzerland / France / West Germany, Claude Goretta, 1977) and *Okupacija u 26 slika* (*Occupation in 26 Pictures*, Yugoslavia, Lordan Zafranović, 1978). The respective countries protested over the damage done to their films, citing the abuse of artistic integrity as unacceptable and a hindrance to the panel's ability to select winning titles. The festival responded by allowing an exclusive preview of uncensored films to a select few: reviewers, critics and panel judges; meanwhile, the crowds only saw censored versions. The festival still received criticism over this censorship and exclusion, as well as criticism over the poor organisation of Elizabeth Taylor's welcome party.

But the fifth festival was a far cry from redemption, in terms of hospitality, inclusion or luxury of any kind. Taking place in 1980, the 5th Cairo International Film Festival coincided with the assassination of Egyptian president Anwar Sadat. The Minister of Culture at the time, Mahmoud Abdel-Radwan Hamid (who later suspended Al Mallakh from his duty as festival director) proposed that the festival did not take place that year, in the wake of the national tragedy. However, the fifth festival did take place, albeit within a condensed timeframe and with minimal screenings – as a deliberate sign of mourning for the late president. Although the official competition was suspended that year, there was still an opportunity to show good films, including *Tre fratelli* (*Three Brothers*, Italy, Francesco Rosi, 1981), *Quartet* (UK / France, James Ivory, 1981), *La mort en direct* (*Death Watch*, France, Bertrand Tavernier, 1981), in addition to a number of films by John Huston, and a selection of Indian cinema.

As the years went by, the date of the festival shifted nearer and nearer to the end of the year. From the sixth festival in 1982 until today, the Cairo International Film Festival has taken place in the last week of November over ten days. The 1982 festival was also attended by stars, including Egyptian and Hollywood legend Omar Sharif, French actress Dominique Sanda and Italian director Mauro Bolognini (nine of whose films were screened). Six French films were shown, such as *Le retour de Martin Guerre* (*The Return of Martin Guerre,* Daniel Vigne, 1982), which was met with such positive reviews, that it led to an Egyptian adaptation by Tarik El Nahri under the title *Rage of the Father* (*El Ab El Tha'ir*, 1988). In addition, films from Finland were screened for the first time in Egypt. As always, neighbouring Arab countries had their own films presented at the festival, amongst which the most prominent that year was *L'Ombre de la Terre* (*Land's Shadow*, Taïeb Louhichi, 1982) from Tunisia. For the first time, there was a marathon of Egyptian films shown, 28 in total, including titles such as *Sawwaq Al utubis* (*The Bus Driver*, Atef El Tayeb, 1982) and *Al azraa wa al shaar al abyad* (*The Virgin and The White Hair*, Hussein Kamal, 1983).

Other films shown at the sixth festival included Costa-Gavras' *Hanna K.* (Israel / France, 1983), and Vanessa Redgrave's *The Fifth War* (UK, 1978). Both films had a political message and triggered much debate amongst critics, particularly *Hanna K.* Meanwhile, tension was just as rife behind the scenes: conflict broke out between the Minister of Culture and Kamal Al Mallakh, the president of the ACWC. Al Mallakh was eventually dismissed from his position, to be replaced by Kamal El Sheikh, who simultaneously took on the presidency of the ACWC and the directorship of the festival. El Sheikh was aided by other members of the ACWC and by other cinematographers in the running of the festival; but since the dismissal of Al Mallakh, the festival has never been independent of governmental rule. Since the sixth festival, the Ministry of Culture not only acted as main sponsor, but also had power to appoint (and dismiss) festival directors. The festival later was moved to the headquarters of the United Arab Actors (UAA). This was a foreshadowing of what would soon follow: Saad El Din Wahba, an influential member of the UAA, monopolised the running of the festival. Almost turning it into a private project, Wahba had sole power over whom to appoint, include or exclude. Wahba also worked adamantly on increasing festival profits, by screening as many uncensored films as possible so as to draw as large an audience as possible. He appointed a crew of film critics to run the ninth festival in 1985, only to replace them with his own people for the tenth festival; Suhair Abdel-Qader, one of Wahba's notable female appointees, was on the managerial panel from 1986 until 2012. The festival ran under the protective wings of the General Union of the Arts, which was headed by Wahba himself.

Wahba's continued efforts to promote the Cairo festival abroad gained it recognition from the FIAPF in 1986.[2] As such the festival managed to create an image and reputation separate from the Ministry of Culture and, from 1987, became a world-renowned festival. The festival welcomed reporters and critics from cities and organisations at the forefront of filmmaking; the artistic and ceremonial themes and aspects of the festival were renewed yearly. Meanwhile, the quality of festival publications improved dramatically, and included catalogues and pamphlets. Moreover, a new category, Children's Films, was introduced to the festival, the popularity of which later led to the establishment of the first Children's Cinema Festival in 1991.

The International Film Festival in Cairo continued to grow in size and popularity. By the late eighties, more countries and films participated than ever before; the panel of judges continued to host prominent figures from the international cinema scene; world-renowned stars and intellectuals continued to grace the festival with their presence. In 1989, the festival welcomed two major Egyptian figures, actor Omar Sharif and author Naguib Mahfouz, winner of the Nobel Peace Prize for Literature earlier in the year. In the same year, and for the first time since 1986, the festival did not run a marathon of Egyptian films, and has not done so since. Instead, in 1989 the festival paid tribute to Syrian and Indian cinemas. In spite of the Iraqi invasion of Kuwait and the subsequent war in the nearby region, the festival went ahead. Not completely blind to political turmoil, the festival hosted talks on the connections between politics and cinema, one of which was a lecture on the effects of the 'pro-strike' legacy on filmmaking in Eastern Europe.

The 1990s heralded a golden age of festival success for Cairo, now a hotspot in the Middle East for all things cinematic. Still under the governance of Wahba, the festival grew to cement relationships with various artists unions, and with the press. In 1992, a large number of actors were welcomed and presented with awards, including Layla

Murad, Magda, Yahya Haqqi and British actor Christopher Lee. The subsequent annual festivals continued to grow in success, climaxing in 1996. Besides marking the centenary of the birth of cinema, 1996 marked two local celebrations for Cairo: the Festival's 20th anniversary, and the election of Cairo as Cultural Capital of the Arab World.

However, Sa'ad El Din Wahba resigned from his post in 1997,[3] and the Ministry of Culture stepped in once more to seize the reins. In addition to sponsoring the festival, the Ministry also appointed Hussein Fahmy as director of the festival. A very popular actor in Egypt, Hussein Fahmy provided a smooth transition. In fact, little appeared different since Wahba's departure: the managerial team aiding Fahmy was more or less Wahba's own crew. Although the festival now bore the logo of the government as opposed to the United Arab Actors, it was run along the same lines, and included various competing categories, lectures, marathons, and there was no decline in the number of participating films or countries. In fact, a new competing category was included for film adaptations of novels by Naguib Mahfouz in 1998. That same year, local and foreign talent within the world of cinema and literature, was warmly welcomed and awarded prizes. Actors Christopher Lee, John Malkovich and Gina Lollobrigida, as well as Syrian-American producer Moustapha Akkad, were amongst the various award-winners that year.

The year 1999 saw the genre of comedy as the main attraction. The usual conundrum of choosing an appropriate film for the opening night was missing from the 1999 festival: the panel unanimously elected *Analyse This* (U.S., Harold Ramis, 1999). The festival that year, besides screening the newest comedy films, also honoured and awarded old and contemporary comedians from Egypt and across the globe. It was a year of mirth, lights, cameras and action – a successful run for Hussein Fahmy, in his second year as festival director.

By 2001, however, Fahmy faced a crisis: he was starting to run low on festival funds. While Fahmy continued to spend as much as before to ensure the festival was run according to the highest standards, there was a decline in interest and attendance amongst the Egyptian audience. The festival's sanctioned screening of nudity, sex and other taboos, no longer held an allure; the internet allowed free access to all that and more. Young Egyptians, who may have felt liberated in front of a screen at the festival, felt even more liberated and in control in front of a computer screen. Internet cafés were spreading fast all over Cairo, providing even the poorest with access to the World Wide Web – for a price that was much cheaper than a ticket to the International Film Festival. As for the cinema lovers and those thirsting for an inter-cultural and international exposure or education, their numbers were simply not large enough to sustain the festival's profits. Swiftly, the festival's audience dwindled, and in 2002, the festival allowed anyone who carried a festival membership card access to all its screenings in a desperate attempt to attract an audience. This not being enough, the festival withdrew its screenings from the various established cinema screens scattered across the capital and confined its few remaining films within the walls of the Cairo Opera House and a few new cinemas nearby. Fahmy was replaced by a new festival director in 2002, Sherif El Shubashy, a journalist for the prestigious national newspaper *Al Ahram*. A passionate film critic, El Shubashy embarked on what seemed like a one-man campaign to revive the festival. He campaigned for funding from various cultural institutes and unions, as well as from film festivals both abroad and closer to home. He was equally active behind the scenes as he was on set, regularly participating in opening and closing ceremonies, at award-givings and all other aspects of the festival. And yet, his name was not as widely circulated as that of his predecessor; he lacked the celebrity status of actor Fahmy. In fact, in 2006, the famous actor Omar Sharif was named 'honorary director' of the festival – perhaps in another attempt to encourage audience attendance. In the same year, El Shubashy was replaced by another popular and long-standing Egyptian actor, Ezzat Abu-Auf, who served as festival director until 2012.

In recent years, the festival has hosted competitions in three categories: International Film, Arabic Film and Digital Film. While the Naguib Mahfouz Adaptation competition is no longer running, entries still compete for staples such as Best Film (the Golden Pyramid Award), the Judges' Favourite (Silver Pyramid Award), Best Actress, Best Actor, Best Director, Best Script, Best Newcomer, Best Artistic Innovation, Best Arab Film – with the winning prize for the latter coming close to U.S.$116,000.

Scene II: International & Mediterranean Film Festivals in Alexandria

It was common practice to showcase films from the Cairo festival elsewhere after 1977, particularly in Alexandria. On such occasions, ticket sales increased in number – and in price. Films with scenes of nudity, such as the Dutch-produced *Het Begin* (*The Beginning*, Orlow Seunke, 1981), were shown repeatedly in an attempt to generate higher profits. But after the Cairo festival acquired A-list status in 1986, FIAPF did not approve of the screenings of Cairo Festival films outside of the capital and they had to be discontinued.

The Cairo festival was as much if not more a commercial project as an artistic endeavour; and it generated big profits for its management.

Meanwhile, though, it also provided its audiences – or, consumers – with goods in the shape of the unfamiliar, the uncensored and the taboo. This was an enticement for Egyptians living outside and within the cities of Cairo and Alexandra. Young Egyptians from the rural areas flocked into the cities at the time of the festival, bringing their yearly savings to spend on watching the uncensored films. All seemed eager to embrace the rare chance to see what was, at all other times, forbidden. It did not take long for the ACWC to decide that it was time to put on a separate, fully-fledged festival in Alexandria – a project supported both by the local governorate in Alexandria and the Ministry of Culture in Cairo.

And so the 1st Alexandria Film Festival was hosted in the old San Stefano Hotel in 1979. From the outset, it was clear that this festival had a flavour all of its own, distinct from that of the Cairo festival. Many local societies collaborated in the running of the Alexandria festival, including the Seventh Art Society (founded 1977), a specifically Alexandrian film appreciation society, which took charge of the festival's publications. Meanwhile, the Tourism Organisation in Alexandria played an active role in providing venues for film screenings and other festival ceremonies. The Alexandria festival seemed, from the outset, to demand a higher spending budget. Festival management and crew required lodgings at the hotels where the festival was hosted, which added to its spending. Alexandrian hotels competed for the privilege of hosting the festival, offering the ACWC and festival affiliates special deals and coveting the publicity they would gain from accommodating international film stars. During the festival, hotel lobbies would be swarmed by cameras from various broadcasting channels – a publicity opportunity not to be missed. The Alexandria Sheraton was particularly successful at hosting the festival, and as a result, its reputation and earnings skyrocketed at the time.

While hotels lent the festival a degree of glitz and glamour, and vice versa, things did not go smoothly for long. Providing full room and board to festival affiliates and guests proved a costly and tricky task. Boarders demanded the fullest attention and highest-quality services at every turn, making it harder and costlier for the ACWC to effectively fund and run all aspects of the festival with equal attention. Controversially, many of the local festival affiliates did not show an interest in attending screenings of foreign films, preferring instead to preview Egyptian films (which were available at the festival prior to their commercial release date). In contrast, participating actors from home and abroad tended to attend most screenings and other lectures and ceremonies taking place throughout the festival.

As for the local Alexandrian crowds, they started applying the 'scene versus story' value-judgements on festival films, as did their Cairo counterparts. Going to the festival became a social pastime rather than an artistic pursuit – a chance for crowds to access the culturally taboo within the legitimate space of the festival. It became a prevalent pattern amongst the audience to attend more than one screening of the same film in one night, especially if it contained any nudity or sexual scenes. Loud and rowdy young Egyptians were magically silenced when the much-anticipated scene came on screen; they held their breath for the next explicit delight. It was as if the Alexandria festival, like the Cairo festival before it, was a pressure-release valve, providing Egyptians with an outlet for sexual frustration.

It was within this social background, then that the 1st first International Film Festival came to Alexandria in the summer of 1979, running from 16 to 22 June. The international scope of the festival, however, was focused purely on countries along the Mediterranean. The festival screened a marathon of French films, including six films new at the time, including *La Femme qui pleure* (*The Crying Woman*, Jacques Doillon, 1979), *Coup de tête* (*Hot Head*, Jean-Jacques Annaud, 1979) and *L'Amour en fuite* (*Love on the Run*, François Truffaut, 1979), and also screen a number of other films by François Truffaut. A number of Italian films were shown, including five from director Vittorio De Sica. In addition, the festival included films from Spain, Yugoslavia, Turkey and Greece. Meanwhile, the panel of judges, headed by Italian film critic Giovanni Grazzini, included French critic Claude-Michel Cluny, Spanish writer Miguel Angel Diaz, Greek director Kostas Ferris and Egyptian director Kamal El Sheikh.

In addition to the films competing in the central Mediterranean category, the festival screened seven Egyptian films, under the category 'Egyptian Nights'. These included, amongst other titles, the films *Darbet shams* (*Sunstroke*, 1978) by Mohamed Khan, *La yazal El tahkik mustamirran* (*Until Proven Otherwise*, 1979) by Ashraf Fahmy, *El Bo'asa* (*The Wretched*, 1978) by Atef Salem (an adaptation of Victor Hugo's *Les Misérables*, set against the backdrop of the Egypt-Israel war) and *Khayfa min shay'in ma* (*Somewhat Scared of Something*, 1979) by Yehia El Elmy. Meanwhile, the festival management team was headed by Kamal El Malakh as President, with Mohammed El Dessouki as Deputy-Director, Hassan Abdel-Rassoul as Press Coordinator, Ahmed Al Hadari as Administrative Director (mudir) and Fawzi Sulaiman as General Secretary.

That year, the festival seemed to strike a good balance between professionalism, camaraderie and leisure. Festival leaders, judges and associates attended screenings, lectures and debates during the day, and whiled away the night at festival concerts or at debating circles.

The prevalent atmosphere of warmth and cheer enveloping the festival members seemed to be a feature unique to the Alexandria festival, and a missing ingredient from the event in Cairo. This atmosphere of warmth and camaraderie continued to surround competitors as they waited for winners to be announced. As the participating nations left for their home-countries, carrying back trophies or fond memories, they were sorry to bid goodbye to Alexandria, and hoped they would reunite again on its shores the following year.

But they did not reunite the following year, or the year after. It was not until September 1982 that the festival reconvened. The festival opened with a screening of Youssef Chahine's *Hadduta misriya* (*An Egyptian Story*, 1982). According to festival publications dating from the time, there were a large number of companies and individuals acting as sponsors, contributing towards the cost of running the festival and towards the monetary awards presented to competition winners. That year, the festival screened films from Spain, Turkey, Morocco and Yugoslavia, amongst other Mediterranean countries. And, once again, France was an integral participant in the festival as it had been in 1979, bringing a plethora of new films to the festival screens, including Pierre Lary's *La Revanche* (*The Revenge*, France, 1981, Henri Verneuil's *I... comme Icare* (*I as in Icarus*, France, 1979) and Michel Deville's *Eaux profondes* (France, 1981). And, as was the case in 1979, the 1982 festival screened a collection of new Egyptian films, hot from the reel. This year, more so than in 1979, the films proved very popular with their audience, and included, amongst other titles, *Al tawous* (*The Peacock*, Kamal El Sheikh, 1982), *Al azraa wa al shaar al abyad* (*The Virgin and The White Hair*, Hussein Kamal, 1983) and *Arzaq ya Dunya!* (*Our livelihoods, O World!*, 1982, Nader Galal).

The festival continued to flourish over the following years. Sixteen Egyptian films were showcased in the festival's third year, between 5 and 11 September 1983, which brought much profit – and publicity – to the festival that year. The popularity of Egyptian films at the festival had grown by the festival's fourth year. In 1984, the festival screened 19 Egyptian films, many of which received high critical acclaim, as well as festival awards. A particularly successful time for Egyptian cinema, the fourth festival still included films from across the Mediterranean. France, as fundamental a participant as ever, brought many films to the scene, including titles by Bertrand Tavernier and Francis Veber. Meanwhile, 1984 marked Lebanon's participation in the Alexandria International Film Festival for the first time.

The festival's continued success over the years grew alongside the popularity of Kamal Al Mallakh, president of the ACWC and festival director. As a journalist for the prestigious national newspaper *Al*

Ahram, Al Mallakh had a strong reputation amongst Egypt's literary circles. A charismatic, level-headed man, and respected widely, Al Mallakh seemed to be the perfect figure to preside over the Cairo and Alexandria festivals. But the Minister of Culture at the time, Mohammed Abdel-Hamid Radwan, thought otherwise. Soon, the behind-the-scenes tension between Al Mallakh and Radwan escalated to new heights, resulting in Al Mallakh's suspension from his position at *Al Ahram*. Stripped of his famous 'last page' column in *Al Ahram*, Al Mallakh's voice would no longer reach Egypt's most influential institutions. Not stopping there, Radwan stripped Al Mallakh from his duties as President of the EAFCWC and ACWC and as Director of the Cairo and Alexandria festivals. The running of the Cairo festival was delegated to Sa'ad El Din Wahba, and, after a period of confusion, Fomil Labib was appointed the new president of ACWC.

The Alexandria festival ceased to run altogether, for several years, until Ahmed El Hadary took charge in 1988. That year, the festival was officially sanctioned by the new Minister of Culture Faruq Husni and for the first time welcomed films from beyond the Mediterranean. To accentuate this new inclusion, the festival opened with a screening of the British film, *Cry Freedom* (Richard Attenborough, 1987). By 1989, the festival opened with an Egyptian production, *El Aragoz* (*The Clown*, 1989) by Hani Lashin. That same year saw the screening of *La Mémoire Tatouée* (*Tattooed Memory*, France / Tunisia, Ridha Behi, 1988) based on the 1971 novel by Moroccan Abdelkebir Khatibi, and some key French films, including A *Man in Love* (*Un homme amoureux*, 1987) by Diane Kurys, a film evolving from the experience of making another film about the life of Italian author Cesare Pavese. Greek films seemed to be very popular with Egyptian audiences, occupying a position second only to Egyptian films. Egyptian films seemed to dominate the festival screens, as well as being the most popular with local audience – which made the festivals of 1988 and 1989 appear to be events for 'national' films with a handful of 'international' titles scattered in between.

With the departure of Kamal Al Mallakh, however, the Association entered a vulnerable phase, being led by a series of men who, in comparison to Al Mallakh, lacked passion and momentum. Al Mallakh's successor required support from a television reporter in an attempt to secure and conduct an interview with the Mayor of Alexandria – a task Al Mallakh would have accomplished without external assistance. Ironically, off stage, Al Mallakh's successor did not seem to be a fan of delegation; he significantly reduced the number of festival personnel, appearing to single-handedly run the festival for over ten years. Nonetheless, Al Mallakh was commemorated by the creation of an award in his name, the

Al Mallakh Award, for Best Debut Feature. The Ministry of Media added to the festival's repertoire a number of awards exclusively granted to Egyptian films. The focus on Egyptian films may have been part of a larger attempt to remedy the restlessness caused by Al Mallakh's departure. Once again, in 1989, Egyptian cinema enjoyed the limelight, with the festival screening a marathon of eleven films. The same year marked the first round of Takrim, or Homage to actors, directors or filmmakers for a particular achievement. Amongst those who were given special mention on stage were director Salah Abu Seif, who had won the National Recognition award that same year, and Kamal El Shennawi, a prominent Egyptian actor. The tradition of Takrim became a solid custom in all years to come, in both international and national film festivals, in Alexandria and other cities. And, as before the departure of Al Mallakh, the festival continued to screen films from around the Mediterranean. Algeria, a newcomer in 1989, participated in the festival with two films, *Louss, warda Al rimal* (*Rose of the Desert*, 1989) by Mohamed Rachid Benhadj, and *El kalaa* by Mohammed Chouikh (*The Citadel*, 1988). It seemed that every year the festival had a different mix of participating Arab countries than that of the year before – almost as if these countries took turns to step in and out of the limelight. Meanwhile, countries like France, Italy and Greece seemed a staple on the Alexandrian Mediterranean Festival programme.

In 1991, the festival once more increased the variety of its menu to serve films from beyond the Mediterranean. Films from Britain, Austria and the United States were included in the 1991 repertoire. In 1992, a Hungarian film was screened on Opening Night: Édes Emma, drága Böbe - vázlatok, aktok (*Sweet Emma, Dear Bobe*) directed by István Szabó. The 1992 festival was labelled as the 8th Alexandria International Film Festival: while a marathon of Egyptian films was screened, the festival included works from Argentina, China, Germany, India, Poland and the U.S. The festival still had a significant number of Mediterranean participants and also attracted prominent filmmakers and stars from Cairo who were particularly eager to attend. It was as if the scope and success of the Cairo festival had flooded onto Alexandrian shores that year, a ripple effect, with the Cairo festival director, Sa'ad El Din Wahba at the centre. In 1993, the Alexandria festival welcomed respected literary figures into its circle, and delegated prominent positions to notable Egyptians. Dr Abdel-Qader El Qitt, author and writer, headed the judges' panel for the Egyptian films category. The panel judging international entries was headed by director Salah Abu-Seif. Meanwhile, notable Egyptian artists to receive awards and Takrim that year included actresses Nadia Lutfi and Magda and director Youssef Chahine.

In the following years, little changed in the way the Alexandria festival was organised and run. As ever, there was an effort on the part of the festival management to include and screen as many films as possible, from as many countries as possible, regardless of genre. But clashes continued behind the scenes, between festival management and festival guests; critics and journalists, in particular, vied for free room and board. Despite the festival's keen attempts to include a wide selection of participants, some critiqued its lack of vision and innovation. This critique went hand-in-hand with a tendency for its guests to view the festival, not as a time for serious contemplation on art, but as an excuse to escape. Spending a week in a glamorous hotel and on the beeches of Alexandria, while an unavoidable aspect of the Alexandria festival experience, was the very same feature that threatened its credibility in some circles. Nonetheless, the festival continued to attract films from all over the world and, in 1996, included notable entries from Japan, Estonia, Azerbaijan and the Netherlands.

In 1998, film critic Rauf Tawfik was appointed new Festival Director. The pace and dynamics of the festival changed, clashes subsided and the festival seemed to run in a calmer manner than before. That year, the festival put on a special celebration to celebrate the birthday of the Spanish poet García Lorca a century earlier. Meanwhile, mainly Egyptian artists were presented with awards in 1999, including actors Mahmoud Yassine and Nelly and director Said Marzouk. That same year, another president was appointed to run the festival, Mohammed Saleh. Saleh managed to significantly improve the festival's financial situation, making it possible to publish good quality festival literature that year. And from then on, the festival would continue to have a new director each year. Iris Nazmi, Mohammed Kamel El Qalyobi and screenwriter Mamdouh El Leithy all served as festival directors at different times. El Leithy, during his time as President of the ACWC and EAFCWC, ran the festival more than once. Across the years, the festival's focus has tended to shift back and forth, from specifically focusing on Mediterranean films, to focusing on international cinema. But by 2008, the festival had returned to its Mediterranean legacy and, in 2009, celebrated its 25th Anniversary.

Scene III: International Film Festivals in Egypt

Under Sa'ad El Din Wahba's leadership, the immense success and popularity of the Cairo Film Festival paved the way for other Egyptian cities to run their own film festivals. The Ministry of Culture oversaw a number of smaller societies and councils organising both national and international festivals, including the International Film Festival for Children (www.ciffc.org) and the Ismailia National Festival for Documentaries and Short Films (www.ismailiafilmfest.com). The Ismailia festival was born out of an attempt to rejuvenate a smaller event that which the National Cinema Centre put on annually to screen and celebrate contemporary documentaries. In addition, Cairo has been hosting the Egyptian National Film Festival since the founding of the ACWC and EAFCWC. In those early years, the Ministry of Culture would have been better labelled as the Ministry of Festivals: its members seemed as keen on the behind-the-scenes organisational aspects of running a festival, as they were in garnering a media-presence; as eager to deliver awards as to receive awards for their dedication to running the festival. Since its beginnings, the Ismailia festival has been overseen by members of the Ministry of Culture. One member in particular was in position from 1987 up to the Revolution in January 2011.

As for the International Film Festival for Children (IFFC), Sa'ad El Din Wahba took on ownership and direction for the first six years of its running. After that Fawzy Fahmy was appointed festival director. A member of the Ministry of Culture, Fahmy holds a significant number of honorary and literary titles, and has overseen the running of the festival for over 15 years.

The IFFC place for the first time in 1991, and was organised by the same crew who oversaw the running of the Cairo festival. At that point, the Cairo festival was run from the headquarters of the United Arab Artists, headed by the ever-present Wahba. The first IFFC took place shortly after the Cairo festival that year, and in the years to come, it became customary to hold the IFFC at the beginning of March, which coincided with the start of the second school term. At the time, it was seen as strange that Egypt would put on a festival dedicated to children's films since the country itself had never produced a single film for children. But the festival director and crew dismissed such remarks, seeing them as offensive and contradictory to the vision of the festival, which was about the act of putting together a child-oriented film event – regardless of where the films themselves came from. In what may have been an attempt to deflect criticism on Egypt's passivity on children's film-production, each festival's publications chronicled activities and events from the previous year, foregrounding the Minister of Culture and the Festival Director, and their roles as activists and advocates for children's cinema.

The IFFC includes two main competition categories: one for films (animation or live-action), and one for short films. Egypt is a prominent participant in the second category, due to the large number of animated shorts produced for local television channels. There are two different judges' panels, each boasting judges from Egypt and other parts of the world. The festival regularly hosts key-speakers, although Egyptian speakers tend to be associated with children's literature and culture rather than children's film. The year 2010 hosted a particularly impressive list of judges, guests and screenings, with the festival's opening ceremony that year taking place in the prestigious Cairo Opera House, and various other screenings being shown in smaller sister-theatres. The festival regularly includes an international judges' panel composed of children. It also usually includes a themed marathon, as well as a spotlight on a particular theme or work. But things came to a halt in the wake of the 2011 Revolution, with no festival taking place that year. In 2012, the IFFC ran once more, but under the supervision of an inexperienced crew. This led to a decline in the number of children attending the festival, which, sadly, led to the festival not taking place in March 2013.

The Ismailia Documentary and Short Film Festival (IDSFF), meanwhile, took place for the first time in 1992, in the small town of Ismailia on the banks of the Suez Canal. The festival was run jointly on behalf of the local Ismailia Council and the Department of Cultural Development, part of the larger Ministry of Culture in Cairo. The festival was created in response to the growing popularity (and proximity) of the Alexandria festival; the festival crew from nearby Alexandria would relocate after their festival to Ismailia and start setting up for that event. At first, festival personnel stayed in hotels, but later on, they were to be hosted by locals. During its first five years the festival was supervised by Samir Gharib, head of the Department of Cultural Development. Later, Ali Abu Shadi took over directorship of the festival for over 15 years, during which time he also oversaw the smaller Egyptian Film Festival, and juggled various other titles and duties within the Ministry. The IDSFF followed more or less the same approach as the other festivals and produced its own literature yearly, including an annual catalogue. In its publications, the festival stated that its goal was to encourage innovation within the field of documentary filmmaking and short filmmaking. And so, for over twenty years, the festival recognised the achievement of various documentary filmmakers, including Qais Al Zubaidi from Iraq, Fouad El Tuhami from Egypt and various others. And as with other festivals, there was a main competition, and judges' panels, and awards. The festival was over-flown with documentaries, animated films of varying lengths from Egypt and various parts of the globe. It continued to run until 1995, before resuming in 2001, when Amir El Umri took over directorship. In 2013, screenwriter Ali Hafzi became Festival Director. The time of year when the festival takes place regularly varies from September to June. The IDSFF continues to regularly include monetary awards reaching up to U.S.$30,000, granted by the Ministry of Culture.

Conclusion

Egypt has become ripe with festivals, with the biggest beneficiaries, perhaps, being those who supervise them. On the one hand, the various festivals are organised by the usual suspects, who take turns circulating through panels, ceremonies and various festival activities. On the other hand, Egyptian cinema began to emerge as a league of its own, particularly with the setting up of the Cairo National Festival for Egyptian Cinema (www.cdf.gov.eg/Arabic/cinema/index_cinema. htm) in 1994, under the directorship of Samir Gharib (followed by Ali Abu Shadi). The Egyptian National Film Festival was a glamorous outlet to showcase the activities and dedication of the ACWC and EAFCWC, through the competitions, funds, publications and monetary awards the societies granted exclusively to competitors in this festival. The festival states that its main goal is to support the growth and development of Egyptian cinema, as part of a larger cultural development project, by supporting high-quality film production. And yet, in the tenth year of the festival, the director admitted that Egyptian cinema has undergone a noticeable decline in the quality and quantity of feature film production. Nonetheless, the festival continues to run, despite the Minister of Culture's disapproval in 2010. Like the IFCC festival, the Egyptian National Film Festival came to a halt with the Revolution of January 2011. For these festivals there was no clear procedure at the time for selecting entries for the main competition category. Most films produced in the previous year were entered into the competition, without much prior evaluation or critique – perhaps due to that decline in the quality of films mentioned above. Most recent entries were flimsy and lightweight comedies that somehow crept into the competition. Ironically, the festival's panel of judges was composed of authors and literary critics – who possessed little or no knowledge of films – and included the likes of Abdel-Qader El Qitt, Mahmoud Amin El Alim, Bahaa'Taher, Ahmed Abdel Mati Hegazi, El Sayid Yassin. It is hard to tell whether those literary judges were aided in any capacity by filmmakers in making their decisions regarding awards. In any case, the inclusion of literary rather than film specialists did not prove popular, and, due to complaints, was discontinued. Perhaps the exclusion of filmmakers from the judge's panel is in itself a reflection of the disregard with which the festival management was starting to view its own festival. Arguably, the festival supervisors' disregard for quality could be seen in the number of lightweight films included in the main festival competition.

Egypt has a varied and diverse range of film festivals. Cairo,

Alexandria and Ismailia are not the only cities to host such events. New festivals are springing up and dying every year. In 2012, Luxor hosted its African Film Festival for the first time, despite Egypt experiencing a difficult time, both economically and politically. With continued effort and dedication, festivals like this one will continue to run successfully, taking their information and drawing lessons from the glamorous or more modest film festivals that have taken place in Egypt since the birth of cinema.

Notes

1   [Editor's note: This famous 1974 song by Dalida tells about Gigi (Giuseppe), a Neapolitan musician who is universally loved by the people who always cheer when he appears ('But when Gigi appears / The hurrahs and the cheers / Come from the crowd'). As at Gigi's appearance, Kassem suggests, the crowds flooding into cinemas in Cairo cheer the arrival of new films.]

2   [Editor's note: FIAPF's 'A' Category accreditation is issued sparingly and is bestowed only on a handful of film festivals around the world. The CIFF is the only festival in the region of the Middle East and North Africa to be awarded such accreditation. Having A-listing from FIAPF, however, is considered a double-edged sword: on the one hand, it spells prestige, while on the other hand, many other festivals treat it disrespectfully. It also comes along with a number of regulatory requirements and restrictions that significantly restrict the flexibility of the festival's management.]

3   [Editor's note: Wahba passed away in 1997. His name appears in various transliterations, such as Saad Eldin Wahba, Sa'ad Eddein Wahba and Sa'ad al Dain Wahba. He is celebrated as one of Egypt's prominent intellectuals (http://www.sis.gov.eg/En/Templates/Articles/tmpArticles.aspx?ArtID=1288).]

Egyptian Film Festivals

Est.	Name	Date	Website	Location	Specialisation
-	Festival of the Film Society for Egyptian Cinema	-	-	-	National competition organized by the Film Society for Egyptian Cinema; 39th edition in 2013
-	National Festival for Egyptian Cinema	17th edition in 2013	-	Cairo	National competition organized by the Cultural Development Fund; Competition for Egyptian feature, short and animation films;
1976	Cairo International Film Festival	November-December	http://www.ciff.org.eg/	Cairo	A-Category film festival; Competition in three categories: official international competition, in addition to Arabic and digital films competitions – Golden Pyramid-award
1979	Alexandria International Film Festival	September-October	-	Alexandria	Competition only for feature films from Mediterranean countries; Additional screenings organized for Panorama of World Cinema

Est.	Name	Date	Website	Location	Specialisation
1991	Cairo International Film Festival for Children	March	http://www.ciffc.org/	Cairo	Competition in three categories: feature films, short and documentary films, animation
1991	Ismailiyya International Film Festival for Documentaries and Shorts	June	http://www.ismailiafilmfest.com/	smailia	Competition in four categories for long and short documentaries, short fiction films and animation
2001	Independent Short Film Festival	October	http://www.goethe.de/ins/eg/kai/acv/flm/2012/de9469662v.htm	Cairo	Not organized in 2013; Competition for short and documentary films
2004	Panorama of the European Film	October-November	http://www.misrinternationalfilms.com/about-panorama	Cairo	Organized by Misr International Film
2008	Cairo International Women's Film Festival	November	http://www.cairowomenfilmfest.com/	Cairo	Focuses on women filmmakers from around the world, including a competition for "Best Film"

2008	Cairo Human Rights Film Festival	December	http://www.cairofilm.org/filmfestival.html	Cairo	Stopped activities since 2011
2009	Arab Shorts	-	www.arabshorts.net	Cairo	Stopped activities since
2011 but kept online database of 2012	Cinemobile Film Festival	September	http://www.cinemobilefilm.com/	Online	Official competition for short films shot with smartphone or tablet
2012	Luxor African Film Festival	February-March	http://www.luxorafricanfilmfestival.com/	Luxor	Competition for African feature and short films – Golden Mask of Tutanchamon-award for each section
2012	Luxor Egyptian and European Film Festival	September	http://www.luxorflmfest.com/en/	Luxor	Competition for feature and short fiction films – Gold Djed-award

Compiled by Koen Van Eynde
Listing is representative, not exhaustive

Damascus and Beirut, or Why Arab Film Festivals Go On and Offline[1]

Stefanie Van de Peer

The pasts and presents of Lebanon and Syria are riddled with political oppression, civil war, religious tensions and the burdens of the on-going state of war with neighbouring Israel. These conditions have had a defining influence on film culture in the two countries, with impacts on production, distribution and exhibition. In this chapter, I look in some detail at how – in spite of these difficult circumstances – both Lebanon and Syria have retained healthy film production rates, but have suffered when it comes to distribution and exhibition of their respective, qualitatively impressive outputs. First, I trace the growth and demise of the larger national film festivals, both materially and online, before offering as a comparison a brief account of the setbacks and successes of the smaller festivals that exist in their shadows.

The Damascus Film Festivals

The first Damascus Film Festival (DFF) (www.damascusfest.com) took place officially in 1979, and was organised by Syrian film director Muhammad Shahin in conjunction with the National Film Organisation (NFO), the government body responsible for film production and censorship. The NFO itself, was established in 1963 as an independent arm of the Ministry of Culture. It adhered systematically to the prevailing ideological mind-set of the ruling Ba'ath Party, which came to power after a coup d'état in 1963 and has been in charge ever since.

Interestingly, the start date of this festival is contested. The festival's website has it beginning in 1979, however, various other sources claim either 1968 (*Caméra Arabe*, Férid Boughedir, 1987) or 1972 (Cousins 2008: 374). The political unrest during the late 1960s and early 1970s, with Ba'ath seizing power and the infighting among its ranks, has obviously severely influenced the historiography of the festival. And it is also possible that other, independently organised film festivals took place in Damascus, bearing the title Damascus Film Festival, yet without being connected to the festival run by the NFO.

The NFO has been, since its inception, a site of hegemony, and its role within the film industry in Syria has been reshaped over the decades to accord with the vision of the person at the helm. According to Rasha Salti, the directorship of Hamid Merei in the 1970s heralded an important new direction in state-funded film production. Under his stewardship filmmakers such as Nabil Maleh were allowed enough freedom to create films like *Al Fahd* (*The Leopard*, 1972). When Marwan Haddad took over in the 1990s things changed, both politically and artistically. And later, Mohamad Al Ahmad's on-going tenure has proven to also be very significant (Salti 2013). A 2012 newspaper article covering the cancellation of that year's DFF, reported:

> Many filmmakers accuse the top echelons of the organization, particularly its general director, Mohammad Al Ahmad, 'of corruption and favoritism – awarding close friends with opportunities and grants, while ignoring others'. Each year, these arguments reach a crescendo as the Damascus Film Festival approaches. This year, however, the festival has been cancelled because of the crisis in the country. (Zarzar)

Miriam Cooke relates a scenario whereby the

> NFO was the only institution that could commission the production of films. Since every stage in the production and direction was submitted to the Censor Board, the NFO knew everything about the films it owned and distributed. The NFO might commission a film but then disable its completion by denying sufficient funding and forbidding filmmakers to seek outside sponsorship. This way of dealing with film production has earned the NFO the title maqbarat al-aflam wa al-sinima'iyin, or the graveyard of cinema and filmmakers. (Cooke: 115)

In any case, according to the state-approved historical discourse, the NFO is the state body that has run DFF since 1979, thereby implying continuity in its political and artistic positioning. The film festival takes place biennially in November, alternating with the Carthage Film Festival in Tunisia (www.jccarthage.com) which speaks to the same audience. In 1968, however, long before its ostensible inauguration, at least some form of DFF was already the nexus of filmmaking in the Arab world and acted as the place where the so-called 'New Arab Cinema' first saw the light of day. Until 1999, the festival's competition explicitly focused on films from Arab countries, Latin America and Asia – that is, on Third Cinema – but has, since 2001, taken on a decidedly international focus.

In the 1960s and 1970s, Damascus acted as a space where dissident artists came together, in spite of prevalent censorship and cultural oppression, precisely because the most respected filmmakers were from there. It is within these paradoxical circumstances that the festival's impact must be understood. Rasha Salti points out in the Introduction to her book *Insights into Syrian Cinema* (2006) that Syrian cinema remains a space of paradoxes: harsh censorship does not seem to prevent the most artistically challenging and well-crafted films from being made in Syria. Whether or not they are then screened (in Syria itself, or elsewhere) is an entirely different matter.

This scenario was most controversially the case with *Al Kompars* (*The Extras*, Nabil Maleh 1993), which, like all Maleh's previous films, was funded by the NFO. It deals with a love affair between two poor, young people who work as extras at a local theatre after their long shifts in a gas station and sewing factory. A friend lends them his apartment for two hours as they are unable to meet anywhere but in public otherwise. These two hours are filmed with incredible intensity and delicacy and lead to a devastating denouement. The film, though initially sponsored by the NFO, was later banned by that same institution, even as it screened in France at the Montpellier Film Festival (MFF) (www.cinemed.tm.fr). Maleh's film *The Leopard*, on the other hand, screened in Syrian cinemas and festivals, including the DFF Festival, to great acclaim, and he has been called a master of cinema because of it. To celebrate his career and classic films, in 1999 MFF dedicated a retrospective to Maleh, screening his earlier films from the 1970s, such as *Flash* (1977), *Fragments* (1979) and *Rijalun tahta ash-shams* (*Men under the Sun*, 1970).

Given this unpredictability within the NFO as to who is in or out of grace at a particular moment, it is not so surprising to see the odd mix of films on DFF's programme. So, with Turkey as the guest country in 2010, a retrospective of eight Turkish films was screened (among which were three films by Nuri Bilge Ceylan: *Uzak* (*Distant*, 2002), *Iklimer* (*Climates*, 2006) and *Üç Maymun* (*Three Monkeys*, 2008)) and guest actress Türkan Şoray made a special appearance. These films appeared alongside *Somewhere* (Sofia Coppola, U.S., 2010) and *Up* (Peter Docter, U.S., 2009).

The festival clearly has a great reputation for screening films that have travelled the festival circuit extensively and received acclaim worldwide; films like *Lung Bunmi Raluek Chat* (*Uncle Boonmee Who Can Recall his Past Lives*, Weerasethakul, Thailand, 2010). Nevertheless, its political affiliations are undeniably and intricately linked with the Syrian Ba'ath government and, accordingly, it reflects contemporary political affiliations (with Turkey) and plays its ambassadorial role very well: the Opening Ceremony in 2010 included a Parade of Respect dedicated to nine Turks who had lost their lives at the Gaza Flotilla Raid in May 2010. This special, self-appointed ambassadorial role, however, failed with the next edition. In 2011, it was announced that the festival for 2012 would go ahead under the special patronage of Bashar Al Assad in a theatre bearing his name. This caused stars and directors from across the Arab world to criticise the festival; the Arab Revolutions in Egypt and Tunisia had encouraged many to oppose oppressive regimes such as Al Assad's, and to affiliate themselves instead with 'the people'. Even though Egyptian stars have historically been the most popular at DFF, it was announced that they would boycott the festival in solidarity with the Syrian people 'who have been suffering for months under the regime's brutal crackdown' (Rahman). The festival's Director Mohammed Al Ahmad claimed these particular Egyptian film stars were 'troublemakers', optimistically announcing that 'despite this growing malcontent, the festival carries on unfazed, periodically announcing activities for the new session, including the most recent for a new award supporting amateur film writers' (Rahman). Of course, the festival in 2012 did not take place.

Since the last edition of DIFF and the advent of the Syrian uprisings, almost all cultural activity in the country has come to a standstill, and DIFF's website – like many other cultural websites – has been closed down completely. However, while the Syrian uprisings have had a detrimental influence on the government-run DIFF, smaller, non-government affiliated film festivals like DoxBox (www.dox-box.org) have resisted the cultural wipe-out and have taken to heart the new digital shape film festivals can now assume. While they could not physically take place in Damascus, the DoxBox Global Days held in March 2012 and 2013 display Syrian filmmakers and festival organisers actively resisting the government's crackdown and accompanying censorship. Films were distributed and exhibited online and on DVDs to a worldwide network of volunteers who coordinated two days of screenings dedicated to Syrian cinema. DoxBox was true to its word in claiming the Global Day would show 'how poverty, oppression and isolation do not prevent humans from being spectacularly brave, stubborn and dignified' (DoxBox).

This festival has completely embraced the power of social networking and online streaming which have enabled it to not only programme a festival of documentaries, but also to counter the portrayal of Syria as a country in which filmmakers suffer under an unconquerable censorship regime. The Global Days screened classics rarely seen anywhere (either in Syria or abroad), clandestinely-produced films and films by filmmakers in exile; even as the event itself unveiled a film festival in exile. The Global Day screenings have taken place on 15 March in 2012 and 2013 to commemorate the Syrian Uprising. The labelling of the showings as solidarity screenings is indicative of the idealism and political activism that inspire the festival. In 2012, the festival was dedicated to the screening of the 'forbidden films' of Syrian documentarist extraordinaire, Omar Amiralay. Prior to 2011, none of

Amiralay's films had ever been screened publicly in Syria. Even so, his reputation had been established from his space in exile in France. His work on, and dedication to, documentary across the entire Arab world is reflected in his setting up of the Arab Institute of Film (AIF) to provide support for young documentary makers through workshops and training. Amiralay was also one of the chief advisors and supporters of DoxBox until his untimely death in February 2011, a few weeks before the uprisings began.

DoxBox is dedicated to the promotion of creative documentary from the Arab region, and was inaugurated in 2007 in Damascus by documentary filmmaker Diana El Jeiroudi from ProAction Film, the only independent Syrian documentary production company. Admission to screenings is free of charge. It is regarded as the Arab world's leading documentary festival, and usually runs in Damascus, Tartous and Homs during the first two weeks of March. In the spirit of its dedication to 'the people', DoxBox has offered the country's very first audience award at a festival. Its aims are markedly more democratic than DIFF's. DoxBox has a very active online presence, through El Jeiroudi, on Facebook and in the Blogosphere. It also works in close collaboration with other documentary festivals around the world, such as the International Documentary Film Festival Amsterdam (http://www.idfa.nl/industry.aspx), the European Documentary Network (hwww.edn.dk), DocPoint Helsinki (docpoint. info/en) and the Copenhagen International Documentary Festival (cphdox.dk/en). This innovative, online, cinematic subversion of, and resistance to government censorship, is illustrative of the flexibility and reflexivity of small film festivals, combining as it does the possibilities of online distribution and voluntary labour with idealism and generosity. DoxBox's online resistance utilises access to a global audience with a potential impact that far outstrips the more limited regional audience to which the festival was accustomed. Its online networking skills and successes have encouraged like-minded organisations and individuals worldwide to embrace the event and even claim the festival as their own.

Beirut Film Festivals

Political unrest, the Civil War (1975-1990) and the continued State of War with Israel meant that film festivals arrived in Lebanon much later than in Syria. The on-going religious tensions in the region are arguably still played out on the territory of Lebanon, and many regard the Civil War as never having really ended; it just paused in 1990. These circumstances have understandably created an unstable space, somewhere far from conducive to the organisation of an annual film festival with international ambitions. Nevertheless, since the end of the Lebanese Civil War in the early 1990s and the subsequent reconstruction of the capital Beirut, that city has been the focal point of the region's cultural life, renowned for its press, theatres, cultural activities and nightlife. Since the late 1990s, when the first festivals began to see the light of day, an abundance of small independent festivals celebrating film throughout the year has sprung to life in the city's many cinemas and film schools.

The Beirut International Film Festival (BIFF) (www.beirutfilmfestival. org) was inaugurated in 1998 by Colette Naufal (Director of the Beirut Film Foundation since 2001). The idea for a festival formed during a conversation with an entrepreneurial friend who encouraged her to start a event dedicated to Lebanese films. This happened in the context of the reconstruction of Lebanon, several years after the end of the Civil War and during what Lina Khatib (2008) has called the Lebanese Renaissance of Cinema.[2] According to Naufal, she had only three and a half months to put together a festival focusing on the history of Lebanese cinema – and screen 15 international films. The festival ran in a big exhibition tent in the centre of the city that was normally used for trade fairs, while downtown Beirut was still in ruins. In an interview in *Al-Monitor* in October 2012, during the 11th edition of the festival, Naufal explains that by the event's third year she had realised that there was not enough production in Lebanon to hold a dedicated competition, so the decision was made 'to go Pan-Arab' (Ghawanmeh).

The festival's ambitions as an annual event have often been thwarted because of the political and religious tensions in the country and in the region at large, although it ran consecutive annual editions between 1998 and 2001. In 2001, the financial backer of the festival pulled out for undisclosed reasons and the 2002 session had to be cancelled. Then Naufal founded the Beirut Film Foundation, and the company has been behind BIFF ever since. The festival re-launched in 2003 with another very successful edition, but in 2004 had to be cancelled at the last minute because of the assassination attempt on Minister of Trade Marwan Hamadeh a few days previous. That attempt is now considered to have been the beginning of the series of deadly attacks on Lebanese politicians and journalists that gave post-war Beirut its reputation as one of the world's most dangerous cities, with car bomb attacks and murders all too common. The continued and increased presence of Hezbollah in the city imparts a sustained sense of religious and political division and tension. In 2005, the hugely popular Prime Minister Rafik Hariri was assassinated, resulting in uprisings throughout the country but especially in downtown Beirut. Again, BIFF had to be cancelled. In 2006, Naufal managed to hold a small festival just six weeks after the war between Hezbollah and Israel ended, but in 2007 Hezbollah closed down the entire downtown area, and therefore she had to cancel the event again. Thankfully, since then, the festival has run continuously, but it has nevertheless been affected by the increased violence in Syria since 2011. Both international and regional guests express concerns regarding their safety and some choose to not travel to Beirut.

Image 7: Colette Naufal, Director of the Beirut International Film Festival
© Colette Naufal

Another hurdle for BIFF has been recurring censorship issues, and not only at the hands of the Lebanese censor. Other governments have taken a dislike to the liberal stance Naufal has assumed regarding her programming strategies. In the notes on festival strategy on the BIFF website, one of the things that stands out is the emphasis on freedom of expression. Nevertheless, as we shall see, in 2011 there were some high-profile problems with a couple of Iranian films, and again in 2013 there was a problem with the portrayal of sexualities in the Lebanese short film *Wahabtoka Al Mutah* (*I Offered You Pleasure*, 2012, Lebanon, Farah Shaer).

Censorship at BIFF takes a number of different forms. Firstly, there is the reputation Beirut and BIFF have regarding its relatively liberal stance on freedom of expression. In 2011, the Iranian government accused the festival of opposing the Islamic Republic of Iran and did not allow 7 filmmakers to leave Tehran to come to the festival. They were stopped at the airport and were taken in for questioning. Each filmmaker subsequently emailed us and asked not to screen his or her film. (Naufal)

Naufal speculates that the reasoning behind this interference began in the previous year when she had planned to screen *Ruzhaye sabz* (*Green Days*, Hana Makhmalbaf, Iran, 2009). As Iranian President Mahmud Ahmadinejad was visiting Beirut during the festival, the Lebanese Censorship Department asked BIFF not to screen it until he had left. However, his visit did not end until the closing night of the festival, so the film was not screened at all. Naufal decided to screen the film later in the year, at a one-off screening, but once again the Iranian Ambassador in Beirut intervened by requesting that the Lebanese government prevent the screening; they conceded. The intertwining of politics with filmmaking and film exhibition in the Arab world becomes clear here: it is a balancing act between being a forward-thinking festival and playing an intrinsic role in the country's ambassadorial endeavours, and thus severely complicates the freedom of the programmer in Lebanon.

Then there is the fact that within Lebanon itself there are several levels of censorship. In our interview, Naufal emphasised that the festival continues to try to break down old barriers claiming that the government-led Film Committee, which makes the final decisions regarding whether the festival can screen a film or not, was established precisely to deal with the festival. This committee was established in 2011 and since then has been in charge of the more controversial films on the programme. It is a separate entity to the censorship board, and is in fact more tolerant. As a result, she believes and hopes, the censorship board will follow suit in its leniency; it has, in fact, already shown signs that it is becoming more indulgent. In support of this contention Naufal cites the screening in 2011 of the controversial film *Michael* (Markus Schleinzer, Austria, 2011).

Such leniency was not apparent in 2012 when Naufal selected *I Offered you Pleasure* for the programme of short films from Lebanon. Her reasons for selecting it, she says, were its topic (temporary marriages that allow young people to have 'legal' sexual relationships) and the courage the young woman filmmaker showed in tackling such a controversial theme. But because the film touched on a very sensitive religious area, the censors were obliged to pass it on to the government committee, which did not allow the screening.

Naufal says that these days, if a film is excluded, it is not usually because of the censorship board but because of the government – political decisions are once again increasingly impacting upon the festival, especially since 2011, and in the wake of the revolutions in the larger Arab region. Naufal has a good relationship with the censors and they do let films through that could potentially be cut as long as she does not publicise their screening too widely. If she does and the government becomes aware of the upcoming screenings, they interfere directly. Still, she says, 'this does not stop us from trying, and many films are passed under the radar, and no one realises it until they have been screened and it is too late to ban them' (Naufal).

A showcase of the festival programme is BIFF's prestigious competition for Middle Eastern Fiction and Documentary. However, and unusually for the Middle East (when compared to the profligacy at Doha or Qatar, for example), there is no cash prize attached to this competition. The young filmmakers who win at BIFF earn a valuable association with the reputation of the festival and its director rather than any monetary reward. Naufal says this is simply due to financial constraints and emphasises that once she figures out a way to attract the right kind of investment for these prizes she will to make sure that they go to the filmmakers rather than to their production companies.

BIFF has one sponsor. The Société Générale de Banque au Liban (SGBL) has been the lone financial backer of the festival since 2011. Prior to that there were a few others but they gave up in the face of the increased instability within the country. What SGBL donates, however, is not enough to run a festival, another reason why the festival has had to downsize over the last three years. Naufal says: 'Believe me, if we only had 10% of what the Gulf festivals spend, we would have the best festival in the region.' She admits that because they cannot invite international guests who would enhance the international profile of the festival and of Beirut, potential sponsors are less interested. Indeed, SGBL itself seems more interested in promoting the festival as a cultural event relevant primarily for the Lebanese people. Still, even though it is the only sponsor and therefore occupies a rather powerful position over Naufal, SGBL does not interfere with the programme or the selection of films for competition.

Alongside the competition, the festival organises a number of specialist strands, such as Human Rights Watch films, Children's Films and a strand dedicated to young Lebanese filmmakers from local film schools and art colleges. The festival's (and Naufal's) emphasis on freedom of speech attracted the attention of Human Rights Watch (HRW). Their agreement is that Naufal makes a selection of films from a list HRW sends her, based on their screenings in New York and London. The section started small, screening only three films in 2010, but by 2012 that had become five after Naufal noticed there was a good audience for such films in Beirut. The HRW films are mostly activist productions and are not always of the highest production standards. Naufal's chief concern is the quality of the films screened, and she has become aware that the Beirut audience has high standards, too, something which she feels she has contributed towards. She says:

> For these kinds of films, I feel that in the beginning one should not only think of being an activist. One must first interest the audience and pull them in, educate them to take an interest in what is happening on the Human Rights level internationally, and we go from there. Obviously there is a big audience for these films in Lebanon, and I am very happy with the results [...] I programme the section, and we have one member of the team who coordinates our panel discussions after the films with HRW. (Naufal)

Another potentially successful strand at BIFF is the Children's Film screenings. The decision to launch a Children's section was made in collaboration with Myrna Maakaron, who curates the Children's section at the Dubai International Film Festival. BIFF launched theirs in 2011, and the response was great. All local schools were invited to attend and games and other events were organised after the screenings, introducing students to the complexities of such topics as the environment. None of the films on this programme are from the Middle East; it is a decidedly international section, most often with films from the Netherlands and Germany. Unfortunately, in 2012 screenings were cancelled due to the deteriorating security situation in Lebanon. The 2013 edition did include a Children's section, but it did very poorly. The increasingly dangerous situation in the region has undoubtedly had a direct influence on the size and composition of the audience. Indeed, Naufal acknowledges that cinema attendance has dropped tremendously in the last two years because of the situation in Syria, and this had a detrimental effect on the festival's latest edition.

The festival enjoys the support and enthusiasm of the many young Lebanese filmmakers who are graduating from several high-profile film schools in Beirut, such as Film and TV School Beirut and the Lebanese Film Academy. Universities such as Saint Joseph University, and both American Universities in the capital, also have flourishing film departments, often with an emphasis on production. In the first couple of years of the festival, all film students used to submit their work for possible screening, as the festival focused on Lebanese productions. However, since 2001, when the festival turned its attention to region-wide and international production, the festival stopped taking as many local Lebanese films as it had in the past. (The students set up their own small student-run film festival instead, which still takes place off and on at the schools or at smaller cinema venues throughout the city.)

The festival has enjoyed very good, close working relationships with the film schools, especially with the Institute d' études scéniques, audiovisuelles et cinématographiques (IESAV) at Université Saint Joseph. In 2002, BIFF hosted a hugely successful workshop with Abbas Kiarostami at IESAV, which has had a great impact on how young filmmakers see the important role BIFF plays both in Beirut and in their own careers. Naufal believes that BIFF has had a major impact, too, on how young Lebanese filmmakers and their films are appreciated throughout the world:

> [O]ne main result of our festival, was Nadine Labaki. She won her first prize in our festival in 1997 with her first short film *11 Rue Pasteur*.[3] This film went on to screen in several international festivals thanks to us. And thanks to BIFF as well she was introduced to her producer Anne Dominique Toussaint, whom we invited to Beirut in 2003. So actually, BIFF is where Nadine's first internationally successful film, *Sukkar banat* [*Caramel*, 2007] was conceived. (Naufal)

Naufal makes even bigger claims with her stated belief that the steady growth of the festival has positively influenced the filmmaking in Lebanon as a whole: 'We have created an awareness of good Lebanese cinema. Due to our festival's success, festivals from all over the world have opened their eyes to Lebanese cinema, as we can see when they continuously contact us for recommendations' (Naufal). It is undeniable that BIFF has been an advocate for great Lebanese films since its inception.

In addition to its focus on young people's films, BIFF also has a productive relationship with Palestinian filmmakers, many of whom live in Beirut.[4] In 2012, BIFF screened *5 Broken Cameras* (Emad Burnat and Guy Davidi, Palestine / Israel / France / Netherlands, 2011). Naufal says the reason for selecting this film for screening was the courage it shows. This is a character trait she believes needs to be encouraged in filmmakers, especially because freedom of expression is far from the norm in 'this part of the world', even in Lebanon, which used to be much more liberal; the situation has deteriorated since 2011. Initially, the Censorship Department was critical of screening *5 Broken Cameras* because it is an Israeli co-production. With Lebanon in a continuous state of war with Israel, there is a reflexive tendency there to boycott any and all Israeli products. However, as the film promoted the Palestinian cause, the censorship board passed it and it screened to 200 people at

BIFF. Naufal says that she hopes one day to be able to screen Israeli films. Again, she emphasises that her first criterion for programming a film is that it has an outstanding quality and / or an admirable cause, regardless of the nationality of the filmmakers.

In 2013, the selection of films was more arduous than usual. Interestingly, the main reason for difficulties was that internet provision in the country was not up to its usual standard as a direct result of the conflict in Syria. Film submissions to festivals have increasingly gone online in the wake of the rise in popularity of Vimeo or via private links to screeners as an alternative to physical DVD submission. But in Lebanon this year there were problems with the speed of the internet. Most of the international, and all of the regional (Middle Eastern) films were submitted online. Naufal says that she had to upgrade the BIFF connection twice, but still the speed was not what it should be in order to watch a film, and so she resorted to buying two new and costly USB dongles for a 3G connection, which also left much to be desired. These problems led to Naufal having to explicitly ask for DVD screeners to be sent by mail. It made the process of programming a time-consuming and expensive experience, more stressful than it should have been. Naufal also notes that films are increasingly being streamed at film festivals, for which a very high quality connection is required. If the internet provision in Lebanon remains the way it is, this might cause serious problems for the festival in the future.

BIFF's online presence is increasingly important if it is to reach its young audience – a situation now common to all festivals around the world – but due to these and other internet problems, the online profile of the festival is not without its shortcomings. The website is very basic and limited when compared to others from the region, and its archives only go as far back as 2003. The archived editions of the festival, moreover, only reveal (if the link is not broken) the different strands and their winners. They do not inform the visitor who the members of the juries were or the rationale behind the curated strands. When I asked Naufal about this she told me that the festival has only really had a website and an email address since 2003. In 2012, the website was hacked and so what is online at the moment is a partial reconstruction of what was lost then. While the festival does attempt to make use of the increased visibility offered by social networking sites such as Facebook, their effectiveness is doubtful. Even during the festival period, posting is very intermittent and inconsistent. Outside of the festival week, postings are rare.

DocuDays presents a different online story. The Beirut International Documentary Festival (DocuDays) promotes itself as a festival with a specific story to tell. It was founded in 1999 with the aim of raising public awareness of the non-fiction genre as an entertaining and informative tool. Like DoxBox, it believes strongly in the growing importance of documentary film as a tool for engagement and the raising of awareness in the region. Lebanon's documentary tradition emphasises engagement with the past – in fact, film is one of the few areas in which the Lebanese are comfortable confronting the traumas of the past. Documentary offers itself as a facilitator of traumatic recall and national healing. The founder of the festival, Mohamad Hachem, was a consultant on the launch of the Al Jazeera Documentary Festival (festival.aljazeera.net) in 2005 and is a mover and shaker in the region. Now based in Doha, Hachem continues to run DocuDays, and has added forums and promoted networking opportunities for documentary makers from across the region. He is entrepreneurial, has strong ideals and is very optimistic about the future of the current revolutions sweeping through the region. In an interview with the Doha Film Institute, Hachem has said that he 'can't in any way disconnect filmmaking from social changes' (DFI Blog 2011), explicit indication of his activism in and for documentary filmmaking.

DocuDays' online presence is streets ahead of that at BIFF. It has a well-designed, attractive website dedicated to the festival and its submissions; it seems to welcome and embrace online submissions and updates its website very regularly. Likewise, its Facebook page is a lively space where information on documentary opportunities are shared among a large community that is more than four times the size of the online audience for BIFF, and much more actively involved in the postings. In his DFI interview, Hachem says

> The digital evolution of the internet in both applications and bandwidth, which led to the democratisation of audio-visual means of expression [is of vital importance]. These tools, previously only available to the elite few, are now available to whoever has a message or a point of view. (DFI Blog 2011)

While this optimism reflects a faith in the possibilities of the internet and its connections, the problems Naufal alludes to regarding connectivity are also important, and central to the survival chances of festivals in regions where political conflict or economic problems impede digital communication in general and internet provision in particular.

Hachem is 'in the process of creating the "Arab Documentary Network", an online portal which aims to serve the Arab documentary community by creating an online network for films, filmmakers and film professionals' (DFI Blog 2011). As such, the DocuDays network continues to grow, its success seeming to depend very much on, and to be very well served by its online networks and the connectedness of the man at its helm. The fact that Hachem is based in Doha is central to an understanding of his optimistic attitude towards the potentialities of the internet. In a rich, young and relatively stable place – politically, at least – the internet can indeed be of prime importance to the continuing growth of festivals, whatever size or however ambitious they may be. The physical reality of the city and country in which a festival takes place traditionally forms the basis of its accessibility and success, but so too, now, does the availability of the online world. And in Syria and Lebanon, this is not self-evident.

Now in their third decade of operation the Beirut International Film Festival (1998) and DocuDays (1999) are still going strong. Still, whereas BIFF has taken measures to downsize since 2011 due to the unstable regional and local situation and also the intermittent availability of its online network, DocuDays has continued to grow. Both festivals aim to showcase international films, but the focus of their respective directorships varies widely. The more careful approach to the political situation undertaken by BIFF reflects the concerns of a director inviting an international contingent of stars, while DocuDays has more modest ambitions internationally and prefers to focus on speaking to a local and an online audience for its international films.

Conclusion

The aim here has been to tackle issues of political and social importance in cinema, and to note how they impact directly on the size and status of film festivals. Examination has been undertaken into how these festivals reflect the political situations in their countries, not only through the films they programme but also by the organisational hurdles their directors have to face. The rise and (partial) fall of the larger Damascus and Beirut International Film Festivals stands in contrast the growth of the smaller, thematic documentary festivals that usually boast large online followings and clearer activist agendas. Downsizing impacts on the potential reception of the festivals, both nationally, internationally and in cyberspace. Historically, the New Arab Cinema has been hugely important to filmmaking in the Arab world, and the festival in Damascus in the 1970s was a defining influence, despite rarely being credited for its role. More recently, the absence of a film festival in Damascus and the downsizing of the Beirut International Film Festival in 2011 and 2012, have had repercussions on the local cultural scene and on the presence of Lebanese and Syrian films at global film festivals. While the bigger festivals' demise and lack of online presence reveals a failure to achieve their international ambitions, the option taken by the smaller festivals to adopt and adapt to online distribution and exhibition processes might prove the saving grace of local film festivals.

Works Cited

Boughedir, Férid (1987) *Caméra Arabe* (Documentary), Argos Films and the British Film Institute.

Chaaban, Jad et al. (2010) 'Socio-Economic Survey of Palestinian Refugees in Lebanon', *UNRWA Report*. On-line. Available HTTP: http://www. unrwa.org/userfiles/2011012074253.pdf (13 November 2013).

Cousins, Mark (2008) *The Story of Film*. London: Anova Books.

DFI Blog (2011) 'People in Film: Mohamad Hachem', *DFI Blog*. March 2011. On-line. Available HTTP: http://www.dohafilminstitute.com/blog/ people-in-film-mohamad-hachem (13 November 2013).

Ghawanmeh, Mohammad (2012) 'The Little Film Festival That Could: Beirut Beats the Odds', *Al-Monitor*, 10 October. On-line. Available HTTP: http://www.al-monitor.com/pulse/originals/2012/al-monitor/beirut-film-festival-interview.html# (13 November 2013).

Khatib, Lina (2008) *Lebanese Cinema: Imagining the Civil War and Beyond*. London: I.B. Tauris.

Miriam Cooke (2007) *Dissident Syria: Making Oppositional Arts Official*. Duke University Press, 2007.

Naufal, Colette (2013) Interview with the author. November 2013.

Rahman, Mohammed Abdel (2011) 'Syrian Film Festival Under Fire', *Al-Akhbar English*. 15 September. On-line. Available HTTP: http:// english.al-akhbar.com/content/syrian-film-festival-under-fire (13 November 2013).

Salti, Rasha (ed.) (2006) *Insights into Syrian Cinema: Essays and Conversations with Contemporary Filmmakers*. New York: ArteEast & Rattapallax Press.

Salti, Rasha (2013) Interview with the author. September 2013.

Zarzar, Anas (2012) 'Syria Censorship: Opposition Directors Under the Axe', *Al-Akhbar English*. On-line. Available HTTP: http://english.al-akhbar.com/node/10329 (11 November 2013).

Notes

[1] I am very grateful to Rasha Salti, Colette Naufal and Elias Doumar for their advice and for answering my questions about the Damascus and Beirut festivals.

[2] 1997 marked the production and release of Ziad Doueiri's film *West Beirut*, which, according to Khatib, initiated a renaissance in Lebanese cinema. From this film onwards, Lebanese filmmakers seemed to gain the confidence that they could address their recent history meaningfully, and cinema became a (tentative) part of a reconstructed country and a reconstructed national identity.

[3]   *11 Rue Pasteur* was Labaki's 1997 graduation project for IESAV, the film department at the University of Saint Joseph.

[4]   The United Nations Relief and Works Agency for Palestine Refugees in the Near East (UNRWA) states that at least 10% percent of the Lebanese population is Palestinian. For more information see Chaaban, Jad *et al.* (2010).

The Stakes of the Argument: Beirut, for Example[1]

Laura U. Marks

[...] I would like to give a final example of curating practice, in order once again to nuance the understanding of the role of argument in programming and curating. At the beginning of this essay I noted that argument helps clarify choices in an environment, like that in North America, where there is simply too much good work to see. By contrast, Beirut, where I lived for the past year, is a city that, like other postwar cities, has a small amount of art and a community eager to see it. Beirut raises the stakes of argument in programming and curating. There is a sense of urgency: first, to get work to audiences, and second and more subtly, to make good arguments – arguments about history, about how to remember the civil war, about citizenship, about individuality, about the relative worth of documentary, fiction, and experimental / personal work to deal with the ideological tangle with which Beirutis live.

This is a city rich in film festivals. The Beirut Cinema Days Arab Film Festival (http://ayambeirut.wordpress.com), held in October 2002, was organised by Beirut DC, an organisation that produces and distributes independent media. Eliane Raheb and Hania Mroué, the festival directors, brought together 95 works by filmmakers and video makers from all over the Arab world, including its diaspora. They created not a dinner party but a wonderful, surfeiting banquet, as good festivals do. At a couple of points, however, I felt that an argument from the presenters' side would have facilitated better digestion among the artists and audience.

Arab audiences are understandably uneasy about what message cinema will give about the Arab world to the outside. As such they seem to spend as much time anticipating Western responses to a work as appreciating it on local terms. We saw Iraqi exile Saad Salman's *Baghdad On / Off* (2002), a fictionalised documentary about a filmmaker's (Salman's) attempt to visit his mother in Baghdad after 35 years of exile, only to have his journey derailed through Kurdish refugee camps, meetings with artists recovering from torture and mysterious concrete bunkers. *Baghdad On / Off* is a stunning and disturbing film. But the audience became inflamed at what kind of tool the film would be in American hands 'at a time like this'. They attacked Salman and ignored the film's cinematic qualities in favour of its ideological portent. Could a curatorial argument have engaged the audience to see the film as made for them and speaking to them, as well as speaking to the West? Could an argument have encouraged a reception of the film as a work of art, not only as a potential ideological tool?

In a charged political context, a solid curatorial argument is crucial to encourage reflective synthesis and avoid clichés. An exemplary case is the work of Ashkal Alwan, the Beirut arts organisation directed by Christine Tohme, which has been organising exquisitely-crafted multimedia events for several years. In 2000, Ashkal Alwan's Hamra Street Project brought a specific argument to the circular logic and strategic amnesia around the Lebanese civil war. Rather than make yet more large statements about the war – statements that end up playing into an audience of outsiders – Tohme invited artists to reflect on the history of one street. Hamra Street was the energetic hub of the city before the civil war. Now, however, Muslim and Christian Beirutis have retreated to West and East Beirut, and Hamra Street has lost its integrating function in the city. Tohme asked artists a series of specific questions designed to elicit argument, such as, 'Why is Hamra Street considered the Champs-Élysées of the East? Is it possible to work on why and how this association came about?' 'Why would we be concerned with the life and death of that street?' 'Why were the Israeli soldiers killed in Wimpy café?'[2] 'Is Hamra Street still able to invent its own image and, more broadly, that of Beirut?' (Tohme and Alwan 2002). Tohme's questioning allowed artists (video makers, writers, photographers and installation artists) to perform an archaeology of Hamra Street. The curatorial argument extended to commissioning works specifically for the project.

The resulting event was a beautiful example of a rigorous curatorial argument that uses every intellectual tool: reason, poetry, memory, color, montage, humor, heartbreak… and audiences flocked to it. I believe the Hamra Street Project was so successful precisely because its political stakes were so high. Indeed, the independent artists' scene in Beirut is one of the strongest critical voices in the contemporary Lebanese political scene. In a country where political crisis is relatively explicit, where artists and curators operate in an environment of evident social and political injustice, clear and compelling arguments are more obviously called for. In the North American context, where crisis and injustice are relatively veiled, the necessity of argument appears less pressing. In such a context, curators and programmers must work to unfold our arguments from the bland normalcy of everyday life.

Yet the Hamra Street Project also understood that argument is hollow without feeling. Its finely-wrought, deeply-felt argument demonstrated that ethics and aesthetics, while not identical, are inextricable. The ethical presenter knows that a good argument passes through the heart.

Notes

1   [Editor's note: This text is an extract taken from Marks, Laura U. (2004) 'The Ethical Presenter: Or How to Have Good Arguments over Dinner', *The Moving Image* (Spring 2004) 4, 1, 34-47.]

2   This shooting in 1980, on the liveliest corner of Hamra Street, marked the beginning of Lebanese resistance to Israel's invasion during the civil war.

Film Festivals in Lebanon

Est.	Festival	Date	Website	Location	Specialisation
1998 (not annually)	Beirut International Film Festival	October	http://www.beirutfilmfestival.org/	Beirut	International
1998	Labil Lekol El Nass Arab Film Festival	June	http://nadilekolnas.org/festival.php	Nadi Lekol El Nass / Club for Everyone	Arab films
1999, biennial	DOCUDAYS: Beirut International Documentary Festival	December	http://www.docudays.com/	Beirut	Documentaries
200	Festival du Film Libanais	August	http://www.metropoliscinema.net/2012/lebanese-film-festival-festival-du-film-libanais-2/	Beirut	Lebanese films
2001 (not annually)	Ayam Beirut al Cinema'iya	March	http://ayambeirut.wordpress.com/	Beirut	Arab films
2009	Cabriolet Film Festival	May / June	http://www.cabrioletfilmfestival.com/	Outdoors in Beirut	Shorts

Est.	Festival	Date	Website	Location	Specialisation
2011	Outbox International Short Film Festival	June	http://www.outboxfilmfestival.com/index.php	Roman Baths, Beirut	Shorts
2011	Forbidden Films Festival	June	https://www.facebook.com/events/209674475743198/	Part of BIFF in 2011	Censored films
2011	Turkish Film Festival	April	https://www.facebook.com/events/369692959813712/	Beirut	Turkish cinema
2013	International Film Festival Tripoli	November	http://tripoliintfilmfestlebanon.wordpress.com/	Tripoli and Beirut	Dissident films

Film Festivals in Syria

Est.	Festival	Date	Website	Location	Specialism
1979	Damascus International Film Festival	September	http://damascusfest.com/ (offline)	Damascus	International
2007	DOXBOX	March	http://www.dox-box.org/	Damascus and worldwide	Documentaries

Film Festivals in Yemen

Est.	Name	Date	Website	Location	Specialisation
2011	Eye To Heart Sana'a Human Rights Film festival, organised by American Islamic Congress (AIC)	March	http://www.eyetoheart.org/	Sana'a	Human Rights Films
2013	Yemen Film Festival	-	http://yemenfilmfestival.com/	Sana'a	International
2014	Yemeni Film and Visual Arts Festival	January	http://www.yemenpeace-project.org/filmfestival/	Sana'a	Peace Films

Compiled by Stefanie Van de Peer
Tables are representative, not exhaustive

The Spotlight and the Shadows: Film Festivals, Israeli Cinema and Globalisation

Matt Sienkiewicz and Heather McIntosh

The State of Israel bears a unique relationship to the flows or 'scapes' that Arjun Appadurai (1996) evokes in his theorisation of the modern era of globalisation. This is most pronounced at the level he identifies as the 'ethnoscape', whereby accelerated rates of travel and immigration have come to fundamentally reshape global society's understanding of both physical and cultural space. Israel was born of both a mass ingathering of Jews and a forced migration of Palestinian Arabs. Perhaps as much as any country, it is a nation built by global movement. In subsequent years, the country not only has served as a destination for tourists and immigrants from across the world, but also has become a point of origin for a post-modern version of the Jewish diaspora, with large numbers of Israeli-born citizens emigrating to America and Europe. Israel's outsized role in the realm of geopolitics thus goes beyond its religious history and its strategically significant location in the Middle East. It is also a nation that, via the increased movements of people over the past century, has developed direct connections, both celebratory and antagonistic, with a disproportionate number of communities across the world.

This chapter analyses how the globalised nature of Israel plays out at the level of international cinema culture, considering the role that the international film festival circuit plays in distributing Israeli films both to audiences with a particular interest in the nation, as well as to more generalised pools of viewers. Using the West Jerusalem-based distribution company Ruth Diskin Films as its main case study,[1] the argument here is that a variety of factors aid in the globalisation of Israeli cinema in ways not experienced by other nations in the Middle East. Two key elements unique to the flow of Israeli films are identified.

The first of these elements is the internationalisation of Israeli cinema via advocacy and protest, whereby little-known films become the subjects of celebratory endorsements and public condemnations. To this end, this chapter offers an analysis of the controversy that erupted over the 2009 Toronto International Film Festival and its Tel Aviv 'City Spotlight' sub-program. We argue that Israeli films that otherwise would go largely unremarked are often spotlighted in the international press by virtue of the ever-present controversies, protests and counter-protests. The second key element is a series of intersecting 'shadow circuits' of regional and thematic film festivals that provide modestly profitable, truly global distribution pathways for Israeli films that are not accepted into higher profile festivals or that do no not receive distribution through other mainstream outlets. Unlike other national cinemas, Israeli cinema is able to access the well-funded and, in North America and Europe, seemingly ubiquitous network of Jewish film festivals supported by local Jewish Federations and Jewish Community Centers. Furthermore, as this analysis of Ruth Diskin Films' marketing strategies reveals, Israeli films are also popular programming selections in human rights film festivals and even Palestinian film festivals. These shadow circuits offer landing spots for niche Israeli films that are not suited for A-list festivals such as Cannes or Sundance, and provide both screening fees and video marketing opportunities to an unusually high number of productions from the country. This unique collection of international venues incentivises distributors such as Ruth Diskin Films to work with a wider variety of films, and thus supports a greater diversity within Israeli cinema.

Festivals, Legitimation and Distribution

Film festivals play a central role in the cultural legitimation, promotion and distribution of national cinemas around the world. This role is particularly important for small national cinemas, such as Israel's, that produce films in languages rarely spoken beyond their own borders. Historically, long-running European festivals such as Venice and Cannes served as venues for highlighting less prominent national cinemas, promoting auteur filmmakers, celebrating national film-art movements and providing moments of international attention often reserved for Hollywood stars and star-makers. As festivals' activities and purposes shifted in the 1970s and again in the 1980s, they began to balance the culture of cinema with the business of film. By the late 1980s, many festivals appeared to be as interested in commerce as they were in film art and culture (de Valck 2007).

Today, industry imperatives appear to dominate the A-list festivals, as seen in their built-in marketplaces and the attention they garner in trade papers such as *Variety* and *The Hollywood Reporter*. Recent Israeli films have benefited considerably from this system. In 2007, Shira Geffen's and Etgar Keret's unusual drama *Meduzot* (*Jellyfish*, 2007) enjoyed success at both Cannes and the increasingly important Toronto International Film Festival (TIFF), parlaying the upsurge in publicity into a modest North American theatrical run organised by the U.S. distributor Zeitgeist Films. In 2011, Joseph Cedar's drama *Hearat Shulayim* (*Footnote*, 2011) rode success at Cannes to a more robust distribution agreement with Sony Pictures Classics. Although historically fiction filmmakers have dominated film festivals, recently top-level festivals such as The Sundance Film Festival (www.sundance.org/festival) have brought similar industry attention to the realm of documentary filmmaking. Furthermore, documentary-specific festivals such as the International Documentary Festival in Amsterdam (IDFA) and HotDocs have become key spaces in which distributors see and acquire films from smaller nations. Emad Burnat's and Guy Davidi's *5 Broken Cameras* (Israel / Palestine, 2011), a documentary often described, as here, as a Palestinian-Israeli co-production, garnered early attention at IDFA before winning a jury prize at Sundance and eventually earning an Academy Award nomination.

The notion of a global film festival 'circuit' provides one scholarly conceptualisation for the mechanism by which films from less prominent national industries are able to gain notoriety and access to wider audiences. The key to this idea is that festivals, with their abilities to weave the artistic, cultural and economic concerns that underpin global filmmaking, provide a unique evaluative space. Marijke de Valck argues that this circuit's importance

> has been dependent on the creation of film festivals as a zone, a liminal state, where the cinematic products can bask in the attention they receive for their aesthetic achievements, cultural specificity, or social relevance. (2007: 37)

Part of maintaining this cultural relevance comes through the rejection of mainstream films, particularly from the United States. Building on the discourses of early film festivals as the 'antithesis' (Wong 2011: 132) of the Hollywood dominance of the global film distribution (de Valck 2007), the festival circuit may be understood as alternative to mainstream film distribution (Iordanova 2009), even as it establishes its own internal hierarchical order. The film festival thus plays a dual role in the realm of distribution, simultaneously providing a space for films that defy Hollywood standards to find an international audience, as well as offering the opportunity, if only rarely, for a film from a small nation to gain access to the profit-driven realm of theatrical distribution.

In doing so, the festival circuit offers another, indirect financial element to the world of international filmmaking. As Ragan Rhyne (2009) notes, a proper understanding of the festival circuit must move beyond the most obvious stakeholders, such as producers, distributors and exhibitors. Perhaps most importantly, governmental bodies increasingly understand the role that national cinema can play not only in promoting domestic arts, but in also fostering perceptions of their nations abroad. Success on the festival circuit has garnered significant, often flattering attention for countries that have become particularly successful during different periods, such as Japan in the 1950s, Iran in the 1990s and Israel in the early twenty-first century (Wong 2011). For countries without a strong cinematic infrastructure, such as Turkey, 'many international film festivals, while opening a window to the world, serve as a platform for national cinemas to dialogue with foreign buyers, journalists and programmers' (Dönmez-Colin 2012: 101).

The variety of festivals appearing on this global film festival circuit offer different ways to construct and promote the connection between national art and national culture. The larger, A-list festivals often offer explicit showcases of national cinemas from both the hosting country and abroad. Czach (2004), for example, analyses how the showcases at TIFF contribute to the understanding of a Canadian national cinema that is both defining and challenging, through programming choices and the debates. Other activities drawing attention include premieres, competition screenings, retrospectives and director sessions. In 2009, for example, TIFF offered a spotlight series on Tel Aviv, which included ten films, accompanied by their filmmakers and, as is discussed below, garnered considerable attention, even if much of it came in the form of protest. Israel's partnership with TIFF has grown over the years, with the total number of Israeli films shown there numbering 42 since 2000 (Kaplan 2013). According to Katriel Schory, Executive Director of the Israeli Film Fund, '[W]e attend TIFF to bring life to our existing pictures and find partnerships' (Kaplan 2013). Like many nations, Israel subsidises the presence of their films and filmmakers at notable festivals, particularly those taking place in nations that represent political allies such as the U.S., Canada and Australia. In 2009, this sponsorship became a point of controversy, as British filmmaker Ken Loach withdrew from the Melbourne Film Festival (http://miff.com.au) in protest of the Israeli government's co-sponsorship of his work ('Director Ken Loach Exits' 2009).

As Bill Nichols (1994) suggests, however, the presence of a nation's filmmakers at A-list festivals must be conceptualised beyond the level of their potential use as advertising or propaganda. The nature of the festival circuit, he contends, is to focus on films that are simultaneously from a nation and yet, at the same time, above that nation. Nichols writes further: 'We are invited to receive such films as evidence of artistic maturity – the work of directors ready to take their place within an international fraternity of auteurs – and of a distinctive national culture' (1994: 16). The film festival circuit thus does not allow nations to easily represent pre-existing national cultures. Instead, the circuit and its negotiation of national and cosmopolitan cultural markers are constitutive of a new sense of how a domestic culture is to be perceived on the global stage. Film festivals play an important role in cultural legitimation, though the process proves both useful and troublesome for discussing global cinemas. On the one hand, inclusion within a festival offers acceptance of a nation's films, maybe even pushing toward the idea of a national cinema. On the other hand, inclusion within a festival outside the nation's borders situates the power of the national identity building within the international festival's programmers, promoters and critics, in that which films these people ultimately choose come to define, in part, what constitutes a film from that nation. As Chan asks, '[D]o nations create cinema or does cinema create nations?' (2011: 255).

Too often, however, scholarly attention falls entirely on the place of major, A-list festivals in contributing to national film cultures. Regional and thematic festivals also play important roles within the global film festival circuit, and are particularly important in the case of Israeli cinema. As a small nation, whose relatively few local cinemas are overwhelmingly stocked with American fare, it is not possible for Israel to foster a robust, successful filmmaking culture entirely on the shoulders of the handful of films that find success at the A-list level. Regional and thematic festivals, including the Jewish, Palestinian and Human Rights programmes in which Israeli films are often featured, play an important dual role. On the one hand, these festivals often come to be the spaces in which truly oppositional visions of national cultures can be expressed. And, while A-list festivals in the past more commonly presented strong political statements with their programming choices (de Valck 2007), this mission now often falls on more regional and thematic festivals, as A-list programming decisions are increasingly influenced by economic concerns.

For example, a film such as *Lir'ot im ani mehayechet* (*To See If I Am Smiling*, Tamar Yarom, 2007), an Israeli documentary featuring female ex-soldiers confronting acts of abuse they perpetrated against Palestinians, found its greatest success at human rights-themed festivals across the world. Passed over by the A-list festivals in part, perhaps, because of the film's complex portrayals of Israel and Israelis, the film was nonetheless able to find a considerable global audience on this alternative or, as we would like to call it, 'shadow circuit'. Jewish film festivals often play a parallel role, offering spaces for some Israeli films that question hegemonic notions of Judaism and Jewish identity. However, it is important to note that economic concerns remain present on these secondary, shadow circuits, particularly as they become increasingly important for filmmakers hoping to find more general audiences. Joshua Gamson (1996), for example, explores these balancing acts within two gay and lesbian film festivals in New York City and suggests that moving away from or toning down oppositionality, appears to enhance both a film's and a film festival's capacity for reaching broader audiences.

There are, of course, multiple points of connection between A-list festivals and regional or thematic festivals. Perhaps most importantly, major festivals often serve as a de facto clearinghouse for smaller festivals, winnowing down programming options through what amounts to a pre-approval process. As Mark Peranson (2009) notes, alongside the straightforward economic potential offered major film festivals, there is also a benefit of cultural affirmation. Thus, A-list festivals, simply by choosing and promoting a film, have a strong tendency to influence the content of regional and thematic 'shadow' festivals. Discursive association with a major festival is often enough to lift a film's status to the point where it is likely to be accepted at a number of smaller venues. 'Film festivals', he writes, 'live by the printed word, they are verbal architectures' (Peranson 2009: 45). An extension of these 'verbal architectures' lies in the online materials on both dedicated websites and social media presences created and maintained by the festivals' staff, which are, hopefully, 'spread' (Jenkins, Ford, and Green 2013) through other sites by motivated users. In an inundated filmmaking environment already saturated with films, the legitimising function of A-list festivals has increased in value. Major festivals thus play a central role in priming a film to be accepted into a variety of smaller festivals.

As Dina Iordanova (2009) argues, it is misleading to suggest that film festivals represent a simple 'feeder' system that helps to usher certain, high-quality productions into mainstream distribution. Festivals play one part in a complicated, intertwined system in which artists, small businesses, non-profit organisations, governments and multi-national corporations, all play important, if sometimes undefined, roles.

However, as we argue below, in the case of Israel there are unique and systematic ways in which the festival system plays an important role in globalising the cinema production of this relatively small nation. First, the political controversies that constantly follow Israeli films to film festivals across the world serve a function of garnering attention for films that might otherwise go unnoticed. Second, Israeli films, due to their relevance to multiple diasporic audiences and deep engagement with issues of geopolitical interest, have access to entire circuits of smaller festivals. These 'shadow circuits', we argue, operate in scaled-down versions of the A-list dynamic, whereby larger Jewish, Palestinian and Human Rights festivals influence smaller, similar events by legitimating certain films. This dynamic allows distributors to find a global audience for a film if they can simply place it in one influential, but by no means A-list, festival, such as the Boston Jewish Film Festival (www.bjff.org), the Human Rights Watch Film Festival (www.ff.hrw.org) or the Palestine Film Festival (www.palestinefilmfoundation.org/festivals.asp?s=next) in London.

Global Publicity, Good and Bad

Given the high profile nature of Israel's politics, its military and its occupation of the Palestinian Territories, it is perhaps unsurprising that the nation's cinema garners global attention disproportionate to its output. From 2007 to 2011, four films put forward by Israel to the Academy of Motion Picture Arts and Sciences were nominated for Best Foreign Language Picture, including three films, *Vals Im Bashir* (*Waltz with Bashir*, Ari Folman, 2008), *Beufort* (Joseph Cedar 2007), and *Ajami* (Scandar Copti and Yaron Shani, 2009), that explicitly deal with the issues of Israeli military action and occupation. To this list can be added a pair of 2012 nominees for Best Documentary Feature, the aforementioned *5 Broken Cameras* and *The Gatekeepers* (2012, Dror Moreh), a film highly critical of Israeli intelligence forces' tactics since the 1967 occupation of the Palestinian Territories. These films received attention for a variety of reasons, ranging from technical innovation to bitter disputes over whether films such as *Ajami* and *5 Broken Cameras* should be labelled as 'Palestinian', 'Israeli' or 'Palestinian-Israeli' (Rohter 2013).

Film festivals, however, have provided even more vociferous and, at times, headline-grabbing controversies surrounding Israeli cinema. The most remarkable example of this phenomenon occurred at the 2009 TIFF, which featured a 'City to City' programme intended to highlight movies from Tel Aviv. Led by Canadian filmmaker John Greyson and journalist Naomi Klein, a protest movement developed around the spotlight series, with Greyson arguing that a boycott should be enacted as a result of Israel's military assault on Gaza in January 2009. In an open letter signed by hundreds of filmmakers titled 'The Toronto Declaration: No Celebration of Occupation', Greyson, Klein and others, condemned the festival not for showing Israeli films, but for putting together a program that failed to feature Palestinian voices and effaced the Arab history of the Tel Aviv-Jaffa region (Aloni, Flanders, et al. 2009).

The story of the protest was picked up across the journalistic spectrum, appearing in mainstream outlets (including Reuters, the *Los Angeles Times*, *Al Jazeera* and *The Guardian*) Jewish and Israeli media (*Haaretz*, *YNet* and *The Forward*) and Palestinian activist sites such as Electronic Intifada. The Palestinian Campaign for the Academic and

Cultural Boycott of Israel released a statement accusing TIFF of allowing itself to be made a 'tool for Israel's apartheid public relations machine' (Palestinian Campaign 2009). Though the festival did not bend to the demands of the protesters, the boycott efforts garnered attention well beyond the rarefied air of art cinema fans and industry insiders who make up the majority of TIFF's audience.

Predictably, the protest evoked a considerable response, with numerous well-known personalities defending the festival and the importance of Israeli cinema. Celebrities such as Jerry Seinfeld and Natalie Portman appeared in advertisements featured in the *Los Angeles Times* and *Toronto Star* emphasising the diverse and often self-critical nature of the films featured in the Tel Aviv spotlight (Zohar and Mozgovaya 2009). Articles in a variety of major outlets not only quoted writers praising the festival for its programming, but also listed the films in question, thus providing considerable additional attention for films that might otherwise have been mere footnotes at TIFF.

Such protests have not been limited to TIFF. Numerous other festivals – for example, the 2006 Locarno Film Festival, the 2012 San Francisco Film Festival (www.festival.sffs.org), the 2012 Toronto Queer Film Festival (www.insideout.ca/initiatives/toronto) and many other events, including numerous Israeli-themed festivals – have been subject to high profile demonstrations. It is difficult to determine the ultimate impact of these protests in terms of screening attendances and festival acceptances. For every protestor who avoids an Israeli film due to a boycott, it is possible that someone else chooses to view the film either as an act of support for Israel or due to the excitement and publicity surrounding the event. What is certain is that Israeli films, by virtue of the controversy that follows them, bring with them a sense of global importance exceedingly disproportionate to the limited film industry from which they emerge.

Ruth Diskin, proprietor of Ruth Diskin Films, Israel's most prominent documentary distribution company, notes that conflict and controversy make up a significant proportion of her business. Describing her catalogue, for which she selects roughly ten new movies a year, Diskin says that her films aim to 'comfort the troubled and trouble the comfortable' (2013). She notes that controversy, on the whole, serves to draw attention to Israeli films, driving interest particularly in documentary projects that take critical stances towards Israeli politics. Despite representing a catalogue stocked with films of which 90% are supported by the Israeli government, Diskin attests that a month never goes by without one of her films being requested by a festival or event themed around critical perspectives on occupation and conflict. It is, in many ways, the polarising nature of Israel and Israeli cinema that allows her to operate a truly global distribution business based on films produced exclusively in one small country.

Big Circuits and Their Shadows

Other factors do contribute to the viability of Diskin's business. In particular, we argue, Diskin's films are uniquely positioned to find financial support as a result of Israel's place at the centre of both global political discourse and multiple diasporic movements. Israeli films, drawing interest from Jewish Film Festivals, Palestinian Film Festivals, Human Rights Film Festivals and Israeli Film Festivals located around the world, have the opportunity to participate not only in the standard festival circuit but also in a number of 'shadow circuits.'

For Diskin, film festivals ideally serve the function described in traditional circuit approaches. Under the most favourable circumstances, she looks for films that will succeed at festivals not specifically looking for Jewish or Israeli content but for those that will achieve A-list legitimisation. Commonly, success at a major festival such as Cannes, Locarno, Tribeca or Sundance, will lead both to success at numerous smaller festivals and, most profitably, theatrical and home distribution agreements. The documentary *The Flat* (Arnon Goldfinger, 2011) represents the rare case in which such a plan was directly actualised. After premiering at the Jerusalem International Film Festival (www.jff.org.il), a prestigious but not Tier-A venue, the film was selected for the eminent and highly industry-focused Tribeca Film Festival. Screening as part of the World Documentary Competition, *The Flat* garnered considerable attention, drawing a large number of potential distributors to its screening. Furthermore, the film was reviewed by outlets that otherwise might never have mentioned it, including *The Hollywood Reporter*, which suggested that the film's 'prospects at the art house' were strong, implying that the film could succeed in a theatrical setting (DeFore 2012). After playing at a handful of smaller festivals, *The Flat* found representation for theatrical runs in both the U.S. and Germany, playing in hundreds of cities and grossing roughly U.S.$500,000 in America alone (IMDB 2013). Though such a figure pales in comparison to major Hollywood films, Diskin's business is funded primarily by festival screening fees and educational DVDs, the majority of which are sold for $300 a copy to American and European universities. The theatrical agreements amounted to more money than a dozen of Diskin's less successful films might gross in a year. For *The Flat*, the conventional film circuit approach worked perfectly, providing

Diskin with a tent pole project that has helped solidify the long-term standing of her distributorship.

However, as Diskin notes, successes like *The Flat* are exceedingly rare. Were her business dependent on identifying Israeli films capable of thriving at A-list festivals and thus finding theatrical distribution, years could pass without finding a profitable project. Instead, simultaneous to her efforts to recruit and promote films capable of finding success at A-list venues, Diskin also cultivates projects that can succeed in self-contained smaller festival circuits. Standing in the shadow of A-list festivals, these shadow circuits operate with a logic very similar to that which films like *The Flat* experience at higher levels.

For Diskin's catalogue, the most prominent shadow circuit is that comprising the hundreds of Jewish film festivals that dot North America, Europe and beyond each year. The very existence of this circuit is remarkable. Although many national cinemas have occasional showcases in cities across the world, Jewish film festivals uniquely comprise a network of well-funded institutions that build off of one another and remain relatively stable from year to year. Jewish film festivals are numerous and lucrative enough that a movie can be targeted entirely towards them and not only gain a global audience, but also recoup significant sums of money. It is, perhaps, the world's most successfully institutionalised shadow circuit. And just as the more mainstream film festival circuit has its A-list showcases, so does the world of Jewish film festivals. Festivals such as the UK Jewish Film Festival (www.ukjewishfilm.org), Toronto Jewish Film Festival (www.tjff.com), San Francisco Jewish Film Festival (www.sfjff.org) and Boston Jewish Film Festival, though secondary in all other contexts, represent for Diskin the keys to a successful business model. Diskin remarks that although even the top Jewish festivals never lead to theatrical distribution, success in these major Jewish venues directly drives programming choices at smaller Jewish festivals that often programme only a handful of films. These minor Jewish events often operate with miniscule staff and budgets, offering little in the way of time to screen the thousands of potential films that might be programmed in any given year. As a result, small Jewish film festivals will often only consider those films that have been approved by the major nods of this shadow circuit, making their selections a subset of those choices made by higher profile programmers. Thus, by targeting a handful of key festivals with her films, Diskin potentially unlocks numerous, if still modest, income sources for them. For example, the film *David* (Joel Fendelman, 2010), one of Diskin's few narrative titles, played at the UK and Boston Jewish Festivals early in its run in 2011. By October of 2013, the film had played at 36 separate Jewish film festivals, receiving on average roughly U.S.$700 as a screening fee at each event. It is rare for any film to play in so many festivals, let alone to receive fees from the majority of festivals at which it plays. However, the Jewish shadow circuit, often funded by local Jewish Federations and community centres, offers a uniquely robust and well-supported series of venues for Israeli films.

Furthermore, as Diskin notes, this Jewish shadow circuit offers films such as *David* an invaluable level of publicity. Although attendance at smaller Jewish festivals can be relatively slight, audiences are often disproportionately comprised of local educators and heads of Jewish institutions. Playing these festivals thus commonly leads not only to subsequent bookings, but also to institutional video sales that add a crucial revenue stream. Thus, for a savvy distributor such as Diskin, the Jewish shadow circuit offers an economic justification to support and promote films with no realistic chance of succeeding at Sundance or Cannes.

As unusual as the Jewish film festival environment is, it does not represent the only shadow circuit to which Israeli films have potentially profitable access. Dozens of major world cities, including Los Angeles (lajfilmfest.org), Miami (www.miamijewishfilmfestival.com/mjff), Montreal and Sydney (www.jiff.com.au), stage Israel Film Festivals separate from Jewish-themed events. These Israeli-branded festivals tend to be marketed, at least in part, to Israeli immigrants living abroad. Perhaps surprisingly, Diskin also represents films such as *Palestine in the South* (Ana Maria Hurtado, Chile, 2011) and *Dubak, Palastinai Yehudi* (*Dubak, A Palestinan Jew*, Ella Alerman, 2008), which have found success at Palestinian film festivals across the world. Furthermore, Diskin has found success with many of her films on the Human Rights festival shadow circuit. Just as is the case with Jewish film festivals, this thematic circuit offers a few key festivals, such as the Human Rights Watch International Film Festival (HRWIFF) that serves as a gatekeeper for a variety of smaller, similar events.

Often, Diskin finds films able to circulate simultaneously on these separate shadow circuits, combining fees from across divergent events in order to drive enough revenue to support her work with the film. For example, the documentary *One Shot* (Nurit Kedar, 2004), which features candid, self-critical interviews with Israeli snipers, began its run at the HRWIFF, a stamp of legitimation that led to it being featured on five subsequent human rights programmes. It also, however, played on the IDFA's 'Reflecting Images' programme, an offshoot of the A-list festival. This contributed to a limited run at mid-range generalist festivals such as the Melbourne International Film Festival and Istanbul International Film Festival. Additionally, *One Shot* was selected to the influential Toronto

Jewish Film Festival, playing at five venues on that shadow circuit. Finally, the film was selected as part of the 2005 Malmö (Sweden) Palestinian Film Festival. Although *One Shot* was perhaps exceptional in its ability to cross circuits, it is, in many ways, a metonymic representation of the totality of Israeli cinema. Though never reaching a mass audience or garnering a single, dependable revenue stream, the film's multipronged connection to global discourses and diasporic communities was enough to piece together an effective distribution strategy.

Conclusion – Always Already Global

Perhaps what is most striking about the globalisation of Israeli cinema is the extremely localised, idiosyncratic nature of the films. Although, of course, movies such as *The Gatekeepers*, *5 Broken Cameras*, *The Flat* and *One Shot*, touch upon themes that can be widely appreciated, they each also require viewers to delve deeply into the complex historical, political and social circumstances of people in a small country in a far-flung corner of the globe. And yet, Israel not only consistently garners international attention for its films, but also supports numerous small production houses and distributorships such as Ruth Diskin Films. The robust, highly globalised nature of the Israeli film industry has much to do, we have argued, with the particulars of the global film festival environment. At both the A-list level and the shadow circuit level, Israeli films benefit from an enhanced relationship to globalisation that predates the release of any particular film. For Israeli films aimed at A-list outlets, the constant controversy that surrounds Israeli film production serves to emphasise the relevance of Israeli content, even if it causes some viewers to enact boycotts. High-profile protestations may be adding a sense of gravitas and immediacy to films that otherwise would be seen as unremarkable instantiations of a small national cinema culture.

Even more remarkable, however, is the strength Israeli cinema draws from the various global shadow festival circuits in which its films participate. Although these festivals offer little hope for a film wishing to break into the mainstream, the sheer number of paying customers available to Israeli projects in the form of Jewish, Israeli, Palestinian and human rights film festivals, represents a unique resource. These outlets not only provide small-scale Israeli productions with access to audiences across the world, but also incentivise distributors such as Ruth Diskin to work with a wider variety of filmmakers.

In an international film environment that funnels enormous amounts of revenue to a few global blockbusters, this situation is of particular scholarly interest. In contrast to the traditional 'feeder' model of film festivals, according to which A-list festivals legitimate and make profitable a handful of films, the shadow circuits described here offer a place for numerous films to make some, if not as much, money. And, although it is perhaps a model that is only applicable in a limited set of cases, it nonetheless offers a strong caution against reductive, one-size-fits-all conceptualisations of the relationship between film festivals and globalisation.

Works Cited

Aloni, Udi, Elle Flanders, Richard Fung, John Greyson, Naomi Klein, Kathy Wazana, Cynthia Wright, and b h Yael (2009) 'Toronto Declaration: No Celebration of Occupation'. On-line. Available HTTP: http://torontodeclaration.blogspot.com/ (16 September 2013).

Appadurai, Arjun (1996) *Modernity at Large: Cultural Dimensions of Globalization*. Minneapolis: University of Minnesota Press.

Box office / business for The Flat (2013) IMDb.com. On-line. Available HTTP: http://www.imdb.com/title/tt2071620/business?ref_=tt_dt_bus (16 September 2013)

'Director Ken Loach Exits Melbourne Film Festival in Protest of Israeli Funding' (2009) news.com.au. On-line. Available HTTP: http://www.news.com.au/breaking-news/director-ken-loach-exits-melbourne-film-festival-in-protest-of-israeli-funding/story-e6frfkp9-1225751688594 (18 July 2013).

Chan, Felicia (2011) 'The International Film Festival and the Making of a National Cinema', *Screen*, 52, 2, 253-260.

Czach, Liz (2004) 'Film Festivals, Programming, and the Building of a National Cinema', *The Moving Image* 4, 1, 76-88.

Dayan, Daniel (2000) 'Looking for Sundance: The Social Construction of a Film Festival'. In Ib Bondebjerg (ed.) *Moving Images, Culture and the Mind*. London: University of Luton Press, 43-52; 45.

DeFore, John (2012) 'The Flat: Tribeca Review', *The Hollywood Reporter*. On-line. Available HTTP: http://www.hollywoodreporter.com/review/flat-tribeca-review-documentary-317893 (29 April 2013).

de Valck, Marijke (2007) *Film Festivals: From European Geopolitics to Global Cinema*. Amsterdam: Amsterdam University Press.

Diskin, Ruth (2013) Personal interview. Interviewed by Matt Sienkiewicz (17 September 2013).

Dönmez-Colin, Gönül (2012) 'Film Festivals in Turkey: Promoting National Cinema while Nourishing Film Culture', in Jeffrey Ruoff (ed.) *Coming Soon to a Festival Near You: Programming Film Festivals*. St Andrews: St Andrews Film Studies, 101-116.

Gamson, Joshua (1996) 'The Organizational Shaping of Collective Identity: The Case of Lesbian and Gay Film Festivals in New York', *Sociological Forum*, 11, 2, 231-61.

Iordanova, Dina (2009) 'The Film Festival Circuit', in Dina Iordanova with Ragan Rhyne (eds) *FFY 1: The Festival Circuit*. St. Andrews: St. Andrews Film Studies and College Gate Press, 23-39.

Jenkins, Henry, Sam Ford, and Joshua Green (2013) *Spreadable Media: Creating Value and Meaning in a Networked Culture*. New York and London: New York University Press.

Nichols, Bill (1994) 'Discovering Form, Inferring Meaning: New Cinemas and the Film Festival Circuit', *Film Quarterly* 47, 3, 16-30.

Nichols, Bill (1991) *Representations of Reality: Issues and Concepts in Documentary*. Bloomington: Indiana University Press.

Palestinian Campaign for the Academic and Cultural Boycott of Israel (2009) 'TIFF Celebrating Israeli colonialism, ethnic cleansing and apartheid! City-to-City Spotlight on Tel Aviv at the Toronto International Film Festival'. On-line. Available HTTP: http://www.pacbi.org/etemplate.php?id=1085 (27 August 2013).

Peranson, Mark (2009). 'First You Get the Power, Then You Get the Money: Two Models of Film Festivals', in Richard Porton (ed.) *dekalog 3: On Film Festivals*. London and New York: Wallflower Press, 23-37.

Rhyne, Ragan (2009) 'Film Festival Circuits and Stakeholders', in Dina Iordanova with Ragan Rhyne (eds) *FFY 1: The Festival Circuit*. St Andrews: St. Andrews Film Studies and College Gate Press, 9-22.

Rohter, Larry (2013) 'A Documentary About a Palestinian Village Sets Off a Dispute', *The New York Times*, 13 February. On-line. Available HTTP: http://carpetbagger.blogs.nytimes.com/2013/02/13/a-documentary-about-a-palestinian-village-sets-off-a-dispute/ (13 February 2013).

Wong, Cindy Hing-Yuk (2011) *Film Festivals: Culture, People, and Power on the Global Screen*. New Brunswick, New Jersey, and London: Rutgers University Press.

Notes

1 In addition to examining the promotional materials put forth on www.ruthfilms.com, the authors also conducted an interview with Ruth Diskin via Skype on 17 September 2013.

Carole Zabar's Other Israel Film Festival

Dina Iordanova

First held in 2007, the Other Israel Film Festival (www.otherisrael.org) abides by a Mission Statement, according to which it

> uses film to foster social awareness and cultural understanding. The Festival presents dramatic and documentary films, as well as engaging panels about history, culture and identity on the topic of minority populations in Israel with a focus on Arab / Palestinian citizens of Israel. Our goal is to provide a dynamic and inclusive forum for exploitation of, and dialogue about, diverse communities in Israel, and encourage cinematic expression and creativity dealing with these themes. (Other Israel)

In addition to Israel's Muslim and Christian Arab populations (close to 2 million people), the festival is concerned with the cinematic treatment of other Israeli minorities. There are Druze, Bedouins, as well as the significant population of foreign workers (nearly half a million) and other non-Jewish immigrants whose experiences constitute an important yet lesser-known part of the country's multicultural context.

Initiated and largely funded by Carole Zabar (of Zabar's, the famous Upper West Side food emporium; http://www.zabars.com), the Other Israel takes place over a week in mid-November and is headquartered at the Jewish Community Centre (JCC) in Manhattan. For a festival that is still in its first decade, it has generated an encouraging amount of media attention, with articles in *The Washington Post*, *The New York Times* and the *Village Voice*, among other publications.[1]

In June 2013, I travelled to New York for a meeting with the festival's team. Our encounter took place on the premises of the JCC and was attended by the festival's founder Carole Zabar,[2] as well as by two other team members – the festival's Director Ravit Turjeman[3] (of Dragoman Films) and the festival's Executive Director Isaac Zablocki (the Director of the Israel Film Center at the JCC in Manhattan).[4] Our conversation lasted over an hour and was recorded on my advanced Samsung Galaxy II phone. Due to my technical ineptitude, however, at the last moment I pressed the wrong button and lost the entire recording. I left thinking I could restore the conversation from memory if I only could work on the transcript sooner rather than later. But within days of my return from New York I suffered a family bereavement, so for me the summer months of 2013 were marked by mourning, a period during which I could not work meaningfully. At the time of this writing, in October 2013, I have no way to reliably reference a recording of the conversation and therefore I cannot present the results of this interview as a transcript. What I have reconstructed here is based on the extensive notes that I took during the meeting. To compensate for this deficiency, I explored much material from the web and printed sources, the festival's leaflets and site, and used research notes that I had assembled in preparation for the interview and in the aftermath. Thus, what I render here is a portrait of the Other Israel Film Festival that is partly based on the June 2013 encounter with the founder and the programming team, and partly on my own research.

Why did I think the Other Israel would be an interesting festival to present in the context of this volume? Perhaps because I know that there is a solid, yet often overlooked body of works that feature the difficult co-existence of diverse groups in Israel, i.e. in what is ultimately a multi-ethnic state that finds it difficult to recognise its own diverse nature. Perhaps because, based on my own past experience working with similar material in the context of the Balkan conflict,[5] I know how influential the type of films they present can be. Perhaps because, like the festival's founder, I believe that equating 'Israeli' with 'Jewish' is counter-productive as it obscures multiple other dimensions that are equally vital and deserving of respect and mindful awareness. Perhaps because I like Zabar's *chutzpah* in creating this festival: even if she is assisted by affluence, this is a woman alone taking on the rigid establishment of American mainstream public opinion in her own delightfully stubborn and idiosyncratic way. And perhaps because I share her views on the importance of understanding and respecting multiculturalism and the power of film.[6] So, here is my report on what I learned about the Other Israel Film Festival.

For whom is the festival? The festival is a mainstay for those New York-based Jews who want to keep an open mind on the conflict, and for those Arab-Israelis who are open to the idea of dialogue. According to *The New York Times*, Zabar's

> one goal [for] the festival was to make American Jews face difficult realities. 'I am doing this for those Jews who go to Israel and see only the fine and rosy parts of life there,' she said. 'I think they have to see this. It is the real Israel. That is the bottom line of why I started this festival.' (Bronner 2012)

Programming team. At this point, the festival is programmed by a team of four: Carole Zabar, Ravit Turjeman, Isaac Zablocki (all three based in Manhattan) and with the close involvement of the Israeli-Arab actor Mohammad Bakri,[7] who is based in Israel and thus interacts with them from a distance. Zabar has frequently spoken publicly of her great friendship with Bakri, which has developed and persevered over the years. She reiterated to me that this is a friendship she particularly cherishes, but she feels her friendship with the other team members is remarkable as well. These relationships are not easy, as all team members differ in their political persuasions. She explains that Bakri usually walks out on the festival at least once every year but always stays on in the end.[8] All things considered, Zabar said, what is most important for the quality of the festival's programme is that members of the team have the freedom to challenge and disagree with one other.

Programming philosophy. For programmer Zablocki, the most important thing is the quality of the films, as it is on quality that the festival's reputation is built. For Zabar, there are other important dimensions: the conversations that take place around the film, the aura that is created, and even the very fact that the festival takes place. According to her, these things may be even more important than the films. The festival generates a kind of community, which sometimes draws in people who may not have attended just a picture show. 'But all these elements would not be as impactful', Ravit Turjeman interjects, 'if the films were not there.' They all concede that, for the festival, the films' content may sometimes be more important than their form.

The programming philosophy relies on showing different takes on life via films from a variety of countries. For an opening night gala the programmers would usually seek to have a film featuring life in a divided country; most often these are films feature the lives of Israeli Arabs. In 2013, the festival opened with the American *Dancing in Jaffa* (Hilla Medalia, U.S., 2013); in 2012, the French *Une bouteille à la mer* (*A Bottle in the Gaza Sea*, Thierry Binisti, France / Israel / Canada, 2011) was received with great interest.

The programme is put together through a selection of films seen at other festivals in Israel (most commonly at Docaviv in Tel Aviv in May (www.docaviv.co.il), at the Jerusalem FF (www.jff.org.il), at the Haifa FF (www.haifaff.co.il) or at other festivals in the U.S., such as the Hamptons International Film Festival (www.hamptonsfilmfest.org) or the Sundance Film Festival (www.sundance.org/festival)). About 20-30% of the programme is selected from among the 100 or so films submitted directly to the open call (in 2012, three out of the 14 films at the festival were selected in this way). Some of the acclaimed films screened in recent times include *Dolphin Boy* (Dani Menkin and Yonatan Nir, Israel,

2011), or *Shom'ray Ha'Saf* (*The Gatekeepers*, Dror Moreh, Israel / France / Germany / Belgium, 2012).

Venues. Most of the festival screenings take place at the JCC in Manhattan (Upper West Side, 334 Amsterdam Avenue; www.jccmanhattan.org). All films also show at the Cinema Village in Greenwich Village (which bills itself as 'specializing in provocative foreign and independent films'; www.cinemavillage.com). In recent years the festival has been running joint projects with the Taub Centre for Israeli studies at New York University (www.hebrewjudaic.as.nyu.edu/page/taub) and some of the screenings have also taken place at NYU facilities. A selection of films is streamed via the website, but access is available only to audiences based in the U.S. (for copyright reasons). The website also streams some of the discussions that take place around the festival.[9]

Beyond New York City? Is there a network that permits at least some of the films to be seen beyond NYC? What is, in this respect, the relationship of the Other Israel to the significant number of Jewish Film Festivals across North America and internationally? Isaac Zablocki runs a network of about 80 Jewish Film Festivals,[10] based chiefly in the U.S., but in other countries, too. In his assessment, about half of the films shown at the Other Israel would play in the context of many of these other Jewish film festivals as well. Also, a variety of festivals and events – sometimes based in remote or unexpected places – get in touch to ask for some of the films: there has been interest from the Netherlands and Brazil, but also from Rome and even from Jaffa in Israel. In this way, Other Israel plays a distribution role of sorts, ensuring a wider spread for such material.

Sidebars and debates. One of the most important features of the festival is the series of talks and encounters organised and presented as part of the Speak Easy Café, an on-going festival project hosted at the Laurie M. Tisch Gallery in Manhattan (www.otherisrael.org/speakeasy), again at the JCC. An example of a recent panel topic is Other Voices of Conscience: Challenging the Status Quo in Israel Today. It was at Speak Easy that, in 2011, actor Mohammad Bakri engaged in dialogue with Ella Shohat, known for her most eloquent writing on matters of the multi-layered Orientalisation and the problematic representation of minorities in Israeli cinema (1989). Other events staged by the festival include informal brunch discussions and a New Generations Shabbat Dinner, intended to provide a platform for 'intimate discussion on activism in Israel with festival guests' (Other Israel). The chief concern for the organisers is to keep the conversation going and ensure that the ensuing dialogue reflects the difference of opinions without excluding anyone.

Otherness. The films selected by the festival form a programme that addresses a broad variety of aspects of 'otherness' and that show the multicultural complexity of Israel. Over the years, films on the programme have dealt with many diverse topics, ranging from African refugees to forbidden love. In 2012, critics praised the selection and suggested a subtle shift towards a more universal understanding of otherness, as suggested by Emmanuel Lévinas (Bronner 2012). Ravit Turjeman confirmed that their aim is indeed to push the conversation a bit further, focusing on peace and reconciliation, yet not to dwell solely on the difficult relationship between Palestinians and Israeli Jews. It would be unfair to the audiences to not bring up those additional dimensions; Lévinas' ideas of otherness are important because they deal with a wider range of issues and not solely with conflict.[11]

TRC? I noticed that the South African Truth and Reconciliation Commission (TRC) is referenced as an inspiration for a difficult yet necessary dialogue, so I asked about it. The response was that this issue had come up in regard to the showing of the film *One Day After Peace* (Erez Laufer and Miri Laufer, Israel, 2012); the team recognise the importance of such cathartic encounters as those known to have occurred in the context of the TRC-led process, yet admit that they do not believe such things are likely to happen in Israel. How can one talk about such matters? There are so many layers of trauma and resentment. 'It is not likely that Israel will ever come to it', Zabar says. Indeed, according to Isaac, such important dialogues may come about on a social level, but only after peace. 'It will take a few generations', adds Ravit.

Partners and supporters: Also founded and partially funded by Carole Zabar at the JCC in Manhattan, is the Israel Film Center (www. israelfilmcenter.org), a major sponsor of Other Israel. The New Israel Fund (www.nif.org), an international organisation 'committed to equality and democracy for all Israelis' is a partner. Another partner is the educational foundation Givat Haviva, whose stated mission is 'furthering equality and understanding between Jews and Arabs and Israel' (www.givathaviva. org).

The bulk of the Other Israel's budget (approx. U.S.$175,000 per annum, which also pays part of Zablocki's salary at the Israel Film Center) comes from Zabar's private funds. Other support comes mainly as in-kind matching funds. I ask why it is that they do not seem to be pro-active in seeking more sponsors. What would happen if, for some reason, Zabar could no longer back the festival? The response of the team is that they are not worried about continuity and they are optimistic about the event's sustainability. For the time being it is not necessary to seek other sponsors; the funding is sufficient. Should Zabar's support cease for some reason, I am assured, there are enough parties out there willing to pick up the bill and ensure that the festival continues. Isaac and Ravit are equally invested in and committed to the festival, and they are sure that the JCC will continue supporting Other Israel, as it is already one of its established brands. Zabar adds that there are also other people in the community who have the means and the desire to step in if required: 'I am not alone.'

Oppositions and rejection. The objections are two-fold: 'The title of the festival proves tricky for everyone', Isaac remarks. First, there is criticism from various Jewish groups. This was most pronounced in the early days. During the first and second year of the festival, for example, there were phone calls expressing suspicion about an anti-Israeli agenda. Somebody even started an organisation – 'one man and a computer', as Isaac puts it – called *JCC Watch*, the purpose of which is the monitoring of the JCC for alleged anti-Israeli activity (www.jccwatch.org). There has been criticism about some of the discussions that take place at Speak Easy, which are recorded and posted on Other Israel's On Demand website (www.otherisraelondemand.com). When the festival sought assistance from the Israeli consulate, someone suggested: 'Why don't you go to the Other Israeli consulate?' Zabar's close friendship with and support for Mohammad Bakri, whose documentary *Jenin, Jenin* (Israel, 2003) had been banned by the Israeli Film Board, which had described it as a 'propagandistic lie' (Pogrebin 2008), has also raised eyebrows among the Jewish community.[12] But whilst there have been tensions, there have so far not been problems major enough to have prevented the festival from taking place.[13] The festival is not yet mainstream, but is now much more established than when it began.

Next, there is the boycott, by Palestinians, and by Arab nations and international individuals, of all things Israeli. 'Efforts by the festival organizers to reach out to Arab groups have met with rejection over the past few years [...] nonetheless reaching across such barriers remains perhaps the central theme of the films being shown' (Bronner 2012).[14] Zablocki confirms that it has been difficult to partner up with Arab organisations. For many, the boycott comes first and they take a 'guilty until proven innocent' stance. The mere fact that the festival titles itself Other *Israel* would be enough to cause some to disassociate themselves from it as a reflex. And even though Zabar's efforts have earned the festival, and herself, the moniker of 'outliers' (Bronner 2012), Palestinian and Arab organisations have traditionally snubbed the event. Arab and Palestinian filmmakers who have taken part have had to make difficult choices: there have been directors who committed to take part but eventually did not come. Nevertheless, and perhaps most importantly, the team is committed to continuing to invite Arab and Palestinian directors, and there are, for the most part, at least *some* who do take part.

Food and film. To me it seemed logical to ask Zabar if she sees a direct link between film and food. After all, some of the most important discussions take place during brunch meetings hosted and catered at her home.[15] She has often expressed the view that the only road to peace is by nurturing contacts between people, and on one occasion she used the metaphor of 'a famous Zabar's lobster salad which only has crayfish in it' (but no real lobster) to describe the uneasy situation of Arab Israelis (Zabar 2011). To her, food is one of the major tools for enabling communication; the breaking of bread and a shared meal can see all manner of borders transcended. She has even written a piece that speaks of 'crossing the cultural divide between Arabs and Jews through food and film' that was published by the *Washington Post*, symbolically, on the 10th anniversary of 9/11 (Zabar 2011). Cultural cross-over and the sharing of worlds is not a fantasy; it has already been achieved to some extent in important ways that are often overlooked, but that can teach us vital lessons. Thus, what some today may regard as traditional Jewish fare, in fact sports Arab roots, viz., the hummus boom of the 1970s, or rise of the falafel.[16] In the context of the current explosion of interest in food, Zabar believes that a new BBC project, Yotam Ottolenghi's *Jerusalem on a Plate* (2013), provides a vivid illustration of how such elusive multicultural conviviality can be effectively brought to the table.

Is this festival activist? 'Absolutely,' affirms Zabar. 'I wanted to have an activist stealth films festival, to present a picture of ordinary Arab-Israelis, to show they are not as scary as many think: they are not only terrorists; I wanted to show their human face.' As she has said elsewhere: 'It is not about taking sides – this festival is about people' (Other Israel). The activism was there from the beginning, and so what is particularly important is the shared experience of viewing films alongside others in the audience, observing how they interact and react – this is as important to Zabar as her own reaction to the films. She also believes the website plays an important role. Zablocki stresses that films screened here are never left to stand alone, the aim is to engage audiences in conversation. 'For us it is not just about bringing in the directors or experts but to have the conversations in the context of the Speak Easy Café.'

Ravit Turjeman observes that a major change in the history of the festival came with the introduction of its Film Fund in 2009 (www.otherisrael.org/film-fund). A number of its funded films have already been shown at the festival, including *Zahara*, by Mohammad Bakri

(Palestine / Israel, 2009).[17] Filmmakers who visit the festival have the opportunity to participate in important discussions. And, significantly, these exchanges take place in New York, far from where the on-going conflict; people feel more at ease, open up and talk. 'We have relations with these filmmakers, we have conversations here that they cannot have there', Zabar says.

Summing up is probably best left to Zablocki, who thinks of the Other Israel Film Festival as 'by far one of the most progressive and creative festivals':

> There may be many other interesting film festivals out there; some have more money, some have better access. Yet our creativity, ingenuity, and vision, the quality of our programming, the dialogues, our understanding and thinking outside the box, make us proud. We are tempted to think that more people go to film festivals than to synagogues, and the added value that is created is enormous.

Works Cited

Bronner, Ethan (2012) 'Films Show an Israel Divided From Its Neighbors and Itself', *The New York Times*. 7 November. On-line. Available HTTP: http://www.nytimes.com/2012/11/08/movies/other-israel-film-festivtal-explores-a-fractured-nation.html (4 November 2013).

Lévinas, Emmanuel (1969) [1961] *Totality and Infinity: An Essay on Exteriority*. Pittsburgh: Duquesne University Press.

Marks, Laura U. (2004) 'The Ethical Presenter: Or How to Have Good Arguments over Dinner', *The Moving Image*, 4, 1, 34-47.

Other Israel Film Festival website (2013). On-line. Available HTTP: http://www.otherisrael.org/about-us. (30 October 2013).

Ottolenghi, Yotam (2013) *Ottolenghi's Mediterranean Feast: Jerusalem on a Plate* (DVD). London: Spirit Entertainment Limited.

Pogrebin, Robin (2008) 'Beyond Them and Us: Films About Israeli Arabs', *The New York Times*, 29 October. On-line. Available HTTP: http://www.nytimes.com/2008/10/29/movies/29fest.html?partner=rssnyt&emc=rss&_r=0 (3 November 2013).

Shohat, Ella (1989) *Israeli Cinema: East / West and the Politics of Representation*. Austin: University of Texas Press.

Zabar, Carole (2011) 'Crossing the Cultural Divide between Arabs and Jews through Food and Film', *Washington Post*, 11 September. On-line. Available HTTP: http://www.washingtonpost.com/blogs/guest-voices/post/crossing-the-cultural-divide-between-arabs-

and-jews-through-food-and-film/2012/11/09/3fae0e24-2aae-11e2-bab2-eda299503684_blog.html (1 November 2013).

Zabar, Carole (2011) 'Other Israel Film Festival Carole Zabar Video Blog: Other Israel in a Tent', On-line. Available HTTP: http://www.youtube.com/watch?v=qNp8n627_y0 (30 October 2013).

'Saul Zabar, Proprietor of Zabar's' (2012) *CityWide*. 17 October. Online. Available HTTP: http://www.youtube.com/watch?v=vB3230RVWgs (3 November 2013).

Notes

[1]   Yet when I asked my New York-based cinéphile friends about the festival, most said they were hearing about it for the first time from me. Another friend commented by email: 'I cannot make up my mind whether I think the festival is doing a great job in sustaining a multi-ethnic awareness among especially U.S.-based Jews (who seem to be the primary target group) or trying to present a more favourable image of Israel than the one many of us are left with due to the Arab-Israeli conflict, like "We certainly have nothing against the Arabs – some of our best friends are Arabs"' (14 January 2014).

[2]   Carole Zabar, described as 'both a great lover of Israel and a harsh critic, especially about its treatment of Palestinians' (Bronner, 2012), was born in Detroit, Michigan, and attended Hebrew University of Jerusalem in the 1960s, graduating in Philosophy and English. She has been active in many Israeli non-profit organisations related to civil rights for over three decades. She worked as a professional photographer, and later completed a Law degree and worked for the City Law Department of New York in the Family Court Division. In 2006, she established the Other Israel Film Festival. Mrs. Zabar is also the co-founder of the Israel Film Center at the JCC in Manhattan. As part of her support for Israeli cultural, social and political causes, Mrs. Zabar serves as board member of the JCC, the New Israel Fund and the American Friends of Meretz. Most recently, she served as Executive Producer of Mohamed Bakri's documentary film *Zahara* (Palestine / Israel, 2009).

[3]   Ravit Turjeman was born in Israel and is now based in the U.S. She founded and runs Dragoman Films (http://www.dragomanfilms.com), a NYC-based boutique distribution company, specialising in the marketing of independent Israeli cinema in North America. Ms. Turjeman also serves as director and programmer of other film festivals in the Tri-State area, including the New York Sephardic Jewish Film Festival (http://sephardicfilmfest.org).

[4]   Isaac Zablocki was born in New York, grew up in Israel and served as an Educational producer at the leading film unit of the Israeli Defense Forces. He studied film at Columbia University and worked for Miramax. Since 2004, Mr. Zablocki has been the Director of Film Programs at the JCC in Manhattan, from where he programmes several different film festivals, including Reelabilites: NY Disabilities Film Festival (http://www.reelabilities.org) which also travels nation-wide across the U.S. to a number of large cities. He is the leading programmer of Israeli films in the U.S. and has developed the largest online database of Israeli films as well as the Israel Film Center Stream, the leading site for streaming Israeli films. He also writes for *The Huffington Post*.

5   See in particular my (2001) *Cinema of Flames: Balkan Film, Culture and the Media* (London: BFI); the writings in 'Balkan Cinema', the special supplement to *Cineaste* (New York) in June 2007. On-line. Available HTTP: http://www.cineaste. com/; and (2008) 'Intercultural Cinema and Balkan Hushed Histories' in *New Review of Film and Television*, 6, 1, 5-16

6   In a Letter from the Founder document posted on the festival's website, Carole Zabar develops her vision of the importance of multiculturalism and the role of film in fostering understanding. It reads:

> The Other Israel Film Festival was founded to be a vehicle for cultural change and social insights into the nature of Israel as a democracy and the complex condition of the lives of its minorities that are living in the Jewish Sate. Israel's largest minority within its midst is the 1.7 million Arabs. In its 60 years of existence Israel has fostered another group of people who have put down roots in Israel and have born their Hebrew speaking children in its boundaries - Israel's 300,000 foreign workers. It is not about the conflict - it is not about taking sides - this festival is about people.
>
> Film can be a powerful tool, it can show new sides, change perceptions, and evoke emotions. Through the use of film we are provided with a human dimension that extends beyond the daily news bulletins. Film can explore the deeper meaning of everyday living. Through these films, the festival aims to present the lives, dreams and strengths of the Arab minority and to show their participation in Israeli life. Foreign workers present a unique condition in Israeli society and we aim to familiarize our audience with the faces of 'foreign workers'.
>
> I care deeply about Israel and its future. Growing up in a democratic Jewish state has without any doubt shaped the cultural and national identity of all of its inhabitants and citizens - who know no other home. These films and artistic expressions are paving the way to co-existence and a new, more inclusive culture in the Middle East.
>
> Sincerely, Carole Zabar Founder
> (http://www.otherisrael.org/about-us).

7   Arab-Israeli theatre and film personality Mohammad Bakri was born in 1953 in North Israel. He is best known for one-man theatrical performances, and he is the director of critically outspoken documentary films such as *Jenin, Jenin* (Israel 2003), a film which won the Best Film award at the Carthage Film Festival, JCC and was subjected to an extensive anti-censorship battle in Israel, and *Zahara* (Palestine/Israel, 2009). A transnational actor, Bakri is also known for his roles in important critical films such as *Hanna K.* (Israel / France, 1983, Constantin Costa-Gavras), *Me'Ahorei Hasoragim* (*Beyond the Walls*, Israel, 1984, Uri Barabash), *Esther* (1986, Austria / Israel / UK, Amos Gitai, where he co-starred with Juliano Mer-Khamis), *Haifa* (Palestine/Germany/Netherlands, 1996, Rashid Mashrawi), *Desperado Square* (Israel, 2001, Benny Toraty), *Private* (Italy, 2004, Saverio Costanzo) and *La Masseria Delle Allodole* by Paolo and Vittorio Taviani (*The Lark Farm*, Italy / France / Spain / Bulgaria / Germany, 2007).

8   Bakri clearly prefers to keep a low profile with regard to his involvement. He is not listed as a member of the programming team on the website, nor as a member of the advisory board, which includes the following personnel: Daniel Chalfen - Filmmaker, DJC Films; Victoria S. Cook – Entertainment Attorney; Gil Kulick – Environmental and Middle East Peace Activist; Richard Lorber –

President, Koch Lorber Films; Richard Pena – Director, Film Society of Lincoln Center. Professor, Columbia University Film Department; Ravit Turjeman – Festival Director (Dragoman Films); Isaac Zablocki – Festival Executive Director (The JCC Manhattan); Carole Zabar – Festival Founder.

9   Some further recordings of discussions can be found on YouTube, for example Brunch with Festival Guests (2009), available at http://www.youtube.com/watch?v=ykcCCwPD7cc

10   In Zablocki's estimation, the number of Jewish film festivals stands at about 150 across North America.

11   For Emmanuel Lévinas (1906-1995), the face-to-face encounter with another human being is a privileged phenomenon, an epiphany, where the other person's proximity and distance are both strongly felt (as discussed in his *Totality and Infinity* (1961)).

12   In a recent example where Jewishness and Israel are considered to be the same thing, in August 2013, Isaac Zablocki came under sustained attack from *The Jewish Press* for allegedly expressing 'anti-Israeli views' in his writing for *The Huffington Post*, an offense particularly exacerbated by the fact that he was a paid employee of a Jewish organisation.

13   There has been no uproar comparable to the one faced by the San Francisco Jewish Film Festival (http://www.sfjff.org), which screened a film about Rachel Corrie, resulting in a public scandal in 2009. Rachel Corrie (1979-2003) was an American pro-Palestinian peace activist who was crushed to death by an Israel Defense Forces (IDF) armoured bulldozer in Rafah, in the Gaza Strip, under contested circumstances at the height of the second Palestinian Intifada.

14   [Editor's note: Nick Denes makes similar remarks in his chapter on the London Palestine Film Festival (http://www.palestinefilmfoundation.org) written for this volume.]

15   This part of our discussion reminded me that it may be a good idea to reference here Laura Marks' piece on festival programming: Marks (2004).

16   In a CityWide interview featured on YouTube, Carole's husband Saul Zabar also discusses his own efforts to change the staff ratio at his store from being primarily Jewish at its onset to the more multicultural balance it enjoys today (Saul Zabar 2012).

17   According to our style guide, we reference all films by the nationality listed on the IMDb. In the case of *Zahara*, however, which is listed with only Palestine as a producing country, I received an indirect communication from Bakri who confirmed that the film ought to be listed as Palestine / Israel – a guidance that I have adopted for this piece.

Film Festivals in Israel

Est.	Name	Date	Website	Location	Specialisation
1983	Haifa International Film Festival	September	http://www.haifaff.co.il/	Haifa	Feature, documentary, animated and short films, retrospectives and tributes. Israeli and International competition.
1984	Jerusalem Film Festival	May-June until 1989. July since 1990	http://www.jff.org.il/	Tel Aviv	Student films. Israeli and International competition.
1986 (held every two years)	Tel Aviv International Student Film Festival	June	http://www.tauflmfest.com/	Tel Aviv	Student films. Israeli and International competition.
1997	Icon TLV - International Fantastic Film Festival	September	http://www.icon.org.il	Tel Aviv	Feature. Competition.

247

Est.	Name	Date	Website	Location	Specialisation
1999	Jerusalem Jewish Film Festival	December	http://www. jer-cin.org.il/ Cinematheque/ The%20Jewish%20 Film%20Festival. aspx	West Jerusalem	Feature, documentary, short, animated, avant-garde films. Special sub-theme on the Holocaust. No competition.
1999	Docaviv – The Tel Aviv International Documentary Film festival	May	http://www. docaviv.co.il/.	Tel Aviv	Documentary films. Israeli, international and student competitions.
2000	Rosh Pina Television and Film Festival	October	http://www. roshpinacine.com/	Rosh Pina	Israeli feature, Israeli and international television.
2001	Animix International Animation Comics & Caricature Festival	August	http://www. animixfest.co.il/	Tel Aviv	Animated films.
2002	Cinema South Festival	June	http://csf.sapir.ac.il	Sderot	Israeli cinema, world cinema and Israeli student films. Graduate competition and young filmmakers' awards.

2003 (Terminated in 2008)	Eilat International Film Festival	Spring (March or April or May)	http://eilatfilmfest.com/ (website not valid anymore)	Eilat	World and Israeli feature films, children's films. Competition for best Israeli film, best foreign film, and best children's film.
2004	Ecocinema	June	http://www.ecocinema.org.il	aifa, Tel Aviv, West Jerusalem	Feature. No competition.
2004	International Women's Film Festival	November	http://www.iwff.net/	Rehovot	Competition for best feature director, best short film director, promising director, grant for a feature script.
2004	Jewish Eye – Jewish World Film Festival	October	http://www.jewisheye.org.il	Ashkelon	Feature, documentary. Competition for the best feature film and best full-length documentary.
2005	Tel Aviv International Children's Film Festival	October	http://kidsfestival.cinema.co.il/	Tel Aviv	Children's films. No competition.

Est.	Name	Date	Website	Location	Specialisation
2006 (Terminated in 2008)	Nazareth International Film Festival	December	http://www.elsana.net/	Nazareth	Competition for international and Israeli/Palestinian Territories films on human rights. Non-competitive section for international films on religion.
2006	Tel Aviv LGBT International Film Festival	June	http://www.tlvfest.com/	Tel Aviv	Feature, short. Competition for best Israeli film.
2007	Tel Aviv Spirit Film Festival	October	http://www.spiritfestival.co.il	Tel Aviv	Feature, documentary and short films.

Compiled by Viviane Saglier
Listing is representative, not exhaustive

An Overburdened 'Brand'? Reflections on a Decade with the London Palestine Film Festival

Nick Denes

Introduction

For festival producers, Palestine can offer considerable scope as a thematic focus. Intensely mediated throughout the era of the moving image, a fascinating expanse of material is available to programmers.[1] Forever topical, new work is being produced at a growing rate, while public interest equates to viable audiences and good prospects for press attention. But these advantages bring certain challenges with them. The unusual extent of Palestine's exposure to image-making practices, its persistent topicality and the kinds of press and audience interest it tends to generate, are each tied to political associations that can impede as much as enable festival production or survival.

This chapter addresses those impediments. It draws on my own experiences as a Director of the annual London Palestine Film Festival (www.palestinefilm.org). Colleagues and peers at similarly themed festivals elsewhere may recognise some or none of the issues I address.[2] No two festivals are alike, and differing contexts can make for very different experiences in each of the areas I focus on. In the first half of what follows, I describe tensions arising between the creative and political fields referenced by the festival. I show how Palestine's tendency to evoke ideas regarding national storytelling and political pedagogy results in definitional and presentational tensions. In the second half of the chapter, I give an account of the impact these tensions can have in areas critical to the viability of a mid-sized independent film festival – curatorial partnerships and festival funding. A brief introduction to the festival and its organising body prefaces this discussion.

The London Palestine Film Festival

The Palestine Film Foundation (PFF) was formed by Khaled Ziada and me in 2004, following a six-year period in which a modest Palestine Film Festival had been produced on an *ad hoc* basis by activists associated with the School of Oriental and African Studies at the University of London. Those initial iterations aimed to engage students, scholars and fellow activists; they involved free screenings of DVD (initially VHS) formats at university, school and community venues.[3] Contact with filmmakers and audiences in this period suggested the viability of an expanded festival. In 2004, the PFF was established as a dedicated curatorial, research and fundraising structure, to facilitate that expansion. This move was partly motivated by a desire to overcome constraints felt to inhere in the earlier 'activist' model. Accordingly, one of the PFF's first aims was to adjust the festival's profile in a way that might enhance prospects for audience growth and diversification, increase access to funding resources and exhibition venues, and broaden curatorial opportunities. In 2005, a key venue partnership was established with the Barbican Cinema at London's iconic Barbican Centre. Over the following years, links were made with other cinemas, partnerships were established with several mid-size festivals and increased funding was obtained from statutory, charitable and private sources.

The repositioning reflected by these processes was effective if assessed in terms of overall festival growth. From 2003 to 2012, average audiences rose seven-fold; between 2005 and 2013, the PFF presented some 380 works at over 250 events, recording attendances in excess of 24,000.[4] With multiple daily screenings over its two-week run each spring (April / May),[5] the festival has grown in size and range to span the exhibition of 30 to 45 international works across most genres; programmes now include a roster of guest speakers, parallel art exhibitions, book talks and academic symposia.[6] The festival regularly generates mainstream UK and international media coverage.[7] Meanwhile improved and improving visibility, presentation and funding, has resulted in curatorial freedoms the previous model militated against – prestigious screen talks with renowned directors, opportunities to present high-profile premières and access to precious archive collections. While it has diversified its audiences and cultivated an inclusive public image, the festival has not foregone its roots in political activism. This is evidenced most clearly in the festival's second week, which sees it return to free-access venues, working closely with academic and activist partners. Importantly, whereas non-cinema exhibition in the previous model restricted programming options, the festival's current form means such screenings offer a latitude that can enrich overall programming by lending space for valuable, but perhaps technically imperfect or highly specialised content.

Definitional Friction: Politics and Branding

Its benefits notwithstanding, the festival's current structure is also indicative of a definitional tension with regard to its political aims and image. The early activist model had wed rudimentary exhibition to a promotional strategy relying heavily on campaign networks. The model risked 'ghettoising' an encounter with Palestine on film, by precluding audience diversification and aesthetically compromising works. The overcoming of this problem definitively supposed, instead, an alloying of the festival to a 'brand' deemed palatable to stakeholders, including: funding bodies averse to suggestions of the political; partner organisations with their own image-management concerns; commercial distributors or status-conscious filmmakers positioning their products; press editors packaging their own brands and stories; and consumer-publics potentially alienated by overt signs of the political. This can be a fraught undertaking. It requires politically conscious festival organisers to appeal to the codes of mainstream cultural valuation, seeking to harness the powers of a neoliberal consumerism that is an anathema to their own motivations. Insofar as the designation 'Palestine' inevitably summons national and political associations, this peculiar dynamic becomes circular, instating a cycle of de- and re-branding of a *cultural* 'product' to counter the weight of its *political* associations. With the decision to retain a base in traditional modes of festival activism, and by retaining links to activist audience networks, this 'branding' circuit is made an internal characteristic of festival production. It sees the PFF regularly mobilising activist networks with which it affiliates, or engaging politically motivated participants with whom it identifies, while consciously projecting a 'brand' shorn of such profane connotations, in order to access or retain other audiences, partners, participants and funds.

The PFF and its annual festival operate in this state of definitional friction: unable (and unwilling) to divest the festival of Palestine's political associations, yet compelled to constantly allay the power of those associations to devalue or delimit the encounters it generates. Unsurprisingly, this is a state replete with impasses; many of which can be traced to an ambiguity over the relationship between politics and culture, art and activism.

Between Activism and Politics

The fourth volume the series *Film Festival Yearbook* series treats film festivals and activism (Iordanova and Torchin 2012). The editors depict a vertical intentionality that largely determines relationships between programmers, artists and audiences in an activist film festival: curators aim to 'correct the record on a certain issue' via works chosen to 'assist in winning over further supporters for the cause' (Iordanova 2012: 13); filmmakers set out to 'mobilise their films in the pursuit of justice and community action' (Torchin 2012: 10); and audiences enact a 'renewal of commitment' in contact with 'empowering stories' and 'equally committed people' (6). This is a powerful normative account of the ways politics and film combine under the sign of activism. The original model of the

London Palestine Film Festival (LPFF) bore little resemblance *in practice* to this vision. But expectations that it *should*, or *would* be consumed by political affirmations and disciplinary aims were pervasive and risked becoming debilitating. As long as funders, partners, participants or audiences, equated the festival with the aesthetic aridity or pedagogic determinism evoked in normative visions of an activist festival, efforts to expand its audience appeal, curatorial scope or funding base, would remain impeded.

The meeting of politics and film found in normative accounts of an activist film festival is not the only such meeting on offer. For some, the normative model must be resisted, not just because it risks reducing culture to instruction, but because it ultimately abjures participatory politics. Considering the documentary filmmaker as a composer of meanings, Trinh Minh-Ha observes that political composition 'is not always synonymous with ordering-so-as-to-persuade'; in fact, arrival at 'meaning can be political only when it does not let itself be easily stabilized' but, rather, appears more consistent with the imprecisions of life (1990: 89). Turning to questions of film spectatorship and persuasion, Michael Renov notes the constant need to ask

> on what basis does the spectator invest belief in the representation, what are the codes which ensure that belief, [...] and *to what extent are these processes to be made visible or knowable to the spectator?*' (1993: 31, emphasis added).

Degrees of instability and invisibility are crucial to the way meaning-making and spectatorship occur. Rather than recycling affirmations and certitudes, a political curatorial ethos might seek to foment disruptions and contradictions, uncertainties and indeterminacies. In this spirit, film's tie to politics might be rethought in terms of the 'politics' Jacques Rancière finds in his account of 'the aesthetic regime' – where artworks offer political space precisely because they neither give lessons nor have any destination' but, rather, rupture familiar artistic *and* political borders, thereby creating 'a new landscape of the visible, the sayable and the doable' (2010: 140, 149).

This understanding of 'politics' offers a marked alternative to the normative image of 'activist' festivals as pedagogic assemblages. Both models are perhaps equally idealistic and hence remote in practice. They constitute the limits of a continuum extending from didacticism to ambiguity. The LPFF operates between these extremes. It is a scene of 'activism' in that it consciously designs spaces conducive to engaged reflections and practices. But it is also a scene of 'politics', as its designs appeal to cinema and spectatorship as sources of uncertainty and disruption rather than merely affirmation or instruction. Working across these conceptions of politics and activism produces tensions and contradictions that can be compounded with the festival's similarly imprecise relationship to ideas of nationhood.

National Cinemas, National Storytelling

The LPFF has been showing international films for 15 years, featuring a dozen or more countries of production annually. Yet it is consistently cited as a *Palestinian* Film Festival. The nationalising misnomer recurs in everything from venue signage and press coverage to partnership accreditation. Too insistent to be attributed to mere technical slippage, the pattern underscores a grip that the national continues to exert over cultural and political imaginaries; a grip hardened by a 'fundamentally national framework' that the film scene's economy of critics, competitions, funders and distributors animates (Hedetoft 2000: 286). Not a problem unique to a Palestine film festival, this insistence on the national only emerges as a specific dilemma once it is wed to a conflation of the cinematic and the national as fields of narration. Expectations then readily arise that a Palestine film festival assays an idea of national identity – that its selections and their arrangement compose a particular story about Palestinian nationhood, past and present.

Histories of pernicious misrepresentation, the inadequacies of mainstream media and a scarcity of alternative forums, can result in a daunting responsibility being placed on filmmakers and other story-tellers, especially given the task of (re)asserting a recognisable national narrative. Such narratives are unsettled and multiple and this can lead to uncertain criteria being applied to films and, by extension, film programmes – both run the risk of being caught in a subjective prism of identification or national recognition. Palestinian filmmaking, in particular, has often been allocated a duty of national narration that can lead partners, audiences, or commentators, to measure work against a chimeric ideal: the 'truly Palestinian film' (Tawil-Souri 2011). Such expectations go beyond the work of Palestinians though, and are not limited to the pressures of 'conational adjudication'. The investments Palestine attracts are myriad; as a result, varying criteria can be at work in deciding a film's fealty to the object of those investments. At its most troubling, such invested spectatorship can lead to repudiations of the veracity (*ergo* legitimacy) of a given work, perhaps for depicting a subject insufficiently conformed to piety, ideology or victimhood. More commonly, an appetite exists for work redressing silences or representational harms. This can lead to excessive demands for realism, narrative explication and political transparency. Enigmatic flair or originality fade as sources of valuation with a sense that the hard-won 'permission to narrate' (Said 1984) is, above all, a chance to rebalance a representational bias – an opportunity too precious to gamble on oblique expression, much less fritter away on personal creative forays. Struggles for Palestine's national survival, history and representation can, as such, foster expectations that both films and festivals function (or ought to function) primarily as a vehicle for national storytelling. As understandable as this may be, it suggests an improbably substantive relationship between the nation's narrative (re)constitution and cinema's qualities as a site of narrative expression.[8] Nation and cinema risk undergoing a correlated reduction toward an untenable ideal of verisimilitude. With their merits weighed accordingly, this leads to films (and film programmes) being perceived largely as tools for relaying a national story effectively into a theatre of narrative contention.

A state of chronic definitional and presentational ambiguity can be traced to the festival's failure to readily corroborate any of these normative claims concerning links between the political, the national and the creative or artistic. To fend off reductive understandings of both the political and the national, the Festival is compelled to separate itself from a 'Palestinian' misnomer, to free itself of a determinism affixed to activism, and to project a cultural 'brand' vacated of political contention. Each of these (re)definitional and (re)presentational undertakings is impossible, circular, permanent. Their paradoxes and contradictions therefore permeate every aspect of the film festival's production and of the PFF's wider activities. In what follows, I explore some practical repercussions of these frictions in the fields of festival partnership and fund-generation. My aim is to show how internal definitional ambiguities and external normative pressures combine and impact on core areas of festival production and organisational development in a manner that hampers the long-term sustainability of the PFF and its annual festival.

Partnerships: Pragmatic and Ideological Impasses

For mid-sized festivals, the development of mutually beneficial curatorial and co-presentation partnerships represents a key mechanism for organisational development. Partnerships can offer valuable audience development opportunities; they deliver access to venues, experience with new forms of presentation and chances to extend professional and personal networks. How each party perceives the other is a fundamental factor determining the appeal or viability of any such partnerships. As such, partnerships are a useful lens through which to assess how the PFF's uncertain 'brand' is perceived, and to ask how Palestine's political and national associations, and the normative understandings deriving thereof, manifest in practice.

Over the past decade, the LPFF has enjoyed a sustained and fruitful partnership with its primary venue, the Barbican Cinema. It has established other lasting and respectful partnerships with UK-based, as well as international venues, festivals, programmers and cultural institutions. But over the same period, it has also faced serious obstacles when assessing or initiating some other partnerships. The impasses that have emerged can be related directly to the types of definitional and normative tensions identified above.

For some prospective partners, the spectre of the political that attaches itself to Palestine instils doubts over alienating audiences, sponsors, board members and so forth.[9] Such wariness is rarely articulated though. It might manifest initially in a failure to make good on verbal commitments or expressions of interest, an avoidance of phone calls or a failure to respond to proposals; only later, often privately and apologetically, is Palestine's political bearing likely to be proffered as explanation. This can be a circuitous process, with a private concession couched in renewed expressions of commitment, and the process resumed. This is rarely a reflection of any coherent ideological reticence. It might best be understood as a form of cost-benefit calculation: a risk felt to inhere (however uncertainly) in the political is not felt to be sufficiently offset by clear benefits to the prospective partner's prestige, revenue or other priorities. In the UK, two perceptual frameworks might explain such a calculation. In the first instance, Palestine evokes mass-mediated images of conflict bracketed by polemic. In the second, it evokes grassroots campaigns; a realm of slogans and badges, *ad hoc* coalitions, spontaneity and passion. If one framework hints at unwanted contention, the other suggests exuberant amateurism. However flawed, these are widely reinforced associations and can make for an off-putting couplet for prospective partners. Directly assuaging such concerns is complicated, with their expression (if at all) only occurring *post factum*, implicitly or in confidence.

Very different challenges can emerge when prospective partners are not wary of the political or national properties they associate with Palestine, but hope, instead, to access and mobilise powers imputed to those properties. In such cases, the PFF has experienced a relatively consistent pattern: an organisation will contact us concerning content they appear confident we will present or promote on their behalf. This is explained by virtue of the content being Palestinian-made or, more commonly, it being 'pro-Palestinian'. As it is with the pragmatic reticence sketched above, the Palestine signifier is seemingly understood as little more than a campaign slogan – a banner before which political homogeneities coalesce as half of a putative pro / anti binary. This involves the troubling claim that beyond the confines of an alleged 'anti-Palestinian' space, an undifferentiated field of culture and politics coalesces; an undiscerning unity readily co-opted to marketing or other ends. Experience suggests that it is with reductive assertions of this type that ideological impasses are more prone to arise.

In 2010, an established (and well-regarded) film festival in London contacted the PFF in the manner described, suggesting we co-present a première at their coming festival. The film was produced by an initiative dedicated to a particular form of Palestinian / Israeli 'coexistence' advocacy.[10] It works with specific stakeholders on set issues, using precise political vocabularies to express a certain ideology. The festival assured us the film was 'pro-Palestinian'. They added that this co-presentation would involve us as well as London's Jewish Film Festival – a match the film's producers were said to be especially keen on. The intention was clear to anyone familiar with the pedagogies of the film or its production body: by enlisting a 'Palestine' (in the PFF) to stand in for 'Palestinian', while equating 'Jewish' with 'Israeli', the joint presentation was devised to enact and endorse the ideological claims surrounding communalism and parity advanced in the film. Declining the proposition prompted a series of ill-tempered responses from the prospective partner, suggesting the PFF was impertinent for querying the integrity or coherence of the proposal, and that its refusal to throw its weight behind the 'pro-Palestinian' project showed it to be implacably opposed to efforts at conflict resolution. That the PFF had been cast as 'the Palestinian' in the proposed scheme suggests this attribution of belligerence was being mapped to larger political cartographies.[11]

The illustration is not as peculiar as it may appear. By reducing the Palestine signifier to a glib pro / anti logos, the mere assertion of 'pro-ness' invalidates questions of difference or discretion, ideology or nuance. It mobilises Palestine as a national, cultural and political designation, yet insists on the self-evidence of those categories as banal and interchangeable. Since the case I've described, the PFF has fielded many propositions sharing this underlying premise. What sets the above example apart, is that it was the last time we attempted to persuade a prospective partner of our concerns. Our actions were misjudged; troubling the pro / anti logos resulted in the PFF, and not that logo, being perceived as an irrational ideological structure. Declining without explanation has proved a less exasperating tactic. There continue to be awkward exceptions, though. More than once, the PFF has been unable to evade partnerships it finds questionable for the reasons described. One such case entailed promoting a film we found troublesome after repeated requests from a cinema chain we were negotiating with regarding events of our own.

As a small, independent body, such partnership decisions involve a struggle to reconcile the pragmatic or strategic with the political or the ethical. As noted, the majority of partnerships have been and remain respectful and straightforward. Contradictions and compromises over content or presentation may be inevitable in any curatorial or venue-related partnership. What seems more specific to the experience of the PFF is that normative claims and / or ideological agendas tend to precede, and to displace, more usual considerations going into forming a mutually beneficial partnership – from aesthetics to scheduling, audience development to funding. Beyond a slowly expanding radius of existing contacts and relationships, the PFF continues to be treated, first and foremost, as a conduit leading to and from imaginary political-national homogeneities, rather than as a discerning curatorial counterpart.

Funding: The Cost of Indeterminacy

Fundraising is another crucial area for festival development where 'brand' perceptions and normative frameworks become evident. Fundraising can require definitional clarifications – making explicit otherwise under-elaborated affinities, motivations and methods. As such, it stands to propel the definitional tensions and contradictions explored above into view. Because fundraising also often involves contact with entities or individuals new to the festival and at a remove from both its activities and public image, it is an area in which normative assertions about film's relationship to nationhood or activism can also exert their greatest impact.

The present economic and political climate in the UK is hostile to medium-sized independent film festivals. Always scarce, statutory funding is now virtually non-existent for festivals not operating industry market places or privileging UK and EU productions. The meagre sums still available to independent non-industry festivals, notably the British Film Institute's Film Festival Fund, are increasingly targeted at private enterprises (e.g. cinema consortia).[12] As of 2013, there was no remaining statutory film exhibition fund for which the PFF was eligible – unless it were to reinvent itself as a private venture or shoehorn UK or EU production quotas into its programmes. Philanthropic grants are, as a result, in shortening supply for independent festivals focusing on non-European content. And the largesse of wealthy donors has inevitably been tempered by the financial crises of the past half-decade. This is a worrying landscape, familiar to anyone operating in the non-commercial margins of the UK's cultural industry.

While funding opportunities have contracted over the last decade, the PFF's budgets have risen in line with the festival's growth in reach, range and size. Producing a 2005 festival cost under £9,000 (U.S. $14,500). In 2013, costs exceeded £25,000 (U.S. $40,450). This remains an inadequate sum with which to produce and promote a two-week festival consisting of upwards of 40 films, a roster of international guest speakers, accompanying art exhibitions, and more. It leaves the festival unable to fund artists' fees, festival staffing or programme-related research and travel; the PFF has no office space and is unable to finance such basic assets as a computer. While these deficits endanger the festival's long-term future, they are not in themselves the gravest threat to viability.[13] That threat resides in the fact that raising the sums on which the festival can survive has become a year-round burden, absorbing vast amounts of time and administrative resources. For an organisation the size of the PFF, the constant search for an already-inadequate budget impinges on its capacity to conceive or produce projects, eroding its very rationale. The state of funding in the UK offers little to arrest this dynamic. But its roots lie in more specific obstacles faced by the PFF; obstacles that are again related to the definitional frictions and normative pressures described.

The PFF has not been successful in acquiring commercial festival sponsorship. The reticence of sponsors can be related to a cost-benefit calculus similar to that rendering the festival unattractive to some venue or curatorial partners. UK-based companies do routinely sponsor festivals of similar size, some of which include political and even controversial films. But such sponsorship generally affiliates sponsors with uncontroversial partner brands: such as, perhaps, 'Surf', 'Documentary', 'Women', 'Green', 'Animation' or 'Human Rights'. Insofar as 'Palestine' offers a narrowing and potentially more emotive set of associations for sponsors relative to festivals of a similar size, the PFF struggles to obtain affiliations that might deliver crucial support in such areas as hotels, transportation, logistical services, catering and so on.

Absent statutory funding prospects, with limited sponsorship opportunities and stalked by inchoate associations with the political and the national, the festival is made heavily reliant on private donors who are sufficiently familiar with Palestine to be motivated, or at least unperturbed, by its resonances. This naturally includes Palestinians themselves. There is a considerable amount of private wealth in London that this focus might correspond with. However, the affluent business elites in question tend to be primarily, and understandably, inclined to focus their resources on humanitarian relief and on longer-term welfare or social initiatives in Palestine or its region. While they may (and do) make modest one-off gestures of support, insofar as cultural patronage is rarely an abiding passion, chances of cultivating substantive relationships remain slight. Moreover, they are accompanied by a powerful re-emergence of the Festival's core definitional tensions. Vera Tamari observes how funding by business elites for Palestinian museums or arts institutions has often been motivated by a sense of 'national duty' (2012). Appealing to donors moved by a sense of national or political purpose before cultural philanthropy *per se*, risks sliding into a register of 'awareness-raising'. If, as a result, the LPFF is mistaken for a simple advocacy project, normative visions of an activist film festival exert their effect: donors may imagine rough-and-ready screenings, online video campaigning, high-impact pedagogic content and an overarching ethos of voluntarism and amateurism. Such misconceptions easily reframe the Festival's meagre budget as incomprehensibly grand. Because access to, and time with, wealthy elites can be tightly restricted, overturning such misapprehensions is not straightforward.[14]

A small group of donors invested in cultural philanthropy exists, and does represent a source of funding. But again, normative understandings of the ways film, politics and nation combine can be an impediment. Arts patronage generally revolves around a monetising of prestige and status. Given the deliberate imprecision of its relationship to politics, and given the normative vision of 'film activism', the cultural capital that the festival offers in this respect is ambivalent. Arts patrons whom the PFF has been in contact with over the years exhibit a willingness to invest in activities involving the prestigious bastions of Britain's cultural establishment. The festival's partnership with the Barbican Centre is thus an appealing asset, one foregrounded in this sort of fundraising. But persisting ties to 'grimier' political spheres and registers stand to dull the sheen acquired with this ratification from the cultural mainstream.

In combination, the impact of these funding impasses is profound. They manifest themselves not just in under-resourced festival production, but also in a lack of durable relationships, a corrosion of curatorial and research capacities, and an inability to underwrite mid- to long-range projects. This leaves festival production reliant on the investment of considerable resources by its organisers; it means the very activities that lend originality and value to programmes (e.g. archive research or subtitling) are steadily set aside as non-urgent or non-critical; it means the PFF is reluctant to undertake long-range partnerships, and that making its own long-range plans remains highly speculative.

Conclusion: Toward a Revised Festival Model

Since its establishment in 2004, the Palestine Film Foundation has operated in a state of mounting contradiction over its definition and even its viability as a curatorial concern. Its annual festival has grown significantly in size, reach and scope. It has also become increasingly costly to run. Throughout this decade, the PFF has struggled to assert a festival identity not determined by a set of nested normative frameworks that combine to suggest film exhibition and political engagement engender aesthetically pedestrian, technically amateurish and curatorially undiscerning pedagogic encounters. The PFF has tried to dodge nationalising misnomers and to avoid being restricted by perceptions of a primary duty that resides in national storytelling or in the redressing of representational harms. Each such external pressure has been amplified and exacerbated by internal contradictions – definitional frictions and impasses deriving from the PFF's inability, and its reluctance, to dissociate itself from a political ethos or to reject outright the representational commitments that can emerge as a result of Palestine's national and political circumstances.

Together, the types of external perception, normative prescription or ideological agendas depicted in this chapter, limit the festival's chances for further development; they impede partnership generation, restrict funding prospects and set limits on audience development and diversification. But it is the internal state of contradiction and indeterminacy attending these pressures that ultimately militates against future development. By resigning itself to, and perhaps embracing, a state of indeterminacy in its relationship to Palestine's political and national connotations, the PFF has located itself at the outer limits of a British cultural mainstream. While this marginality offers certain freedoms, it produces a fatal paradox: the festival's costs are now increasingly dictated by its location *within* this fantastically expensive industry, while the PFF's capacity to generate funds remains dictated by its location *without* that industry – in a sphere of political activism accompanied by radically opposing economic norms. This has set in place an untenable impasse, with rapidly debilitating effects. As a result, after ten years in its current form, the PFF is poised to embark on a process of radical organisational change in pursuit of a fresh and more viable festival model.

Works Cited

Hedetoft, Ulf (2000) 'Contemporary Cinema: Between Cultural Globalisation and National Interpretation', in Mette Hjort and Scott MacKenzie (eds) *Cinema and Nation*. London and New York: Routledge. 278-97.

Iordanova, Dina (2012) 'Film Festivals and Dissent: Can Film Change the World?', in *FFY4: Film Festivals and Activism*. St Andrews: St Andrews Film Studies. 13-30.

Iordanova, Dina and Leshu Torchin (2011) *FFY4: Film Festivals and Activism*. St Andrews: St Andrews Film Studies.

Minh-Ha, Trinh T. (1990) 'Documentary Is / Not a Name', *October*, 52, 76-98.

Rabinowitz, Dan (2001) 'Natives with Jackets and Degrees: Othering, Objectification and the Role of Palestinians in the Co-Existence Field in Israel', *Social Anthropology*, 9, 1, 65-80.

Rancière, Jacques (2010) *Dissensus: On Politics and Aesthetics*, trans. Steve Corcoran. London and New York: Continuum.

Renov, Michael (1993) 'Toward a Poetics of Documentary', in Michael Renov (ed.) *Theorizing Documentary*, New York: Routledge, 12-36.

Said, Edward (1984) 'Permission to Narrate', *Journal of Palestine Studies*, 13, 3, 27-48.

Tamari, Vera (2012) 'Tawfik Canaan – *Collectionneur par excellence*: The Story Behind the Palestinian Amulet Collection at Birzeit University', in Sonja Mejcher-Atassi and John Pedro Schwartz (eds) *Archives, Museums and Collecting Practices in the Modern Arab World*, Farnham: Ashgate Press, 71-91.

Tawil-Souri, Helga (2011) '*A Space Exodus*: A Truly Palestinian Film', *Jadaliyya*, Online. Available HTTP: http://www.jadaliyya.com/pages/index/1099/a-space-exodus_a-truly-palestinian-film (24 October 2013).

Torchin, Leshu (2012) 'Networked for Advocacy: Film Festivals and Activism', in *FFY4: Film Festivals and Activism*. St Andrews: St Andrews Film Studies, 1-12.

Notes

[1] Naturally, not all this material is suited for traditional festival programming. As history suggests, much is politically or artistically compromised; a large portion is made for television (or online) spectatorship rather than cinema exhibition; and uneven preservation is an impediment with respect to certain historical periods.

[2] The London Palestine Film Festival is one of several longstanding festivals dedicated to the subject of Palestine. Other festivals of a similar size and focus include the Boston Palestine Film Festival (http://www.bostonpalestinefilmfest. org), Chicago Palestine Film Festival (http://palestinefilmfest.com), and Toronto Palestine Film Festival (http://tpff.ca), which have been functioning for between 7 and 12 years respectively. Newer initiatives include a Madrid Palestine Film Festival (http://muestracinepalestino.com), Bristol Palestine Film Festival (http://www.bristolpff.org.uk), Houston Palestine Film Festival (http://www.hpff.org) and the Al Ard [doc] Film Festival in Sardinia (http://www.sardegnapalestina.org). Many more Palestine-themed festivals and film cycles have either come and gone over the years or have appeared to be organised on an ad hoc rather than regular annual basis – locations have included Bangkok, Oslo, Nairobi,

Kuala Lumpur and Johannesburg. In the U.S., Palestine-related film and arts events are organised regularly in locations that include Ann Arbor, Washington DC and New York. A smaller number of festivals dedicated to Palestinian cinema have also appeared in recent years, such as the Australian Palestinian Film Festival (http://palestinianfilmfestival.com.au).

3   Khaled Ziada initiated and supervised these early iterations from 1998. My involvement dates from 2004.

4   Figures based on audience survey and box office data collated by the PFF between 2004 and 2013.

5   The LPFF has always taken place in April / May, but in 2014 will change its dates on the calendar to November / December.

6   Recent examples include the exhibition 'Navigations: Palestinian Video Art, 1988-2011' (2012, Barbican Centre, London), and the conference 'Palestine and the Moving Image' (2013, SOAS, University of London).

7   In recent years, the LPFF has been covered by mainstream papers including the *New York Times* and the *Guardian;* it has been profiled by broadcast channels including BBC World, BBC Arabic, and Al Jazeera English; and it has been featured in Arabic newspapers, including *Sharq Al Awsat* and *Al Quds Al Arabi.*

8   This is not to deny the importance of narration in constituting nationhood, kinship or identities. Nor is it to discount film's contributions therein. It is, rather, to question the stability or self-evidence (and hence the possibility of simple adjudication) applied to narrative powers and effects.

9   For obvious reasons, prospective partners with whom relationships have not been satisfactorily established will remain unnamed.

10   For an account of the political pedagogies involved in the 'coexistence' industry that emerged in Israel during the mid-1990s, see Rabinowitz (2001).

11   Our interlocutor found it pertinent to stress that, in contrast to the LPFF, the Jewish Film Festival had been willing to play its role, a distinction made to carry a clear, if absurd, inference.

12   Eligibility changes effecting the current emphasis on private enterprise were introduced in the wake of UK Government funding cuts in 2013. This prevented the PFF from applying to the only government funding stream it had previously been eligible for, and which had provided some funding over preceding years.

13   Working to financial constraints does not automatically impinge on the festival's quality. It can even impel curatorial experimentation and open pathways to innovative creative partnerships.

14   A certain hesitancy in grasping the financial dimensions of film festival production mustn't be confused with a lack of cultural appreciation or sophistication on the part of prospective donors amongst this affluent business elite. The non-commercial film industry can involve financial models so at odds with the larger market forces they overlay as to appear irrational on any close inspection. But they risk seeming especially odd when first encountered by business executives with an eye for the laws of the markets. As such, a lack of familiarity with the peculiar economics of film exhibition can combine with an acute familiarity with market forces more broadly to render a non-commercial film festival's financial structure alien and off-putting, if not outright delusional.

Film Festivals and Palestine

Apart from those represented in this table, there are many other irregular screening cycles and previously active festivals dedicated to Palestine. Rather than include all of these, we have opted to focus on the ones that are on-going and annual as a way to ensure a certain consistency.

Est.	Name	Date	Website	Location
1998	Al-Ard Festival of Palestinian and Arab Documentary Film	November	http://www.sardegnapalestina.org/?p=2242	Sardinia, Italy
1999	London Palestine Film Festival	November	http://www.palestinefilm.org/	London, UK
2002	Chicago Palestine Film Festival	April – May	http://palestinefilmfest.com/	Chicago, Illinois, U.S.
2007	Boston Palestine Film Festival	October	http://www.bostonpalestinefilmfest.org/	Boston, Massachusetts, U.S.
2007	Houston Palestine Film Festival	May	http://www.hpff.org/	Houston, Texas, U.S.
2008	Toronto Palestine Film Festival	Sept – October	http://tpff.ca/	Toronto, Canada

Est.	Name	Date	Website	Location
2009	Palestinian Film Festival Australia	November	http://palestinianfilmfestival.com.au/	Sydney, Melbourne, Brisbane and Perth, Australia
2010	Muestra de Cine Palestino	November	http://muestracinepalestino.com/	Madrid, Spain
2011	Bristol Palestine Film Festival	December	http://www.bristolpff.org.uk/	Bristol, UK
2011	Washington DC Palestinian Film and Arts Festival	Sept – October	http://dcpfaf.org/	Washington, District of Columbia, U.S.
2012	Kuala Lumpur Palestine Film Festival	May	http://vpm.org.my/events/events/66-the-kl-palestine-film-festival	Kuala Lumpur, Malaysia

Film Festivals Regularly Taking Place in the Occupied Palestinian Territories

Est.	Name	Date	Website	Location
2005	Shashat Women's Film Festival in Palestine	Sept – December	http://www.shashat.org/new/etemplate.php?id=642	Palestine-wide
2005-2010	Al-Kasaba Film Festival	October	http://www.alkasaba.org/festival2010/#	Ramallah, Palestine
2011	Shortat: International Short Film Week	November/Dec.	-	Ramallah, Jerusalem, Jenin, Gaza
2013	Karama Human Rights Film Festival in Ramallah	December	http://karamafestival.org/new/	Ramallah
2009[defunct]	Palestinian Mobile Cinema Series	-	http://pscaa.wordpress.com/	Mobile, West Bank

Compiled by Nick Denes and Stefanie Van de Peer
Tables are representative, not exhaustive

Film Festivals in Iraq

Est.	Name	Date	Website	Location	Specialisation
2005	Baghdad International Film Festival	October	http://www.baghdadfilmfest.com/	Baghdad	International competition
2005 (second planned for 2011, never took place)	Iraq Short Film Festival	24 – 29 September	http://isff-iraq.org/en-index.html	Baghdad	Short films
2012	Baghdad Eye Human Rights Film Festival	February,	http://baghdadeye.org/	Baghdad	Human Rights Films
2013	International Kelar Short Film Festival	-	-	Sulaymaniah	Short Films

Compiled by Stefanie Van de Peer
Listing is comprehensive, not exhaustive

The Gulf Region

Red Carpet Education: The Persian Gulf Approach to Film Festivals

Alia Yunis

Within weeks of arriving in the United Arab Emirates (UAE) in 2008 to teach Video Production and Film Criticism at Zayed University in Abu Dhabi, I found myself overwhelmed by the flow of film festival executives calling me (and other film and media production professors), offering free screening tickets for all my classes and the chance to meet the celebrities the festival was flying in. Any one of my Emirati students was also welcome to volunteer to escort VIPs on the red carpets. The festivals were anxious to fill up the seats and to have the venue spaces decorated with enough Gulf nationals to give them a local flavour. Indeed at this time, the festival executives who contacted me were not themselves locals; most were Western expats. They offered tea with Susan Sarandon, front row seats with Naomi Watts and a workshop on directing with Spike Lee.

As someone who had just come from Los Angeles, where people are in a constant frenzy to get an actor's attention to pitch their latest projects, it was almost like a parallel universe: the prize was an audience with the students, rather than with the talent. By my second year, I was not surprised when the new Artistic Director of the Abu Dhabi Film Festival, Peter Scarlet – the former head of the Tribeca Film Festival in New York – called to suggest that Catherine Deneuve have an audience with my students.

I could fit Deneuve into my class schedule but I couldn't find any student enthusiasm: they had no idea who she was and the idea that any good film could have been made outside of Hollywood or before they were born was a relatively alien concept. This lack of interest was perhaps even more shocking for the festival organisers, most of whom had been recruited from well-known festivals, particularly the Toronto International Film Festival, at very high salaries: around U.S.$22,000 a month for mid- and upper-level management. Scarlet was brought in for five million AED dirhams (U.S.$1.36 million) over five years.[1]

Education Before Glamour

But in the Gulf, a lot changes in five years. Today there are few free tickets left, most of the seats are full and the salaries for expats at the festivals have decreased significantly. Most importantly, the students who didn't know who Spike Lee was in 2008 are making their own films today. This is, in significant part, a result of workshops and other educational and funding opportunities by the three major film festivals in the region.

Like so much in the Gulf, in the festivals' first three years glamour came before education. Over the past decade, the Persian Gulf has purposefully worked at developing a reputation for rolling out the red carpet for a plethora of cultural and sporting events, including the launch of its three major film festivals: the UAE's Dubai International Film Festival (DIFF), founded in 2004, Abu Dhabi Film Festival (ADFF), founded originally as the Middle East International Film Festival in 2007, and Qatar's Doha Tribeca Film Festival, founded in 2009 and now split into two new festivals.[2] Dubai, Abu Dhabi and Qatar have been engaged in a game of one-upmanship since they emerged onto the international stage after the U.S. invasion of Iraq, and that competition includes film festival education. All three have been competing with each other to be the incubators and nurturers of a local film industry.

At the launches of these festivals, the red carpets were packed such stars as Omar Sharif, George Clooney, Demi Moore and the most famous actors of Arab cinema, including Hend Sabry, Ahmed Helmy and Yousra. Most were paid to visit for a day or two to enliven parties and screenings, even though they did not have a film playing. But soon the festivals needed more substance behind them to generate both local and international attention – and to prevent them from becoming merely freebie seven-star junkets for even the most insignificant of Hollywood guests. As Jay Weissberg, film critic for *Variety* who attends all three festivals regularly, says of the early days:

> The films were almost an afterthought, and little attention was paid to fostering cinema culture in the region. Of course there were lone voices working hard for the sake of cinema, but they were drowned out by the thirst for glitz. (Weissberg 2013)

As these cities competed to become global destinations, it was not their budgets that was an issue, but their substance. All three began with relatively open-ended budgets. Doha is believed to still have fairly unlimited resources, while DIFF today relies on significant sponsorship deals, with Abu Dhabi somewhere in the middle, spending perhaps around U.S.$13.6 million a year in addition to sponsorship.

What they did not have was a viable source of regional production or even a festival-going native population to tap into. These countries barely even had cinemas until the late-1990s development of the mall culture and its consequent multiplexes. The festivals were struggling for an identity along with their nations: the UAE and Qatar, less than 40 years old at the time of the festival launches, were and are still creating their modern national identity from the top down. To borrow from the film *Field of Dreams* (U.S., Phil Alden Robinson, 1989), it is a 'build it and they will come' approach to nationhood. This applies both locally and internationally, as the countries have to be marketed both at home and abroad for the purpose of tourism and the formation of a clearer national identity.

By the mid-2000s, seeking alternatives to oil and in order to diversify their national identities, the UAE and Qatar began to pump billions of dollars into new industries, primarily tourism and the festival / event and film production businesses. These industries were virtually non-existent – particularly in Qatar and Abu Dhabi – before the new millennium.

While there is no public agenda to interconnect the film festival, tourism and production sectors, they are interdependent: hotels and the national airlines provide sponsorship for the festivals and the regional production companies host many workshops. Additionally, in the Gulf these sectors are mostly government-owned and operated. The mutually-beneficial support between these industries is not a complicated web of bureaucracy, particularly as these are small countries run by an even smaller group of people.

But this sense of collaboration quickly came up against a significant lack in film education. For example, the UAE made international industry headlines when the government-owned Abu Dhabi Media Company announced the formation of Image Nation (www.imagenationabudhabi.com). Image Nation is a billion-dollar-funded production company that, since opening in 2008, has co-financed several Hollywood productions with its partners, including Warner Bros and Participant Media, with whom it made *The Help* (Tate Taylor, U.S., 2011) and several other less successful studio films, such as *Contagion* (Steven Soderbergh, U.S., 2011), *The Double* (Michael Brandt, U.S., 2011) and *Shorts* (Roberto Rodriguez, U.S., 2009).

But Image Nation's movies were not local, nor were they festival films. Indeed, over the last decade, the handful of feature length films shot at least in-part in the Gulf were Hollywood films, such as *The Kingdom* (Peter Berg, U.S., 2007) and *Syriana* (Stephen Gaghan, U.S., 2007), hardly flattering or even accurate portraits of this part of the world. The more complimentary *Mission Impossible 4: Ghost Protocol* (Brad Bird, U.S., 2011) was the only one of these Hollywood films to be shown at DIFF, with a lavish premiere, in which the ruler of Dubai joined Tom Cruise at the screening.

Qatar's only venture into feature length filmmaking to date has been the U.S.$55 million *Black Gold* (Jean Jacques Annaud, 2011), starring Antonio Banderas as a bumbling Arab sheikh, which debuted at the Doha Tribeca Film Festival to brutal international reviews.

Local production in the Gulf was not really local because there was so little local skilled film or production culture in place. So the festivals set out to create this film culture, primarily reaching out to higher education, another sector that is also mainly government-owned. Even quasi-private universities have at their head a high-ranking member of a ruling family (Wilkins 2011).

In 2004, when DIFF launched, there were virtually no film history or filmmaking courses in the country. As a result of outreach from the festivals, which provided an outlet for student work, the attention in video production courses has shifted from a focus on talk shows and broadcast news to narrative and documentary filmmaking. Today, Film History is a course offered at all three of the major federal universities and all but a handful of the scores of private universities and film institutions that have opened their doors since the start of the new millennium, institutions that began developing themselves just as the festivals were doing the same (Yunis & Duthler 2011).

The development of higher education and of the festivals have fed off each other, and have helped all three festivals foster their shared niche: Arab film education and funding. While educating young people, the festivals' initiatives also allow for them to have debut screenings of their films. To build momentum quickly, the festivals' offer of support to film productions locally was aimed at the wider Middle East and North Africa, which was in need of attention and financial assistance. In these other Arab countries, unlike the Gulf, there was already a small pool of experienced filmmakers to tap into: Egypt had a 100-year old studio film history that had suffered from government interference, and the Arab countries around the Mediterranean had developed cottage film industries with sporadic international recognition.

Dubai International Film Festival: Stable and Steady

The first film festival in the Arab Persian Gulf was the Emirates Film Competition (EFC) held in Abu Dhabi in 2002. It was not a festival so much as a chance for a cooperative of young Emirati filmmakers, many self-taught, to have the opportunity to show the films they had been working on to a small audience of friends and family and to screen a collection of shorts and features from around the Arab world. A quick look through the Emirati films in this first competition, now housed at the UAE National Film Library and Archive, reveals that the line-up consisted mainly of shorts resembling home movies or high school projects, with plotlines that were weak at best and showed little proof of technical

proficiency.[3]

However, EFC was the only place in the Gulf where one could see Arabs on screen through the eyes of Arab filmmakers. There were films coming out of the Egyptian studio system, but they were formulaic. The concept of self-representation, or of Arabs behind and in front of the camera in *independent* films, was a foreign concept when DIFF began. The model DIFF had formulated by 2008, of balancing international productions with an emphasis on Middle Eastern independent film development, would be followed by Abu Dhabi and Doha.

DIFF is the most organically-developed of the three UAE film festivals and, compared to the other two, has been stable and steady in its growth. It is still overseen by the two Emirati men who have been there since the beginning: its Chairman and Deputy, Abdulhamid Juma, who is also the Deputy Director of the Dubai Technology and Media Free Zone, and Masoud Amralla Al Ali, the festival's Artistic Director.[44] Al Ali, a poet, artist and filmmaker, was one of the founders of EFC, so he had been personally invested in developing an Emirati film culture for many years.

However, DIFF started out primarily promoting the modern Gulf agenda of big and lavish showcases. The following extract is typical of the local press coverage of its 2004 debut:

> With DIFF, the Middle East confirms its move from chronic savoring of the purest imitation of life – cinema – to having finally sunk its teeth into the culture, décor and ambiance of this important medium of art [...] more than 800 VIP guests walked the 40-meter red carpet. (The Emirates Network 2004)

Relying heavily on the popularity of Western films, the first DIFF featured 76 films, including 20 Arabic feature films and several more shorts, five of which were Emirati. However, all the Arab feature films had already played extensively elsewhere and the quality of the shorts, particularly those from the Gulf, was questionable.

The festival needed and wanted a distinct niche, and so it began creating it: By 2008, DIFF featured 181 films from 66 countries, 82 of which were Arab language films – many having been funded or work-shopped through DIFF to compete for prize money totalling over U.S.$500 million, a first in the Arab world. The festival's focus had turned to creating incentives for young Arab filmmakers to go out and make their own fil

Each year, DIFF rolls out more unprecedented opportunities to entice Arab filmmaking. In 2006, it launched the Muhr Awards to recognize regional and international Arab filmmakers, with prize giveaways totalling U.S.$300,000, which are selected by a prestigious international jury. The awards are categories [sic] into *Muhr Feature Film Award*, *Muhr Documentary Award*, and *Short Films Award*, and the winning films will be shown on the last day of the festival. (www.diff.ae)

In 2007, DIFF made a pivotal decision to get itself more involved in creating content for the festivals by founding the Dubai Film Connection (DFC) as its co-production arm.

DFC aims to raise the visibility of Arab filmmakers and stimulate the growth of film production originating from the Arab world. DFC brings international and Arab film professionals together to collaborate on the realization of approximately 15 selected projects each year. An annual guest list of more than 80 international film industry professionals from over 20 countries are invited to attend the DFC each year. (DIFF website 2013)

Since the first DFC, more than 30 projects have been completed and a further 13 are in various stages of production (UAE National Film Library & Archive, UNFLA). Success stories include the first feature length Saudi film, *Wadjda (Saudi Arabia / Germany, 2012)* by Haifaa Al Mansour and *Lamma shoftak (When I Saw You, Palestine / Jordan / Greece / UAE, 2012)* by Palestinian Annemarie Jacir, which have both won several prizes at international film festivals.

DFC partnered with a number of European and other organisations to create more specific awards for filmmakers. In 2012, DFC gave U.S.$25,000 development awards to three filmmakers, as well as the Film Clinic / DIFF Debut Feature Award of U.S.$10,000, the U.S.$10,000 Euro ARTE Award to a filmmaker for exceptional originality and writing style, the U.S. $10,000 Front Row / KNCC Award, and U.S.$7,000 from the Organisation Internationale de la Francophonie (www.francophonie. org) for a film produced in a Francophone Arab country. The ten Arab producers selected for DFC in 2013 also received accreditation for the Producers Network at Cannes. The filmmakers receiving these awards were all from the Levant and Maghreb countries.

To push the availability of original programming even further, in 2008 DIFF debuted the Enjaaz Awards, a division of the festival that gives post-production completion money to films, the caveat being that the films' premiere must take place regionally at the festival. Enjaaz has partially funded nearly 40 films that have premiered at its festival in the past four years. The highest profile Enjaaz success story is Palestinian Hani Abu Assad's *Omar* (2013), which was awarded the Un Certain Regard Jury Prize at the 2013 Cannes Film Festival. In 2012. DIFF gave out the first U.S.$100,000 IWC Schaffhausen Gulf Filmmaker Award to Iraqi director Maysoon Pachachi for her script *Nothing Doing in Baghdad*, which is in development with DIFF.

In an effort to get the general student population of the UAE interested as well, DIFF runs the annual Young Journalist Award, in which a group of university students are selected to work with journalists as their professional mentors, covering film festivals. Another DIFF program allows Emirati university students to cover the red carpet events for DIFF's Twitter, YouTube and other social networking channels.

Abu Dhabi Film Festival:
Giving International Legitimacy to Arab Filmmaking

Neighbouring Abu Dhabi and Doha's histories have been more chaotic as they have alternately grown and shrunk and evolved in the past five years. Launched in 2007, ADFF functioned under the same government organisation as Image Nation, the billion-dollar film fund, and its first two editions, run by local Egyptian talk show celebrity Nashwa Al Ruwaini, emphasised style over substance. In 2008, attendees were left baffled by a three-hour gala opening that included random circus and dance acts, and an overwhelming amount of money given to relatively mediocre, mostly European films, through the Black Pearl Awards.

Today the Black Pearl Awards are still generous: in addition to over U.S.$400,000 in awards for documentaries and short films, there are awards for Best Narrative Film (U.S.$100,000), Best New Narrative Director (U.S.$50,000), Best Middle Eastern Narrative Film (U.S.$100,000), Best New Middle Eastern Narrative Director (U.S.$50,000), Best Actor (U.S.$25,000), and Best Actress (U.S.$25,000). But today the quality of the competition is much higher. The festival's standards have become increasingly selective as it has become more recognised as a lucrative showcase for filmmakers around the world.

International legitimacy was brought to the ADFF in 2009 with the appointment of Festival Director Peter Scarlet. For three years, his team built the festival up to include more UAE films, specifically incorporating the grassroots EFC. His team focused on both the festival and film education. Its festival internships for university students were adapted to suit the students' hours, rather than the festivals' needs.

The festival partnered with New York Film Academy Abu Dhabi, which opened in 2008, to run workshops for students. It also invited

Arab directors to hold student workshops during the festivals. Film students from the UAE have arguably more opportunities to learn from professionals than anywhere else in the world. Indeed, neither they nor their professors can keep up with the offers. Filling the workshops beyond a handful of people, particularly with such a small population being offered so many opportunities, was difficult, and today the workshops have decreased to one or two a day to maximise attendance (Yunis & Duthler 2011).

The ADFF also became the primary sponsor of the Zayed University Middle East Film Festival (ZUMEFF, www.zumeff.com), the only region-wide student film festival. ZUMEFF is taught as a full course and ADFF executives visit the class to lecture students on programming, marketing and promotions. They also make themselves available throughout the process to mentor students.

In 2010, ADFF launched SANAD, grants for pre-production (for which it usually offers approximately U.S.$2,800) and post-production (usually U.S. $14,000). SANAD offers support to around 30 films a year, selected from about 200 submissions.

While SANAD acknowledges the money is not excessive, organisers note that every year the festival also arranges for the winners to take part in workshops, training session and discussion panels. In addition, the festival helps to set up meetings for them with distributors and other funders, thus assisting filmmakers even as it enhances its own international image. In the past three years, ADFF has premiered 17 films that have received some funding from SANAD. SANAD success stories sometimes overlap with DIFF, such as Annemarie Jacir's *Lamma shoftak* (*When I Saw You, Palestine, Jordan / Greece / UAE, 2012). The* SANAD-supported *Alam laysa lana* (*A World Not Ours*, Mahdi Fleifel, Lebanon / Denmark / UK / UAE, 2012) has also garnered much international attention on the festival circuit.

Educational efforts continued internally as well, with another focus being on 'Emiratizing' the festival itself. In other words, Scarlet and his team were training the young Emirati staff to take over their places. This took precedence particularly in 2012, when the festival was moved under the umbrella of the government's TwoFour54, an organisation whose primary goal is to foster Emirati talent in all media. Scarlet's contract was paid out early in 2012 and most of the other foreigners were let go or left of their own accord. Sudden and unexplained changes in management are very common in the Gulf region across all industries as they push 'Gulfization', the hiring of citizens. As such, Scarlet's early departure was not a shock to the film community here. Many of the key positions in the festival are now held by Emiratis. Scarlet's place was taken by Ali Al Jabri, who – like Al Ali at DIFF – is one of the original founders of the EFC.

Even before the merger in 2012, when ADFF moved to TwoFour54, six of the Emirati films that played at the 2012 ADFF had been developed at TwoFour54 workshops. In addition, TwoFour54 continues to hold numerous student workshops throughout the year that create content for the festival. This indicates an extraordinarily close collaboration and cross-pollination between the government, the festival management and staff, and the students at the local universities.

ADFF's undisclosed budget was severely cut when Scarlet left. So, too, were budgets across the country as the after effects of the economic collapse in Dubai in 2008 began to ripple through the rest of the country. The glamour factor of the festival has diminished accordingly. Meanwhile, though, the educational imperatives and funding continue to provide improved and increased content for the film festivals. Previously, ADFF screened almost any Emirati film that was submitted, in order to be able to claim its full support for local film production. Now, it can be relatively selective, accepting in 2013 around half of the approximately 100 submissions it received.

Doha: Transition Toward a More Comprehensive Film Culture

Doha's film festival history has been even more erratic than those of Dubai or Abu Dhabi. However, of the three festivals, it is the event that foregrounds its role in and agenda for film education. A year after its launch, the Doha Tribeca Film Festival became part of the Doha Film Institute (DFI), a governmental non-profit organisation established in 2010 with whom the festival shared offices. In 2012, Tribeca and Doha split just weeks after the departure of festival founder Amanda Palmer, an Australian national. No official reasons were given, but it is generally assumed that the reasons behind the moves were similar to the departure of Scarlet in Abu Dhabi: a need for Qatarisation. Palmer was replaced by young Qatari banking executive Abdulazia Al Khater. Then Doha announced at Cannes in 2012 that it would divide the original festival into two festivals. The Qumra Film Festival, 'a committed advocate of first- and second-time directors' and the Ajyal Film Festival 'to foster film appreciation among youth'. The latter event is being modelled after Italy's Giffoni Film Festival (www.giffonifilmfestival.it), with whom Doha has a partnership agreement (Doha Film Institute 2013).

The two new festivals will continue to operate under the DFI banner, which sponsors numerous film workshops that used to fuel the Doha Tribeca Festival's emphasis on Gulf cinema. DFI's most notable success came during the 2010 tenure of Oscar-nominated Palestinian director Scandar Copti as head the DFI's education department. Under Copti, the festival developed a very strong slate of Qatari short films created in DFI's workshops (AMEinfo 2011).

DFI also has a production-funding strand, which receives about 400 submissions, like Enjaaz, and it similarly provides up to U.S.$50,000 per film during its two annual funding cycles. Its success stories include four films selected for the 2013 Toronto International Film Festival: Syrian Mohamad Malas's *Soullam ila dimashk* (*Ladder to Damascus*, 2012), Bosnian Jasmila Žbanić's *Za one koji ne mogu da govore* (*For Those Who Can Tell No Tales*, 2012), Tunisian Néjib Belkadhi's *Bastardo* (2012) and Palestinian Mais Darwazah's *Habibi bistanani and il bahar* (*My Love Awaits Me by the Sea*, 2012). In 2013, DFI shifted focus. Instead of supporting all filmmakers, it has changed its agenda to state that the DFI Grants initiative 'aims to identify new talents worldwide and focus its support on first- and second-time filmmakers' (Doha Film Institute 2013).

Conclusions

The Dubai, Doha and Abu Dhabi festivals arguably did not so much start out with a passion for film, as a passion for a festival to assist in building the nation's identity as a tourism and business hub. Now film and festival education, primarily of Gulf Arabs, continues to be their almost frenzied obsession, as these countries work towards achieving a global city status for their festival homes that incorporates the native populations into the process. The festival initiatives are less than a decade old, but as local quality and content develop further, films generated by the festivals' education initiatives and incentives create a national cinema identity for consumption at home and abroad.

Equally important is the contribution they have made to fostering Palestinian, Lebanese, Egyptian and North African independent films, many of which would have never had a platform or even gone into production without the financial and mentoring support of the festivals.

However, the outlook is not all optimistic. Undoubtedly, the Gulf film festivals have come far in developing film production in the UAE and Qatar. One has to remember that in these countries in which 90% of the residents are foreign guest workers – from labourers to CEOs – the remaining 10% local population of Emiratis and Qataris only began to go to the cinema a decade ago. However, while the UAE has gone from no multiplexes fifteen years ago to a box office of U.S.$129 million in 2012, with 11.8 million admissions (*The National* 2013), there are still no independent cinemas in the Gulf region.[5] Local audiences have no exposure to the festival-produced films beyond the festivals themselves. This raises issues as to the production / distribution / exhibition ratio and poses the question 'if you make them, who will watch them?'.

In UAE, the audiences for the three festivals consist mainly of expats. The reason is straightforward: cinema is much more embedded in their home cultures. But these expats are a temporary audience; expats by definition come and go. As Weissberg states:

> All three festivals have now undergone painful structural changes, but what's still lacking is a committed initiative towards year-round programming. DFI seems to be more engaged with this idea than the others, establishing regular screenings outside the festival and partnering with embassies and cultural institutes like the Goethe Institute and the British Council. More needs to be done however, since a film festival existing in a cinéphile desert is doomed to finding itself faced with empty screening rooms, or cinemas filled only with festival guests rather than locals. (Weissberg 2013)

So perhaps what these festivals still need to do is work as platforms for educating *the public* on the existence and history of Arab cinema. In this sense, DFI's partnership with the famous Italian film festival for children, Giffoni (www.giffonifilmfestival.it), may be one of the most significant steps for the Gulf, as it has the potential to help build a framework for the understanding of film at a younger age, thereby giving its citizens a longer lead-in time to develop an appetite for independent film. Alaa Karkouti, who runs Mad Solutions, a film marketing business based in Cairo, echoes filmmakers when he says:

> The Gulf film festivals have created more and more talent, more projects, more networking, and have put more Arab cinema on the map regionally and internationally. They have very good programs but they are not working on the distribution part, which is most important for the industry to survive. Local filmmakers are making films to be seen only in film festivals and maybe online, but not based on a business model. Imagine what would happen if one of the Gulf festivals stopped funding and education? There would be a big drop in projects and films, as most of the Arab films now count on Gulf funds and awards. This is an unhealthy structure and relationship. If there is no real market soon for Arab films, even on small scale, then all of this will be a fake industry. When it comes to money, the total budget of

all film festivals in the whole Arab world (MENA) is between U.S.$75m and U.S.$100m. This can produce at least 100 well made films yearly. (Karkouti 2013)

While all the arts to some extent count on maecenas, this situation of production without distribution causes a crucial imbalance in the film world locally and at large. Indeed, non-Gulf Arab filmmakers still need to seek funding elsewhere. For example, Enjaaz has partially funded nearly 40 films that were screened at DIFF in the past four years. But most of the filmmakers received the majority of their financing elsewhere, primarily in Europe. Even when films are funded, the money comes with certain explicit and implicit rules and regulations. A Palestinian filmmaker who has received funding from both DIFF and Doha says, under the condition of anonymity, 'Money in the form of grants is helpful. But the money is limited – and the U.S.$30,000 to 50,000 for production cannot really be considered production money. It's more like start-up funding.'

Censorship also comes into play in the educational process. The film festivals are funded by the government, which practices censorship. Consequently, the grants given out and the workshops organised by the festivals fall within the comfort zone of censorship and self-censorship. Proposals would not be accepted if they dealt negatively with issues around Gulf politics or religion, thus limiting Gulf filmmakers more than those from elsewhere.

In fact, films funded by festivals are split fairly evenly between documentaries and narrative films, and they tend to be about looking back at, for example, the Lebanese civil war, displacement in post-war Iraq, North African emigration and women's rights; and the perennial issue of Palestine. This is perhaps because within the Gulf these are safe topics with little controversy for the Gulf government to deal with and so for its population to be exposed to.

There is a particular audience discomfort in seeing films that portray local people and events in an unflattering light. This is indeed the first decade that Gulf locals have been able to see themselves in stories on screen told by themselves. Local audiences do not have the experience to be critical of the actual filmmaking at the festivals but they are sensitive to any negative representation of their nation's culture, a culture that is still very much developing and growing. This is illustrated by the sarcastic judgement of one Emirati filmmaker: 'Emiratis are all angels.' He is just one of many who feel frustrated by the taboo of tarnishing the nation's self-image. He continued: 'Eventually we will learn from the Iranian model of how to work creatively around censorship.'

In the Middle East, including the Gulf, an estimated 60% of the population is under the age of 25, and unemployment is staggeringly high, with even some of the Gulf countries' figures at 25% (Booz and Company 2012). Indeed, while the current unrest sweeping the rest of the Middle East is removed from daily life in the UAE and Qatar, Gulf youth are growing up in a rapidly changing region. The limitations of perfection will likely be expressed in the future stories these youth wish to tell on film. If the incentives to make films and the educational activities that inform such filmmaking continue to come from the festivals, we are likely to see the Gulf's filmmaking become more sophisticated locally, resulting in more assertive and creative storytelling of the world as the locals know it.

Works Cited

AMEInfo (2011) 'Doha Film Institute Films Compete for Prizes at Gulf Film Festival', *AME Info*. 11 April. On-line. Available HTTP: http://www. ameinfo.com/261947.html (1 September 2013).

Booz and Company (2012) 'The Arab World's Soaring Youth Unemployment Rate Requires Immediate Action by Large Employers', *Booz*. On-line. Available HTTP: http://www.booz. com/me/home/press_media/management_consulting_press_ releases/article/50813650 (1 September 2013).

Doha Film Institute (2013) 'Financing'. On-line. Available HTTP: http:// www.dohafilminstitute.com/financing/grants/guidelines#mena (1 September 2013).

Emirates News Network (2004) 'Dubai International Film Festival [DIFF] 2004', *The Emirates News Network*. On-line. Available HTTP: http://movies.theemiratesnetwork.com/diff/2004/ (1September 2013).

Hamid, Triska (2013) 'Superheroes a Box Office Marvel', *The National*, 9 January. On-line. Available HTTP: http://www.thenational.ae/ business/industry-insights/media/superheroes-a-box-office-marvel-as-uae-cinema-takings-top-dh475m (1 September 2013).

Karkouti, Alaa (2013) Interview with author. 13 September 2013.

UAE National Film Library & Archive (UNFLA), Zayed University, Abu Dhabi, UAE.

Weissberg, Jay (2013) Interview with author. 13 September 2013.

Wilkins, Stephen (2011) 'Who Benefits from Foreign Universities in the Arab Gulf States', *Australian Universities' Reviews*, Volume 53, Issue 1. 73-83.

Yunis, Alia & Duthler, Gaelle (2011) 'Lights, Camera Education', *Journal of Middle East Media*, 7, 1. On-line. Available HTTP: http://www2.gsu.edu/~wwwaus/JMEM_archive_Vol7_Issue1.html. (17 October 2013)

Notes

[1]   Scarlet's salary is on the public record and was covered by all local media. However, most other budget issues are not on the public record and the information contained here is gleaned from private conversations with those working with the festivals or related organisations. Figures are only cited if I have them from more than one source. I have in past years interviewed several filmmakers and executives, but (with only rare exceptions) on the condition of their anonymity.

[2]   The United Arab Emirates (UAE) is a country that includes seven emirates, the two biggest of which are Abu Dhabi, the capital city, and Dubai. Citizens of the UAE are referred to as Emiratis. Qatar is separate country with its capital of Doha.

[3]   The UAE National Film Library & Archive opened at Zayed University in Abu Dhabi as a research and preservation centre in May 2013, and houses over 230 UAE-funded or produced films, including the handful of films remaining from the first three EFC festivals, as well as the catalogues of all the UAE film festivals.

[4]   DIFF has had a relatively stable team, with many top staff members in place since 2004. A notable controversy was Neil Stephenson, the first CEO of the festival who also claims, although these are unsubstantiated, to be its creator and who left in 2006, suing the festival for calling him a racist. Juma countered that he was let go because of his different vision for the festival's future. The case was dropped (Dixon, Guy (2008) 'Canadian sues Dubai Film Fest Organizers' *The Global and Mail* (4 December) On-line. Available HTTP: http://www.theglobeandmail.com/arts/canadian-sues-dubai-film-fest-organizers/article1067229), and the festival no longer has a CEO position. DIFF continues to maintain a steady team of programmers from around the world who work with the Dubai-based team. Briton Sheila Whitaker was the most notable of the expats. Eventually taking the title of Head of International Programming, her experience in the arts in Europe and the Middle East helped shaped the festival from 2004 to 2013, when she sadly passed away. (Jeavons, Clyde (2013) 'Sheila Whitaker Obituary', *The Guardian* (2 August) On-line. Available HTTP: http://www.theguardian.com/film/2013/aug/02/sheila-whitaker).

[5]   Because of the huge population of Indian labourers and the long trade history with India, Bollywood films still play on TV and are popular as DVD rentals. There is even a handful of rundown independent film theatres that cater to the labour populations. These cinemas, built in the late 1970s / early 1980s are not now, nor were they in the past, frequented by the native population. Bollywood's presence is further enhanced by the many Bollywood stars with homes in Dubai or who vacation there under much media attention.

'Our Festival is our Window onto Others': An Interview with Abbas Arnaout, Director of the Al Jazeera International Documentary Film Festival

Asma Ajroudi & Zena Al Tahhan[1]

18 April 2005 marked the official inauguration of the notable Al Jazeera International Documentary Film Festival (www.festival.aljazeera.net). The initiative, which has grown to prominence over the years, managed to carve out a name for itself within the Middle East and North Africa region, and globally. By its fifth anniversary, the festival boasted participation from 94 different countries. The competition, which was originally titled Al Jazeera Television Production Festival, was developed by the Qatar-based, government-funded news broadcaster Al Jazeera Media Network as a move to add cultural flavour to the organisation's heavy news substance. The inception of the Al Jazeera Media Network began with the 1996 launch of Arabic-language news broadcaster Al Jazeera Satellite Channel, upon the closure of Saudi-based BBC Arabic television station. The Al Jazeera Media Network is now a multinational multi-platform corporation that is a parent to the Al Jazeera Satellite Channel and its joint networks, which includes Al Jazeera International Channel and Al Jazeera Sports Channel. Although Al Jazeera Media Network also established a documentary channel, the relationship between the festival and the channel remains one of cooperation and not of dependency. With its expanded media outlets, such as the 2013 launch of Al Jazeera America, the network now appeals to a very diverse, international and regional audience.

Although the festival was initially designed to cater to Qatar's multinational residents and Al Jazeera's regional viewers, the success of the first edition widened the scope of the festival, luring international filmmakers and television stations. This spawned the addition of the word 'international' to the festival's title. The title evolved once more when the organisers noted the overwhelming majority of documentary-based films that were submitted; Al Jazeera International Documentary Film Festival became the new title. As the programme evolved, new categories were added, such as the festival's trademark New Horizon Competition, a category aimed at encouraging student filmmakers.

The festival owes its success largely to Abbas Arnaout, its founder and director. The Jordanian specialist dedicated 18 years to working in TV drama production, while also gaining much experience in film directing and documentary production. Upon his graduation from the Arts University Bournemouth in Britain, with a degree in Film Production, Arnaout joined Jordan TV to become a director. Three years later, he joined Dubai TV in the United Arab Emirates where he directed prominent drama series such as *Suleiman Al Halabi* (Abbas Arnaout, UAE, 1976) and *Antar* (Abbas Arnaout, UAE, 1978). In 1996, Arnaout moved to Al Jazeera where he established the production department for the then-infant Al Jazeera Satellite Channel. Arnaout's contributions to the TV network developed when he recognised the news network's need for a cultural dimension, and consequently he founded the Al Jazeera International Documentary Film Festival in 2005. He has been successfully running the festival for seven years now. 'I've loved cinema since childhood... perhaps because film symbolises a beautiful world to me and incorporates things that are often closer to fiction than reality,' said Arnaout, in an interview with Zena Al Tahhan on 26 September 2013.

The following is a joint effort in which Asma Ajroudi and Zena Al Tahhan formulated the interview questions, transcribed, translated and co-authored the profile. However, because Asma was spending a semester abroad, Zena conducted the interview on her own. Al Tahhan met with Arnaout to discuss the Al Jazeera festival's establishment and structure, its role as a platform for cultural and knowledge exchange, as well as the challenges and criticism involved in running the event.

Festival History

Zena Al Tahhan: *Can you describe the exact moment you decided to set up the Al Jazeera International Documentary Film Festival?*

Abbas Arnaout: Al Jazeera became famous as a news channel and needed to give itself a new dimension. This was before the launch of Al Jazeera Documentary Channel and the network's expansion in recent years. It needed a cultural dimension. The public thought of Al Jazeera as a channel only specialised in providing political substance. But this was not true because it has another role; one of the network's most important objectives is to spread Arab culture and knowledge. Al Jazeera was perhaps the only channel that thought of launching a festival specifically for documentary films. This field is not very common in the Arab world. It was an honour for me to be the person who was entrusted with it, and it was an honour to launch this festival.

ZT: *What did you offer audiences and participants to ensure the growth of the festival?*

AA: In my estimation, neutrality and honesty in work were the most important and distinctive foundations on which the Al Jazeera International Documentary Film Festival was based. I participate in other festivals where winners and awards are predetermined. For example, they would specify the countries they want to award. This is unfortunately common in Arab festivals. Frankly, I refuse to work in this manner. For instance, I remember some of my former colleagues from the Jordanian television, who participated in the first edition of the festival and expected to win golden awards because I worked at their station – but that was not going to happen. Being the only festival that did not soften to compliments, I believe that we were able to build a good reputation by the second edition. On these grounds, I think the festival reached a certain level of credibility. And, credibility is the basis in every piece of artwork.

ZT: *How did you advertise and establish yourselves in the media arena?*

AA: We are lucky that we work for Al Jazeera Network. Firstly, the name is very powerful and prominent in the arena. Secondly, we had the opportunity to place commercials on a channel that attracts a large number of

ZT: *What is the relationship between the Al Jazeera Media Network and the Al Jazeera Film Festival?*

AA: We used Al Jazeera's slogan right from the start – 'The Opinion and the Other Opinion' – and it still remains. In other words, the slogan signifies the acceptance of other viewpoints and of allowing people to know these opinions. We sought the same goal. We are not in any way separated from Al Jazeera; we are a part of the same concept.

Structure and Finance

ZT: *How do you obtain funding?*

AA: We are part of Al Jazeera. We get our funding from the network just like it funds its other divisions. This has, of course, changed over the years due to the growing size of the festival. Consequently, financial matters changed to match our progress. We organise this festival for cultural and artistic goals. So it is subordinate to Al Jazeera, which sponsors it for the same goals, and not for any profit.

ZT: *Are there others sources of funding?*

AA: We rely mainly on Al Jazeera. But some companies want to participate by giving out awards in their names. Let's take for example the Al Jazeera Children's Channel; it might want to give out an award for the Best Children's and Family Movie. This helps promote its channel. We help in that process. But this does not make up our main source of funding.

ZT: *What was your budget when you started?*

AA: We had no budget. Because it was an experiment, the budget was not set. As a result, the budget evolved accordingly. In the first year, we received substantial financial support from the channel and we had the liberty to work as we pleased. By the second year, things became clearer.

ZT: *Can you tell me about the different departments that fall under the umbrella of the Festival?*

AA: What is special about our festival is the way it combines a group of departments working at Al Jazeera. They work together as a team with the unified goal of making one project succeed. At the outset, we had what we called the Operations Department, which is mostly an engineering department. In other words, this department helped us with equipment, printing, translation and typing – with all the technical work. Additionally, there was, and still is, a very big role for other supporting services such as the Public Relations Department that takes care of receiving guests, handling them, and organising their travel. Therefore, there is a group of departments from Al Jazeera that are working with us indirectly for temporary periods throughout the year, whenever we need them. For example, in typical instances when we receive guests for the festival, there is no doubt that the PR Department would issue the visas, receive the guests at the airport and organise their stay. So, that particular department from Al Jazeera would have a specialised role to play in specific months during the year. The only department that works all year-round is the Festival Department. During the work period, we reach certain periods when we must contact the other departments for assistance in operating specific aspects of the festival that we are not as capable of running.

ZT: *Can you tell me about your staff?*

AA: The festival is divided into two parts. There is the management work dealing with the festival organisation. That is, contacting people and sending out invitations, and answering their questions – let's call it organisational communication. This is an essential part of our work that is constantly operating, from the first day of the festival until the last. It works throughout the festival, to prepare, make the necessary arrangements for people and attend to their comfort and service, from the moment that the guest writes to us expressing his or her desire to attend, to the moment that we drop them back at the airport; such organisational matters have a corresponding team to carry out the work involved.

The second part of our work is the technical part. For example, when we need to copy a film, organise meetings with the jury to view the films, or create translations of the films to render them suitable for our audience. We deal with two languages in the festival: Arabic and English. If the movie is in English we translate it into Arabic, and vice versa, for foreigners to be able to understand as well. Sometimes the film is in another language such as German or French, so we translate it into both Arabic and English, as they are the primary languages of the festival. We have a technical team to assist and monitor, but usually translations are done by outside experts.

ZT: *What are the senior roles in running the festival?*

AA: There are none. There are no unimportant individuals. I always say that our work resembles a relay race, where the racer holds the baton and passes it over to the next racer. The first racer runs the first hundred meters then passes it over to the next person, and then the next person runs the next hundred meters, and so on. The nature of our work is like that. For example, we can say that the individuals that usually carry out the editing or translation are not important at that specific moment in time, in the sense that they are not under work pressure. However, in the following month, these individuals will be working the hardest out of us all. In another month, the public relations employees will be the ones working the most, and so on. The stages of work move from one team to another.

ZT: *How long do you take throughout the year to prepare for the upcoming festival?*

AA: The termination of the festival means the commencement of a new working year. If the festival ends today, then it is the beginning of a new working year. We start with the new cycle immediately after the end of the festival. The nature of our work does not follow the same pace every year. Of course, we first take a break to regain our energy. I take advantage of this period to travel and see other festivals, and participate in the jury of other festivals. It is my chance to see what is happening in the outside world and to see the work of others. Following that stage, we announce the launch of that year's festival. After that, people start submitting their films and that is when the pressure gets high. The last four months of work before the festival are very demanding.

Festival Objectives / Philosophy

ZT: *Do you ever see the film festival becoming self-sufficient?*

AA: Every project has a primary goal. When we launched the Al Jazeera Film Festival, financial gain was not our objective. This should be kept clear when talking about the festival.

ZT: *Is there a certain image or agenda that the festival tries to communicate as part of the artistic and cultural goals?*

AA: The image that I personally insist upon reflecting is this: we are a civilised people, in a civilised country, and we treat knowledge with respect. Some of the people who contact us, or whom we invite to the festival, ask absurd questions such as: 'Do you have cars or streets?' A lady once asked me if she was required to wear black! [The traditional attire for local women in Qatar]. They hold a negative image of us that the international media might have had a hand in generating. But then, they come here and realise that we are ordinary people. It is very important to me that we reflect our reality. I have come across people that inquire as to whether or not we have a film festival – they don't process the idea at first. But when they come here, they return home as our ambassadors, promoting us.

ZT: *Have you met the goals and expectations set in the initial aims stated in the paperwork you submitted when you proposed the idea of a film festival?*

AA: I recall our first interview nine or ten years ago, when we were asked, 'Why are you establishing this festival?' I simply answered them: 'We hope for this festival to be our window onto others. When others come to present their work, civilisation, culture and films, we would be able to see them through this window called Al Jazeera Film Festival.' But this is not enough. This festival should also be their window onto us — they should be able to see us too. We should be presenting something for the world to see; ourselves, our movies, productions, even our streets and the country they are visiting. For the first edition (2005), only 14 countries submitted entries. By the 6th edition (2010), the festival attracted 94 countries. We have received films from China, Japan, the U.S., Sweden, Germany and France. We did not anticipate that we would be expanding in such a rapid manner. The festival truly became a window through which we prospered. The notion of this festival as a window still holds till today — our slogan for our most recent festival (April 2013) was in fact 'Windows'.

Film Selections

ZT: How is the selection process for the films carried out?

AA: The first phase is to collect the participating films. Any film received by the festival must firstly be assessed for its technical quality. For example, the film must comply with acceptable production standards; it must be suitable for screening. If, for example, the audio or the image is inadequate, the film will not qualify. After that, we delve into the content aspect of the films. We ask, 'Has the film's topic been constructed in a good way?', 'Has the topic been studied and assessed in an objective and strong manner?', 'Is the film topically weak?' and 'Is it suitable or not?'. There are some topics that we cannot pursue in the festival; for example, a topic that verbally attacks celestial religions, or a specific religion or a specific race or nationality. We do not show such films in our festival. We are neutral in our vision. The director must tackle an issue in a respectful and objective manner for it to be included in our festival. However, we do not have many censorship regulations in comparison with other festivals. On the contrary, we are more open than many other festivals in the world, provided that the topic is treated with respect and professionalism. If these two factors are not present, the film cannot be shown.

I will take, for instance, a very controversial topic in the Arab world: the Palestinian issue. We may receive two films in the same year that have conflicting views on the matter; a film that supports the notion of peace, and a film that rejects it. We would screen both films. The two would have to be produced in good (technical) quality, and both would have to have discussed the matter objectively and intellectually – without the use of offensive language, for example. If the director analyses the topic and provides his / her point of view in an objective and scientific manner, the film will be shown. The films screened at the festival reflect the director's opinion and not our personal opinion.

ZT: How do you ensure diversity in the films that get selected?

AA: Our business is not to ensure that the same film topics do not get repeated. I have nothing to do with the making of the films. However, when I select a film, I choose the one that treats the topic in the best way. If I wanted to talk solely about the Palestinian conflict, I would say that it is multifaceted to an incredible extent. I personally learned about the number of different angles of this conflict from the number of different films we receive. For example, last year, we screened a film named *Sacred Stones* (Muayad Alayan and Laila Higazi, Palestine, 2011), centring on a struggle occurring in the Palestinian territories about the stones used to build houses. The whole film's construction revolves around these stones, and their importance. I had never seen a film about such a topic in my life. It was a new topic, despite the fact that it was about the Palestinian conflict. Another example is of a film we screened two years ago by a Swedish director, also about the Palestinian conflict. It was called *Israel vs. Israel* (Terje Carlsson, Sweden, 2010) and spoke about the divisions in Israeli society concerning the Palestinian issue. When I watched this film, it was the first time that I came across such information.

ZT: *Do you try to enforce some sort of representative selection?*

AA: No, we choose the elite of films. However, if there was a country participating for the first time in the festival, we make it somewhat easier [accessible] for them, hoping that they would join again.

ZT: *Can you tell me about your jury?*

AA: Since the launch of the festival, we have not repeated the same jury members. The jury changes every year. What distinguishes this panel is that it is composed of 15 judges, each from a different country. Every judge holds a different nationality – it is impossible to find two judges from the same country. This is done to ensure some sort of neutrality and multiplicity in vision, to ensure a wide-ranging vision. We choose our jury in a number of different ways. So the jury members are chosen for their reputation as well-known judges. Also, when I travel to attend other festivals and meet distinguished jury members, I invite him or her to attend and become a jury member for our festival. There is also a tradition in festivals, in which the directors of excelling films that have won first place golden awards are invited to become jury members for the upcoming festivals. Finally, we also select jury members through our relationships with individuals. This is our tenth anniversary, so we will be re-inviting some of the best judges who have participated previously, as a commemoration of our tenth anniversary. We collaborate; the same people who are working for the festival are the ones that select the jury.

Challenges and Criticism

ZT: *Some people might argue that although Qatar's art and culture sector is evolving, Qatari locals are not very involved in the field, and that such initiatives are, in light of the country's very recent and rapid development, usually targeted at the foreigners rather than the locals. From your experience in the festival, do you see that most guests and participants are foreigners or are there locals too?*

AA: I meet a lot of people who inquire about the festival dates. I know Qataris who take time off to attend the festival and watch all the films – start to end. The enthusiasm to attend and watch the films and experience cultural work is immense. Also, there have not been any festivals in the past that have not included a locally produced film. So, I think this question involves some kind of injustice. But, of course we are talking about a new field in the Arab world. The documentary film is not a feature film. For example, many people go to feature film festivals to see the stars or a certain actor. On the other hand, documentary pieces are more education-based. Documentary work does not involve stardom or any of the factors we see in the cinema. This is not only prevalent in Qatar, or Jordan and Egypt, but all over the world. Documentary films do not spread as fast as feature films. Feature films host some type of entertainment, and people are generally more welcoming and accepting of entertainment. As for documentaries, they are more educational. Therefore, the demand for them, internationally, is less than the demand for feature films. For this reason, you do not see the same rush and excitement as people have to attend feature film festivals, which include stars and entertainment – this needs to always be taken into consideration. However, I believe that this is the importance of the Al Jazeera Film Festival: that in this commercial ambiance prevailing throughout the world, we offer an educational festival with an educational nature. Therefore, if we sometimes have fewer individuals attending our festival, it does not mean anything. On the contrary, this is normal and a good thing.

ZT: *For the international entries that are selected, do the directors of such films usually attend the festival?*

AA: When we choose the films, we invite the directors and the production houses, because one of the festival's primary goals is to establish a type of connection with these individuals – one that strengthens the professional relationships between those working in the same field. Sometimes, the number of films selected is larger than usual, resulting in special cases where we cannot invite everyone. However, around 80% of directors whose films are selected and who are invited to attend, personally participate in the festival. We sometimes take care of their tickets, and other times we do not.

ZT: *Some argue that this film festival is Middle East-focused.*

AA: Sorry, but I am not willing to hear such criticism. When I say that 90+ countries have participated, how can it be region-focused? Even if all the Arab countries were to participate, they are only 22 states and would only make up 25%; a quarter. This is not true. When you see the films being shown, you will know that the Arab world is sometimes underrepresented in this film festival. And the reason for this is simply professionalism. We do not take sides. Unfortunately, the documentary film industry is more advanced in Europe than in the Arab world. The majority of the films shown are European or foreign.

ZT: *How do you handle films that tackle topics that are culturally and religiously sensitive to the Middle East? Do you screen them or not?*

AA: I will recall a film that dealt with rape cases in Congo. The film spoke of some soldiers who raped African women. This film, which hosts a very human and respectful message about rape, included a scene in which a lady, after being raped, heads out to the sea to bathe. The scene is shot in a very refined way without any audacious nudity, or any kind of purposeful temptation, as we know it. On the contrary, it is a very sad scene; she is trying to get rid of the soldiers' odour. It is a scene that will make you cry and feel pain. When we contemplated showing this scene or not, my personal opinion was that we should show it because it does not contain inappropriate material. Its aim is not to seduce or tempt the viewer. Instead, the goal is a very noble one of expressing an extremely painful humanitarian tragedy. I thought that that was a great thing. To me, the film is all about that one scene; it is the strongest point in the film. The film was screened, and it received an award because of this specific scene. We do not think of things in a shallow manner. We assess the motive behind any scene in any film. We ask: 'Why was this shot filmed?' 'What was the motive behind this scene?' The same shot may have two goals: it may have cheap and seductive purposes, or its goal may be to express and communicate a humanitarian tragedy. At the end of the day, it is the same scene, but you must assess the motive behind it.

ZT: *Say, for example, a homosexual man wants to give a human face to the topic of homosexuality.*

AA: I have not seen a film that expresses what you are speaking about. We have previously received films that deal with sensitive topics in our societies, as in all human societies. I, personally, in all these years, have not come across a technically and artistically sophisticated film that deals with such topics. Unfortunately, they were all trivial films. I did not select them, [not] because they were silly, and not because they deal with sensitive topics. The topic must be dealt with in a humane and in-depth manner, and not like a cheap sex film. The festival displays the elite selection of films in the world. We receive a thousand films but we only show a hundred of them. The other 900 that we do not screen are not displayed because they are of lower quality in comparison to the rest.

ZT: What would you say are the challenges and rewards of running a festival?

AA: Every year is a new challenge. We cannot say, 'We succeeded in the 6th Festival and therefore, that is enough'. No, we must succeed in the 7th Festival too. Every year is a test for us. The rewards consist of the happiness we feel during the closing ceremony of the festival, knowing that we delivered a good message, and that the guests we hosted are leaving with a good impression of us – that is the most important reward for us.

Notes

[1]   This interview and its resultant chapter were closely supervised by Dr. Joe F. Khalil, Associate Professor in Mass Communication & Media Arts at Northwestern University in Qatar.

Film Festivals in the Gulf Region

The nations that belong to the Persian Gulf are: Saudi Arabia, Kuwait, Bahrain, Qatar, UAE and Oman. The 7 United Arab Emirates are: Abu Dhabi, Ajman, Dubai, Fujairah, Ras al-Khaimah, Sharjah, and Umm al-Quwain. The capital of UAE is Abu Dhabi.

Film Festivals in United Arab Emirates

Est.	Name	Date	Website	Location	Specialisation
2004	Dubai International Film Festival	December	www.dubaifilmfest.com	Dubai	All types of films
2008	Gulf Film Festival	April	www.gulffilmfest.com	Dubai	All types of films
2007	Abu Dhabi Film Festival	October, November	www.abudhabifilmfestival.ae	Abu Dhabi	All types of films
2010	The Green Caravan Film Festival	March	www.thegreencaravan.com	Dubai	Line-up of award winning films
2011	Heritage Film Festival organised by Goethe Institut Gulf Region	April (February)	http://www.goethe.de/ins/ae/abu/kul/prk/hff/013/enindex.htm	Abu Dhabi	Emirati and German films
2013	Abu Dhabi International Environmental Film Festival	April	www.adieff.com	Abu Dhabi	All types of films – a platform for dialogue and artistic dialogue on the environment
2013	Sharjah International Children's Film Festival	February	http://www.sicff.ae/index.php?lang=en	Sharjah	Children's films

297

Film Festivals in Bahrain

Est.	Name	Date	Website	Location	Specialisation
2007	Sawari International Film Festival	November	-	Manama	International
2008	Bahrain Human Rights International Film Festival	May	http://www.oneworld.cz/2013/hrfn	Manama	Human Rights Films
2012	Japanese Film Festival organised by the Embassy of Japan and the Shaikh Ebrahim bin Mohammed Al Khalifa Centre for Culture & Research	November	http://www.bh.emb-japan.go.jp/cultureEducation.htm#99	Manama	Japanese Films

Film Festivals in Qatar

Est.	Name	Date	Website	Location	Specialisation
2005	Aljazeera International Documentary Film Festival	April	http://festival.aljazeera.net	Doha	Documentary
2006	Tasmeem Film Festival	March	http://www.tasmeemdoha.com/film-festival.html	Doha	International
2009	Doha International Film Festival	March / November	http://www.dohafilminstitute.com/filmfestival	Doha	International Films
2011	THIMUN Qatar Northwestern Film Festival	March 2012	http://qatar.thimun.org/film-festival	Doha	Students Films
2012	Doha Turkish Film Festival	June	http://www.doha.emb.mfa.gov.tr	Doha	Turkish Films
2013	Aijal Film Festival for the Young	November	http://www.dohafilminstitute.com/filmfestival	Doha	Young Filmmakers
2013	QSFF - Qatar Sports Film Festival	May	http://www.qsff.org	Doha	Sports Films

Est.	Name	Date	Website	Location	Specialisation
2013	Qumra Film Festival	March	http://www.dohafilminstitute.com/filmfestival	Doha	Support for first-time filmmakers
-	Italian Film Festival	July	http://www.giffonifilmfestival.it	Doha	Italian Films

Film Festivals in Kuwait

Est.	Name	Date	Website	Location	Specialisation
2008	Indian Film Festival organised by the Indian Embassy	-	-	Kuwait City	Indian Films
2010	The Green Caravan Film Festival	March	www.thegreencaravan.com	Kuwait City	Line-up of award winning films
2010	Kuwait Young Film Festival	Last time in May 2011	www.kuwaitfilmfest.com	Kuwait City	Supports young filmmakers
2012	Kuwait International Film Retreat	August	www.kuwaitfilmretreat.com	Kuwait City	Short and feature film for filmmakers and enthusiasts from around Kuwait
2012	GCC Film Festival	May	-	Kuwait City	Films from the six GCC states
2012	The Future Shorts Festival	August, November	www.kuwaitup2date.com/2012/10/31/future-shorts-film-festival-autumn-season-nov-4/	Kuwait City	Short films, part of worldwide pop-up festival network

Est.	Name	Date	Website	Location	Specialisation
2013	French Short Film Festival	April	-	Kuwait City	French Films: screened in partnership with Cinescape and the International Festival of Short Films at Clermont-Ferrand

Film Festival in Saudi Arabia

Est.	Name	Date	Website	Location	Specialisation
2013	Television & Film Festival organised by the King Abdul Aziz Cultural Centre	May	-	Jeddah	International

Film Festivals in Oman

Est.	Name	Dates	Website	Location	Specialisation
2006	Muscat International Film Festival	March	http://www.m-iff.com/Home.aspx	Muscat	International
2013	Bait al Zubair Independent Film Festival	October	http://www.baital-zubairmuseum.com/	Muscat	

Compiled by Marion Fohrer and Stefanie Van de Peer
Listing is representative, not exhaustive.

Maghreb

Between Tangier and Marrakech: A Short History of Moroccan Cinema through Its Festivals

Jamal Bahmad

The story of Moroccan cinema revolves around its annual festivals. In a manner similar to the festive Moroccan social life, which revolves around a regular cycle of *Iydouden* and *Moussems* (carnivals and festivals in celebration of food, drink, women, saints, horses and so forth), the onscreen life of the nation is projected and pondered in film festivals year-round. Even though the North African country boasts around 50 annual film festivals at present, the tale of a rapidly evolving Moroccan cinema and society can be related through the story of the origins and evolution of two seminal festivals in two important cities. The National Film Festival in Tangier (www.ccm.ma/fnf14) and the Marrakech International Film Festival (www.festivalmarrakech.info) came into existence at various stages of Moroccan (cinema's) history, are run in different fashions and target divergent audiences. The first National Film Festival was held in 1982 in Rabat in response to a growing crop of quality films and the perceived need for a national debate on the country's visual and cultural identities. Twenty years later, Morocco had witnessed dramatic political and social transformations; so much so the need arose for the projection of Moroccan images to the world through a platform up to the challenges of cultural globalisation. Launched in 2001, the Marrakech International Film Festival (MIFF) has rapidly grown in size and influence to become an important annual event for Moroccan and international cinema.

This chapter examines the industrial and historical backgrounds to the rise and growth of the Tangier and Marrakech film festivals with a focus on what they reveal, on the one hand, about the place of festivals in a national cinema's life cycle, and on the other, how a country's images of itself are cultivated and altered by the transnational dynamics of festival organisation in these two Moroccan cities. A critical history of self-defined 'national' and 'international' film festivals reveals how both nostalgia for the national and the uncritical celebration of transnationalism as the cultural logic of globalisation are not only often unconvincing but also uncritical. A lot of 'translational' scholarship in film studies, for example, can be short on concrete detail about the contingent processes of film production and exhibition in specific contexts and within complex economies of difference. As Will Higbee cogently remarks, transnational approaches are often 'not specific enough or sufficiently politically engaged' (2007: 85). This chapter demonstrates how the national film festival lives on and is the scene of the most important debates on Moroccan self-images away from the spectacle of Marrakech's international film festival. Both events are important and their lessons, renewed every year, are as crucial for Moroccan cinema as they are for the study of film festivals and what they disclose about the life and magic of cinema in an increasingly interconnected world. In what follows, the role of the National Film Festival, which has had a fixed home in Tangier since 2005, in national identity construction is explored, before moving on to explore Moroccan culture's global circulation through the international film festival in Marrakech. The chapter concludes with critical reflections on the increasing overlap and necessity of both events and their articulation of Moroccan-ness for national and transnational audiences.

The Colonial Night

Morocco is a common topos on international film screens, even if it often goes unnoticed as such. The country is a convenient backdrop for movies set almost anywhere around the world. Ever since the invention of cinema, Morocco has attracted international filmmakers and production companies to its unspoilt beauty and stunning scenic diversity. Natural light, cultural diversity, polyglotism, hospitality, cheap labour and the availability of technical expertise, have also made the country a favourite destination for film producers. The story began with the Lumière brothers' *Le Chevrier Marocain* (*The Moroccan Goatherd*, 1897). In 1912, Morocco became a French and Spanish protectorate. Film production was seen by the French in particular as not only an important economic resource but also a means of imperial control. The coloniser invested heavily in the production of films that dehumanised natives by painting them through an Orientalist lens as a backward people in need of Western enlightenment. Under Resident-General Henri Hubert Gonzales Lyautey's auspices 'a Franco-Moroccan film industry arose and thrived, producing travelogues, ethnological docudramas, and narrative fiction' (Slavin 1998: 128). The Centre Cinématographique Marocain (CCM) was set up and housed under the Ministry of the Interior in 1944 by the French colonial regime. Its mission was to organise the film trade and promote colonial propaganda to counter the surge of Egyptian cinema and its promotion of Pan-Arabism in the late colonial era. The CCM was also tasked with consolidating the burgeoning sector of international film production and distribution.

The exoticisation of Moroccans in colonial cinema was much to the taste of metropolitan Western audiences; even today only a certain type of Moroccan cinema is popular, while radically original films are often unheard of, let alone seen or appreciated to any great extent. The origins of this enshrined way of seeing Morocco and North Africa are to be found in the ontology of the colonial gaze. Cinema-going flourished in colonial Morocco (1912-1956), particularly in the cities where film theatres and disposable income were in supply. J. P. Pichon's *Mektoub* (1918), Jacques Sévérac's *Sirocco* (1930) and *Razzia* (1931), Jean Benoît-Lévy and Marie Epstein's *Itto* (1934) and Jacques Becker's *Ali Baba et les quarante voleurs* (*Ali Baba and the Forty Thieves,* 1954), are just a few of the French colonial films made in and about Morocco to wide acclaim. Hollywood discovered Morocco around the same time and has made it a favourite destination for location shooting ever since. *Morocco* (Josef von Sternberg, 1930), *Casablanca* (Michael Curtiz, 1942), *A Night in Casablanca* (Archie Mayo, 1946) and *Outpost in Morocco* (Robert Florey, 1949) are popular examples of the American film industry's colonial Morocco. Other international film productions have also anchored Morocco as a cultural geography in the global cinematic imagination.[1]

Alongside colonial films and Hollywood movies, the country also attracted some independent-minded filmmakers who had twisted the conventional codes of misrepresentation at play in international cinema. Orson Welles' *Othello* (1952) is a unique example of this original mode of filmmaking. Made on a shoestring budget as a collaborative effort by Italy and Morocco, the film was not only sensitive to non-Western ways of seeing in its narrative and visual construction, but also won the Palme d'Or under the Moroccan flag at Cannes in 1952. *Othello* established a lasting connection between Moroccan cinema and festivals. Since its amateur beginnings in the 1950s through to its professionalisation from the 1970s onwards, Moroccan cinema has been seeking international visibility as a postcolonial art form and entertainment industry. As will be seen in the next sections of this chapter, Moroccan filmmakers and other players in the film field have been striving towards national and international festival visibility for and recognition of Morocco as a nation of cinema.

Decolonising the Gaze: The National Film Festival

In the face of the influence and scale of Western representations of Morocco on the big screen, Moroccan filmmakers have devoted themselves since the end of the colonial period to the production of authentic images of the country. The question of how to exhibit these national self-images has been at the centre of Moroccan cinema. The first film festival in post-colonial Morocco dates back to 1968. The International Mediterranean

Film Festival (IMFF) in Tangier was organised by the Fédération Nationale des Ciné-Clubs du Maroc (FNCCM), the National Federation of Film Clubs. The Centre Cinématographique Marocain (CCM), Morocco's national film board, produced two national feature films for the occasion. Mohamed Tazi Ben Abdelouahed and Ahmed Al Mesnaoui's *Al-Hayat Kifah* (*Life is Struggle*, 1968) and Latif Lahlou's *Shams al-Rabie* (*Spring Sun*, 1969) are widely regarded as the country's first postcolonial features even if Mohamed Ousfour's *Al Ibn al bar* (*The Cursed Sun*) had been made between 1956 and 1958. The IMFF signalled the official birth of national cinema and set the bar high for the nascent nation's filmmakers to produce cinematic articulations of a society in transition. Morocco became independent only in 1956 and most filmmakers had been born and received their education in metropolitan Europe as students from the colonies. It therefore seems only natural that the colonial experience should dominate the first postcolonial images of Morocco on the big screen. However, Moroccan cinema was markedly different from that of neighbouring Algeria, where a cult of the collective hero emerged under the aegis of the one-party regime. The dramatic length and violent end of Algeria's colonial experience meant that its postcolonial filmmakers were more involved in reflecting on that condition than their Moroccan and Tunisian counterparts. The release of Gillo Pontecorvo's *La battaglia di Algeri* (*The Battle of Algiers,* Italy-Algeria, 1966) and the award of a Palme d'Or at Cannes 1975 to Mohamed Lakhdar-Hamina's historical epic *Chronique des années de braise* (*Chronicle of the Years of Fire*, Algeria, 1975) defined the image of Algerian cinema on the international scene. Early Moroccan filmmakers had both the advantage and misfortune of living in Algeria's shadow. The fact that the Moroccan state was averse to funding feature filmmaking until 1980, meant that filmmakers had to make heroic efforts to produce films and strive to have them screened at national and international festivals.

In 1982, just two years after CCM introduced the Fonds de Soutien à la Production Cinématographique (Support Funds for Film Production) to galvanise feature cinema, the 1st edition of the National Film Festival (NFF) took place in Rabat (the national capital). The event was the first major *rendez-vous* of Moroccan national cinema. It was held in different cities on an irregular basis, on the one hand as a reflection of the insufficient quantity of films produced in that early period, and on the other as the expression of a desire to celebrate cinema in all the four corners of the country. Despite the accolades garnered by Moroccan films at international festivals in the 1970s, the NFF brought together filmmakers and other actors in the national film sector for the first time. The event soon became a primary platform for lively debates on national cinema and identity. Moroccan films were not commercially distributed before the 1990s, despite a growing production volume thanks to increased state support.[2] The distributors were not interested in local films because they cost many times more than Hollywood, Bollywood and Egyptian movies. However, one national distributor who attended the 3rd NFF, held in Meknès in 1991, decided to distribute Abdelkader Lagtaâ's *Hub fi Dar al-Beida* (*A love Affair in Casablanca*, 1991). It was a risky undertaking, but the rewards far surpassed everyone's expectations and changed the history of Moroccan cinema forever. *Love Affair* did very well at the national box office. The distributor's decision, made at the NFF, revealed the existence of a broad audience niche for Moroccan films. Kevin Dwyer ascribes this audience interest to the dynamics of cultural globalisation:

> Homegrown films are increasingly popular in Morocco, reflecting the changing tastes of film audiences and their growing desire to see themselves and their own society represented on the large screen, rather than yet another representation of life in the West. (2002: 351)

Moreover, Moroccan filmmakers became determined to cater to this new audience. National films have crowned the box office ahead of Hollywood and Bollywood fare since the late 1990s. The distribution of Lagtaâ's first feature film has therefore created a unique situation in Morocco where national cinema surpasses the world's most powerful film industries in terms of audience numbers and revenue.

Further proof of the transformational role of the NFF occurred in June 1995. The fourth edition of the event in Tangier, which coincided with the centenary of cinema, remains a watershed date in the history of Moroccan cinema. New filmmakers from the diaspora, mostly second-generation Moroccan immigrants from Europe, were especially invited to screen their short films at the festival. The new cineastes met with their older compatriots, discussions flourished about the state and future of Moroccan cinema, and the CCM promised to cast the net of its funding recipients wider to incorporate the new diasporic filmmakers. Their productions over the years have changed the face of this cinema. Some of the diasporic filmmakers discovered at the national film festival have gone on to win prizes at prestigious international film festivals. Prominent examples include Nabil Ayouch (*Mektoub*, 1997; *Ali Zaoua*, 2000; *Khail Allah / Horses of God*, 2012), Narjiss Nejjar (*Allen Zwanin / Dry No More*, 2003; *L'amante du Rif / The Rif Lover*, 2011) and Noureddine Lakhmari (*Casanegra*, 2008; *Zero*, 2012).

Organised and sponsored by the CCM, the NFF is an occasion for national film critics to debate the state and future of national filmmaking.[3]

These formidable participants are the de facto kingmakers or king slayers of national cinema. Their rarefied praise for, and common attacks on certain works and filmmakers, have lasting echoes in the national press and on the funding decisions of the CCM. Take, for example, the filmmaker Hakim Noury. His prolific production record in pursuit of a broad audience in the 1990s led to his stigmatisation as the creator of cheap, commercial films unworthy of public funds through the CCM. Noury entered a long period of silence in the 2000s. Another significant example of the role of the NFF in national life is Leila Marrakchi's *Marock* (*Morocco?*, 2005). The film stirred a big debate between supporters and detractors at the festival in Tangiers, and subsequently at festival screenings around the world. It was attacked by Islamists and the conservative press for its alleged misrepresentation of Islam. Between the conservative attacks and the silence of intellectuals on the Left, *Marock* touched a nerve about Morocco in the early twenty-first century by depicting the existential insecurity of an upper-class isolated by wealth in exclusive suburbs. In a less intentional way, it also unveils the spectral resistance of large masses dispossessed by neoliberal globalisation.

In recent years, the NFF has been the stage of serious attempts to foster the identity of Morocco as a pluralistic, tolerant and modern nation. In 2007, for example, the festival screened Mohamed Mernich's *Tilila* (2007), a feature film in Tamazight (the Berber language). After many decades of the official repression of this indigenous language spoken by the majority of Moroccans, the regime was forced by local and transnational civil society activism to acknowledge the multilingual identity of the country. The NFF put itself at the forefront of national debates by screening Mernich's film years before the constitution was amended to recognise Tamazight as an official language in Morocco in 2011. In another instance of the festival's role in promoting multiculturalism, the poster for its 2010 edition (see Image 8) was designed by a Marrakech film school student in the country's three main languages (Tamazight, Arabic and French). The festival has further fostered considerations of Morocco's Africanness in response to the hitherto predominant Pan-Arabist ideological framework of conceiving national identity. As well as including African film directors and actors in its juries, the NFF has been used to launch future editions of FESPACO, Africa's longstanding biennial film and television festival.

Held annually in Tangier since 2005, the NFF projects from this transnational city the identity of an increasingly confident nation. Tangier sits at the meeting point of the Mediterranean Sea and the Atlantic Ocean and is only a few miles south of Europe. Both Gibraltar's and Spain's southern shores are within unassisted sight of Tangier. The legacy of the city as an International Zone (1923-1956) and its reputation for housing some of the finest literati and artists of the twentieth century, make it an ideal site for projecting cinematic images of Morocco as an open nation, striving to face its own past and present in an increasingly interconnected world. Despite its fast-changing urban landscape, Tangier has a stable cinephilic audience, which makes the NFF a success every year. This success is marked by the controversies and debates that emanate from the festival's crop of screened films, which represent the entirety of films produced in or co-produced with Morocco. In February 2012, the festival

Image 8: Poster for the 12th Edition of the National Film Festival 2011

made global headlines by screening the Franco-Moroccan filmmaker Kamal Hachkar's documentary film *Tinghir-Jérusalem: Les échos du Mellah* (*Tinghir-Jerusalem: Echoes of the Mellah*, 2011). The film attracted the ire of Islamists and Pan-Arabists, who accused the young director of promoting a Zionist agenda (Bahmad 2012). The work relates Hachkar's journey in search of remnants of his native town's Jewish community from Tinghir to Israeli cities and villages. The NFF once more placed itself at the forefront of national debates about Moroccan cultural identity through the selection and award of a prize to Hachkar's debut film, which is a tribute to inter-faith tolerance and the importance of preserving the memory of a multicultural country.

Morocco Goes Global: The Marrakech International Film Festival

In 2001, a nation drunk with the faith that a new era was at its doorsteps, cheered as the first Marrakech International Film Festival (MIFF) opened to much fanfare in global media. In addition to the presence of the cream of international film stars and legends, the festival distinguished itself through its colossal character. Nothing is done on a small scale in Marrakech. The city has rapidly emerged as the country's most urban centre. Marrakech is the face of a half-real, half-fictionalised Morocco: open, merry and proud of its millennial traditions and cultural heritage. What is taken by visitors to Marrakech to be Moroccan authenticity is often a carefully spectacle staged for the unwary foreign tourist looking for easy access to and gratification in a different culture (see Image 9). Marrakech gives the average international visitor the elusive gift of cross-cultural understanding. In their book *Paris-Marrakech: Luxe, pouvoir et réseaux* (2012), Ali Amar and Jean-Pierre Tuquoi unveil the invisible networks and monies behind the spectacle. Postcard Marrakech is global capital incarnate. MIFF is shot through with the capitalisation of the city's cultural heritage and built environment. The worldliness of Marrakech is displayed too in the embeddedness of the international film festival not only within the ubiquitous dynamics of globalisation but also in the local structures of power. That the festival foundation is presided over by Prince Moulay Rachid, King Mohammed VI's brother, and functions under the high patronage of the King himself, is not lost on keen observers of Moroccan political life. The prestige of the attendees, dinner receptions and the accolades received from the Prince or, indeed, the King inscribe the festival within a political economy of cultural distinction and political hegemony.

Image 9: Marrakech International Film Festival 2013 Poster

Marrakech is particularly well-known for its age-old marketplace, Jamaa El Fnaa, where musicians, dancers, storytellers, snake charmers and food sellers gather everyday to perpetuate a perennial festival for the senses. Spectacle and performance have become intricately woven in Morocco's identity as a gateway to Africa. MIFF has built its reputation on the city's growing fortunes as an everyday spectacle event with transnational visibility. Film is spectacle too, of course: from the big screen projection to the audience rituals. To seal this link between the spectacle of the city and cinema's spectacularity, a big film screen is installed in Jamaa El Fnaa for the duration of the festival. Hundreds of Moroccan and international tourists halt their evening walks in the medina to watch films instead. The party is even livelier when big-name stars such as Shah Rukh Khan, Martin Scorsese, Leonardo DiCaprio, Nicole Kidman or Emir Kusturica are in attendance.

The transnational identity of the festival is further enshrined in every edition's celebration of a national or regional cinema and honouring a coterie of its best-known faces with medals of honour on the festival stage. The cinemas honoured in recent years include the French, British, South Korean, Mexican, Indian and Scandinavian. Yet another facet of the festival's transnationalism is embodied by the composition of the jury members. In his editorial to the festival website's presentation of the 2013 edition, HRH Prince Moulay Rachid, writes:

> Universality is more present than ever this year, with a retrospective dedicated to Scandinavian cinema that will allow us to immerse ourselves in some exceptional oeuvres from the Northern European imagination. Similarly, the talents and diversity of the Jury, presided over this year by Martin Scorsese, bear witness to the vision and international perspective of our festival.

Other prominent presidents and members of the festival's juries for short and feature-length films in recent years include Abbas Kiarostami (Iran), Emir Kusturica (Serbia), Abdelkebir Khatibi (Morocco), Chantal Akerman (Belgium), Ousmane Sembène (Senegal), Elia Suleiman (Palestine) and Roman Polanski (Poland). Among the members of Scorsese's jury for the 2013 edition were Fatih Akin (Turkey-Germany), Marion Cotillard (France), Amat Escalante (Mexico), Golshifteh Farahani (Iran), Anurag Kashyap (India), Narjiss Nejjar (Morocco) and Park Chan-wook (South Korea). The prestigious jury members undoubtedly attract global media attention. However, MIFF's transnationalism is represented by diverse elements from the city of Marrakech to the quality and diversity of the films screened in and out of competition.

The international festival meets national cinema in master classes and Moroccan film competitions. The former are often given by famous film directors like Martin Scorsese (2006) and Abbas Kiarostami (2006, 2013). The festival organisers consider the classes as both a sign of the event's openness to the world and a chance for young Moroccan talent to learn the art of cinema from its masters. In his aforementioned editorial, the President of the Marrakech International Film Festival Foundation explains that the 2013 edition

> [...] will include some exceptional master classes hosted by Abbas Kiarostami, James Gray, Nicolas Winding Refn and Bruno Dumont, that will allow movie lovers to share the

films and thoughts of some of our greatest directors as well as philosopher Régis Debray. This spirit of openness towards the world is further underscored by the films of the Official Selection, that will transport us through those emotions and realities that make cinema a global art form that helps us better understand one another. (Rachid 2013)

Within this framework of transnationalisation and cross-cultural understanding, the festival showcases Morocco for the world by including Moroccan films in both official and sidebar competitions, particularly the Cinécoles Competition for short films made by Moroccan film school students. However, and especially as far as the selection of Moroccan feature-length films is concerned, the selection process betrays a certain proclivity to works with a touristic gaze on the country. The selected films in recent years can leave local audiences puzzled about whether the festival organisers are promoting Moroccan cinema or rather fostering Westernised views on the country.

A Nation in Translation

In conclusion, this comparative journey through Morocco's two foremost film festivals has revealed how these annual gatherings are about more than stars walking on red carpets in Marrakech and barely visible national filmmakers in a darkened room in Tangier lamenting how the dawn of globalisation has crushed the short night of decolonisation. Instead, the Tangier and Marrakech film festivals reveal a nation actively negotiating its place in the world through cinematic images and events in tune with the challenges of our modern world. The National Film Festival in Tangier is an occasion to mark the growing influence of Moroccan cinema as a medium for the negotiation of national identity and debates on the country's past, present and future from the distracting glamour of Marrakech and its spectacular globalisation. The national festival stages Morocco for Moroccans and an elite of international film scholars and observers. The Marrakech International Film Festival operates according to different dynamics and needs. With a basic budget of over MAD 60 million (U.S.$8 million), Morocco's biggest film festival is a de facto transnational event from conception to consumption. Its location in Marrakech taps into the city's cultural heritage and international visibility to translate Morocco for the world and the world for Moroccans in an effort to marry globalisation to local cultural authenticity. Neither festival, as we have seen, is completely immune from controversy, nor has either had its last word. The Tangier and Marrakech film festivals are rapidly evolving in tune with a world rapidly marching into an unknown future. The two film festivals are apposite screens and fora where this change is mirrored, debated and translated by local and global actors.

Works Cited

Amar, Ali, and Jean-Pierre Tuquoi (2012) *Paris-Marrakech: Luxe, pouvoir et réseaux* | *Paris- Marrakech: Glamour, Power and Networks*. Paris: Calmann-Lévy.

Bahmad, Jamal (2013) 'Tinghir-Jerusalem-Tangier: The Jew, the Imam and the Camera in Morocco', *Africultures*. On-line. Available HTTP: http://www.africultures.com/php/?nav=article&no=11305 (13 February)

Dwyer, Kevin (2002) 'Moroccan Film-making: A Long Voyage through the Straits of Paradox', in Donna Lee Bowen and Evelyn A. Early (eds) *Everyday Life in the Muslim Middle East*. 2nd ed. Bloomington: Indiana University Press, 349-59.

Higbee, Will (2007) 'Beyond the (Trans)national: Towards a Cinema of Transvergence in Postcolonial and Diasporic Francophone Cinema(s)', *Studies in French Cinema*, 7, 79-91.

Rachid, Prince Moulay (2013) 'Editorial of His Royal Highness, Prince Moulay Rachid', Festival Marrakech. On-line. Available HTTP: http://en.festivalmarrakech.info/Editorial-of-His-Royal-Highness-Prince-Moulay-Rachid_a686.html (15 November).

Slavin, David H. (1998) 'French Colonial Film before and after Itto: From Berber Myth to Race War', *French Historical Studies*, 21, 1, 125-155.

Notes

1   Examples of such popular films include Alfred Hitchcock's *The Man Who Knew Too Much* (U.S., 1956), David Lean's *Lawrence of Arabia* (UK, 1962), Henri Verneuil's *Cent mille dollars au soleil* (*Greed in the Sun*, France / Italy, 1964), Jean-Luc Godard's *Le Grand escroc* (*The Great Swindler*, France, 1963), Pier Paolo Pasolini's *Edipo re* (*Oedipus Rex*, Italy, 1967), John Huston's *The Man Who Would Be King* (U.S. / UK, 1975), Mustapha Akkad's *Ar-Risalah* (*The Message*, Morocco / Libya / UK / U.S., 1976), Franco Zeffirelli's *Gesù di Nazareth* (*Jesus of Nazareth*, UK / Italy, 1977), Carroll Ballard's *The Black Stallion Returns* (U.S., 1979), Claude Lelouch's *Édith et Marcel* (*Edith and Marcel*, France, 1982), Raul Ruiz' *L'île au trésor* (*Treasure Island*, France / Chile, 1986), Martin Scorsese's *The Last Temptation of Christ* (U.S. / Canada, 1987), Bernardo Bertolucci's *The Sheltering Sky* (Italy / UK, 1990), Ridley Scott's *The Gladiator* (U.S. / UK, 2000) and *Black Hawk Down* (U.S., 2001), Oliver Stone's *Alexander* (U.S., 2004), Alejandro González Iñárritu's *Babel* (U.S. / Mexico / France, 2006), and Xavier Beauvois' *Des hommes et des dieux* (*Of Gods and Men*, France, 2010).

2   Moroccan national film production has increased from an average of five feature films per year in the 1990s to an annual rate 20 to 25 features today. Short films are also encouraged and sponsored by the CCM at a variable rate of 50 films every year.

3   There is no precise information regarding the budget of the festival. The organiser, CCM, is a public institution that does not disclose its budget for this festival despite calls in the local press for more clarity on this matter.

A Festival of Resistance and Evolution: Interview with Mohamed Mediouni, Director of the Journées Cinématographiques de Carthage / Carthage Cinema Days[1]

Javier H. Estrada

Most of the world's cinéphiles are not aware that the Carthage Film Festival / Journées Cinématographiques de Carthage or JCC (www. jccarthage.com) is the longest running festival outside of Europe. Every two years, for almost half a century, this festival has consistently shown a panorama of Arab and African cinemas, promoting challenging films (in terms of politics and aesthetics). It was created in 1966 by the Tunisian Ministry of Culture as a response to the expectations of the local cultural elite. The initiative to set up a big film festival was consistent with the spirit of other Tunisian cultural associations that were very active immediately after independence, but that, since the start of the twentieth century, have ceased to exist in Tunisian public life. This elite, and specifically the militants in these associations, was responsible for the different sections of the Ministry of Culture that was established in 1961, four years after the country's independence. Theatre and cinema occupied a privileged position in their plans for the cultural growth of the newly independent country. The spirit that dominated the activities of this elite was similar to that which they had contributed to the colonial authorities years before: the implementation of a national cultural policy that would allow Tunisian people to express their authenticity and become a modern society. The JCC was built upon these ideals. It was a great challenge if we consider that the country recovered its independence just a few years before and that, therefore, its cultural facilities and economic resources were very limited.

Significant figures, such as Tahar Cheriaa, Ahmed Attia and Dora Bouchoucha, among many others, have led the JCC through the years, demonstrating that film festivals must enlighten the evolution of cinema, but also reflect on the political and cultural mutations of their societies. We can find an exceptional example in the present. Mohamed Mediouni became Director of the JCC in 2012 when the effects, promises and uncertainties of the Tunisian Revolution were still latent. The 2012 edition of JCC took place in a tremendously tense atmosphere, as Mediouni explains in this interview. He was the right person for such a complicated job. A specialist not only in Arab and African cinemas, but also in the theatres of the region, Mediouni was President of the Fédération Tunisienne des Ciné-Clubs from 1993 to 2000, the Director of the Carthage Theatre Festival in 1999 and also the founder and Director of the Festival International du Court Métrage de Tunis from 1994 to 2000. In his first edition as a director of JCC, he insisted on furthering the festivals' goals and tasks by turning to the youth of Tunisia and new media.

I met Mohamed Mediouni for the first time in March 2013, some months before the interview project was assigned. We were both members of the jury at the Ibn Arabi Film Festival (IBAFF) in Murcia, Spain. We understood each other easily despite the fact that I am not fluent in French and he is not in English. During the interview we experienced some idiomatic issues but in the end the key language prevailed: our mutual, inexhaustible passion for the culture and the cinemas of Africa and the Middle East.

Javier H. Estrada: We could begin by talking about the origins of the festival. How important was the impact of the first edition?

Mohamed Mediouni: Both official (embassies and diplomatic representations) and unofficial (ciné-clubs) organisations made efforts to invite and enthuse filmmakers from all around the world to participate in the new event that was going to put the independence of a culturally mature Tunisia on the map. In the end, 31 countries answered the call: ten from the Arab and African countries (Ivory Coast, Guinea, Senegal, Zaire, Lebanon, Algeria, Morocco, Libya, Kuwait, Tunisia) and 21 from the rest of the world. The programme consisted of 29 features and 22 short films. The festival has enjoyed a positive and constructive atmosphere since its very beginning.

Well-known directors and film critics were involved: the great French film historian Georges Sadoul and Italian director Enrico Fulchignoni (responsible at that time for the film department at UNESCO) coordinated the festival's symposium, of which the theme was Mediterranean and Arab cinema. Turkish film critic Semih Tuğrul was part of the jury, as well as Antoine Bohdziewicz, President of the International Federation of Ciné-clubs. Films such as *De man die zijn haar kort liet knippen* (*The Man Who Had His Hair Cut Short*, André Delvaux, Belgium, 1966) and *Der junge Törless* (*Young Törless*, Volker Schlöndorff, West Germany, 1966) were included in the programme. The awards of that edition were a testament to the quality of the selected films and announced the kind of cinema the festival was committed to showing in order to have a long life: the Golden Tanit was awarded to the Senegalese film *La noire de...* (*Black Girl*, Ousmane Sembène, 1966) and the Silver Tanit to the Czech film *Krik* (*The Cry*, Jaromil Jireš, 1966).

JHE: *The festival was created by film critic Tahar Cheriaa (1927-2010). What kind of project did he have in mind?*

MM: Tahar Cheriaa belonged to the Tunisian elite that contributed to the cultural establishment in general and to forms of artistic expression in particular, which were among the priorities in the fight for the independence and the construction of the country and its future. It is not a coincidence that Cheriaa was the President of the Fédération Tunisienne des Ciné-clubs (FTCC, the Tunisian Federation of Ciné-Clubs),[2] created in 1950. This federation played a significant role in the diffusion of film culture among young Tunisians. It also contributed, along with the Fédération Tunisienne des Cinéastes Amateurs (FTCA, Tunisian Federation of Amateur Filmmakers) to the training of most of those directors that the country would soon become famous for. I'm talking about the Golden Age of Tunisian cinema and concretely about directors such as Férid Boughedir, Selma Baccar, Nouri Bouzid, Taïeb Louhichi, Ridha el Behi, Naceur Khemir, Moncef Dhouib, Mohamed Dammak, Mohamed Zran and Khaled Barsaoui, among others.

A cultivated cinéphile, Tahar Cheriaa had the character of the cultural organiser who used pedagogy and experience to connect young (and not so young) people with the cinema. He was – like most of the artists of his generation – a confirmed Third-Worldist. He fought for the emergence of a different cinema that could reflect on the questions that concerned the people of these countries, a cinema that would take part in their battles and conflicts for independence and respectability, a cinema able to move its audience and connect with their sensibilities. His book *Ecrans d'abondance ou cinéma de libération en Afrique* (1979, *Screens of Abundance or Cinema of Liberation in Africa*) perfectly illustrated this tendency, and gave a clear idea of the activist spirit that marked his particular point of view. The analysis he made of the film industry and the system of distribution, particularly in the countries of the Third World, was a way to report the domination of American majors on the African markets and distribution companies, even if they took the form of French companies such as Gaumont or UGC. It was a way of participating in the battle for real change in favour of African and Arab cinema. The creation of the JCC represented for him and his colleagues at FTCC and FEPACI (Pan-African Federation of Filmmakers) an appropriate frame for this transformation.

Cheriaa was the absolute leader of the festival during its five first editions: he took the responsibility as Director of the JCC, was part of jury, intervened in symposiums, and sometimes he even conducted the debates on the films in competition. Cheriaa marked the festival forever because he understood very early on that it was useless trying to imitate European and U.S. festivals. In his mind and in the minds of his colleagues, the JCC should look for a different philosophy. It was irremediably located among the alternative festivals which tried to show emerging cinema by encouraging and discovering new talent. This was, of course, a very difficult task...

JHE: *How has the identity of the festival developed since 1966?*

MM: The success of the first edition silenced the sceptics and gave an opportunity to the organisers to show not only that it was *possible* to organise a film festival in Tunisia, but also that it was *necessary*. Despite the fact that the main ideas were clear from the first edition, the exact identity of the festival was defined in 1968 with its second edition. The foreword to the awards ceremony of this second edition clearly indicated the nature of the event:

The JCC is not a festival like the others. It tries to testify to a specific idea of cinema: it is a tool that must work for the collective struggle in this segment of the world, which is the Third World. It must help people to finally decide their own destiny, to become aware of their problems. This perspective requires huge efforts. The JCC must support a cinema that shows a clear vision on sociological realities. It should suggest, if not certain solutions, at least critical reflections on how to find those solutions. (JCC 1976: 11-13)

The peculiarity of the festival relies on the geographical and historical position of Tunisia, a country that is both African and Arab. Therefore, Tunisia was an ideal place to function as a meeting place for both cultures from which to lead the battle to build a cinema for Arab and African people. Since then, the official competition of the festival is reserved to Arab and African filmmakers.

JHE: *Why is the festival biennial? Carthage alternates with the Damascus Film Festival. Do you collaborate with them in any way?*

MM: In my opinion, the fact that we are biennial has nothing to do with a possible alternation with the Damascus International Film Festival (DIFF). They started in 1979, 13 years after the JCC's first edition. The executives of DIFF thought it was useful to alternate it with the JCC. As for the collaboration between JCC and the festival in Damascus, it obviously happened, but not in an official way. We attended both events and the participation of Tunisian and Syrian filmmakers in the two festivals is very common. The reasons for the two-yearly basis of the JCC could be found, perhaps, with the pace of Arab and African film production during the 1970s. Film production was rather slow, so it was difficult to find enough quality films each year. A true alternation was established with FESPACO after the birth of this festival in 1969. According to many African filmmakers, the first ideas of establishing something like FESPACO germinated during the JCC itself.

JHE: Could you introduce us to the figure of Ahmed Attia and also talk about the legacy he has left to the festival?

MM: Well, firstly, at the time he joined the team of JCC in 1992, Ahmed Attia was the most successful Tunisian producer. One of the founding fathers of FEPACI, he innovated Tunisian film production in terms of its financial set-up and supported a significant number of Tunisian and African film directors to accomplish their best films. He also succeeded in assuring an appropriate distribution network for the films he produced. He became Director of the JCC, continuing in the same spirit he had for his production activities. Without ignoring the peculiarities of the festival, he put the emphasis on the professional dimensions of cinema and the unique problems that people from this field were facing at that time. Therefore, he focused the debates of the festival on production and distribution issues. He tried to add an economic dimension to the cultural achievements of the JCC, hoping to turn the festival into 'a hub for the exchanges South-South and North-South' (Attia 1992: 8).

A certain pragmatism seemed to guide his approach. For him, the problems in the local film industry were no longer a question of accusing the dominant system or discussing production and distribution matters between film critics and representatives of the *government. These accusations had often defined the debates at the festival* since its 5th edition in 1974. He thought, rather, that it was a question of going further by gathering 'influential people from the North and the South in order to build a sustainable cooperation between them' (Attia 1994: 8). In this sense, Attia restructured the Carthage Film Market (first organised in 1974) for the 1992 edition and established L'Atelier des projets (Projects Workshop) so as 'to help to materialise the best screenplays presented by Arab and African filmmakers in a selection made by the festival' (Attia 1992: 8). In the following edition in 1994, he announced the creation of a similar project, entitled Marché International du Produit Audio-Visuel de Carthage (MIPAC, International Market of Audio-Visual Products in

Carthage). Unfortunately, this was just an ephemeral initiative and was soon discontinued, but the Atelier remained a very important element for the subsequent editions of the JCC.

JHE: *How important has the prestigious film distributor and producer Tarak Ben Amar been for the festival?*

MM: Tarak Ben Amar was a special adviser for the 2004 edition of the JCC. Apart from this he has never held any official role at the festival, but he has definitely provided valuable help in terms of facilitating contacts and helping to solve logistical problems. He was honoured as 'Parrain de la session' (Supporter of the session) in the 2010 edition of the festival.

JHE: *What about Tunisian producer Dora Bouchoucha?*

MM: She joined the team of the JCC in 1992 as Attia's assistant. In that edition she was in charge of the Film Market. In 1994 she became part of the programming team for the festival. When she became a film producer at Nomadis Images in Tunis, she also assumed the direction of the JCC for the 2008 and 2010 editions.

JHE: *How important has the festival been in the development of African and Arab cinemas through the years?*

MM: The JCC is the oldest international film festival organised outside of Europe and America and the only one to be held regularly since its creation in 1966. The JCC was very involved with the development of Arab and African cinemas, partly because of its pioneering position and also due to the objectives appointed by its founders. This is, at least, what is suggested in the forewords for the awards of the first editions. The first festival took place in a particularly optimistic and revolutionary atmosphere that put the members of jury in a position in which they became the messengers of a project. They were defenders of a particular cause: the necessity of the emergence of a distinctive cinema coming from the African and Arab countries.

For them [the members of the jury], each edition seemed to be an opportunity to make a point about the evolution of this project, a chance to assess, encourage, accompany and to claim that the JCC was not a festival like the others. They had the mission to guide Arab and African filmmakers towards a type of filmmaking that would allow them to create a genuinely new cinema.

It also happened that in some editions the jury took the decision not to award the Golden Tanit to any film. This was the case in the

2nd and 5th editions [in 1968 and 1974, respectively]. As a reason they declared that 'no film contained the necessary qualities to contribute to the struggle of the Third World, to its existence and dignity'. The last paragraphs of the forewords to the 3rd edition's awards (1970) sum up the revolutionary spirit of the time very well:

> The criteria of selection of the films is based on the expectations offered by certain filmmakers and national cinemas, and it is also based in the quality of their actual research in the expression of a social or cultural, genuinely African or Arab reality. Africa and the Arab countries are a world in quick mutation. Cinema must be a weapon to protect ancient cultures, a weapon to confront the future. (JCC 1976)

But times have changed. Other festivals appeared and showed interest in the African and Arab cinema in different ways, sometimes with bigger resources than JCC. The cinema in the Arab and African countries has also evolved. The structure of the JCC has not been altered too much and in my opinion it is still playing an essential role in the development of Arab and African cinema.

JHE: *Since its foundation, the festival has shown and awarded extremely important films such as* La noire de... [Black Girl, *Senegal, Ousmane Sembène, 1966*], Al-ikhtiyar [The Choice, *Egypt, Youssef Chahine, 1970*], Finyè [The Wind, *Souleymane Cissé, Mali, 1982*], Urs al-jalil [Wedding in Galilee, *Michel Khleifi, Palestine, 1987*], Bab El Oued City [*Merzak Allouache, Algeria, 1994*] *and* Daratt [Dry Season, *Mahamat Saleh Haroun, Chad, 2006*], *among many others. Do you think the awards contributed to the local and international reputations of those films?*

MM: The JCC played a key role in the development of many Arab and African filmmakers. It revealed unknown talents to the world, but also helped others to be acknowledged in their own countries. The reaction of the Egyptian filmmaker Hossam Eddine Mostafa when he accused the JCC in some circles [at the beginning of the 1970s] of favouring 'left-wing anti-Nasserists', such as Tewfik Saleh, at the expense of traditional Egyptian cinema, shows that the festival was prepared to go off the beaten path in order to contribute to the promotion of the new voices of African and Arab cinemas. In this sense, apart from the films you mentioned, I would point out titles such as *Al-makhdu'un* (*The Dupes*, Tewfik Saleh, 1972), *Sawak al utubis* (*The Bus Driver*, Atef El Taieb, 1982) and *Arack el balah* (*The Sweat of the Palm Trees*, Radwan El Kashef, 1998) from Egypt; *Ahlam el madina* (*Dreams of the City*, 1984) and *Al lail* (*The Night*, 1992) by Syrian director Mohamed Malas; *Nyamanton, la leçon des ordures* (*Lessons from the Garbage*, Cheick Oumar Sissoko, 1986) from Mali; *Halfaouine* (Férid Boughedir, 1990) from Tunisia; and *Po di Sangui* (*Tree of Blood*, Flora Gomes, 1996) from Guinea-Bissau.

JHE: Were those significant filmmakers (Sembène, Chahine, Khleifi, etc.) involved in the festival? How important is the presence of the directors for the festival?

MM: There was a special relationship between many of the filmmakers who came to the JCC. They felt part of the family. Guadeloupian director Sarah Maldoror once said:

> Carthage, the city where we learnt to look at our films, our dances, our stories, our love affairs and our dreams. We understood our differences by looking at each other. Today, film culture and television are universal, so let's cultivate our differences and remain faithful to the JCC. (Maldoror 2004: 28)

Usually, filmmakers were involved with successive editions. The winners of the Golden Tanit are automatically included as members of the jury for the following edition. This is a way to honour them and to strengthen their relationship with the festival.

JHE: You became Director of the festival for its 24th edition in 2012. How was this first e

MM: The 24th edition was organised under very special circumstances. It was the first festival to be held after the Revolution of 14 January 2011, which is not finished yet. In 2012, there were huge political, security and economic problems, but also other challenges to overcome. Some attacks against artists and against cultural and artistic places were perpetrated by so-called Salafi groups. Also, an aggressive discourse was orchestrated by political parties against the arts and artists, with total *tolerance* by the new government. The Ministry of Culture handled these problems in a very poor way and there was a poisonous atmosphere.

The violent attack committed by radical groups against the U.S. Embassy in September 2012 as a response to the well-known and repulsive islamophobic film *Innocence of Muslims* (Sam Bacile, 2012), ended in a tarnishing of the world's image of Tunisia, and resulted in the loss of very important economic and cultural assets. This violent mood led to a crisis of trust between the Ministry of Culture and many artist and filmmakers who felt betrayed. They thought the sector would now face even more complicated problems than the existing ones.

This atmosphere pushed some associations and individuals to deem the JCC less important. Some even expressed doubt that the 2012 edition would take place. This extreme position was well-planned, but it involved serious risks for many parties. To cancel the JCC that year would have meant to betray the founders of the festival and to surrender to the obscurantism that was seizing Tunisia. It would also be a betrayal of a society that struggles to protect the contemporary values of a modern Tunisia and to advance in the direction of freedom and dignity. It was a great challenge to organise this edition in time. These were the questions we posed to ourselves when working on the festival: which vision, which new proposals, which perspectives of the future can we offer in reply to the numerous and legitimate expectations of the audience? In particular, how can we answer the expectations of Tunisian youth which has witnessed all over the world the concepts of freedom, justice and respectability in action?

To answer to all these questions, the team in charge of the 2012 edition put art and culture at the centre of their concerns. They assumed this mission with a commitment to defend art and the right to make art. This is the only concept that dictates their direction and choices. One idea was a certainty for us: youth will be at the heart of the edition. We created a programmed space for young artists: 'Ecrans d'avenir' (Screens of the Future), a section that will become a regular part of the festival. It was conceived as a forum for the exchange of people and ideas and is devoted not only to young Arab and African filmmakers, but to young talented artists from all over the world as well.

JHE: *How does the festival work in terms of its programming? Do you have consultants in every country?*

MM: We do not have official delegates, but we have very useful contacts in those countries that help us in the film selection.

JHE: *How many people work for the festival?*

MM: The festival does not have a permanent administration. For each edition we form a project team of approximately 50 people in total.

JHE: *How many sections do you have in the festival and how many films per section?*

MM: Since the first steps were taken by the festival to assist with the exhibition of films from those countries to the South, the JCC aimed to evolve, to express itself and to adapt to the social, political, aesthetic and technological changes. Growing in size and importance, the JCC expanded its frame from edition to edition, becoming more demanding and showing work from all around the world. For the official competition of the 2012 edition (for which films needed to have been made after 2010) we selected 19 features, 23 short films, 16 documentaries plus 28 films in Perspectives, our non-competitive section. Aside from those screenings, we had several retrospectives: a celebration of the 50th anniversary of Algerian Independence through 19 films; and special tributes to Souleymane Cissé and Malian cinema, Egyptian Tewfik Saleh and Tunisian Taïeb Louhichi. Also, we screened eight so-called cult films from the Arab and the African worlds, in a section we have named Cinéma retrouvé, focusing on films that have recently been restored; we showed 47 local films in the section Panorama du cinéma tunisien; and work from other parts of the world in Cinémas du monde. Finally, for this edition we inaugurated a new section: Ecrans d' à venir (18 films) was dedicated to new, young filmmakers and professionals from Africa and the Arab World.

JHE: Do you still promote special activities such as master classes, debates and industry meetings?

MM: Of course. Since the 1st edition professional meetings have had a privileged space in the festival's programme. During the last edition we held the Producers Network, an initiative to promote features and documentaries by Arab and African producers in the development phase. We also ran workshops to find financial resources for the development of these projects and we organised a meeting of different national film centres in order to inaugurate the Tunisian Centre. Lastly, we had a symposium on the he Pan-African Fund for Cinema & the Audiovisual, organised in collaboration with the International Organisation of the Francophonie (Organisation Internationale de la Francophonie). Also, the JCC consistently pays tribute to great filmmakers by showing complete retrospectives, promoting encounters with the audience and organising master classes. During the last edition these masters were Tewfik Saleh from Egypt, Souleymane Cissé from Mali and Seyyed Reza Mir-Karimi from Iran.

JHE: How is the festival financed?

MM: The largest part of the budget is provided by the Ministry of Culture and the rest comes from different public and private partners.

JHE: *Does the festival get subjected to any kind of censorship (from the government, social agents or religious institutions)?*

MM: The people responsible for the festival have always campaigned to avoid any kind of censorship.

JHE: *Could you talk about the evolution of the festival in terms of attendance and its importance in Tunisia's cultural life?*

MM: The strongest point of the JCC has always been its audience. We have cultivated a cinema audience in Tunisia that consists of all strata of society. Theatres are packed every day of the festival. Also, the discussions organised by the Tunisian Confederation of ciné-clubs reinforces the cinéphile dimension of the festival. It definitely occupies the most prominent place among the different festivals in the country.

JHE: *What is the most important problem you face when working on the festival?*

MM: If I were to point out a single problem, I'd say that the most important one is, without any doubt, the timing. Often the preparation process starts very slowly because of the absence of a permanent and sufficiently independent structure. The consequences are sometimes devastating to our plans. Periodicity is also a problem related to the timing. In a world where a huge number of festivals are celebrated every year and with the continuous increase of film productions, the fact of being biennial could seriously affect our capacity to attend to all the interesting films.

JHE: *What do you think about the other film festivals in the region? Do you collaborate with them?*

MM: The number of festivals is constantly growing, both in Tunisia and in the region at large. JCC sees itself as the leader of the festivals in the region, and sees its goal as creating connections with all these festivals. We know about all initiatives in cinema worldwide, and in the Arab and African worlds in particular. We are open to all representatives of these festivals, the way they are open to us, and we accept their invitations as and when it is possible for us to do so.

JHE: What role do you feel big film festivals such as Cannes, Venice, Berlin or Rotterdam play in the development and distribution of Arab and African films? Do you collaborate with those festivals in some way?

MM: Those festivals have their own logic and, as a result of their own internal pressures, none of them seem particularly concerned with Arab and African cinema. But this does not prevent them from programming, from time to time, one or two films from the region. For them, in general, it is considered as the ultimate achievement, even if to us it seems ephemeral. However, the programmers of the JCC always pay attention to what takes place there, in order to react appropriately.

JHE: In what way do you think the Arab Revolution is affecting the cinemas of the region?

MM: The Tunisian Revolution is not finished yet. It is now facing a critical moment. The political situation is very complex for different reasons, but the most important aspects are related to freedom of speech. Also, we must give the opportunity to our young people to take advantage of the technological progress that could allow them to create the images they want, and to find new ways of production and distribution.

JHE: How do you see the future of the JCC, and what kind of aspects of the festival would you like to change in the future?

MM: It is absolutely necessary for the future of the JCC to achieve financial independence. Also, it must become an annual festival and work harder for new cinema, especially for those films made by young people.

Works Cited

Attia, Ahmed (1992) 'Editorial', *JCC Catalogue*. Tunis: JCC. 8.
Attia, Ahmed (1994) 'Editorial', *JCC Catalogue*. Tunis: JCC. 8.
Cheriaa, Tahar (1979) *Ecrans d'abondance... ou cinemas de liberation en Afrique? [Screens of Abundance or Cinema of Liberation in Africa]*. Tunis: Société Tunisienne de Diffusion.
Journées Cinématographiques de Carthage (1976) *Rétrospective Sessions 1966-1974*, Catalogue edited by the festival for its sixth edition.
Maldoror, Sara (2004) 'Témoignages', in *Journées Cinématographiques de Carthage, Quatre décennies (1966 – 2004)*. Tunis: Ministry of Culture.

Notes

1   The author would like to thank Ana Mirtha for her help with the translation of the text from the original French.

2   [Editor's note: The FTCC and FTCA were of vital importance to the rapid growth of the importance of cinema in independent Tunisia. They overlapped and formed an independent group of young critics and amateur filmmakers, active mostly in the fifties and sixties, which cultivated cinéphiles such as Férid Boughedir and Tahar Cheriaa, and activist filmmakers such as Nouri Bouzid and Selma Baccar. They were all friends or acquaintances who supported one another's work and formed teams of filmmakers collaborating on one another's projects.]

A Film Festival in the Polis:
An Interview with the Organisers
of the Festival du Film Arabe de Fameck

Sally Shafto

We wanted to give back to the families their culture 'usurped' in the name of economics and labour. We wanted to encourage young Maghrebins to find their roots, to keep them and to nurture them. (Mario Giubilei)[1]

The Festival du Film Arabe de Fameck (FFAF) (www.cinemarabe.org) is today considered the most important festival of Arab film in France. Since its inception in 1990, it has screened over 500 films. Originally programmed in November, now in October, the festival occurs over a 10-day period, selling on average 10,000 tickets.

It takes place in the town of Fameck in the Moselle department in the Lorraine, a border area in North-eastern France that in the nineteenth and twentieth centuries frequently changed hands between France and Germany. Nearby Metz is the regional capital, an architecturally impressive city where the Germans left their mark under Bismarck, and where, in 2010, the Centre Pompidou opened a satellite museum. Fameck's approximately 13,000 inhabitants represent an astonishing melting pot of some 48 nationalities that includes a large Maghrebi constituency (Moroccan, Algerian and Tunisian). These immigrants came to work in the local steel and iron industries.

The Fameck festival is not the first community film festival in the Moselle; that honour goes to the Festival du film italien de Villerupt, which this year celebrated its 36th edition (www.festival-villerupt.com). Perhaps inspired by this festival, in 1990, an Italian-born priest named Mario Giubilei, who was a *prête-ouvrier* (a working priest) working directly in the factories, had an idea ('Carte Blanche' 2010). Collaborating with two youths of Mahgrebi origin who were dissatisfied with the dearth of cultural offerings for their community, they organised the 1st edition of the Festival du film Arabe de Fameck at the Fameck Cité Sociale (Fameck Community Centre). Shortly thereafter, the Fameck Cité Sociale partnered with the Fédération des Œuvres Laïques de la Moselle – Ligue de l'Enseignement (Federation of Secular Works in the Moselle – Teachers'League) to make this cultural event an annual activity. In a town like Fameck – *sans* hospitality (no hotels and no restaurants) – that grew pell-mell in the sixties and seventies as a ZUP (that is, a 'zone à urbaniser en priorité' or priority development area) to meet the housing needs of its burgeoning population, the achievement of these two associations is a noteworthy feat. What began as a local initiative of screening VHS cassettes quickly developed into a larger endeavour with national and international echoes (Fameck 2011).

In France, there are many thematic festivals, all of them younger than FFAF. Organised by the Ecran Cinéma of Saint-Denis and Indigènes Films, the Panorama des cinémas du Maghreb et du Moyen Orient (www. pcmmo.org) has existed since 2005. There is also the Maghreb des Films (www.maghrebdesfilms.fr), active since 2009 and whose extensive programming covers Paris and other regions in France.[2] And in nearby Switzerland, there is the Festival du film oriental de Genève (www.fifog. com) that in 2014 will celebrate its 10th edition.[3]

At the heart of the Fameck festival is the Greek idea of the *polis*, of promoting the common good. While A-list international festivals such as Cannes or Toronto are organised for film professionals, festivals like Fameck have developed from the bottom-up, desirous to address the local population. In telling the story of this festival, it would be hard to underestimate the role of the Teachers' League.[4] The Fameck organisers are proud that their festival's top prize is awarded by the audience. Other prizes include a Young Jury Prize and a Press Prize. In 2013, the festival inaugurated a prize for Short Films in which I participated as juror. Every year, Fameck spotlights the film production of a different Arab country and invites numerous directors to present their films in exchanges that are widely appreciated by the public.

In 2011, Anne-Marie Botkovitiz succeeded Mario Giubilei as the Festival's President. My own acquaintance with the Fameck festival dates to my meeting in January 2011 with Anne-Marie and several other Fameck volunteers at the Festival National du Film de Tangier (www.ccm. ma/fnf14).

This interview was conducted via Skype on 5 November 2013. I was in Ouarzazate, Morocco, and my interviewees were at the Fameck Cité Sociale. I had sent them my questions several days beforehand. The interview was conducted and recorded in French and subsequently translated by me into English. My interlocutors then had an opportunity to read and emend the English version.

Interview with:

- Anne-Marie Botkovitz, President of the Festival du film Arabe de Fameck and of the Fameck Cité Sociale;

- René Cahen, Vice-President of the Fédération des Oeuvres Laïques la ligue de l'enseignement and co-founder of the Festival du Film Arabe de Fameck;
- Blandine Besse, Programmer for the Festival du Film Arabe de Fameck from the Fédération des Oeuvres Laïques – la Ligue de l'Enseignement
- Mahjouba Galfout-Aït Benasser, Consultant and programmer for the Fameck festival from the Fédération des Oeuvres Laïques Ligue de l'enseignement. Currently on maternity leave, she was unable to join us on 5 October, but was sent a transcript of the interview for review.

Sally Shafto: *René, Blandine tells me that you were made a Chevalier des Arts et des Lettres earlier this year by the Minister of Culture, Aurélie Filippetti, in recognition of your life contribution in the cultural sector. I know that after being a resistance fighter at the end of the Second World War, you immediately became involved with cinema. Before we talk about the Fameck festival, could you say a few words about film culture in the Moselle after the war? Then, could you tell us about how you became involved with the Fameck film festival?*

I took part in the founding of the Maison des jeunes et de la culture and in 1945, I helped establish the first ciné-club in Metz at the Maison des jeunes. In a movie theatre, we screened regular films in 35mm and also films in 16mm in a ciné-club for young people at the Maison des jeunes.

SS: *Did you know Jean-Marie Straub in those days?*

Of course. He was one of the first members of our cine-club. I still see him from time to time. Last year, we devoted a two-month programme to his and Danielle's films.[5] After the German Occupation, we discovered various national cinemas (American, Soviet, Japanese, Nordic, South American, Italian neo-realism) and then we were transported by the French phenomenon of the New Wave that coincided with the increasing popularity of our ciné-club. We were programming 12 to 15 films every year, 30 films altogether, if you include the ciné-club des jeunes. It doesn't seem like much when you consider that on television today you can watch 50 films a week! Still, we had an impact. The rapid development of our ciné-club came from an avid desire to discover new cinemas.

SS: *Tell us how you became involved with the Fameck festival.*

When Mario [Giubilei] founded it in 1990, I was already working at the

Fameck Cité Sociale where I was a board member. I was involved with the Cité Sociale before Mario Giubilei joined us. The first year of the festival was occasioned by Mario's meeting a group of young persons whose origins were on the other side of the Mediterranean. Mario at the time organised activities at the Cité Sociale. Together, they had the idea – You're familiar with the French expression 'On n'est plus d'ailleurs et on n'est pas encore d'ici' ['We're no longer from the old country and not yet from here.']. That's really true, all the more so today, and it stands for all expatriates. It was with a small number of young persons that Mario had the idea to create a cultural event focused on film. They then met the Delegate for the Fédération des Œuvres Laïques – La Ligue de l'Enseignement, Denis Darroy, who immediately put the Federation and the Cité Sociale at their disposal. I think nine films were shown that first year.

SS: *Not bad for the first year.*

Yes, there were already some productions. Still, that first year was pretty elementary; we didn't even have a screening room. Guests were welcomed in the back kitchen, etc. But very quickly, the programming became more consequential.

SS: *Where does your budget come from and how has it evolved over the years?*

Our annual budget is currently at about €220,000-230,000 [U.S.$297,000-310,500]. It's been fairly stable for the past few years with roughly a 5% increase every year to meet inflation. Of course, we rely heavily on the administrative staff of the Cité Sociale. And we pay part of the salary of someone who works with us from the Ligue de l'Enseignement. All the rest are volunteers. When you compare our budget to that of other festivals, ours is definitely Spartan. Our overhead is incredibly low when you consider the work involved to put on a ten-day film festival. This is perhaps the moment to pay homage to the 200 persons who work for the Cité Sociale and who donate their time to the festival. Without all of these volunteers, we wouldn't be able to do it.

The Val de Fensch is an agglomeration that comprises ten towns around Fameck. The town of Fameck delegates to this regional office the cultural sector, including the distribution of subsidies. Fameck thus plays a big role in the financial and technical aspect of the film festival. We also occasionally receive a grant from Med Screen, which still exists but operates differently now.

The festival is divided into different sectors. Before the start of each festival, Mahjouba calls a meeting and then divides us into groups. And here in Fameck, Anne-Marie works on ticketing and the organisation of meals. Anne-Marie also oversees the organisation of the Opening Ceremony and the organisation and invitation of the different jury members.

We organise ourselves into groups for the programming, for contacting the distributors, another for the filmmakers; then we have several persons who take care of stocking the bookstore for the festival, a group that takes care of welcoming visitors and, of course, a group that caters the meals during the festival. And another group that takes care of the transport to and from Metz.

SS: *Do you collaborate with other film festivals in France? With the Festival des trois Continents de Nantes, for instance? Or the Maghreb des Films in Paris? I read that last year Algeria was specially honoured during your festival for the 50th anniversary marking the end of the Algerian War and that you screened, in partnership with the Centre Pompidou-Metz, Jacques Panijel's film,* October in Paris, *a film that Gérard Vaugeois, one of the organisers of the Maghreb des Films is distributing (Shafto 2011).*

We have a partnership with the Institut du Monde Arabe [www.imarabe. org] in Paris that gives us access to their exhibitions free-of-charge. Marianne Weiss of the Institut du Monde Arabe regularly comes and organises two-day workshops, pro bono, for local children during our festival. We also have partnerships with the Festival de Carros [www. cinealma.fr] and the Festival de Besançon [www.festival-besancon. com]. The festival of Besançon, the home of the Lumière Brothers, which takes place in November, calls itself 'Lumières d'Afriques' [www.lumieresdafrique.com]. The Festival of Carros emphasises the Mediterranean, so they have a number of films that are of interest to us. Our relationship with the Carros organisers is informal; often, for instance, we will compare notes on films during the National Film Festival of Tangier. Sometimes we invite the same guest filmmakers, which has led to us sharing transportation costs. We also have a partnership with the Centre Pompidou in Metz, but this year we didn't organise an event together. It depends on the year. Last year, it was René who initiated the joint screening there of Jacques Panijel's film *Octobre à Paris* [*October in Paris*, France, 1962]. René contacted Gérard Vaugeois.

SS: *Which international Arab film festivals do you attend to help you prepare your programme?*

Every year, we attend the Cannes Film Festival and the Moroccan National Film Festival of Tangier. Once in awhile, we also go to Marrakech [www.festivalmarrakech.info]. We're not going this year; Marrakech is less interesting for our needs. Then there is also the Rencontres cinématographiques de Béjaïa in Algeria [https://www.facebook.com/events/586871971323909/?ref=3] that Mahjouba has attended. It's an interesting film festival with a miniscule budget that takes place in June.

SS: *And the Carthage Film Festival (Journées Cinématographiques de Carthage)?*

Yes, but not regularly. There is also the Festival international du film arabe d'Oran [www.fofafestival.org], which is still young, but has the merit of being the only Arab festival entirely devoted to Arab film. Unfortunately, we missed Oran this year.

SS: *What is your guiding principle in selecting films?*

First, we're interested in Maghrebi filmmakers who have already achieved a certain prominence and with whom we are friends. The artistic quality of individual films is also a decisive factor. We aim for a balanced programme. We also consciously choose to feature films that don't yet have their exportation visa. This year, for example, 15 out of the 38 feature films we showed didn't have exportation visas and thus were shown at Fameck as new releases. We also do our best to programme films recommended to us by our friends. Last year, for instance, you [Sally Shafto, the interviewer] encouraged us to show Mounia Meddour's excellent documentary on the blossoming of short films in Algeria.

It's important to add that our selection is also dictated by what films have French subtitles. This criterion alone immediately reduces the number of possible films. When we see films at Cannes or in other festivals, most of the time they are subtitled in English for the international market. That is one of our biggest obstacles.

SS: *Do you ever work with soft or electronic subtitles?*

We're not really set up for that. That could change, but for the time being we don't do it. With regard to the choice of films, we programme on our intuition. I'm a big believer in what we call in French 'le feeling', which definitely exists.

SS: *Are there French distributors who come especially to Fameck for the festival to see what films you are showing?*

No, we don't have a market specifically for film distributors. Maybe it's something we should think about. In any case, for the first time this year we inaugurated a Professional Day, devoted to meetings between filmmakers, producers and distributors. Maybe in the future with the Pôle Image in Lorraine we can expand our activities.

SS: *This year, Moroccan cinema, although not officially honoured, was nonetheless very present in the festival: I counted 13 Moroccan films, shorts and feature altogether out of a total of 50. Does the fact that one of your programmers, Mahjouba Galfout-Aït Bennasser, is herself Moroccan, influence your programming? Or do you believe that Moroccan cinema is simply the most dynamic in Arab filmmaking today?*

Yes, that's right: Morocco certainly appears to be the country that currently has the most active film production. We're regulars at the National Film Festival of Tangier, which allows us to discover in January or February the latest crop of Moroccan films.

SS: *Most of the Maghrebi families in the region used to work in the mines or the factories. But in recent years, most of these have closed. How does this population now make its living?*

It's important to remember that there are many, many nationalities in Fameck. I personally don't like it when I hear someone described as a 'Français issue d'immigration' [French of immigrant descent] or if someone is referred to as a 'Maghrebi'. The Maghrebi population, which grew tremendously in the 1970s, is now third- or even fourth-generation French.

In the 1960s Edgar Pisani, the Minister of Public Works, designated Fameck as a ZUP (zone à urbaniser en priorité), for the creation of housing for immigrant workers; not just Maghrebi, but workers in general. Pisani at one point was even the President of the Institut du Monde Arabe.[6] In the 1970s the population of Fameck swelled to 17,000. Of course, the increase in population was also due to the family reunification policy. Earlier, workers lived in communal boarding houses. Now we're heading into another topic, which is rather vast, of post-war immigration. But don't forget that Italian immigrants also lived in wooden barracks for many years.

These immigration narratives are all part of the back-story of our festival. In recent years, there has been a significant loss of jobs in the Lorraine, in an area that once employed literally thousands and thousands of people. Already in the 1980s, the factories and mines started closing, after the oil crisis. Now there are perhaps no more than two or three thousand jobs in all. All you have to do is look at what happened to companies like Arcelor Mittal. These days, more and more young people go to work in nearby Luxembourg or Germany. A recent phenomenon is the development of parking lots for carpooling, for people commuting to work in Luxembourg. This is an important safety valve, even if the economy in Luxembourg is also starting to go downhill. But here in the Lorraine unemployment is over 10%.

SS: *Every year, your festival highlights one Arab cinema in particular. This year, Lebanon was honoured. In fact, Fameck featured Lebanese cinema already in 2006 (Moïse 2013). What changed, if anything, between these two events?*

Thematically, the Lebanese films we screened this year, even if the war remains present in the background, emphasised identity and memory. In 2006, we didn't have any particular problem. The war began in July but we had already ordered the films and they fortunately arrived in time for the festival.

SS: *Since the founding of your festival, the Arab world has undergone many changes. The Fameck festival opened during the first Gulf War, then there was the war in Lebanon for many years, followed by 9/11 and, of course, more recently the 'Arab Spring'. Is it possible to follow the evolution of the Arab world by attending your festival?*

That's not our mission. Our festival is above all a militant festival, that is, we endeavour to promote freedom of expression, equality between men and women, secularity and democracy. In addition, we purposely choose to show films that have been censored in their own countries. And we accompany our filmmaker-friends in their individual undertakings. These are the values we defend with our festival.

SS: *Have you decided the country you want to focus on next year?*

We're thinking about Jordan or perhaps one of the Gulf countries. Up until now, we've generally focused on the Maghreb, so it's perhaps time to open the festival up to new areas. The Sultanate of Oman is also a possibility.

SS: *So now you'll be going to the Gulf festivals like Dubai or Abu Dhabi?*

Yes, that's the idea, but for the time being, we don't have the financial resources to do that.

SS: *It's worth stressing that your festival is much more than just a festival of films. What are the other activities that take place during your festival?*

That's right. Besides our film screenings, we also have exhibitions and a bookstore in the Cité Sociale that thematically accompanies each edition. The festival includes several round-tables and exchanges with filmmakers and others. With the Ligue de l'Enseignement, we also organise numerous on-going workshops throughout the year on photography, video, film analysis, etc. And perhaps last, but by no means least, there are the teas and dinners every day during the festival. The catering is a key element in providing the festival with a certain conviviality.

SS: *I read in the programme that this year you invited the well-known Kabyle[7] singer, Iddir, to give a concert. Do events like this help you to balance the budget?*

We used to regularly organise events like the concert with Iddir, but we stopped two years ago. Although they're very popular with the public, they're never money-makers for us, even when the event sells out. This year, a partnership was proposed to us by the organisers of a neighbouring venue, La Passerelle. That's how we came to co-host the concert with Iddir. In fact, he had already done a concert with us several years ago. In earlier years, we also used to organise Raï[8] concerts, and with them we maybe earned a little bit. We couldn't continue them, however, because they attracted too many people: 900 persons in a hall that should hold no more than 600 is incredibly dangerous. Before he became well-known, the comedian Fellagh would come to Fameck, too. He would stay with Mario. His performances were always packed. One year, we invited him as the President of the festival. Now that he's become such a star, we can't afford him.

SS: *Anne-Marie told me that the festival sells generally around 10,000 tickets per festival, which seems really good. But there seems to be a paradox here. According to your 2003 commemorative catalogue, in 1997, 80% of your public was of Maghrebi origin; two years later, that figure plummeted to 37%. How do you account for such a dramatic drop? I've just participated in the 24th edition of your festival where I didn't notice a large number of Maghrebis in the general public. Every year you put on this incredible programme of Arab films: how can you better target those of Maghrebi origin to draw them in for a screening?*

Where did you get those statistics? I'm not familiar with them.

SS: *They're at the back of your blue anniversary catalogue that you gave me.*

Hmm. I don't know what to say. Those figures don't seem right. Anyway, as René said, at this point in the festival's history, we are no longer interested in determining the ethnic background of our public. We're more interested in generations. Before, Maghrebi women of a certain age would never come to the festival. Then, they started coming with their daughters. And now they come in groups! We create a cultural offering of quality and we need the public in order to share our passion for the films we've programmed. We do our best to promote the festival throughout the region. The local population continues to discover Arab films via our festival. Publicity, though, is paramount and there again we're constrained by the extreme limitations of our budget.

SS: *What is the cost of a ticket to see a film? And how many screening rooms do you have at your disposal?*

A film ticket costs €5 [U.S.$6.75], but we offer a discount if more than 3 tickets are bought (the price then drops to €4 [U.S.$5.4] instead of €5 [U.S.$6.75]). And we also have a special offer, where for €15 [U.S.$20.25] you can see a film and then have dinner afterwards.

We have five theatres, all in close proximity, for the festival:

Victor Hugo Screening Room in Fameck	300 seats
Screening Room of the Fameck Cité Sociale	150 seats
Jean Morette screening room in the Fameck Cité Sociale	180 seats
Cinema Grand Ecran in Seremange	300 seats
Cinema Palace in Hayange	300 seats

And next year, we'll have two more screening rooms in nearby Thionville. This is an important addition, because Thionville is a town of 40,000 inhabitants.

SS: *This year I know that Blandine was annoyed that the Prix du Public was given to Laïla Marrakchi's* Rock the Casbah *(Morocco, 2013). First, tell me how you gather the input from the audience on the in-competition films? Then I would like to know why you are surprised that this film won instead of a more personal film that doesn't have distributor, since* Rock the Casbah *is precisely made to seduce a large audience?*

We ask the audience to vote on the way out of the films in competition. We do it by percentages. The fact that a film has had a very large audience doesn't guarantee that it will win the Prix du Public. Even a film that's been seen by only 50 spectators has a chance of winning; the public grades a film on how much they liked it on a scale of one to ten. So the film that wins is really independent of the number of people who've seen it. If fifty people have seen an unknown film, but they all loved it, it would win over a bigger film seen by a large public that triggered only a lukewarm reaction. And our other prizes are also meant to balance out the Prix du Public. There's the Prix du Jury Jeune where a group of high school students are the judges. Then there is the Prix de la Presse. In addition, we, the organisers of the festival, reserve the right to discern a Special Mention, if we believe a film really merits it.

SS: *Next year, you are going to celebrate your 25th anniversary. Do you already have some ideas in mind for this milestone?*

Next week, we plan on having a meeting to assess this year's festival and to start thinking about next year's. Of course, our programme is dependent on what we'll find on the market. In any case, we're not intending to revolutionise the festival's organisation for its 25th edition.

SS: *Do you believe that the particular history of the Lorraine has rendered its citizens perhaps more open than people in other communities in France to promote this ambitious idea of the peaceful coexistence between different nationalities?*

The migratory flows in the Lorraine have obviously played an important role in its development. The German annexation from 1871 to 1918, and then again during the Second World War has also left its mark. It's certain that our particular historical past has had an effect on our consciousness and even our subconscious. We are bordered by four countries in total.

I'd also like to note that we're extremely pleased that it's becoming more common to see a Maghrebi or Arab film in the theatres. A decade ago, such films were a rarity. And of course this year Abdellatif Kechiche won the Palme d'Or for his new film *La vie d'Adèle* [*Blue is the Warmest Colour*, France, 2013]. And way before Kechiche, there was Mohammed Lakhdar-Hamina's *Chronique des années de braise* [*Chronicle of the Years of Fire*, Algeria, 1975], which won the Palme d'Or for Algeria in 1975, followed by Youssef Chahine's wins for Egypt.[9]

SS: *To finish then, can you summarise in a few sentences the goals of your festival?*

The Festival of Fameck is the offspring of, on the one hand, the Fameck Cité Sociale and on the other, the Fédération des Oeuvres Laïques de la Moselle – Ligue de l'Enseignement: they are two different, complementary entities that have made and continue to make our festival possible. Over the years, we have grown, but our goal remains the same: to continue organising the oldest film festival of Arab film in France, together with the Institut du Monde Arabe. And to increase our reputation nationally as well as internationally.

We're proud of our verbal logo by Walibah Ibn Al Hobab: 'Better than either pearl or coral are the gestures of one man towards another.' In closing, I would like to cite the words of Claude Julien, a journalist who is a former director of Le Monde diplomatique, who paid our festival a great compliment when he wrote: 'Peace is in your hands here in Fameck. You are contributing to a world that is more just and more equitable.'

* * *

In Memoriam René Cahen

The *Festival du cinéma Arabe de Fameck* has just lost one of its principal founders, René Cahen (1926-2014).

Image 10: René Cahen and Madame Filippetti © DR

Called the 'the father of the cinephile movement in Metz and in the Moselle', Cahen was a Metz native. At age 18, he joined the French Resistance in the south of France where he was a member of the Maquis de l'Aveyron. His passion for civic and secular associations dates from this period. In 1947, he took part in the founding of the Maison des Jeunes et de la Culture de Metz and served as its president for twenty years. Later, as Vice President of the Fédération des Œuvres Laïques de la Moselle, he managed its cultural department. With his modern outlook on culture, he organised, from 1953 onwards, workshops where ski, culture and cinema were often combined. In 1989, he oversaw the establishment of the Festival du Cinéma Arabe de Fameck in his role as Vice President of the Cité Sociale de Fameck.

Space, unfortunately, does not allow us to summarise all of René's many activities, devoted to the promotion of film culture in the Moselle. In 2013, the French Minister of Culture, Aurélie Filippetti awarded him the Orders of the Chevalier des Arts et des Lettres.

– Michel Seelig and Pierre Jullien[10]

Works Cited

'Carte blanche à... Mario Giubilei' (2010) *Le Républicain Lorrain*, 19 October 2010. On-line. Available HTTP: http://www.republicain-lorrain. fr/actualite/2010/10/19/mario-giubilei (20 November 2013).

'Fameck, capitale du film arabe, Entretien avec Mahjouba Aït Benasser' (2011) *My Lorraine*. On-line. Available HTTP: http://www.mylorraine.fr/article/fameck-capitale-du-film-arabe/9273 (20 November 2013).

Giubilei, Mario (2003) 'Mémoire', in *Festivals du Film Arabe de Fameck*. Fameck: Cité sociale.

La Ligue de l'enseignement (2013) 'Rejoindre la ligue', *La Ligue*. On-line. Available HTTP: http://www.laligue.org/rejoindre-la-ligue/ (20 November 2013).

Moïse, Joan (2013) 'La Société libanaise décryptée avec finesse', *Le Républicain Lorrain*, 8 October 2013. On-line. Available HTTP: http://www.republicain-lorrain.fr/actualite/2013/10/08/la-societe-libanaise-decryptee-avec-finesse (20 November 2013).

Shafto, Sally (2011) 'An interview with Jacques Panijel on the Making of Octobre a Paris' *Framework Online*. On-line. Available HTTP: http://www.frameworkonline.com/panjeli/panijel-interview.html   (20 November 2013).

Seelig, Michel and Jullien, Pierre (2014) 'Disparition de René Cahen directeur du festival du film Arabe de Fameck', *Africultures*, 14677. On-line. Available HTTP: http://www.africultures.com/php/index. php?nav=murmure&no=14677 (20 March 2014).

Notes

1   'Mémoire', in *Festivals du Film Arabe de Fameck*, after an idea by Mario Giubilei, Fameck: Cité sociale, 2003, n.p.

2   Le Maghreb des Films, unlike the Fameck Festival or the Saint-Denis Panorama, does not award prizes.

Sally Shafto

3   There are also several festivals devoted to Mediterranean cinema. The oldest
    is Cinemed: International Mediterranean Film Festival of Montpellier (http://
    www.cinemed.tm.fr/cgi-bin/newtest.pl?name=1_1&rubrique=festival&lng=en
    &titre=29th+festival+%3E+infos), which just celebrated its 35th year. The town
    of Carros, near Nice, hosts a festival of Mediterranean film, now in its 8th year,
    whose dates coincide with those of the Fameck festival: Cinéalma: L'äme de la
    Méditerranée (http://cinealma.fr). In Brussels, there is the Festival Cinéma Mé-
    diterranéen de Bruxelles – Cinémamed (http://www.audiovisuel.cfwb.be/index.
    php?id=6487) that marks its 13th edition this year.
4   In 1866 during the Second Empire, the journalist Jean Macé founded La Ligue
    française de l'enseignement or French Teachers' League, a movement of popu-
    lar, secular education in a first step towards liberating national education from a
    religious tutelage. Today, the League comprises 30,000 associations, 1.6 million
    members and 102 departmental federations in France. According to its web-
    site, the League is 'More than a simple observer in the evolution of society, it
    encourages all individuals and collective initiatives that develop education and
    training at every stage of life, including culture and sports for everyone and
    vacations for as many as possible' (La Ligue de l'enseignement, 2013) for more
    information, please visit: http://www.laligue.org/
5   [Editor's note: Jean-Marie Straub and Danièle Huillet made films together be-
    tween 1963 and 2006.]
6   Born in Tunis in 1918, Pisani moved to Paris in the 1930s to continue his studies.
    He directed the Institut du Monde Arabe from 1988-1995.
7   Kabylia is a region in Northern Algeria, and has a famous tradition of singing in
    the old Berber language.
8   Raï is a genre of popular music in Algeria, evolved from folk music that origi-
    nated in Oran with Bedouin shepherds. It is now a genre often associated with
    political dissent
9   Chahine received the Lifetime Achievement Award at Cannes in 1997.
10 This is a fragment, translated and adapted by Sally Shafto from French, of a piece
    written by Michel Seelig and Pierre Julien for a Metz newletter and published
    in *Africultures* on-line: Seelig, Michel and Jullien, Pierre (2014) 'Disparition de
    René Cahen directeur du festival du film Arabe de Fameck', *Africultures*, 14677,
    March. On-line. Available HTTP: http://www.africultures.com/php/index.
    php?nav=murmure&no=14677 (20 March 2014).

Film Festivals in the Maghreb

Morocco

Est.	Name	Dates	Website	Location	Specialisation
1977	African Film Festival of Khouribga	June	www.festivalkhouribga.com	Khouribga	African Films
1982	Festival National du Film de Tanger	February	http://www.ccm.ma/fnf13/index.html	Tangiers	Moroccan Films
1985	Tetouan International Festival for Mediterranean Cinema	March	http://www.festivaltetouan.org/page.php?187	Tetouan	Mediterranean Films
1996	Festival of Sidi Kacem for Moroccan cinema	May	www.festivalsidikacem.au.ma	Moroccan Films	
1998	Azrou Summer Moroccan Short Film Encounter	August	www.cineazrou.org	Azrou	Short Film

Est.	Name	Dates	Website	Location	Specialisation
1999	International Festival of Short Film and Documentary Moroccan and Latin American Martil	June	www.martilfilmfestival.ma	Martil	Shorts and Documentaries
2001	Festival International du Film de Marrakech	November	http://en.festivalmarrakech.info/	Marrakech	International Competition
2000 – 2010	National Festival of Amazigh Film Short Film Encounter	December	www.amrec.ma	Agadir	Berber Films
2002	Mediterranean short film festival Tangiers	October	http://www.ccm.ma/11fcmmt/	Tangiers	Short Films
2003 – 2008	Safi Francophone Film Festival	–	http://www.ccm.ma/en/festsafi.asp		Francophone Films
2004	International Film Festival of Women in Salé	September	www.fiffs.ma	Women's Films	
2004	Agadir Cinema Festival of Migration	February	www.festivalagadir.com	Agadir	Cinema of Migration

2004	Meknès International Festival for Animation Films	March	www.ficam-maroc.com	Meknès	Animation
2004	International Meeting Of The Trans-Saharian Film	November	http://www.zagorafilm.com/	Zagora	International
2008	International Student Film Festival (ISFF)	June	https://www.facebook.com/pages/Casablanca-International-Student-Film-Festival-2011/121057787971167	Casablanca	Student Films
2008	International Documentary Festival Agadir	April	http://www.fidadoc.org/en/	Agadir	Documentary
-	Errachida Student Film Festival		No website	Errachida Oasis	Student Films
2009	Festival International du Film Documentaire	November	http://afifdok.org/?page_id=129	Khourigba	Documentary

Est.	Name	Dates	Website	Location	Specialisation
2010	Festival du Film de Fes	June or November	http://asso-soleil-fes.blogspot.co.uk/2012/05/le-festival-de-cinema-le-12-et-le-3.html	Fes	International
2012	Festival Maghrebin du Film Documentaire	May	http://www.fmfdo.cerhso.com/default_fr.html	Oujda	Documentary
-	Festival Oujda du Court Metrage Maghrebin	June	https://www.facebook.com/FOCMoujda	Oujda	Short Films
2012	International Festival of Cinema South Ifni	September	www.azartassociation.org	International	

Algeria

Est.	Name	Dates	Website	Location	Specialisation
1976	International Arab Film Festival	July	-	Oran	Arab
1998 (not in 2001)	International Film Festival of Timimoun / Festival International du Film de Timimoun	December / January	http://www.festivaldetimimoun.fr.fm/	Timimoun	International
2001	Annual National Cultural Festival of Amazigh Film / Festival Culturel National Annuel du Film Amazigh (FCNAFA)	January / March	http://film-amazigh.net/fr/index.php	Tizi-Ouzou	Berber Films
2003	The Bejaïa Film Workshops / Rencontres Cinématographiques de Bejaïa	June	https://www.facebook.com/events/586871971323909/?ref=3	Bejaïa	International
2003	Sahara International Film Festival	October	http://www.festivalsahara.com/index.php/en	Tindouf	International

Est.	Name	Dates	Website	Location	Specialisation
2004	The Nights of Saouira Festival in Béni Abbès / Festival Les Nuits de la Saouira à Béni Abbès	December / January	-	Saouira	International
2006	Ciné d'Aubervilliers a Bab-El-Oued	-	-	Bab-El-Oued	International
2007	Festival International du Film Arab à Oran/Annual Oran Arab Film Festival(FIFAO)	September	http://www.fofa-dz.org/www.cinearabfestival.org (broken link)	Oran	Arab Films
2007 – 2011	Documentary Film Festival in Bejaïa / Rencontres du Film Documentaire a Bejaïa	-	http://www.bejaiadoc.com/	Bejaïa	Documentary
2008	Festival of Amazigh Film in Sétif / Festival du Film Amazigh à Sétif	-	www.film-amazigh.org	Sétif	Berber Films
-	Festival of Amazigh Film in Tlemcèn / Festival du Film Amazigh a Tlemcèn	-	www.filmazigh.org	Tlemcèn	Berber Films

Tunisia

Est.	Name	Dates	Website	Location	Specialisation
1964	International Amateur Film festival in Kélibia / Festival International du Film Amateur de Kélibia (FIFAK)	July	http://www.ftca.org.tn/	Kélibia	Amateur Films
1966	Days of Cinema in Carthage / Journées Cinématographiques de Carthage	October (every two years)	http://www.jccarthage.com/index.php	Tunis	International
1975	Karraka Film Festival in La Goulette / Festival Karraka De La Goulette	July / August	https://www.facebook.com/pages/Festival-m%C3%A9diterran%C3%A9en-de-la-Goulette/23283276065408	La Goulette	
1991	International Film festival for Children and Young People in Sousse / Festival International du film pour L'Enfance et la Jeunesse de Sousse	March	http://www.fifej.com/index.php/en/	Sousse	Children and Young People's Films

Est.	Name	Dates	Website	Location	Specialisation
1994	Festival of European Film / Journées du Cinéma européen	May – June	https://www.facebook.com/events/1240387844467531	Tunis	European Films
2001	Cinema de la Paix / Cinema of Peace	March	www.laftcc.org	Tunis	Peace Films
2003	International Environment Film Festival in Kairouan / Festival International de Film d'environnement à Kairouan	February	http://www.latosensu.tv/festival-internationnal-du-film-denvironnement-de-kairouan-artisans-du-changement/	Kairouan	Environment Films
2006	International Documentary Film Festival in Tunis / Festival international du film documentaire de Tunis	April	http://docatunis.nesselfen.org/	Tunis	Documentary
2006	Film Nights of Nabeul in Hammamet / Les nuits cinématographiques Nabeul - Hammamet	August	-	Hammamet	International

2007	International Film Festival in Tunis / Le Festival International du Film de Tunis	September	https://www.facebook.com/fift2010	Tunis	International
2007	Digital Animation Festival/Festival des Arts Numériques	June	http://festival-arts-numeriques.com/	Nabeul	Animation
2009	Schools' Festival of the Image and Cinema in Tataouine / Festival National de l'image et du cinéma en milieu scolaire à Tataouine	December	-	Tataouine	School Films
2010	Contemporary Italian Cinema Days/Journées du cinéma italien contemporain	March	http://www.cinematunisien.com/index.php?option=com_content&task=view&id=2067&Itemid=64		Italian Cinema
2010	International Film festival of the Arab Film in Nabeul / Festival International De Cinéma Arabe À Nabeul	September / October	http://www.nabeulien.com/actualites/culture/1eres-rencontres-internationales-du-cinema-arabe-de-nabeul.html	Nabeul	Arab Films

Est.	Name	Dates	Website	Location	Specialisation
2010	Mediterranean Film festivals of the short comedy film in La Marsa / Le Festival Méditerranéen du Court Métrage d'humour in La Marsa	September	https://www.facebook.com/pages/Festival-M%C3%A9diterran%C3%A9en-du-court-m%C3%A9trage-dhumour/27626749 3826	La Marsa	Short Comedy
2011	Cinema Days for Children in Monastir / Les Journées du cinéma pour enfants à Monastir	December	-	Monastir	Children's Films
2012	Tunisian Mobile Film Festival	April	http://www.tmff.tn/	La Marsa	Mobile Phone Films
2013	Festival international du film des droits de l'Homme Tunis	September	www.human-screen.com	Tunis	Human Rights Films
-	Young People's Film Week in Bizerte / Semaine du film de jeunesse à Bizerte	October	-Bizerte	Young People's Films	
-	French Film Festival in Tunis / Le festival du film français de Tunis	December	-	Tunis	French Films

-	Festival of the Historical and Mythological Film in Djerba / Festival du film historique et mythologique à Djerba	August (every two years)	http://mediterraneen.crdp-aix-marseille.fr/mediter12/arret-surimage/asi_djerba.htm	Djerba	Historical Films
-	Elyes Zrelli Festival / Festival Elyes Zrelli	August	-	-	International
-	Cinema Days in Sfax / Journées cinéma-tographiques à Sfax	May	-	Sfax	International

Libya

Est.	Name	Date	Website	Location	Specialisation
2012	Tripoli Human Rights Film Festival	December	https://www.facebook.com/tripolihrff	Tripoli	Human Rights Films
2012	International Mediterranean Film Festival for Documentaries and Short Films	June	-	Tripoli	Documentaries and Short Films
2013	Benghazi Mobile Phone Film Festival	October	-	Benghazi	Mobile Phone Films

Compiled by Stefanie Van de Peer
Table is representative, not exhaustive

Thematic Bibliography:
Film Festivals and the Middle East

Amber Shields

Abbass, Hiam (2013) 'Hiam Abbass, Actress/Director (Abu Dhabi Film Festival)', interviewed by Geoffrey Macnab. *Screen International,* 25 October.

Abdulla, Danah (2009) 'Toronto's Different Spotlight (Toronto Palestine Film Festival)', *Washington Report on Middle East Affairs*, 28, 9, 48.

Abt, Sinai (2012) 'Can Documentaries Change the World? Interview with Israel's Docaviv Director, Sinai Abt', *Urban Times*, (9 May). On-line. Available HTTP: http://urbantimes.co/2012/05/can-documentaries-change-the-world-interview-with-sinai-abt/ (22 October 2013).

'Abu Dhabi Festival Launches $500,000 Production Fund' (2010), *Screen International*, 21 April.

'Abu Dhabi Film Festival Becomes Part of Twofour54' (2012), *Screen International*, 22 March.

'ADFF Opens with *Monsieur Lazhar*, Hosts Eight World Premieres' (2011), *Screen International*, 22 September.

Al Ali, Masoud Amralla (2008) 'Interview: Festival Director Masoud Amralla Al Ali (Dubai)', *Screen International*, 5 December.

'Ali Al Jabri, Abu Dhabi Film Festival' (2012), *Screen International*, 11 October.

'Ankara 2004' (2004), *FIPRESCI-Festival Reports*. On-line. Available HTTP: http://www.fipresci.org/festivals/archive/2004/ankara/ankara_ndx.htm (23 October 2013).

'Ankara 2005' (2005), *FIPRESCI-Festival Reports*. On-line. Available HTTP: http://www.fipresci.org/festivals/archive/2005/ankara/ankara_ndx.htm (23 October 2013).

'Ankara 2006' (2006), *FIPRESCI-Festival Reports*. On-line. Available HTTP: http://www.fipresci.org/festivals/archive/2006/ankara/ankara_ndx.htm (23 October 2013).

'Ankara 2007' (2007), *FIPRESCI-Festival Reports*. On-line. Available HTTP: http://www.fipresci.org/festivals/archive/2007/ankara/ankara_ndx.htm (23 October 2013).

'Arab Spring Makes Way for New Look Cairo Film Festival' (2012), *Screen International*, 25 May.

Armes, Roy (1997) 'The Third Biennale of Arab Cinemas, Paris, 21-29 June 1996', *Screen*, 38, 1, 84-87.

Asfour, Nana (1999) 'The International Beirut Film Festival', *Cinéaste*, 24, 2/3, 69 & 77.

D'Azevedo, Amandine (2013) 'Marrakech, un hommage', *Cahiers du Cinéma*, 686, 83-90.

Aziz, Anwar Syed and M. Sadiq Sohail (2004) 'Festival Tourism in the United Arab Emirates: First-time Versus Repeat Visitor Perceptions', *Journal of Vacation Marketing*, 10, 2, 161-170.

Bachmann, Gideon (1973) 'In Search of Self-Definition: Arab and African Film at the Carthage Film Festival', *Film Quarterly* 26, 3, 48–51.

Ballylinch, Anne (2004) 'Un espoir à Ramallah', *Cahiers du Cinéma*, 593, 51.

Barde, Bruno (2010) 'Bruno Barde (Marrakech)', interviewed by Sarah Cooper. *Screen International*, 9 December.

Báron, György (2011) 'Abu Dhabi Film Festival', *FIPRESCI-Festival Reports*. On-line. Available HTTP: http://www.fipresci.org/festivals/ archive/2011/abu_dhabi/abu_dhabi_11_ndx.htm (23 October 2013).

Begley, Alex (2011) 'Smithsonian Rings in 15th Year of Iranian Film Festival', *Washington Report on Middle East Affairs*, 30, 5, 57-58.

Bell, James (2007) 'Meeting at the Bridge (Istanbul)', *Sight and Sound*, 17, 6, 8.

Biénzobas, Pamela (2012) '31st Istanbul International Film Festival, 2012', *FIPRESCI-Festival Reports*. On-line. Available HTTP: http://www. fipresci.org/festivals/archive/2012/istanbul/istanbul_12_ndx.htm (23 October 2013).

Blaney, Martin (2007a) 'Big-spending Dubai and Rome Festivals Under Fire from Berlinale', *Screen International*, 10 January.

___(2007b) 'Talent Campus Abroad Could be Extended to Sarajevo and Marrakech', *Screen International*, 21 March.

Borg, Wayne (2013) 'Wayne Borg, Twofour54'. Interviewed by Wendy Mitchell. *Screen International*, 22 October.

Brown, Colin (2012) 'The Power of Three: The Gulf Festivals are Playing a Central Role in the Arab Film-making Renaissance', *ScreenDaily*, 11 October.

Caillé, Patricia (2012) 'A Gender Perspective on the 23rd Edition of the JCC', *Journal of African Cinemas*, 4, 2, 229-233.

'Cairo 2005' (2005), *FIPRESCI-Festival Reports*. On-line. Available HTTP: http://www.fipresci.org/festivals/archive/2005/cairo/cairo_ndx. htm (23 October 2013).

'Cairo 2006' (2006), *FIPRESCI-Festival Reports*. On-line. Available HTTP: http://www.fipresci.org/festivals/archive/2006/cairo/cairo_06_ ndx.htm (23 October 2013).

'Cairo International Film Festival 2012' (2012), *FIPRESCI-Festival Reports*. On-line. Available HTTP: http://www.fipresci.org/festivals/archive/2012/cairo/cairo_12_ndx.htm (23 October 2013).

'24th Carthage Film Festival, 2012' (2012), *FIPRESCI-Festival Reports*. On-line. Available HTTP: http://www.fipresci.org/festivals/archive/2012/carthage/carthage_12_ndx.htm (23 October 2013).

Carver, Antonia (2006a) 'Cairo Festival Resurrects Market as Egyptian Production Grows', *Screen International*, 12 September.

__ (2006b) 'Post-war Beirut Festival Welcomes 40 International Guests', *Screen International*, 28 September.

__ (2007a) *The Third Day* Scoops Fajr International Film Festival, '*Screen International*, 14 February.

__(2007b) "Dubai Announces Dates, Beefed-up Roles for Amralla and Field', *Screen International,* 28 February.

__ (2007c) 'Abu Dhabi Announces Inaugural Film Festival and New Film Fund', *Screen International*, 18 May.

__ (2007d) 'Charity amfAR Comes on Board for Dubai Film Festival', *Screen International*, 22 May.

__ (2007e) 'Arab Film Festivals Launch Guild to Share Expertise', *Screen International*, 3 July.

__ (2007f) 'Jon Fitzgerald to Head New Abu Dhabi Film Festival', *Screen International*, 16 July.

__ (2007g) 'Amralla Named Artistic Director at Dubai Festival', *Screen International*, 13 August.

__(2007h) 'Film Financing Circle Announced for Abu Dhabi Festival', *Screen International*, 11 September.

__ (2007i) 'Beirut Film Festival Cancelled', *Screen International*, 13 September.

__ (2007j) 'Middle East Festival adds iPod Competition, More Industry Delegates', *Screen International*, 21 September.

__ (2007k) 'Abu Dhabi Unveils Competition Line-up', *Screen International*, 28 September.

__ (2007l) 'Haggis' *Elah* to Close Inaugural Abu Dhabi Festival', *Screen International*, 4 October.

__ (2007m) 'Abu Dhabi Festival to Include Talks with Weinstein and Haggis', *Screen International*, 9 October.

__ (2007n) 'Al Shaibani and Al Muhairi Take Emirates Awards in Abu Dhabi', *Screen International*, 18 October.

__ (2007o) 'Ben X Takes Grand Jury Prize at First Abu Dhabi Festival', *Screen International*, 21 October.

Cassidy, Kevin (2008) 'Money and Movie Stars in the Middle East', *MovieMaker*, 15, 74, 30.

Cengiz, N. Buket (2004) '23rd International Istanbul Film Festival', *Middle East*, 346, 56-59.

__(2005) 'Istanbul Film 2005', *Middle East*, 357, 60-61.

__(2006) '25th Istanbul Film Festival', *Middle East*, 368, 60-61.

__(2008) 'The 27th International Istanbul Film Festival 5-20 April 2008', *Film International*, 6,4, 86-90.

__(2009) 'East, West and More in the 28th International Istanbul Film Festival', *Senses of Cinema*, Festival Reports, 51. On-line. Available HTTP: http://sensesofcinema.com/2009/festival-reports/istanbul-iff-2009/ (19 September 2013).

Chudy, Jolanta (2007) 'Films, Names, Networking Give Life To Startup MEIFF', *Hollywood Reporter—International Edition*, 400, 8-10.

__(2008) 'Cultures Connect at Middle East Fest', *Hollywood Reporter—International Edition*, 406, 46, 40-41.

Ciecko, Anne (2006) 'Bridges Between: Reflections on Dubai and its International Film Festival', *Asian Cinema*, 17, 2, 17-25.

__ (2007) 'Cinema "Oriental": Asian and Arab Films at the Cairo International Film Festival', *Asian Cinema*, 18, 2, 288-293.

Cooper, Sarah (2013) '*Life of Crime* Opens Abu Dhabi', *Screen International*, 1 October.

Dams, Tim (2004a) 'Ramallah Festival Revs up with Motorcycle', *Screen International*, 8 July.

__ (2004b) 'Dubai Festival Unveils Programme Line-up', *Screen International*, 29 November.

__ (2005) 'Arab Festivals Co-ordinate to Avoid Date Clashes', *Screen International*, 10 May.

Diawara, Manthia (1993) 'Whose African Cinema is it Anyway? (Carthage)', *Sight and Sound*, 3, 2, 24-25.

Dickinson, Kay (2005) 'Report on the First Ramallah International Film Festival', *Screen*, 46, 2, 265-273.

'DIFF Showcases Arab Cinema at London Shubbak Festival' (2011), *Screen International*, 5 July.

Ditmars, Hadani (1997a) 'Talking Too Much with Men (Fajr)', *Sight and Sound*, 7, 4, 10-12.

__(1997b) 'Fajr Festival '97', *Middle East*, 267, 40-42.

Dönmez-Colin, Gönül (2009a) '14th Festival on Wheels-Kars Nov. 7-13 2008', *Asian Cinema*, 20, 1, 228-229.

__(2009b) '45th Antalya Golden Orange and 4th International Eurasia Film Festivals (Oct. 10-20, 2008)', *Asian Cinema*, 20, 1, 230-232.

__ (2012) 'Film Festivals in Turkey: Promoting National Cinema While Nourishing Film Culture', in Jeffrey Ruoff (ed.) *Coming Soon to a Festival Near You: Programming Film Festivals*. St. Andrews: St Andrews Film Books, 101–116.

Dore, Shalini (2011) 'UCLA Fest Spotlights Iranian Pix', *Variety*, (6 August). On-line. Available HTTP: http://variety.com/2011/film/news/ucla-fest-spotlights-iranian-pix-1118040940/ (22 October 2013).

'Dubai Reveals Dates for 2013 Fest' (2013), *Screen International*, 21 January.

Earle, Harriet (2003) '70 Iranian Features Submitted for Fajr International Film Festival', *Screen International*, 15 January.

Eder, Klaus (2003) 'I Am-You Are: The 20th Jerusalem Film Festival', *FIPRESCI-Festival Reports*. On-line. Available HTTP: http://www.fipresci.org/festivals/archive/2003/jerusalem_2003/jerusalem_2003_keder.htm (23 October 2013).

__ (2006) 'Istanbul 2006', *FIPRESCI-Festival Reports*. On-line. Available HTTP: http://www.fipresci.org/festivals/archive/2006/istanbul/istanbul_ndx.htm (23 October 2013).

__ (2007) 'Istanbul 2007', *FIPRESCI-Festival Reports*. On-line. Available HTTP: http://www.fipresci.org/festivals/archive/2007/istanbul/istanbul_ndx.htm (23 October 2013).

__ (2009) 'Istanbul 2009', *FIPRESCI-Festival Reports*. On-line. Available HTTP: http://www.fipresci.org/festivals/archive/2009/istanbul/istanbul_2009_ndx.htm (23 October 2013).

__ (2011) 'Istanbul 2011', *FIPRESCI-Festival Reports*. On-line. Available HTTP: http://www.fipresci.org/festivals/archive/2011/istanbul/intro.htm (23 October 2013).

Elley, Derek (2007) 'Istanbul Festival Hands Out Awards', *Variety*, (20 April). On-line. Available HTTP: http://variety.com/2007/scene/markets-festivals/istanbul-festival-hands-out-awards-1117963536/ (22 October 2013).

Fainaru, Dan (2004) '*Thirst, Or* Share Top Jerusalem Prize', *Screen International*, 18 July.

Fainaru, Edna (2002) 'Winning Films Narrowly Avoid Ban at Istanbul Film Festival', *Screen International*, 30 April.

__ (2005) 'Israel Experiences Festival Outbreak', *Screen International*, 7 April.

__ (2013) 'Alesia Weston to Quit Jerusalem Fest', *Screen International*, 3 May.

Farahmand, Azadeh (2002) 'Perspectives on Recent (International Acclaim for) Iranian Cinema', in Richard Tapper (ed.) *The New Iranian Cinema: Politics, Representation and Identity.* London: I.B. Tauris, 86-108.

___(2006) 'At the Crossroads: International Film Festivals and the Constitution of the New Iranian Cinema', PhD thesis, University of California, Los Angeles. Ann Arbor: University of Michigan Dissertations Publishing.

___ (2010) 'Disentangling the International Festival Circuit: Genre and Iranian Cinema', in Rosalind Galt and Karl Schoonover (eds) *Global Art Cinema: New Theories and Histories.* New York: Oxford University Press, 263–283.

Farouky, Saeed Taji (2006) 'Don't Mention the War (Beirut)', *Sight and Sound*, 16, 12, 8.

Feeney, Lauren (2007) 'Arabic Translation (Al Jazeera International Documentary Film Festival, Qatar)', *Release Print*, 30, 4, 32-33.

'Festival on Wheels Rolls Out' (2011), *Variety*, (26 August). On-line. Available HTTP: http://variety.com/2011/film/news/festival-on-wheels-rolls-out-1118041586/ (22 October 2013).

'Film Festival Index for the Middle East' (2008), *Film Festival World*. On-line. Available HTTP: http://www.filmfestivalworld.com/middle_east#start (16 November 2013).

Frater, Patrick (2004) 'Dubai Plans Festival Splash with Royal Backing', *Screen International*, 17 May.

Frodon, Jean-Michel (2008) 'Prouver le cinéma arabe en le montrant (Dubai)', *Cahiers du Cinéma*, 630, 52-53.

Forde, Leon (2003) 'Fuse Lights up Marrakech Jury', *Screen International*, 9 October.

Genç, Kaya (2013) 'Let the Battle Commence (Istanbul)', *Sight and Sound*, 23, 6, 25.

Goodridge, Mike (2012) '12 Israeli Premieres Compete at Docaviv in May', *Screen International*, 20 April. On-line. Available HTTP: http://www.screendaily.com/festivals/-12-israeli-premieres-compete-at-docaviv-in-may/5040697.article (22 October 2013).

Gorvett, Jon (2000) 'Celluloid Civilisations (Istanbul)', *Middle East*, 302, 48.

Gündoğdu, Mustafa (2010) 'Film Festivals in the Diaspora: Impetus to the Development of Kurdish Cinema?', in Dina Iordanova and Ruby Cheung (eds) *FFY 2: Film Festivals and Imagined Communities.* St. Andrews: St. Andrews Film Studies. 188–197.

Hadouchi, Olivier (2011) ' "African Culture Will be Revolutionary of Will Not be": William Klein's Film of the First Pan-African Festival of Algiers (1969)', *Third Text*, 25, 1, 117-128.

'Haifa 2004' (2004), *FIPRESCI-Festival Reports*. On-line. Available HTTP: http://www.fipresci.org/festivals/archive/2004/haifa/haifa_ndx. htm (23 October 2013).

'Haifa 2005' (2005), *FIPRESCI-Festival Reports*. On-line. Available HTTP: http://www.fipresci.org/festivals/archive/2005/haifa/haifa2005_ ndx.htm (23 October 2013).

'Haifa 2006' (2006), *FIPRESCI-Festival Reports*. On-line. Available HTTP: http://www.fipresci.org/festivals/archive/2006/haifa/haifa_06_ ndx.htm (23 October 2013).

Hamedani, Nina (2008) 'Smithsonian Shows Iranian Films', *Washington Report on Middle East Affairs,* 27, 3, 59.

__(2009)'Annual Festival of Iranian Films (Washington, D.C.)', *Washington Report on Middle East Affairs*, 28, 3, 54.

Harris, Brandon, (2012) 'Abu Dhabi Film Festival', *Filmmaker: The Magazine of Independent Film*, 20, 2, 109.

Hatron, France (2008) 'Ankara 2008', *FIPRESCI-Festival Reports*. On-line. Available HTTP: http://www.fipresci.org/festivals/archive/2008/ ankara/ankara_ndx.htm (23 October 2013).

Hay, Rod (2006) 'A Matter of Translation', *Metro*, 149, 76-83.

Hazelton, John (2007) 'Other Israel Film Festival Set for Nov. Dates in New York', *Screen International*, 27 June.

Hercules, Olia (2009) 'Dubai International Film Festival Announces 2009 Dates', *Screen International*, 9 March.

'Horrors of the Gulf' (2010), *Screen International*, 23 April.

Howard, Cerise (2009) 'Flying Dreams of a Fledgling Festival: The 3rd Middle East International Film Festival', *Senses of Cinema*, Festival Reports, 53. On-line. Available HTTP: http://sensesofcinema. com/2009/festival-reports/flying-dreams-of-a-fledgling-festival- the-3rd-middle-east-international-film-festival/ (19 September 2013).

'Iran-Fajr Film Festival at 25' (2007), *Screen International*, 26 January.

'Istanbul 2003' (2003), *FIPRESCI-Festival Reports*. On-line. Available HTTP: http://www.fipresci.org/festivals/archive/2003/istanbul_2003/ istanbul_2003_ndx.htm (23 October 2013).

'Istanbul Film Festival 2003' (2003), *Middle East*, 335, 60-64.

'Istanbul 2004' (2004), *FIPRESCI-Festival Reports*. On-line. Available HTTP: http://www.fipresci.org/festivals/archive/2004/istanbul/istanbul_ ndx.htm (23 October 2013).

'Istanbul 2005' (2005), *FIPRESCI-Festival Reports*. On-line. Available HTTP: http://www.fipresci.org/festivals/archive/2005/istanbul/istanbul_ ndx.htm (23 October 2013).

'Istanbul 2013' (2013), *FIPRESCI-Festival Reports*. On-line. Available HTTP: http://www.fipresci.org/festivals/archive/2013/istanbul/istanbul_2013_ndx.htm (23 October 2013).

Jaafar, Ali (2004) 'The Lights Go Down (Carthage)', *Sight and Sound*, 14, 12, 5.

___(2006) 'Arabian Nights Meets Las Vegas (Dubai)', *Sight and Sound*, 16, 2, 10.

___(2009) 'Film Festivals Bloom in Middle East: Events Have Sprung Up over the Last Decade', *Variety* (2 September). On-line. Available HTTP: http://www.variety.com/article/VR1118008038.html (21 October 2013).

Jabri, Ali Al (2013) 'Ali Al Jabri, Director, Abu Dhabi Film Festival', interviewed by Geoffrey Macnab. *Screen International*, 23 October.

Jacir, Annemarie (2006) ' "For Cultural Purposes Only": Curating a Palestinian Film Festival' in Hamid Dabashi (ed) *Dreams of a Nation: On Palestinian Cinema*. London: Verso, 23-31.

James, Nick (2008) 'Starless and Mao Red (Istanbul)', *Sight and Sound*, 18, 7, 8.

___ (2009) 'Living for the City (Istanbul)', *Sight and Sound*, 19, 6, 13.

___(2010) 'Gulf of Credibility (Doha)', *Sight and Sound*, 20, 1, 8.

Jayyusi, L. (1978) 'The Middle East Film Festival', *MERIP Reports*, 69, 21-23.

Jensen, Jacob Wendt (2008) 'Haifa 2008', *FIPRESCI-Festival Reports*. On-line. Available HTTP: http://www.fipresci.org/festivals/archive/2008/haifa/haifa_ndx.htm (23 October 2013).

Joniken, Heikke (2011) 'Dubai International Film Festival 2011', *FIPRESCI-Festival Reports*. On-line. Available HTTP: http://www.fipresci.org/festivals/archive/2011/dubai/dubai_11_ndx.htm (23 October 2013).

Kamin, Debra (2011) 'Abu Dhabi Blends Talents', *Variety*, (8 October). On-line. Available HTTP http://variety.com/2011/biz/news/abu-dhabi-blends-talents-1118043804/ (21 October 2013).

___(2012a) 'Doha Org Commits to Region', *Variety*, (10 November)/ On-line. Available HTTP http://variety.com/2012/film/news/doha-org-commits-to-region-1118061752/ (21 October 2013).

___(2012b) '"Fundamentalist" Opens Doha Fest', *Variety*, (17 November). On-line. Available HTTP: http://variety.com/2012/film/news/fundamentalist-opens-doha-fest-1118062351/ (21 October 2013).

___(2012c) 'Arab Femme Helmers Find Oasis in Doha', *Variety*, (24 November). On-line. Available HTTP: http://variety.com/2012/film/news/arab-femme-helmers-find-oasis-in-doha-1118062528/ (21 October 2013).

Kenny, Eleanor (2008) 'Tribeca Film Festival Doha to be Launched November 2009', *Screen International*, 24 November.

Keser, Robert (2011) 'Dispatch from the Desert: The Fifth Abu Dhabi Film Festival', *Bright Lights Film Journal*, 74, 13.

Kiarostami, Abbas (2010) 'Judgment Kiarostami-Style', interviewed by Ali Nour-Mousavi. *Film International*, 15, 3/4, 104-107.

Kocer, Suncem (2013) 'Making transnational publics: Circuits of Censorship and Technologies of Publicity in Kurdish Media Circulation', *American Ethnologist*, 40, 4, 721–733.

De Lacharrière, Barbara Lorey (2012) 'Abu Dhabi Film Festival, 2012', *FIPRESCI-Festival Reports*. On-line. Available HTTP: http://www.fipresci.org/festivals/archive/2012/abu_dhabi/abudhabi_12_ndx.htm (23 October 2013).

Langer, Adam (1998) 'African and Middle Eastern Film Festivals: Big Continent, Small Festivals', in Adam Langer *The Film Festival Guide: For Filmmakers, Film Buffs, and Industry Professionals*. Chicago: Chicago Review Press, 239-246.

Langford, Michelle (2007) 'Iranian Cinema Looks Inward: The 25th Fajr International Film Festival', *Senses of Cinema*, Festival Reports, 44. On-line. Available HTTP: http://sensesofcinema.com/2007/festival-reports/fajr-iff-2007/ (19 September 2013).

Lawrenson, Edward (2009) 'Sands of Time (Marrakech)', *Sight and Sound*, 19, 3, 8-9.

Legein, Saskia (2007) 'Haifa 2007', *FIPRESCI-Festival Reports*. On-line. Available HTTP: http://www.fipresci.org/festivals/archive/2007/haifa/haifa_ndx.htm (23 October 2013).

Lodderhose, Diana (2011) 'Fresh Fests Step up in Middle East', *Variety*, 425, 5, 18-19.

__(2012) 'Abu Dhabi Film Festival Joins Twofour54', *Variety*, (22 March). On-line. Available HTTP: http://variety.com/2012/film/news/abu-dhabi-film-festival-joins-twofour54-1118051773/ (21 October 2013).

Lounas, Thierry (1997) 'Carthage s'enflamme pour l'enjue scénario', *Cahiers du Cinéma*, 510, 13.

Lucia, Cynthia (2002) 'The Istanbul International Film Festival', *Cinéaste*, 27, 3, 49-51.

Lumholdt, Jan (2007) 'Marrakech International Film Festival 19 December 2006', *Film International*, 5, 2, 88-89.

Macaulay, Scott (2009) 'Dubai International Film Festival', *Filmmaker: The Magazine of Independent Film*, 17, 3, 94-95.

MacMillan, Scott (2005) 'First Feature Film to Come Out of Yemen Shows at Cairo', *Screen International*, 7 December.

Macnab, Geoffrey (2006) 'Beirut Film Festival Makes Plans for October Event', *Screen International*, 6 September.

Malamud, Randy (2011) 'In Dubai, a Cinematic Door to the Mideast', *Chronicle of Higher Education*, 57, 26, 12-15.

Malandrin, Stéphane (1995) 'Souviens-toi de Carthage!', *Cahiers du Cinéma*, 487, 75-81.

Malausa, Vincent (ed) (2011) 'Jeunesses des cinémas arabes', Special Dossier in Honour of the 5th Abu Dhabi Film Festival, *Cahiers du Cinéma*, October, 671, 1-15.

Masters, Charles (2007) 'Dubai Festival Sparks Local Film Projects', *Hollywood Reporter-- International Edition*, 402, 36, 6.

McCarthy, Andrew (2011) 'The New Movie Mecca; Is The Doha Tribeca Film Festival Qatar's Latest Play For A Place On The Culture Map?', *Atlantic Monthly*, 307, 2, 27-28.

Menashe, Louis (2006) 'The Istanbul International Film Festival', *Cinéaste*, 31, 4, 100.

'Middle East Film Festivals' (2012) *Inside Film Magazine Festival Directory*. On-line. Available HTTP: http://www.insidefilm.com/middleeast.html (16 November 2013).

Mitchell, Wendy (2006a) 'Field and Al Ali Named Artistic Directors for Dubai Festival', *Screen International*, 23 May.

__(2006b) 'Dubai to Open Third Festival with *Bobby*', *Screen International*, 20 November.

__(2007) 'Dubai to Start New Gulf Film Festival in April', *Screen International*, 12 November.

__(2008) 'Abu Dhabi Festival to Open with *The Brothers Bloom*', *Screen International*, 17 September.

__ (2012) 'Ali Al Jabri Becomes Festival Director in Abu Dhabi as Peter Scarlet Departs', *Screen International*, 7 August.

__ (2013a) 'Doha, Tribeca End Partnership', *Screen International*, 30 April.

__(2013b) 'Doha Confirms First Youth Festival Dates', *Screen International*, 8 July.

__(2013c) 'New Advisors Join Doha's Qumra Festival', *Screen International*, 8 September.

__(2013d) 'Abu Dhabi Film Festival Kicks Off With Forest Whitaker Honours', *Screen International*, 25 October.

__(2013e) 'Amritraj Predicts Arab Film Boom in Next 10 Years', *Screen International*, 26 October.

__(2013f) 'Middle East Needs to Grow Infrastructure', *Screen International*, 26 October.

Monceau, Nicolas (1999) 'Situation du cinéma turc (Istanbul)', *Cahiers du Cinéma*, 538, 16.

Mullenneaux, Lisa (2012) 'New York Film Festival Spotlights Israel's Minorities (Other Israel Film Festival)', *Washington Report on Middle East Affairs*, 31, 1, 47-48.

Murdoch, Blake (2004) 'Dubai Festival Fetes The World', *Hollywood-Reporter—International Edition*, 385, 27,8.

Neidhardt, Irit (2011) 'From the Field: Co-Producing the Memory. Cinema Production Between Europe and the Middle East', *Global Media Journal*, 1, 1. On-line. Available HTTP: http://www. globalmediajournal.de/volume-1-no-1/ (23 October 2013).

Nichols, Bill (1994) 'Discovering Form, Inferring Meaning: New Cinemas and the Film Festival Circuit', *Film Quarterly*, vol. 47,3. 16-27.

Nochimson, Martha P (2008) 'The Istanbul Film Festival', *Cinéaste*, 33, 4, 81-82.

Nour-Mousavi, Ali (2009) 'Backed By Petrodollars (Middle East International Film Festival)', *Film International*, 14, 4, 138-141.

__(2010) 'From New York to Abu Dhabi', *Film International*, 15, 3/4, 126-129.

__ (2011) 'Farewell Middle East, Hello Abu Dhabi!', *Film International*, 16, 3/4, 126-133.

Ostria, Vincent (1997) 'Dernières tendances du cinéma turc (Istanbul)', *Cahiers du Cinéma*, 513, 9.

Padgaonkar, Latika (2011) 'Ankara Flying Broom International Women's Film Festival 2011', *FIPRESCI-Festival Reports*. On-line. Available HTTP: http://www.fipresci.org/festivals/archive/2011/ankara/intro.htm (23 October 2013).

Palmer, Amanda (2010) 'Amanda Palmer (Doha)', interviewed by Liz Shackleton. *Screen International*, 11 November.

Panijel, Jacques (n.d) 'An Interview With Jacques Panijel On The Making Of *Octobre A Paris*', interviewed by Gérard Vaugeois. Shafto, Sally (trans.) (n.d.). *Framework The Journal of Cinema and Media*. On-line. Available HTTP: http://www.frameworkonline.com/panjeli/panijel-interview.html (13 November 2013).

Paquet, Andre (1975) 'Toward an Arab and African Cinema: the 1974 Carthage Film Festival', Delforge, Renée (trans.). *Cinéaste*, 7, 1, 19-21.

__ (1979) 'The 7th Carthage Film Festival', *Cinéaste*, 9, 3, 39.

Pasquini, Elaine (2008) 'Arab Film Festival Wows Audiences With Dynamic Films on Hot-Button Issues', *Washington Report on Middle East Affairs*, 27, 1, 42-43.

__(2009) 'Eclectic, Inspiring New Films Highlight Arab Film Festival's Twelfth Season (San Francisco)', *Washington Report on Middle East Affairs*, 28, 1, 42-43.

__(2011) 'Arab Film Festival's Most Ambitious Season Offered Humor, Realism, Originality (San Francisco)', *Washington Report on Middle East Affairs*, 30, 1, 36-37.

__(2012) 'Youthful Creativity, Exuberance Dominate Annual Arab Film Festival (San Francisco)', *Washington Report on Middle East Affairs*, 31, 1, 30-31.

Peachment, Chris (1985) 'Istanbul Juryman', *Sight and Sound*, 54, 4, 234.

Peary, Gerald (1988) 'Jerusalem', *Sight and Sound*, 57, 4, 222.

__ (1993) 'Istanbul Film Festival', *Cinéaste*, 20, 1, 50-51.

Peña, Richard (1999) '1999 Tehran Film Festival: Being There', *Film Comment*, 35, 3, 70-71.

Portis, Larry (2008) 'The twenty-ninth annual Mediterranean Film Festival in Montpellier, France: Under Bombardment in Montpellier (among other films from Greece, Lebanon, Palestine, Israel, Algeria, Spain, and elsewhere', *Film International*, 6, 2, 94-97.

__(2009) 'Cinema, the Mediterranean and the Middle East The Mediterranean Film Festival, Montpellier, France, 24 October-2 November 2008', *Film International*, 7, 2, 88-91.

Porton, Richard (2004) 'The Istanbul Film Festival', *Cinéaste*, 30, 1, 73.

'The Power of Three (Gulf Festivals)' (2012), *Screen International*, 11 October.

'Preview: Dubai International Film Festival' (2008), *Screen International*, 5 December.

Quilty, Jim (2010) 'Middle East Fest Preview', *Variety*, 420, 3, 20-21.

Rapfogel, Jared (2007) 'The Istanbul Film Festival', *Cinéaste*, 32, 4, 73-74.

Rastegar, Roya (2012) 'Difference, Aesthetics and the Curatorial Crisis of Film Festivals', *Screen*, 53, 3, 310-317.

Razlogov, Kirill (2008) 'Istanbul 2008', *FIPRESCI-Festival Reports*. On-line. Available HTTP: http://www.fipresci.org/festivals/archive/2008/istanbul/istanbul_ndx.htm (23 October 2013).

Reichart, Wilfried (2007) 'Cairo 2007', *FIPRESCI-Festival Reports*. On-line. Available HTTP: http://www.fipresci.org/festivals/archive/2007/cairo/cairo_2007_ndx.htm (23 October 2013).

Rigg, Julie (2012) '9th Dubai International Film Fesitval, 2012', *FIPRESCI-Festival Reports*. On-line. Available HTTP: http://www.fipresci.org/festivals/archive/2012/dubai/dubai_12_ndx.htm (23 October 2013).

'Rob Marshall's *Nine* Launches 6th Dubai Film Festival' (2009), *Screen International*, 9 December.

Rosenstone, Robert (2012) 'Mediterranean Encounters in Rabat: Rencontres mediterranéennes cinéma et droits de l'homme', in

Dina Iordanova and Leshu Torchin (eds) *FFY 4: Film Festivals and Activism*. St Andrews: St Andrews Film Studies, 157-164.

Rosser, Michael (2013) 'ADFF: Arabs are the New "Red Scare"', *Screen International,* 29 October.

Rossing Jensen, Jorn (2007) 'New Abu Dhabi Festival to Offer Film Financing with Top Awards', *Screen International*, 9 August.

Roy, Jean (2008) 'Dubai 2008', *FIPRESCI-Festival Reports*. On-line. Available HTTP: http://www.fipresci.org/festivals/archive/2008/dubai/dubai_ndx.htm (23 October 2013).

Ruoff, Jeffrey (2008) 'Ten Nights in Tunisia: Les journées cinématographiques de Carthage', *Film International*, 6, 4, 43-51.

Saadi, Meyrem (2014a) 'A Festival is not Only About Money: Interview with Melita Toscan du Plantier', *Tel Quel* (Morocco) 597, 6–12. Translated by Sally Shafto for *Framework: The Journal of Cinema and Media*, 55, 1. On-line. Available HTTP: http://www.frameworkonline.com/festivals/FIFM2014/MelitaToscanInterview.html (10 February 2014).

__(2014b) 'Interview with Nour-Eddine Saïl: The Moroccan Model is Beginning to be Copied', Tel Quel (Morocco) 606, 42-43. Translated by Sally Shafto for *Framework: The Journal of Cinema and Media*. On-line. Available HTTP: http://www.frameworkonline.com/festivals/FNFMorocco2014/NourEddineSail_interview.html (4 April 2014).

Salti, Rasha (2006) *Insights into Syrian Cinema: Essays and Conversations with Contemporary Filmmakers*. New York: ArteEast & Rattapallax.

Salti, Rasha, and Fawz Kabra (2013) 'Curating Film.' *Ibraaz*, January. On-line. Available HTTP: http://www.ibraaz.org/usr/library/documents/essay-documents/curating-film.pdf

Sandwell, Ian (2012) 'Abu Dhabi Film Festival Names Saleh Karama as New EFC Director', *Screen International*, 24 September.

__(2013) '*Wadjda* to Open Gulf Film Festival', *Screen International*, 26 March.

Santaolalla, Isabel, and Stefan Simanowitz (2010) 'A Cinematic Refuge in the Desert: The Sahara International Film Festival', in Dina Iordanova and Ruby Cheung (eds) *FFY 2: Film Festivals and Imagined Communities*. St. Andrews: St Andrews Film Studies, 136–150.

__ (2012) 'A Cinematic Refuge in the Desert: Festival Internacional de Cine del Sahara', in Dina Iordanova and Leshu Torchin(eds) *FFY 4: Film Festivals and Activism*. St Andrews: St Andrews Film Studies, 121–132.

'Scarlet Joins Middle East International Film Festival', (2009), *Screen International*, 31 March.

Scott, A. O. (2004) 'Film Festival Review; A Portrait of Al Jazeera, Reporting the War Its Way', *New York Times*. (April 2). On-line. Available HTTP: http://www.nytimes.com/2004/04/02/movies/film-festival-review-a-portrait-of-al-jazeera-reporting-the-war-its-way.html (24 October 2013).

Sekler, Joan (2008) 'Middle East International Film Festival: Abu Dhabi and the Dubai International Film Festival', Documentary. On-line. Available HTTP: http://www.documentary.org/content/middle-east-international-film-festival-abu-dhabi-and-dubai-internaitonal-film-festival (23 October 2013).

Shackleton, Liz (2013) 'Doha Unveils New Festival Format', *Screen International*, 18 May.

Shafto, Sally (2011a) 'Celebrating Amazigh Culture: The 5th National Festival of Amazigh Film', *Senses of Cinema*, Festival Reports, 58. On-line. Available HTTP: http://sensesofcinema.com/2011/festival-reports/celebrating-amazigh-culture-the-5th-national-festival-of-amazigh-film/ (19 September 2013).

__(2011b) 'Moroccan Cinema Alive: The 12th Festival National du Film, Tangier', *Senses of Cinema*, Festival Reports, 58. On-line. Available HTTP: http://sensesofcinema.com/2011/festival-reports/moroccan-cinema-alive-the-12th-festival-national-du-film-tangier/ (19 September 2013).

__(2011c) 'The Arab Spring and Maghrebin Cinema: The 6th Panorama des Cinémas du Maghreb, Saint Denis', *Senses of Cinema*, Festival Reports, 59. On-line. Available HTTP: http://sensesofcinema.com/2011/festival-reports/the-arab-spring-and-maghrebin-cinema-the-6th-panorama-des-cinemas-du-maghreb-saint-denis/ (19 September 2013).

__(2011d) 'In Praise of the Short Film: The Mediterranean Short Film Festival in Tangier', *Framework: The Journal of Cinema and Media*. On-line. Available HTTP: http://www.frameworkonline.com/festivals/in-praise-of-the-short-film-the-mediterranean-short-film-festival-in-tangier.html (3 November 2013).

__(2011e) 'October in Paris: A Review of the 2011 "Maghreb des films, Rencontres Cinématographiques" (Paris and Elsewhere in France)', *Framework: The Journal of Cinema and Media*. On-line. Available HTTP: http://www.frameworkonline.com/festivals/4th-maghreb-des-films.html (3 November 2013).

__(2012a) 'It All Began in Khouribga: The 15th Festival du Cinéma Africain de Khouribga', *Senses of Cinema*, Festival Reports, 64. On-line. Available HTTP: http://sensesofcinema.com/2012/festival-reports/it-all-began-in-khouribga-the-15th-festival-du-cinema-africain-de-khouribga/ (19 September 2013).

__(2012b) 'Between Europe and Africa, Inch'allah: Morocco and Its 13th National Film Festival in Tangier', *Framework: The Journal of Cinema and Media*. On-line. Available HTTP: http://www.frameworkonline.com/festivals/tangiers-film-festival.html (3 November 2013).

__(2012c) ' "Hollywood is in Salé, Morocco": A Review of the Festival International du Film de Femmes de Salé, Morocco (September 17-22, 2012)', *Framework: The Journal of Cinema and Media*. On-line. Available HTTP: http://www.frameworkonline.com/festivals/sale2012/sale-2012-morocco-film-festival.html (3 November 2013).

__ (2013a) 'On Moroccan Identity: the 14th Festival National du Film', *Senses of Cinema*, Festival Reports, 67. On-line. Available HTTP: http://sensesofcinema.com/2013/festival-reports/on-moroccan-identity-the-14th-festival-national-du-film/ (19 September 2013).

__(2013b) ' "It's Not Just About the Money": The 16th Festival du Cinéma Africain de Khouribga, Morocco (FCAK) June 22-29, 2013', *Framework: The Journal of Cinema and Media*. On-line. Available HTTP: http://www.frameworkonline.com/festivals/FestivalKhouribga2013/FestivalKhouribga2013.html (3 November 2013).

__(2013c) 'Why Are There So Few Great Women Filmmakers?: Festival International du Film de Femmes de Salé (FIFFS) (September 23-28, 2013)', *Framework: The Journal of Cinema and Media*. On-Line. Available HTTP: http://www.frameworkonline.com/festivals/FIFFS2013/FIFFS2013.html (22 November 2013).

__(2013d) ' "Towards a United Mediterranean": The 11th Edition of the Festival du Court Métrage Méditerranéen de Tanger (October 7-12, 2013)', *Framework: The Journal of Cinema and Media*. On-Line. Available HTTP: http://www.frameworkonline.com/festivals/FCMMT2013/FCMMT2013REview.html (20 November 2013).

__(2014a) 'Marrakech Mon Amour: A Review of the 13th Annual Marrakech International Film Festival', *Framework: The Journal of Cinema and Media*. On-line. Available HTTP: http://www.frameworkonline.com/festivals/FIFM2014/FIFM2014.html (11 February 2014).

__(2014b) 'Fifteen and Counting: The Fifteenth Edition of the Moroccan National Film Festival', *Framework: The Journal of Cinema and Media*. On-line. Available HTTP: http://www.frameworkonline.com/festivals/FNFMorocco2014/15thNFFReview.html (4 April 2014)

Shohat, Ella and Robert Stam (1995) 'The Carthage Film Festival', *Cinéaste*, 21, 3, 56.

Simon, Alissa (2000) 'Meditations on Morality (Fajr)', *Sight and Sound*, 10, 5, 6.

__ (2013) 'Fest Notebook: Titles Rank, Tensions Flare at Istanbul', *Variety*, (4 May). On-line. Available HTTP: http://variety.com/2013/film/news/fest-notebook-titles-rank-tensions-flare-at-istanbul-1200454514/ (22 October 2013).

Simpson, Catherine (2011) '"Like Opium": The 30th Istanbul Film Festival', *Senses of Cinema* (June), Festival Reports, 59. On-line. Available HTTP: http://sensesofcinema.com/2011/festival-reports/%E2%80%9Clike-opium%E2%80%9D-the-30th-istanbul-film-festival/ (19 September 2013).

Sobera, Lucia (2009) 'Dreamers Without Borders *Irakischer Film nach Saddam,* Hamburg, 6-14 October 2007 and Off-Line Baghdad (Not Just Another Film Festival), Milan, 13-16 December 2007', *International Journal of Contemporary Iraqi Studies*, 3, 3, 321-329.

'Special Feature-Dubai International Film Festival at Five—The Fifth Element' (2008), *Screen International*, 3 October.

Szremski, Kristin (2002) 'More Than 20 Films Screened At Chicago's First Palestinian Film Festival', *Washington Report on Middle East Affairs*, 21, 4, 71-72.

Tabak, Yesim (2012) 'Flying Broom International Women's Film Festival 2012', *FIPRESCI-Festival Reports*. On-line. Available HTTP: http://www.fipresci.org/festivals/archive/2012/ankara/ankara_12_ndx.htm (23 October 2013).

Tartaglione-Vialatte, Nancy (2007) 'Marrakech to Open with *Elizabeth* and Close with *The Neighbor*', *Screen International*, 28 November.

Thirion, Antoine (2009) 'Promesses Marocaines (Marrakech)', *Cahiers du Cinéma*, 641, 50.

Toubiana, Serge (1998) 'Impressions de Carthage', *Cahiers du Cinéma*, 530, 6-7.

Uçansu, Hülya (2012) *Bir Uzun Mesafe Festivalcisinin Anıları* (Memoirs of a Long Distance Festival Manager). İstanbul: Doğan Kitap.

Van Reeth, Magali (2013) 'Flying Broom International Women's Film Festival 2013', *FIPRESCI-Festival Reports*. On-line. Available HTTP: http://www.fipresci.org/festivals/archive/2013/ankara/ankara_2013_ndx.htm (23 October 2013).

Vivarelli, Nick (2012a) 'Abu Dhabi Sets Bows', *Variety*, 316, 61, 10.

__ (2012b) 'Cairo Film Fest Chief Ousted', *Variety*, (3 September). On-line. Available HTTP: http://variety.com/2012/film/news/cairo-film-fest-chief-ousted-1118058595/ (21 October 2013).

__(2012c) 'Showcase for Arab Film (Abu Dhabi)', *Variety*, (6 September). On-line. Available HTTP: http://variety.com/2012/biz/news/ showcase-for-arab-film-1118059656/ (21 October 2013).

__(2012d) 'Gulf Films Boost Dubai Fest Slate', *Variety*, (8 December). On-line. Available HTTP: http://variety.com/2012/film/news/gulf-films-boost-dubai-fest-slate-1118063134/ (21 October 2013).

__(2012e) 'Dubai Fest Backs Funding Initiatives', *Variety*, (11 December). On-line. Available HTTP: http://variety.com/2012/film/news/ dubai-fest-backs-funding-initiatives-1118063422/ (21 October 2013).

__ (2013a) 'Tribeca, Doha Film Institute End Partnership', *Variety*, (30 April). On-line. Available HTTP: http://variety.com/2013/ film/international/tribeca-doha-film-institute-end-partnership-1200427812/ (21 October 2013).

__ (2013b) 'Doha Rethinks its Festival Set-up', *Variety*, (18 May). On-line. Available HTTP: http://variety.com/2013/film/news/doha-rethinks-its-festival-set-up-1200483575/ (21 October 2013).

__ (2013c) 'Arab Film Fests: The Big Three Work to Boost Regional Biz', *Variety*, (1 September). On-line. Available HTTP: http://variety. com/2013/biz/news/arab-film-fests-the-big-three-work-to-boost-regional-biz-1200595203/ (21 October 2013).

__ (2013d) 'Qumra Doha Film Fest Sets Dates, Beefs Up Team', *Variety*, (2 September). On-line. Available HTTP: http://variety. com/2013/film/news/qumra-doha-film-fest-sets-dates-beefs-up-team-1200603579/ (21 October 2013).

__ (2013e) 'Abu Dhabi Fest to Open With "Life of Crime"', *Variety*, (1 October). On-line. Available HTTP: http://variety.com/2013/ film/international/abu-dhabi-fest-to-open-with-life-of-crime-1200684327/ (21 October 2013).

__ (2013f) 'Abu Dhabi: Festival Mandate is to Nurture New Regional Pics', *Variety*, (16 October). On-line. Available HTTP: http://variety. com/2013/biz/news/abu-dhabi-festival-mandate-is-to-nurture-new-regional-pics-1200728731/ (21 October 2013).

Whitaker, Sheila (2001) 'A Woman's Touch (Fajr)' *Sight and Sound*, 11, 5, 10.

__(2002) 'Girls and Guns (Fajr)', *Sight and Sound*, 12, 5, 5.

__(2008) 'And Life Goes On (Fajr)', *Sight and Sound*, 18, 4, 12.

Wilson-Goldie, Kaelen (2008) 'Forbidden Images (Middle East Women Film

Wiseman, Andreas (2011) 'Gulf Film Festival Adds Shorts Competition', *Screen International*, 7 February.

__(2013) 'Sarajevo and Doha Festivals Link Up', *Screen International*, 19 August.

Wong, Silvia (2007a) 'Antalya Golden Orange Film Festival Unveils Line-up', *Screen International*, 28 September.

__(2007b) 'Turkey's Antalya Fest Has Double-header Opening', *Screen International*, 21 October.